RETROACTIVITY AND THE COMMON LAW

This book analyses the common law's approach to retroactivity. The central claim is that when a court considers whether to develop or change a common law rule the retroactive effect of doing so should explicitly be considered and, informed by the common law's approach to statutory construction, presumptively be resisted. As a platform for this claim a definition of 'retroactivity' is established and a review of the history of retroactivity in the common law is provided. It is then argued that certainty, particularly in the form of an ability to rely on the law, and a conception of negative liberty, constitute rationales for a general presumption against retroactivity at a level of abstraction applicable both to the construction of statutes and to developing or changing common law rules.

The presumption against retroactivity in the construction of statutes is analysed, and one conclusion reached is that the presumption is a principle of the common law independent of legislative intent. Across private, public and criminal law, the retroactive effect of judicial decisions that develop or change common law rules is then considered in detail. 'Prospective overruling' is examined as a potential means to control the retroactive effect of some judicial decisions, but it is argued that prospective overruling should be regarded as constitutionally impermissible.

The book is primarily concerned with English and Australian law, although cases from other common law jurisdictions, particularly Canada and New Zealand, are also discussed. The conclusion is that in statutory construction and the adjudication of common law rules there should be a consistently strong presumption against retroactivity, motivated by the common law's concern for certainty and liberty, and defeasible only to strong reasons.

Retroactivity and the Common Law

Ben Juratowitch

HART PUBLISHING
OXFORD AND PORTLAND, OREGON
2008

Published in North America (US and Canada) by
Hart Publishing
c/o International Specialized Book Services
920 NE 58th Avenue, Suite 300
Portland, OR 97213-3786
USA
Tel: +1 503 287 3093 or toll-free: (1) 800 944 6190
Fax: +1 503 280 8832
E-mail: orders@isbs.com
Website: www.isbs.com

Hart Publishing, 16C Worcester Place, OX1 2JW
Telephone: +44 (0)1865 517530 Fax: +44 (0)1865 510710
E-mail: mail@hartpub.co.uk
Website: http://www.hartpub.co.uk

British Library Cataloguing in Publication Data
Data Available

ISBN: 978-1-84113-761-2

Typeset by Hope Services, Abingdon
Printed and bound in Great Britain by
TJ International Ltd, Padstow, Cornwall

FOREWORD

Although even Parliament itself cannot actually change what has happened in the past, it can change the legal significance of past events. For example, a statute can provide that something which was lawful when it was done should be treated as having been unlawful, or conversely, that what was unlawful at the time should be treated as having been lawful. Similarly, a statute can change the result of a court case and, in effect, hand substantial victory to the party who actually lost. When the House of Lords ruling on damages for victims of mesothelioma provoked a backlash from trade unions and victims' groups, Parliament quickly passed section 3 of the Compensation Act 2006 changing the law, but only in mesothelioma cases. Section 16 provided that section 3 was to be treated as having always had effect and enabled claimants to have the result of their case altered in line with the new provision. But, by very careful drafting, Parliament was able to ensure that the legislation did not disturb past cases.

That retroactive legislation was widely welcomed. Generally, however, such legislation is treated with suspicion. This suspicion is reflected in the presumption that a statute is to be interpreted as not having retroactive effect. On the other hand, we readily accept that legislation reducing the penalty for an offence should apply to offences committed before the legislation was passed. In his book, Ben Juratowitch not only gives an account of the operation of the presumption, but also teases out the policies which underlie the different rules. This is particularly welcome. Lawyers and judges often seem less than sure-footed when confronted by questions in this field. By giving us an insight into the policies, the author provides a basis for more satisfactory decision-making in the future.

Questions of retroactivity are not confined to the area of statute law. In recent years judges have been forced to think much more carefully about what they are doing when they overrule established rules in the common law. The marital rape case, *R v R*, in the criminal law, and the *Kleinwort Benson* and *Deutsche Morgan Grenfell* cases, in the civil law, are perhaps the best known examples. An increased awareness of the implications of such decisions has stimulated debate about the possibility of courts in this country overruling decisions with prospective effect only. In *Spectrum Plus*, with varying degrees of enthusiasm, the judges in the House of Lords were prepared at least to contemplate the possibility of adopting that course in exceptional cases. Again, it is remarkable how little thought was given to some of these issues in the past – by practitioners and judges, at least. The author not only discusses the recent cases but examines the question in the light of authority in other Commonwealth jurisdictions and with due regard to the more theoretical literature. This is a valuable contribution to what is an important current debate in the law.

Happily, Ben Juratowitch has succeeded in making his study not only useful, but interesting and enjoyable. I wish his book every success.

Alan Rodger
House of Lords
November 2007

ACKNOWLEDGEMENTS

When fellow lawyers discovered the topic of this book, many enthusiastically pointed me towards a case in their own field of specialty raising an issue of retroactivity. Many commented that they had spotted the issue but been frustrated by the lack of treatment afforded to it. This was both a useful research resource and an affirmation of my view that there is a need for a general work dealing with the common law's approach to retroactivity.

Thanks are due to Richard Hart for his enthusiasm to publish this book and, with his staff, to whom I am also grateful, for guiding it through the stages of publication.

A number of people provided helpful comments on drafts of my work. For their time and suggestions I would like to thank Nick Barber, John Cameron, Christopher Curran, Anne Davies, Albert Dinelli, Rosalind Dixon, James Edelman, Timothy Endicott, Nicholas Ferreira, Birke Haecker, Rohan Hardcastle, Daniel Klineberg, John Lovell, Warren Newman and Michael Rush.

This book is mostly based on my doctoral thesis at the University of Oxford. Particular thanks are due to Paul Craig and Lord Rodger, who examined my thesis and suggested ways to develop it for publication as a book.

My greatest guidance, from the conception of the project onwards, came from my thesis supervisor, Andrew Ashworth. I thank him for his generosity with his time and advice, for his thoroughness, and for his insights.

CONTENTS

TABLE OF CASES

Australia

Canada

European Court of Human Rights

European Court of Justice

Hong Kong

International Judicial and Arbitral Decisions

New Zealand

Privy Council Decisions from Other Jurisdictions

United Kingdom

United States of America

TABLE OF LEGISLATION AND INTERNATIONAL INSTRUMENTS

New Zealand

South Africa

United Kingdom

Introduction

This book is about the relationship between law and time. Laws, or at least interpretations of laws, change over time. The law at the time of judicial adjudication of a dispute may differ from the law at the time of the event under consideration. If so, two questions arise. First, whether the law at the time of adjudication or the law at the time of the event should apply. Second, and crucially, what should the law at the time of the event be deemed to have been? Common law courts have provided different answers to these questions according to whether the law under consideration is a statute or a common law rule.

Where a party to a dispute alleges that a statute deems the law, at a time prior to the entry into force of that statute, to have been different from what the law actually was at that prior time, that party has the burden of rebutting a presumption against retroactivity. This presumption rests on the view that retroactive laws are generally, because of their disrespect for legal certainty and individual liberty, bad laws.

If a court develops or changes a common law rule, the new rule will apply to the facts giving rise to the litigation, even though those facts occurred prior to the announcement of the new rule. This phenomenon may be termed 'adjudicative retroactivity'. It is traditionally justified by the declaratory theory, which posits that judges do not make law but rather declare what the law is and, by implication, what it always has been, notwithstanding any contrary prior judicial decisions. According to this theory, there is no retroactivity involved because the law at the time of the relevant events is deemed to have been the same as the law announced in the decision to which those events gave rise. This theory is of no comfort to litigants who suffer detriment because of a newly announced rule.

This book will examine these starkly different approaches to retroactivity and consider whether the rationales for the presumption against retroactivity in the construction of statutes should also motivate explicit judicial consideration of, and caution about, the retroactive effect of developing or changing a common law rule. Much has already been written on the general matters that courts should take into account when considering whether to overrule existing authority.[1] This book will ultimately focus specifically on the concern that should be shown about the retroactive effect of judicial decisions that develop or change a common law rule.

[1] Eg J Harris 'Towards Principles of Overruling—When Should a Final Court of Appeal Second Guess?' (1990) 10 Oxford Journal of Legal Studies 135; JD Heydon 'Limits to the Powers of Ultimate Appellate Courts' (2006) 122 Law Quarterly Review 399; *Jones v Secretary of State for Social Services* [1972] AC 944, 966 (HL); *John v Commissioner of Taxation* (1989) 166 CLR 417, 438–9.

'Retroactive' is often used as a pejorative epithet. For this to be justified, values anterior to a general presumption against retroactivity must be considered. It is those values, to which the third chapter of this book is devoted, that provide a theoretical platform for an exploration of whether there is scope for the operation of a presumption against retroactivity in the adjudication of common law rules as well as in the construction of statutes.

One development encouraging such an exploration, at least insofar as criminal laws in the United Kingdom are concerned, is the incorporation of article 7 of the European Convention on Human Rights (ECHR) into domestic law by force of the Human Rights Act 1998 (UK). This prohibits retroactive criminal laws regardless of whether conduct is made criminal by statute or by the common law. The role in English law of article 7 of the ECHR, thought Lord Woolf MR, has given 'added urgency' to 'the need for an examination of our present approach to the retrospectivity of judicial decisions'.[2] Beyond criminal law, Fuller identified the difficulty and significance of the problem of retroactivity when he wrote that:

> Curiously, one of the most obvious seeming demands of legality—that a rule passed today should govern what happens tomorrow, not what happened yesterday—turns out to present some of the most difficult problems of the whole internal morality of law.[3]

More recently, Lord Rodger commented of the subject 'intertemporal law'[4] that, in continental Europe, the:

> combination of history, jurisprudential theory and practice seems to act like a magnet for doctoral students. In the German-speaking lands a *Habilitation* candidate might go missing for years in the labyrinth.[5]

Except in public international law and private international law, Lord Rodger observed, 'by comparison the literature in English is exiguous'.[6] Encouraged by the view that the common law's approach to retroactivity presents an unsolved puzzle that requires attention, but conscious of Lord Rodger's warning of the fate of those who attempt to address intertemporal issues without clearly identifying the boundaries of their attention, this book will adopt the following approach.

The law of England and Wales (abbreviated as English law), and the law of Australia,[7] will be the focus, though cases and academic writing from some other common law jurisdictions, particularly Canada and New Zealand, will be referred

[2] *R v Governor of Brockhill Prison, ex p Evans (No 2)* [1999] QB 1043, 1059 (CA).

[3] L Fuller *The Morality of Law* (Revised edn Yale University Press New Haven CT 1969) 44.

[4] 'Intertemporal' is a term used only sporadically in legal English: *Island of Palmas Case (Netherlands v USA)* (Decision of Max Huber The Hague 1928) II Reports of International Arbitral Awards 829, 845; Lord Rodger 'A Time for Everything under the Law: Some Reflections on Retrospectivity' (2005) 121 Law Quarterly Review 57, 60–2.

[5] Lord Rodger 'A Time for Everything under the Law: Some Reflections on Retrospectivity' (2005) 121 Law Quarterly Review 57, 61.

[6] *Ibid.*

[7] The complexities caused by the federalism of which are for these purposes reduced by the decision of the High Court that there is one common law of Australia: *Lange v Australian Broadcasting Corporation* (1997) 189 CLR 520, 563.

to. There is no comprehensive treatment of any area of the law, but rather an analysis of issues of retroactivity that arise across many areas. The first chapter addresses terminological difficulties that can beset analysis of intertemporal matters, an exercise that is intrinsically linked to defining relevant conceptual issues and setting the limits of the argument. In the second chapter, the history of approaches to retroactivity will be reviewed. Third, rationales for a general presumption against retroactivity will be established. Fourth, the law applicable to the question of whether a court should construe a statute as having retroactive effect will be examined. The fifth chapter will analyse approaches to retroactivity in the adjudication of common law rules. The sixth chapter will consider the possibility of prospective overruling.[8] The seventh and concluding chapter will focus on whether there should be a general presumption against retroactivity, applicable both to judicial decisions about the construction of statutes and to judicial decisions about whether to develop or change a common law rule.

[8] An umbrella term that includes a number of techniques to control the intertemporal effect of decisions, some of which were described by Lord Nicholls in *Re Spectrum Plus (in liquidation)* [2005] 2 AC 680, [8]–[10] (HL).

1

Concepts, Labels and Limitations

A Introduction

The potential complexity of the relationship between time and human activity can make difficult the accurate representation in language of particular intertemporal effects. Conscious of Lord Steyn's reminder that '[c]ategorisation is an indispensable tool in the search for rationality and coherence in law',[1] conceptually distinguishing between types of intertemporal effect and adopting a label for each is a foundational step. This is important both to identify precisely the phenomenon to be analysed and because of the inconsistency of terminology in existing literature. Though ultimately the discussion will extend to both common law adjudication and statutes, because the terminology in the existing literature most commonly refers to statutes, that will be the starting point.

Statutes can have at least three types of temporal effect. The first applies only to events occurring after the entry into force of the statute. The second operates only after the entry into force of the statute but in doing so affects settled expectations that arose, or vested rights that accrued, prior to the entry into force of the statute. It does not deem the law at the time that the expectation arose or the vested right accrued to have been otherwise than it actually was, but only affects the existing expectation or right from the entry into force of the statute. In this way it differs from the third type of effect, which arises when a statute deems the law at the time of a past event to have been as provided in the subsequent statute, where the law at the time of the event was actually something different. A simple illustration of these distinctions follows.

A traffic law entering into force on Wednesday that prohibits all parking on High Street from Thursday onwards is an example of the first type of effect. The availability and purchase of a week long parking permit for High Street on the preceding Monday would mean that exactly the same law would then fall into the second category. A law entering into force on Wednesday making it an offence to have parked on High Street from the preceding Monday onwards would fall into the third category. A recurring difficulty with labelling the latter two categories is the meaning to be ascribed to each of the terms 'retroactive' and 'retrospective'.

[1] *Boddington v British Transport Police* [1999] 2 AC 143, 170 (HL).

B Retroactivity

There are numerous conceptual and terminological alternatives available for the latter two categories described. In choosing between them, consistency with common judicial usage, and analytical precision are both desirable. Unfortunately these two desires do not always point towards the same outcome.

Driedger's approach to the distinction between 'retroactive' and 'retrospective' statutes, which has been approved and applied by the Supreme Court of Canada,[2] provides a sound starting point:

> A retroactive statute is one that operates as of a time prior to its enactment. A retrospective statute is one that operates for the future only. It is prospective but it imposes new results in respect of a past event. A retroactive statute *operates backwards.* A retrospective statute *operates forwards* but looks backwards in that it attaches new consequences for *the future* to an event that took place before the statute was enacted. A retroactive statute changes the law from what it was; a retrospective statute changes the law from what it otherwise would be with respect to a prior event.[3]

Building on Driedger, Salembier identifies three categories of statute similar to those in the traffic law example above and appears to favour 'prospective' to describe 'acting in the future on future events'; 'retrospective' to describe 'acting in the future on past events'; and 'retroactive' to describe 'acting in the past on past events'.[4] This usage is etymologically sound. As Salembier notes, 'prospective' is from the Latin *prospicere* meaning 'to look forward' and 'retrospective' is from the Latin *retrospicere* meaning 'to look back'. Salembier suggests that 'retroactive' is from the Latin *retro* meaning 'backwards' and *activus* meaning 'acting',[5] but *activus* is not really a Latin word and *retroagere*, meaning 'to reverse', is a better candidate for the Latin basis of retroactive.[6]

Notwithstanding the logic of Salembier's taxonomy, it does not, as he concedes, reflect current usage. Jurists use both 'prospective' and 'retrospective' to describe statutes falling into his category of 'acting in the future on past events'; and use both 'retrospective' and 'retroactive' to describe statutes falling into his category of 'acting in the past on past events'.[7] Ultimately Salembier suggests that the wisest terminological course may be to eschew the use of 'retrospective' and if it must be

[2] See, eg, *Benner v Canada (Secretary of State)* [1997] 1 SCR 358, [39]; *Canada (A-G) v Hislop* [2007] SCC 10, [124]–[132].

[3] EA Driedger 'Statutes: Retroactive Retrospective Reflections' (1978) 56 Canadian Bar Review 264, 268–9.

[4] JP Salembier 'Understanding Retroactivity: When the Past Just Ain't What it Used to Be' (2003) 33 Hong Kong Law Journal 99, 102, 104.

[5] *Ibid* 105.

[6] CS Bobbett 'Retroactive or Retrospective? A Note on Terminology' [2006] British Tax Review 15, 18.

[7] JP Salembier 'Understanding Retroactivity: When the Past Just Ain't What it Used to Be' (2003) 33 Hong Kong Law Journal 99, 105–6.

used, to use it as no more than a synonym for 'retroactive', leaving the label 'prospective' to describe laws in his first and second categories, though those prospective laws in his second category may attract the presumption against affecting vested rights.[8]

There are examples of judicial usage of the term 'retrospective' in a way that corresponds with the meaning attributed by Driedger to 'retroactive'.[9] The difference is terminological, not conceptual. In *Gustavson Drilling v The Minister of National Revenue* Dickson J thought that the statute under consideration 'although undoubtedly affecting past transactions, does not operate retrospectively in the sense that it alters rights as of a past time'.[10] He emphasised that:

> it does not reach into the past and declare that the law or the rights of parties as of an earlier date shall be taken to be something other than they were as of that earlier date. The effect, so far as appellant is concerned, is to deny for the future a right to deduct enjoyed in the past but the right is not affected as of a time prior to enactment of the amending statute.[11]

The same approach was taken in a criminal law case by Isaacs J:

> A retroactive law, that is, a retrospective law in the true sense, is one which 'provides that as at a past date the law shall be taken to have been that which it was not'. That does not include an Act which only alters existing rights as from the date of the Act.[12]

The words quoted by Isaacs J were spoken by Buckley LJ in the private law case of *West v Gwynne.*[13] There are, then, authoritative examples in public, criminal and private law of the judicial delineation of the concept referred to by Driedger as retroactivity, even though the word 'retrospective' has sometimes been used to describe it. This terminological difficulty might be assuaged by an idea worth further exploration: that retroactivity is a specific kind, and the most extreme kind, of a range of intertemporal effects that may broadly be described as 'retrospective'. Isaacs J might have had something of this kind in mind in *R v Kidman* when he referred to a 'retroactive law' being a law that was 'retrospective . . . in the true sense' and Dawson J may have thought similarly when he said that an Act was 'truly retrospective—that is to say, retroactive—in its application to past events'.[14]

Just as there are examples of usage of the word 'retrospective' to describe the concept delineated by Driedger as 'retroactive', there are also examples of the use

[8] *Ibid* 119.

[9] Including *Maxwell v Murphy* (1957) 96 CLR 261, 267; *Polyukhovich v The Commonwealth of Australia* (1991) 172 CLR 501, 540, 642; *Staska v General Motors-Holden's* (1970) 123 CLR 673, 675 (PC); *Waddington v Miah* [1974] 1 WLR 683, 695 (HL); *Wilson v First County Trust (No 2)* [2004] 1 AC 816, [186]–[187] (HL). Cf Tucker J's observation in *DPP v Lamb* [1941] 2 KB 89, 104 that 'I agree that the word used by my Lord, "retroactive," is more correct. I merely use the word "retrospective" for convenience, as it has so often been used.'

[10] [1977] 1 SCR 271, 279.

[11] *Ibid* 279–80. See also, eg, *A-G (Quebec) v Expropriation Tribunal* [1986] 1 SCR 732, [45]–[58].

[12] *R v Kidman* (1915) 20 CLR 425, 443.

[13] [1911] 2 Ch 1, 12 (CA).

[14] *Polyukhovich v The Commonwealth of Australia* (1991) 172 CLR 501, 642, see also 540 (Brennan J). See also *TAC v Lanson* (2001) 3 VR 250, [45].

of the Latin term ex post facto to describe the same concept.[15] Conversely, the term has also been used where it could be replaced by 'after the fact'.[16] The term ex post facto was immortalised by its appearance in sections 9 and 10 of article 1 of the Constitution of the United States, but shortly after that appearance, *Calder v Bull*[17] established that the term was not used in a literal way. Justice Chase remarked that the term ex post facto:

> necessarily requires some explanation; for, naked and without explanation, it is unintelligible, and means nothing. *Literally*, it is only *that a law shall not be passed concerning*, and *after the fact, or thing done, or action committed.*[18]

He continued:

> The prohibition, in the letter, is not to pass any law concerning and after the fact; but the plain and obvious meaning and intention of the prohibition is this; that the Legislatures of the several states shall not pass laws, after a fact done by a subject, or citizen, which shall have relation to such fact, and shall punish him for having done it.[19]

As Willes J observed in *Phillips v Eyre*, statutes that 'voided and punished what had been lawful when done' are 'loosely spoken of as ex post facto laws'.[20] Because it is only through loose language or a non-literal meaning associated with its appearance in the Constitution of the United States that the term ex post facto refers to the concept that Driedger calls retroactivity, the term ex post facto is not a strong candidate as a choice for an analytically precise label for that concept. Apart from its particular meaning in the Constitution of the United States, it may be preferable if the term ex post facto is used simply to denote something occurring 'after the fact'.

The appropriate usage of the word 'retrospective' awaits further discussion, but the meaning given to 'retroactive' by Driedger, which is consistent with the concept identified, for example, by Dickson J, Isaacs J and Buckley LJ, and with some non-literal usages of the term ex post facto, refers to an identifiable type of law, accords with the meaning of 'retroactive' that will be utilised in this book, and describes the only type of intertemporal effect with which this book will ultimately deal. There is no overwhelming reason to prefer the term 'retroactive' to 'retrospective' for this purpose. 'Retroactive' is slightly preferable because it more

[15] *Wilkinson v Meyer* (1724) 2 Ld Raym 1350, 1352; 92 ER 379, 380; *Wright v Hale* (1860) 6 H & N 227, 231; 158 ER 94, 95; *Polyukhovich v The Commonwealth of Australia* (1991) 172 CLR 501, 642; *Maxwell v Murphy* (1957) 96 CLR 261, 285; J Austin *Lectures on Jurisprudence* R Campbell (ed) (5th edn Revised John Murray London 1911) vol 1, 485–6; W Blackstone *Commentaries on the Laws of England* (16th edn Cadell London 1825) vol 1, 45; CK Allen *Law in the Making* (7th edn Clarendon Press Oxford 1964) 465; HLA Hart *The Concept of Law* (2nd edn Clarendon Press Oxford 1994) 276; FAR Bennion *Statutory Interpretation* (4th edn Butterworths London 2002) 267.

[16] *Gardner v Cone* [1928] Ch 955, 966; *R v J* [1991] 1 All ER 759, 768 (CC); *R v Knuller* [1973] AC 435, 480 (HL); A Ashworth *Principles of Criminal Law* (5th edn Oxford University Press 2006) 70; J Waldron 'Retroactive Law: How Dodgy was Duynhoven?' (2004) 10 Otago Law Review 631, 635.

[17] 3 US (Dallas) 386 (1798).

[18] *Ibid* 390.

[19] *Ibid.*

[20] (1870) LR 6 QB 1, 25 (Exch).

accurately captures the essence of what such laws purport to do—ie to act in the past, and because 'retrospective' is commonly used to describe a much broader category of laws.

C Retrospectivity

Though 'retrospective' has sometimes been used to denote the confined concept here designated as 'retroactivity', it has more commonly been deployed to include a broader range of intertemporal effects. In an often cited passage, Justice Story, construing the term 'retrospective laws' appearing in the Constitution of New Hampshire, asked:

> Is it confined to statutes, which are enacted to take effect from a time anterior to their passage? or does it embrace all statutes, which, though operating only from their passage, affect vested rights and past transactions?[21]

He gave this extremely wide answer:

> It would be a construction utterly subversive of all the objects of the provision, to adhere to the former definition. . . . Upon principle, every statute, which takes away or impairs vested rights acquired under existing laws, or creates a new obligation, imposes a new duty, or attaches a new disability, in respect to transactions or considerations already past, must be deemed retrospective.[22]

Lord Rodger used 'retrospective' as a word conveniently inclusive of a range of intertemporal issues. In using 'retrospective', Lord Rodger included:

> under that umbrella both the way in which changes in the law affect situations before the change occurs and the way in which such changes affect situations which begin before, but continue after, the change occurs. And, of course, I include both changes made by legislation and changes made by judicial decisions.[23]

This extra-curial statement contrasts with the distinction drawn by Lord Rodger in *Wilson v First County Trust (No 2)* between legislative provisions that 'actually affect the position before the legislation came into force', which 'can conveniently be described as "retroactive" '[24] and legislation that affects a vested right but does not deem the right to have been other than what it in fact was prior to the commencement of the legislation,[25] which may be covered by a broad use of the word 'retrospective'. Similarly broad use of the word 'retrospective', to include all

21 *Society for the Propagation of the Gospel v Wheeler* 22 Fed Cas 756, 767; 2 Gall 105, 139 (NH Cir 1814).

22 *Ibid.* See also *Re School Board Election for the Parish of Pulborough* [1894] 1 QB 725, 737 (CA).

23 Lord Rodger 'A Time for Everything under the Law: Some Reflections on Retrospectivity' (2005) 121 Law Quarterly Review 57, 59.

24 [2004] 1 AC 816, [187] (HL).

25 *Ibid* [188]–[197]. See also [160] (Lord Scott).

backward looking laws, including but not limited to retroactive laws, is apparent in tomes on statutory interpretation[26] and in other judicial pronouncements.[27]

It seems, therefore, that 'retrospective' has become a protean word, used with various and sometimes inconsistent meanings by different jurists in different circumstances. For some it is only what is here being described as 'retroactive'. For others it covers interference with vested rights, the application of new law to events that started before and continued after that law,[28] and similar intertemporal effects, but excludes retroactivity. For yet others it encompasses both retroactivity and less severe intertemporal effects. Driedger's mistake was to attempt to give 'retrospective' a precise meaning. Salembier's mistake is to assume that a word without a precise meaning should be eschewed. The frequent diversity of its usage indicates that the better view may be that 'retrospectivity' should be seen as a generic word, which includes all intertemporal issues relying on or affecting past events. It includes, as its most extreme example, retroactivity, as well as less severe intertemporal effects, such as interference with vested rights. Accordingly, there are *degrees* of retrospectivity.[29] The antonym of this very general understanding of 'retrospective' is the equally general 'prospective', however the specificity of the meaning of 'retroactive' means that 'prospective' is not its precise antonym.[30] 'Non-retroactive' may be the most accurate available antonym of 'retroactive'. On this approach to 'retrospectivity', whenever it is used, more will be required to specify the precise nature of the backward looking intertemporal effect in question.

There are those, however, who support the view that once something has broadly been labelled as retrospective, there is no need to or utility in further defining the precise intertemporal effect in question. Savigny seems at first glance to have acknowledged the distinction between retroactivity and interference with vested rights. He separated two 'formulas'.[31] First: 'No retroactive effect is to be attributed to new laws.'[32] Second: 'New laws leave acquired rights unaffected.'[33]

[26] D Greenberg (ed) *Craies on Legislation* (8th edn Sweet and Maxwell London 2004) 389, especially fn 28; P St J Langan (ed) *Maxwell on the Interpretation of Statutes* (12th edn Sweet and Maxwell London 1969) 215; E Wilberforce *Statute Law* (Stevens & Sons London 1881) 157.

[27] Eg *Re Athlumney* [1898] 2 QB 547, 552; *Secretary of State for Social Security v Tunnicliffe* [1991] 2 All ER 712, 724 (CA); *Yew Bon Tew v Kenderaan Bas Mara* [1983] 1 AC 553, 558 (PC); *Maxwell v Murphy* (1957) 96 CLR 261, 285; *Ku-ring-gai Municipal Council v A-G (NSW)* (1957) 99 CLR 251, 269; *Coleman v Shell* (1943) 45 SR (NSW) 27, 31.

[28] Eg *R(Haw) v Secretary of State for the Home Department* [2006] QB 780, [17]–[29] (CA).

[29] *L'Office Cherifien des Phosphates v Yamashita-Shinnihon Steamship Co* [1994] 1 AC 486, 527 (HL); *Secretary of State v Tunnicliffe* [1991] 2 All ER 712, 723 (CA); *Gardner v Cone* [1928] Ch 955, 966; *Reid v Reid* (1886) 31 Ch D 402, 408; CK Allen *Law in the Making* (7th edn Clarendon Press Oxford 1964) 463–4.

[30] Contra J Waldron 'Retroactive Law: How Dodgy was Duynhoven?' (2004) 10 Otago Law Review 631, 633.

[31] FC von Savigny *Private International Law and the Retrospective Operation of Statutes: A Treatise on the Conflict of Laws and the Limits of their Operation in Respect of Place and Time* W Guthrie (tr) (2nd edn T&T Clark Edinburgh 1880) 334.

[32] *Ibid.*

[33] *Ibid.*

Expanding on the second formula, Savigny explained that 'legal relations should be preserved in their original nature and efficacy'.[34] Savigny did not, however, ultimately consider there to be a meaningful conceptual distinction between his two formulas. Rather, he thought that there was an 'intimate relation' between them.[35] Of the first formula, he stated that:

> It is evident that it is not to be taken in a literal, material sense. This would mean that what has happened should be undone,—the past annihilated. But as this is impossible, no rule of law is needed to prevent it. The retroaction must therefore be taken in a juridical or formal sense; and it thus means that the retroactive law would draw under its dominion the *consequences* of past juridical facts, and therefore influence these consequences.[36]

For Savigny a principle of non-retroactivity 'absolutely denies the influence of the new law on the consequences of past facts, and that in every conceivable degree'.[37] Thus, according to Savigny, on the basis of a general principle against giving retroactive effect to new laws, rights existing prior to the commencement of a new law persist, even though they would not be afforded to persons seeking to acquire them for the first time after the commencement of the new law. A rule of this breadth subsumes the presumption against interference with vested rights and indicates that Savigny ultimately did not see a meaningful distinction between retroactivity and interference with vested rights. Indeed, he argued that 'in fact, there is in both formulas only one and the same principle contemplated and described from different sides'.[38]

Savigny's error lay in the unjustified leap from a principle that 'no retroactive effect is to be attributed to new laws' to the conclusion that this principle 'absolutely denies the influence of the new law on the consequences of past facts, and that in every conceivable degree'. Such a conclusion is not substantively different to that which can be reasoned from a principle objecting to the interference with vested rights, but Savigny was wrong to think that it flowed naturally from a general principle of non-retroactivity.

Sampford more explicitly adopts the idea that once something can broadly be classed as retrospective, there is no need to pursue any further distinctions. He defines retrospectivity as a law that 'alters the future legal consequences of past actions or events'[39] and, after referring to Driedger's distinction between retroactive and retrospective laws, adds that:

[34] *Ibid* 341.
[35] *Ibid* 339.
[36] *Ibid.*
[37] *Ibid* 340.
[38] *Ibid* 341.
[39] C Sampford *Retrospectivity and the Rule of Law* (Oxford University Press 2006) 17, 22, 37. See also A Palmer and C Sampford 'Retrospective Legislation in Australia—Looking Back at the 1980s' (1994) 22 Federal Law Review 217, 220.

> it must be pointed out that the distinction between *retroactivity* and *retrospectivity*, while describing a real difference in the verbal form in which retrospective law is expressed, lacks normative and practical significance.[40]

Sampford thinks that the *effects* are the same for both.[41]

One way to consider whether it is important to distinguish between the broad category of retrospective laws and the more precise definition of the most extreme class within that category, retroactive laws, is to assess whether there are different theoretical rationales for a specific presumption against retroactivity as compared to a more general presumption against retrospectivity. The third chapter of this book is devoted entirely to the examination of rationales for the presumption against retroactivity. Because in all of its forms other than retroactivity, retrospectivity does not deem the law to be other than what it in fact was, it does not alter someone's liberty to have acted in a certain way after that person has so acted. In this respect it differs from retroactivity. The implications of retrospectivity for the ability to rely on the law, whilst closer to those affected by retroactivity, may be of a different order of magnitude.[42] All types of retrospectivity involve change to the status quo, effective from the time the change is made. Thus a presumption against retrospectivity would be based on the desirability of stability of the law.[43] Retroactivity has the added feature that from the time of the change,[44] the changed law is deemed to have been applicable in the past. This gives rise to difficulties specific to that extreme form of retrospective effect, further exploration of which is the core task of this book.

The contention is not that there is not, or that there should not be, a presumption against interference with vested rights or a presumption against other forms of intertemporal effect that come under the umbrella of retrospectivity. The contention is a more limited one: that such intertemporal effects are meaningfully different to retroactivity—so different as to demand separate categorisation.

D Confusing Usage

In addition to jurists who have used 'retroactive' and 'retrospective' in ways that diverge, in principle, from the preferred usage here adopted, there are also examples of the terms being used in ways that do not reveal precisely the concept that is

40 C Sampford *Retrospectivity and the Rule of Law* (Oxford University Press 2006) 21, see also 257–8. Contra A Palmer and C Sampford 'Retrospective Legislation in Australia—Looking Back at the 1980s' (1994) 22 Federal Law Review 217, 218.

41 C Sampford *Retrospectivity and the Rule of Law* (Oxford University Press 2006) 21.

42 Contra A Palmer and C Sampford 'Retrospective Legislation in Australia—Looking Back at the 1980s' (1994) 22 Federal Law Review 217, 235.

43 J Raz 'The Rule of Law and its Virtue' (1977) 93 Law Quarterly Review 195, 199.

44 *Bowen v Georgetown University Hospital* 488 US 204, 217 (1988).

intended to be represented. Simply to illustrate the level of terminological confusion in this area, a few examples may be mentioned. Mason CJ used the phrase 'retrospective or retroactive'[45] and Finnis used 'retrospective and retroactive',[46] possibly suggesting that they considered the two terms to indicate different ideas, but it is not immediately apparent the particular distinction, if any, either of them had in mind.[47] Fuller also used 'retrospective' and 'retroactive' interchangeably, with no apparent difference in meaning,[48] though he was of course aware of distinctions between different types of intertemporal issues.[49] It is not the case that 'retrospective' is a British term whilst 'retroactive' is North American. Nor is it the case that 'retrospective' is a dated term whilst 'retroactive' is modern. Both suggestions are disproved by the fact that in 1891 Lord Coleridge CJ used the two terms interchangeably.[50]

E Problematic Usage

Although throughout the discussion so far in this chapter objections have been made to usages of 'retrospective' and 'retroactive' that do not conform to the meanings here attributed to them, there are two examples that invite particular attention.

1 Waldron on Criminal Sentencing

On the basis of Salembier's analysis of the difference between 'retroactive' and 'retrospective',[51] but ignoring that Salembier, in the end, recommended against its usage,[52] Waldron discusses *R v Pora*,[53] which involved an increase between commission of an offence and sentencing, of the minimum non-parole period provided by statute. Waldron considers this change to have been *retrospective* rather than *retroactive* on the basis that:

[45] *Polyukhovich v The Commonwealth of Australia* (1991) 172 CLR 501, 534.

[46] JM Finnis 'The Fairy Tale's Moral' (1999) 115 Law Quarterly Review 170, 171. See also *Australian Coal & Shale Employees Federation v Aberfield Coal Mining Co* (1942) 66 CLR 161, 185.

[47] See also FAR Bennion *Statutory Interpretation* (4th edn Butterworths London 2002) 266–7.

[48] L Fuller *The Morality of Law* (Revised edn Yale University Press New Haven CT 1969) 51–62. See also *Wilson v First County Trust (No 2)* [2004] 1 AC 816, [11]–[12] (HL).

[49] L Fuller *The Morality of Law* (Revised edn Yale University Press New Haven CT 1969) 59.

[50] *R v Griffiths* [1891] 2 QB 145, 148.

[51] J Waldron 'Retroactive Law: How Dodgy was Duynhoven?' (2004) 10 Otago Law Review 631, 632–8.

[52] JP Salembier 'Understanding Retroactivity: When the Past Just Ain't What it Used to Be' (2003) 33 Hong Kong Law Journal 99, 119. See Ch 1 Pt B.

[53] [2001] 2 NZLR 37 (CA).

> To increase the punishment associated with an offence is to change what we do now in respect of something that happened in the past, which makes it retrospective, but it need not require the fiction that the law then was as we are saying it should be now.[54]

Waldron considers that the point of distinction is that the 'status'[55] of the event did not change, though the 'legal consequence'[56] to be attached to the event did change. Waldron concedes that his distinction is 'a delicate one'[57] and summarises it thus:

> Increasing the penalty is retrospective, because what it does is attach a new consequence for now to an action that society already had the right to punish. Imposing a penalty on an act previously regarded as innocent is retroactive, because it changes the status of the action *ex post facto* from innocent to criminal.[58]

Waldron's distinction between the *status* and *legal consequences* of a past event and his attempt to use that distinction to justify an argument that exposure to a penalty which did not exist at the time of the commission of the crime is *retrospective* but not *retroactive*, despite its considerable intuitive appeal, requires further examination. Though he cautions against supposing that 'what I am calling retroactivity is necessarily worse than retrospectivity',[59] when specifically discussing criminal law it is clear that he considers *retroactive law* 'problematic',[60] which he contrasts with 'a mere retrospective variation in the penalty'.[61]

There is an important difference between a holding of criminal liability and the imposition of a sentence on the basis of that liability, but it is difficult to see how both are not legal consequences of the same factual event. A finding of criminal liability is a *legal consequence* of the act of throwing a punch just as much as it is a finding as to the *status* of that act. Thus a finding as to *status* is a type of *legal consequence*. It cannot be that Waldron is referring to sentencing as a *legal consequence* of the conviction as opposed to the event giving rise to it because such a distinction would mean that *status* and *legal consequence* refer to different events and so any analytical legitimacy the distinction might otherwise have would be defeated. A conviction would determine the *status* of the factual event whereas sentencing would be a *legal consequence* of the conviction, not the event justifying it. The purported distinction between status and legal consequence is not, in this context, an analytically sound one. There is, however, a more fundamental problem with Waldron's analysis.

Conviction of a crime does not usually involve exposure to an indefinite punishment regime. It typically involves exposure to a punishment regime set down in

[54] J Waldron 'Retroactive Law: How Dodgy was Duynhoven?' (2004) 10 Otago Law Review 631, 633. Cf C Sampford *Retrospectivity and the Rule of Law* (Oxford University Press 2006) 20, 28.

[55] J Waldron 'Retroactive Law: How Dodgy was Duynhoven?' (2004) 10 Otago Law Review 631, 633, 636.

[56] *Ibid* 634.

[57] *Ibid* 635.

[58] *Ibid.*

[59] *Ibid* 633.

[60] *Ibid* 637.

[61] *Ibid.*

advance.[62] Yet Waldron refers to society's 'right to punish' as though it is an unlimited right, including the right to vary the applicable punishment after an offence has been committed. Waldron considers that, in contrast to *retroactive* laws, laws which alter the possible punishment for an offence after it has been committed do 'not require the fiction that the law then was as we are saying it should be now'. The use of 'fiction' as shorthand associated with *retroactive* laws is common and may be useful on occasions. However, there is no actual 'fiction' involved. 'Deeming' is a more apt description.[63] Concluded judgments made in accordance with the law at the earlier time are generally not disturbed by retroactive laws, not least because of the doctrines of res judicata and merger. It is only that present law is empowered, in present controversies, to reach back to apply to prior situations which, had they given rise to litigation at the time that they occurred, would have had different law applied.[64]

Though a finding of criminal liability is a necessary intervening step between the commission of a crime and the imposition of sentence, the legitimacy of the imposition of the sentence is dependent on the event creating criminal liability, although once its imposition is justified by that event the sentence may usually take into account matters other than the specific crime committed. To create a disjuncture between the law applicable to conviction and the law applicable to its dependent process of sentencing deems the person convicted to have been exposed to a different regime than that which operated at the time of the completed criminal event. Thus an alteration with respect to either is properly labelled *retroactive.* An analogy between the state's power to tax and the state's power to impose criminal sentences may illustrate this point.

To say that changing the applicable sentence between commission of a crime and a sentence being imposed for that crime is not retroactive because it does no more than change the consequences that the state may now impose in response to an event that already gave rise to criminal liability, is like saying that if in 2007 one is subject to liability for tax, and the rate was 35 percent, that if in 2008 the state imposed tax liability on income earned in 2007 at 50 percent, then it would not be retroactive because the state already had an entitlement to tax income, and all it was doing was altering the amount payable in the present. With income tax and with criminal sentencing, the exposure to the power of the state is intimately connected to the magnitude of that exposure.

Waldron's argument is relevant not just to issues of terminology, for which reason it has been discussed here, but also to the explication of rationales for a general presumption against retroactivity and so will be discussed again later for that purpose.[65] For present purposes it is sufficient to note that alteration of the applicable penalty subsequent to the commission of a criminal offence will be considered as an example of retroactivity.

62 See further Ch 3 Pt C(4)(b).

63 Cf *Hunter Douglas Australia v Perma Blinds* (1970) 122 CLR 49, 65.

64 Cf *TAC v Lanson* (2001) 3 VR 250, [45].

65 See Ch 3 Pt C(4)(b).

2 Fuller on Tax Liability

Fuller contrasted a criminal statute 'commanding a man today to do something yesterday'[66] with:

> a tax law first enacted, let us say, in 1963 imposing a tax on financial gains realized in 1960 at a time when such gains were not yet subject to tax. Such a statute may be grossly unjust, but it cannot be said that it is, strictly speaking, retroactive. To be sure, it bases the amount of the tax on something that happened in the past. But the only act it requires of its addressee is a very simple one, namely, that he pay the tax demanded. This requirement operates prospectively. We do not, in other words, enact tax laws today that order a man to have paid taxes yesterday, though we may pass today a tax law that determines the levy to be imposed on the basis of events occurring in the past.[67]

Nor do we enact criminal laws ordering someone to pay a fine yesterday—though we may enact a retroactive law that today deems someone to have been criminally liable for something done yesterday, which was legal when done, the outcome of which is that today she is commanded to pay a fine. On this latter understanding of retroactivity, Fuller's tax law example is within it.

Although the obligation to pay in Fuller's example is, and only can be, created by the new statute, that obligation arises because gains not subject to tax at the time they were realised are deemed to have been subject to tax at that time. Presumably in Fuller's example and certainly in some actual legislation of its kind, the quantum of the obligation to pay is calculated on the basis that liability is deemed to have arisen at the time of the event said to trigger liability.[68] When describing the relevant law it would be artificial to sever the legislative command of liability (which is deemed by the law to have accrued at an earlier time) from the legislative command to pay (which arises at the time that it is imposed).

Fuller's examples, phrased in the language of sovereign command, appear to have been directed towards distinguishing between interference with vested rights, and retroactivity. This is confirmed by his subsequent example, which he wrongly placed in the same category as his tax example, that 'a man unable to read or write' who became 'a real estate broker at a time when oral brokerage contracts' were enforceable would not, because of the presumption against retroactivity, 'be protected against a later law that might require such contracts to be evidenced by a signed writing'.[69] The presumption against retroactivity would not be engaged by such a statute, but it would be engaged if the statute purported to nullify oral contracts already made, just as it would be engaged by a statute taxing gains already realised or criminalising conduct that had already occurred.

[66] L Fuller *The Morality of Law* (Revised edn Yale University Press New Haven CT 1969) 59.

[67] *Ibid.* See also J Waldron 'Retroactive Law: How Dodgy was Duynhoven?' (2004) 10 Otago Law Review 631, 632.

[68] Contra *The Commonwealth of Australia v SCI Operations* (1998) 192 CLR 285, especially 309.

[69] *Ibid* 61.

It is one thing for affairs set in place in reliance on one legislative regime to be subjected to a new and different regime, effective from its commencement, regardless of when the affairs were set in place. Such a regime, whatever its impact on vested rights, and regardless of whether it could be labelled 'retrospective', would not be, on the terminology to be used in this book, a retroactive one. It is a different thing for a law, say a tax law, commencing in 2008 to apply to transactions occurring in 1998 so as, in 2008, to create tax liability *deemed to have accrued at the time of the transactions* and payable, for the first time, in 2008. That would be retroactive. As would a law that in 2008 changes the amount of tax payable or the severity of an applicable criminal sentence in relation to an event that in 1998 was already subject to tax liability or criminal liability of a different degree of severity.

F The Scope of this Book

It has been acknowledged throughout that there are intertemporal legal issues other than retroactivity, many of which may broadly be described as involving retrospectivity. It remains to justify the limitation of this book to retroactivity only. The phenomenon sought to be studied in relation to common law adjudication is that decisions that develop or change a common law rule, apply to facts arising at an earlier point in time, as though such decisions represent what the law was at that earlier time. This effect corresponds to the effect of retroactive statutes and does not have a counterpart in other types of retrospectivity. In order to ensure that the same phenomenon is being studied in relation to both statute and the common law, this book is limited to discussing laws, including in that term both statute and common law rules, which are or have a claim to be retroactive, meaning that such a law applies or purports to apply to a past event as though it was applicable at the time of that event. As has been noted, some jurists use the word 'retrospective' to describe what is here termed 'retroactive'. Their words will be reproduced faithfully without returning to the terminological point on every occasion.

G Illustrations of Conceptual Distinctions

Though terminology has been chosen and concepts delimited, this has largely been done in a theoretical context. Little further assistance on matters of terminology is to be found in the decided cases. There are some judgments however, consideration of which further elucidates the *concept* of retroactivity, and illustrates the impact that analysis of intertemporal issues can have on the outcome of litigation. In none of these cases was the law retroactive in the sense used here, but in examining what retroactivity is not, the intention is to clarify what it is.

1 Cases Relating to Contractual Rights

Ward v British Oak Insurance[70] demonstrates the potentially severe practical consequences of purporting to apply the presumption against retroactivity in the construction of a statute that *could not* have had retroactive effect. In November 1927 the plaintiff was injured at work. In 1929 he obtained judgment against his employer. His employer was insured by the defendant insurance company. A resolution for the voluntary winding up of the employer was made in December 1927. The liquidation was later completed but the judgment debt in favour of the plaintiff was not paid. The Third Parties (Rights Against Insurers) Act 1930[71] relevantly provided in section 1(1) that where a company was insured against liabilities to third parties and a resolution was made for the voluntary winding up of the insured company:

> if, either before or after that event, any such liability as aforesaid is incurred by the insured, his rights against the insurer under the contract in respect of the liability shall, notwithstanding anything in any Act or rule of law to the contrary, be transferred to and vest in the third party to whom the liability was so incurred

Relying on this provision, the plaintiff employee sued his employer's insurers. Counsel for the plaintiff submitted that it was not necessary to show that the statute had 'retrospective' operation as the plaintiff's rights existed when the statute was passed.[72] Counsel for the plaintiff nonetheless proceeded to submit that the statute was 'retrospective'. Charles J thought that the plaintiff could only succeed if 'the Act is held to be retrospective'.[73] He gave no reasons for that statement, simply proceeding to consider whether it was 'retrospective' or not. In doing so Charles J quoted Maugham J in *Gardner v Cone* who stated:

> An Act may be called retrospective because it affects existing contracts as from the date of its coming into operation; and this section is an instance of that. It may be more properly described as retrospective, because it applies to actual transactions which have been completed, or to rights and remedies which have already accrued.[74]

The difficulty with this statement is that *affecting* or *applying to* existing or completed transactions and accrued rights and remedies is not sufficient to render an Act retroactive. It means no more than it says—that it applies to existing states of affairs. It has no quarrel with the past. Here the statute transferred a right already in existence. It did not alter that right for a time past, only transferred it from the time of the statute onwards. Whether the statute attracted a presumption against interference with vested rights is a separate question, and even then it must be observed that the plaintiff had an existing right against his employer and his

[70] [1931] 2 KB 637, affirmed on appeal at [1932] 1 KB 392 (CA).
[71] (UK) 20 and 21 Geo 5 c 25.
[72] [1931] 2 KB 637, 638.
[73] *Ibid* 639.
[74] [1928] Ch 955, 966.

employer was insured for such a liability by the defendant, so it is difficult to imagine what vested right of the insurance company would have been affected by the statutory assignment, though it is true that the insurance company became subject to a statutory provision that was inapplicable at the time the contractual arrangement commenced.

Driedger took a grammatically technical approach to *Ward* and considered it to be correctly decided on the basis that use of the statutory phrase '[w]here . . . a person is insured' justified the decision that the statute applied only to insurance contracts entered into after the Act commenced.[75] This grammatical approach overlooks the common usage of the term 'is insured', which is that it refers to the *state of being insured* not the *act of becoming insured*.[76] Moreover, a purposive approach to the statute would favour its application to existing policies of insurance on the basis that the statute sought to protect workers from having the usefulness of their legal rights obliterated by the insolvency of an employer. It did this by transferring to a worker his employer's claim against the employer's insurer, where the insurer was already liable to the subsequently liquidated employer for that amount, and the debt owed to the worker was not paid in the winding up process.

It was artificial and inconsistent with the statutory purpose to insist that the statute applied not to all claims made after the statute but only to those claims that involved a policy of insurance commenced after the statute. In this case the fact that *an* intertemporal issue arose seems to have lured Charles J, and the Court of Appeal that affirmed his decision, into applying the presumption against retroactivity, which was held to preclude the application of a statute to a factual situation that was clearly within the protective function of that statute.

A different view of retroactivity, which is in accordance with the view taken in this book, is apparent in *West v Gwynne*.[77] Section 3 of the Conveyancing Act 1892[78] enacted that 'in all leases' containing a covenant against assignment or subletting without the lessor's consent, such a covenant would be deemed to be subject to a proviso that no fine would be payable for such consent unless the lease contained express provision to the contrary. The question was whether that section was, in the words of Cozens-Hardy MR, 'of general application, or whether its operation is confined to leases made after the commencement of the Act'.[79] Joyce J at first instance considered that its meaning was 'quite plain to everyone but a

[75] EA Driedger 'The Retrospective Operation of Statutes' in JA Corry, FC Cronkite and FC Whitmore (eds) *Legal Essays in Honour of Arthur Moxon* (University of Toronto Press 1953) 20.

[76] Cf *Customs and Excise Commissioners v Thorn Electrical Industries* [1975] 1 WLR 1661, 1664–5, 1669–70, 1676–8 (HL), in which the applicability of the statute turned on the phrase 'are supplied', which was held to refer to rented goods that were first delivered prior to the statute's commencement and remained with the renter after the statute commenced. Supply, like insurance should have been held to have been in *Ward*, was ongoing.

[77] [1911] 2 Ch 1 (CA). Applied, eg, in *George Hudson v Australian Timber Workers' Union* (1923) 32 CLR 413, 431–3, and see 446–450.

[78] (Eng) 55 and 56 Vict c 13.

[79] [1911] 2 Ch 1, 10 (CA).

lawyer'.[80] In dismissing the appeal against Joyce J's holding that the Act applied to leases agreed prior to the Act, Cozens-Hardy MR recorded the argument of counsel for the appellant that 'a statute is presumed not to have a retrospective operation unless the contrary appears by express language or by necessary implication' and stated:

> I assent to this general proposition, but I fail to appreciate its application to the present case. 'Retrospective operation' is an inaccurate term. Almost every statute affects rights which would have been in existence but for the statute.[81]

He observed that the statutory provision in question:

> does not annul or make void any existing contract; it only provides that in the future, unless there is found an express provision authorising it, there shall be no right to exact a fine. I doubt whether the power to refuse consent to an assignment except upon the terms of paying a fine can fairly be called a vested right or interest. Upon the whole I think s 3 is a general enactment based on grounds of public policy, and I decline to construe it in such a way as to render it inoperative for many years wherever leases for 99 years, or it may be for 999 years, are in existence.[82]

Buckley LJ took the same view of the meaning of retroactivity as Cozens-Hardy MR. Buckley LJ began his speech with this powerful statement:

> During the argument the words 'retrospective' and 'retroactive' have been repeatedly used, and the question has been stated to be whether s 3 of the Conveyancing Act, 1892, is retrospective. To my mind the word 'retrospective' is inappropriate, and the question is not whether the section is retrospective. Retrospective operation is one matter. Interference with existing rights is another. If an Act provides that as at a past date the law shall be taken to have been that which it was not, that Act I understand to be retrospective. That is not this case. The question here is whether a certain provision as to the contents of leases is addressed to the case of all leases or only of some, namely, leases executed after the passing of the Act. The question is as to the ambit and scope of the Act, and not as to the date as from which the new law, as enacted by the Act, is to be taken to have been the law.[83]

Applying that approach, Buckley LJ held that the statutory term 'all leases' included 'both existing leases and leases to come into existence'.[84] The judgments in *West v Gwynne* illustrate the conceptual distinction between the presumption against affecting vested rights and the presumption against retroactive application. Neither was operative on the facts of the case, but the elucidation of the confined meaning of 'retrospective' accords with the meaning of retroactivity adopted in this discussion.

[80] [1911] 2 Ch 1, 5.
[81] [1911] 2 Ch 1, 11 (CA).
[82] *Ibid.*
[83] *Ibid* 11–12.
[84] *Ibid* 13. Cf *Ex p Dawson* (1875) LR 19 Eq 433, 435; *Customs and Excise Commissioners v Thorn Electrical Industries* [1975] 1 WLR 1661, especially 1672 (HL).

2 Cases Relating to Personal Status

The division of the Court of Appeal in *Re School Board Election for the Parish of Pulborough*[85] illustrates the distinction between a broad understanding of 'retrospective' and the narrower meaning of retroactivity. A man who was and remained an undischarged bankrupt under the Bankruptcy Act 1869[86] had been elected a member of a school board. Ten years after he was adjudged bankrupt, the Bankruptcy Act 1883[87] entered into force, section 32 of which provided that:

> where a debtor is adjudged bankrupt he shall be disqualified for . . . being elected to or holding . . . the office of member of a school board.

The question was whether section 32 of the 1883 Act applied to the respondent, whose election to a school board occurred prior to the passage of that Act.

Lopes LJ said that from a purely 'grammatical standpoint' the words 'is adjudged bankrupt' in section 32 should be read 'is adjudged bankrupt under this Act'.[88] Lopes LJ made the overly broad statement that it 'is a well-recognised principle in the construction of statutes that they operate only on cases and facts which come into existence after the statutes were passed, unless a retrospective effect is clearly intended'.[89] In a passage that accords with the broad approach to retrospectivity discussed above, which conflates numerous different kinds of intertemporal issue, labelling them all 'retrospective', Lopes LJ continued:

> This principle of construction is especially applicable when the enactment to which a retrospective effect is sought to be given would prejudicially affect vested rights or the legal character of past transactions. It need not be penal in the sense of punishment.
>
> Every statute, it has been said, which takes away or impairs vested rights acquired under existing laws, or creates a new obligation, or imposes a new duty, or attaches a new disability in respect of transactions already past, must be presumed to be intended not to have a retrospective effect.[90]

Davey LJ also thought that the case turned on the construction of the words 'is adjudged bankrupt',[91] holding that the 1883 Act did not apply to the case at hand. Davey LJ's judgment falls into the category of confusing usage of the relevant terminology for the reason that he drew a distinction between 'retrospective effect' and the imposition of new disabilities, with a similar presumption applying to each when he said:

[85] [1894] 1 QB 725 (CA).
[86] (Eng) 32 and 33 Vict c 71.
[87] (Eng) 46 and 47 Vict c 52.
[88] [1894] 1 QB 725, 736 (CA).
[89] *Ibid* 737.
[90] *Ibid.*
[91] *Ibid* 740.

> It is a well-known principle in the construction of statutes, that where the words admit of two constructions you are not to construe them so as to produce a retrospective effect, or *impose disabilities not existing at the passing of the Act.* [Emphasis added][92]

However, the distinction was not pursued and Davey LJ did not specify which of these two potential alternatives led him to hold that the Act was inapplicable. If Davey LJ did not mean them to be true alternatives, then the emphasised portion of Davey LJ's words demonstrates the excessively broad way in which a presumption can be formulated if a distinction is not made between retroactivity and other kinds of intertemporal issue.

Lord Esher MR dissented in *Pulborough* on the basis that the Act was not penal and, more importantly, that it was 'not, in the true sense of the term, retrospective'.[93] He quoted *Ex p Pratt*[94] about which he said:

> the case seems to me to shew that when the present tense is used in this statute [the Bankruptcy Act 1883] the time to be considered is the time at which the Court has to act, and not the time at which the condition of things on which it has to act came into existence.[95]

Properly putting the question of retroactivity logically prior to the question of whether the enactment was penal, Lord Esher applied to the case at hand the principle that he took from *Pratt*:

> the important time is that at which it has to be considered whether the person is disqualified from being elected to or exercising any office. If that is the true construction of the Act it is not retrospective, but prospective, for it relates to a time after the passing of the Act. Therefore, on the authority of this Court, and on the ordinary rules of construction, it seems to me that we cannot say this section is retrospective; and even if it could be said that it is retrospective, its enactments are solely for the public benefit, and the rule that restricts the operation of a penal retrospective statute does not apply, because this statute is not penal.[96]

The lack of agreement in *Pulborough* was caused by the Lord Justices' differing conceptions of the meaning of retroactivity and differing views about whether there is a presumption against intertemporal effects falling short of retroactivity. The second issue is not here under discussion, but the first goes to the heart of the relevant terminological and conceptual issue. Lopes LJ and perhaps Davey LJ considered statutes to be 'retrospective', and to attract a presumption against such operation, which are here considered not to be retroactive. Lord Esher's conception of 'retrospective', by contrast, aligns with the meaning allotted to 'retroactive' in this book. Lord Esher considered that the presumption against retroactive operation applied only when this conception was engaged. An approach similar to Lord Esher's was taken in the final three cases to be discussed in this chapter.

92 *Ibid* 741.
93 *Ibid* 733.
94 (1884) 12 QBD 334 (CA). See especially 337.
95 [1894] 1 QB 725, 735 (CA).
96 *Ibid.*

The statute under consideration in *The Queen v The Inhabitants of St Mary, Whitechapel*[97] provided that no widow could be removed for twelve months after the death of her husband from the parish in which she resided with her husband if she so long remained a widow.[98] The question was whether the statute protected from removal a woman widowed less than twelve months prior to the commencement of the statute. The parish sought to justify its removal of the woman on the basis that the statute should be presumed not to be retroactive. Lord Denman CJ held that the statute was 'prospective, as it relates to future removal only'.[99] The statute was not, according to Lord Denman CJ, a retroactive statute merely 'because a part of requisites for its action is drawn from time antecedent to its passing'.[100] Lord Denman CJ continued: 'The clause is general, to prevent all removals of the widows described therein after the passing of the Act; the description of the widow does not at all refer to the time when she became widow.'[101]

Because a statute protecting a class of persons into which she fell was operative at the time of her removal, that removal was unlawful. The statute did not purport to alter the law applicable to widows at a time prior to the statute's commencement, so the presumption against retroactivity was not engaged. Rather, the woman was a widow prior to the passage of an act that protected widows. She was rightly not denied protection merely because she first fulfilled the status attracting the protection prior to the passage of the Act. All that mattered was that she still held that status at the time of the Act and was protected by the Act from its commencement onwards.[102]

In *The Queen v Vine*[103] the statute in question disqualified 'every person convicted of a felony' from selling spirits by retail. By a majority the court held that a person who had been convicted of a felony before the Act was passed became disqualified on the passing of the Act. Cockburn CJ said:

> If one could see some reason for thinking that the intention of this enactment was merely to aggravate punishment for felony by imposing this disqualification in addition, I should feel the force of . . . [counsel for the appellant's] . . . argument, founded on the rule which has obtained in putting a construction upon statutes—that when they are penal in their nature they are not to be construed retrospectively, if the language is capable of having a prospective effect given to it and is not necessarily retrospective. But here the object of the enactment is not to punish offenders, but to protect the public against public-houses in which spirits are retailed being kept by persons of doubtful character.[104]

[97] (1848) 12 QB 118; 116 ER 811.

[98] An Act to Amend the Laws Relating to the Removal of the Poor 1846 (Eng) 9 and 10 Vict c 66 s 2.

[99] (1848) 12 QB 118, 127; 116 ER 811, 814.

[100] *Ibid.* Applied in *Master Ladies Tailors Organisation v Minister of Labour and National Service* [1950] 2 All ER 525, 527 (KB).

[101] (1848) 12 QB 118, 127; 116 ER 811, 814.

[102] Cf *Benner v Canada (Secretary of State)* [1997] 1 SCR 358, [39]–[59]; *Canada (A-G) v Hislop* [2007] SCC 10, [124]–[132]; *The Queen v Birwistle* (1889) 58 LJ (MC) 158, 160–161; *Dubbo Base Hospital v Jones* [1979] 1 NSWLR 225, 233–4.

[103] (1875) LR 10 QB 195.

[104] *Ibid* 199.

The legislature having decided that its purpose of controlling the type of person allowed to retail spirits was best pursued by the disqualification measure that it enacted, Cockburn CJ considered that 'it matters not for this purpose whether a person was convicted before or after the Act passed, one is equally bad as the other and ought not to be intrusted with a licence'.[105] Mellor and Archibald JJ agreed with Cockburn CJ and added their own brief reasoning. Lush J dissented on the basis that the Act was 'a highly penal enactment',[106] that the words of the Act on its face were ambiguous about whether it was intended to apply to convictions prior to the Act and so the presumption against retroactivity applied.

Superficially, it might be thought that the division in the court was only on the question of whether the Act was penal, and some language in Mellor and Archibald JJ's reasons supports that conclusion. However, the difference between Lush J and the majority was more fundamental than that. It rested on the meaning of retroactivity. For Cockburn CJ it was important not just that the Act was protective rather than penal but also that 'the only question for the magistrates would be whether he had or had not been convicted of a felony'.[107] Thus the Act attached a present and future consequence, which was disqualification, to a completed and past event, which was the conviction of a felony. The disqualification was a separate process coming after the conviction. This form of disqualification differs in kind, not just in degree, from the imposition of a sentence consequent upon conviction. A sentence is imposed as a direct consequence of a finding of criminal liability and is imposed for the same reason that the proscribed conduct is criminal (though it may also take into account additional factors). The disqualification in *Vine* was imposed under a statute distinct from the legal basis for the felony conviction and was imposed for the reason of public protection in the area of retailing spirits, not for a purpose necessarily related to the felony itself. Most importantly, there was no attempt to apply new law to a past event as though it was the law applicable at the time of the event. Thus the Act was not retroactive.

The final case to be discussed in this chapter is *Re a Solicitor's Clerk*.[108] The disciplinary committee of the Law Society had directed that no solicitor should employ the appellant clerk without the society's written permission. It made this order pursuant to section 16(1) of the Solicitors Act 1941[109] as amended by section 11 of the Solicitors (Amendment) Act 1956.[110] Under the 1941 Act, before it was amended, an order of the kind made could be justified only by a conviction for larceny or similar offences related to the money or property of the solicitor by whom the clerk was employed or of any client of that solicitor. The 1956 Act

[105] *Ibid* 200.
[106] *Ibid* 201.
[107] *Ibid* 200.
[108] [1957] 1 WLR 1219 (QB). Applied, eg, in *La Macchia v Minister for Primary Industry* (1986) 72 ALR 23, 26–27, 33; and *Nicholas v Commissioner for Corporate Affairs* [1988] VR 289, 295–9, 300–4. Cf *R v Field* [2003] 1 WLR 882 (CA), discussed in Ch 4 Pt G(2)(a)(ii).
[109] (Eng) 4 and 5 Geo 6 c 46.
[110] (Eng) 4 and 5 Eliz 2 c 40.

amended the 1941 Act by enabling such an order to be made regardless of to whose money or property such offences related. The appellant's conviction for larceny in 1953 involved property belonging to neither his employer nor any client of his employer. He submitted that the 1956 Act should not be applied to his conviction as to do so would be to make its operation 'retrospective'. Lord Goddard CJ, with whom Barry and Havers JJ agreed, provided a good exposition of the meaning of retroactivity:

> in my opinion this Act is not in truth retrospective. It enables an order to be made disqualifying a person from acting as a solicitor's clerk in the future and what happened in the past is the cause or reason for the making of the order, but the order has no retrospective effect. It would be retrospective if the Act provided that anything done before the Act came into force or before the order was made should be void or voidable, or if a penalty were inflicted for having acted in this or any other capacity before the Act came into force or before the order was made. This Act simply enables a disqualification to be imposed for the future which in no way affects anything done by the appellant in the past.[111]

The 1956 Act did not purport to have the effect of deeming the law at the time of the appellant's larceny to be something other than it actually was. The conviction and sentence for that larceny were not disturbed. Rather, the integrity of the legal profession and concomitant protection of the public were decided by the legislature to require that the disciplinary committee of the Law Society have the power to disqualify persons meeting certain criteria. The Act was 'concerned with past history as a condition of present fitness'[112] to practice. That a disqualification order, taking effect no earlier than the time that it was made, was made on the basis that the criteria for disqualification were met by facts occurring prior to the formation of the criteria might have been thought by the appellant to make their application to him unfair as a matter of legislative policy, but, as in *The Queen v The Inhabitants of St Mary, Whitechapel* discussed above, it did not make such application retroactive.

H Conclusion

The discussion in this chapter of academic literature and decided cases reveals a degree of confusion surrounding types of intertemporal issues, distinctions between them, and the appropriate terminology for each. As the discussion of the cases demonstrates, these issues are important not just for theoretical interest, but may have a decisive impact on the resolution of actual disputes.

111 [1957] 1 WLR 1219, 1222–1223 (QB). *Contra Secretary of State for Social Security v Tunnicliffe* [1991] 2 All ER 712, 724 (CA); *Dental Council of New Zealand v Bell* [1992] 1 NZLR 438, 446 (HC).

112 *Traill v McRae* (2002) 122 FCR 349, [211].

An attempt to consider all intertemporal issues is too large an undertaking for one piece of work. The importance of this chapter lies in the annunciation of the particular type of intertemporal issue with which this book seeks to deal: the application of a new law to a past event as though it was the law at the time of that event; and the attachment of a label to that issue: retroactivity.

2

Historical Review

A Introduction

Although Jerome Hall's assertion that:

> there has probably been no more widely held value-judgment in the entire history of human thought than condemnation of retroactive penal law[1]

was hyperbole, it is true that the presumption against retroactivity is longstanding and widely accepted in general terms, at least as it is applicable to the construction of statutes, and particularly in criminal law. The rationales for and contours of the presumption will be developed later. As a precursor to those endeavours, the present task is to conduct an historical review of its reception and development in the common law.

For both statutory construction and adjudicative retroactivity, much, though not all, of the relevant history is concerned with criminal law. However, the implications of this history have application beyond criminal law as well as within it. The general history of opposition to retroactivity, and the history specifically relating to statutory construction until the end of the nineteenth century will be reviewed, followed by the history of adjudicative retroactivity until the same time. There is a body of literature on the history of the approach to retroactivity on the European continent.[2] As this book focuses on the common law, the approach to retroactivity in other legal systems will be considered only insofar as such consideration informs the common law position.

B General History and Statutory Construction

A common starting point for consideration of the common law's approach to retroactivity is clause 39 of Magna Carta 1215, which prohibits, amongst other

[1] J Hall *General Principles of Criminal Law* (2nd edn Bobbs-Merrill Indianapolis IN 1960) 59.

[2] Some of the scant examples in English are J Hall '*Nulla Poena Sine Lege*' (1937) 47 Yale Law Journal 165; Lord Rodger 'A Time for Everything under the Law: Some Reflections on Retrospectivity' (2005) 121 Law Quarterly Review 57; A Cadoppi '*Nulla Poena Sine Lege* and Scots Criminal Law: A Continental Perspective' [1998] Juridical Review 73; G Hornung '*Nulla Poena Sine Lege* in German Law: A Reply to Cadoppi' [2002] Juridical Review 237.

things, imprisonment or persecution of a person 'except by the lawful judgment of his peers and by the law of the land'.[3] There are two difficulties with this starting point. The first is that the prohibition in clause 39 of Magna Carta is concerned with the limitation of arbitrary exercise of *executive* power, not directly with the problem of retroactive law making. The second is that the common law was influenced by the Roman law on the subject and so consideration must commence, at least briefly, with Roman law.

The Digest of the *Corpus Juris Civilis* recorded that:

> Whenever an investigation is made into an offense, it is accepted that the accused should suffer, not the punishment which his status allows at the time when sentence is passed on him but that which he would have undergone if he had been sentenced at the time he committed the offense.[4]

More generally, the Code of the *Corpus Juris Civilis* stated that it:

> is certain that the laws and constitutions regulate future matters, and have no reference to such as are past, unless express provision is made for matters which relate to past time but are still pending.[5]

This was cited by Bracton, writing before 1258, who, of the Constitution of Merton relating to the grant and usage of pastoral tenements, stated: 'Time must be considered, since every new enactment ought to impose a rule on future matters not on past.'[6]

In 1877 Fournier J considered that the rule against retroactivity of statutes is the same in English law as in French law because it derives from the same source, Roman law.[7] Whether there is truly congruence would be an interesting comparative inquiry, but for present purposes it is sufficient to note that the common law was influenced by Roman law on this topic. Having established the fact and something of the nature of this influence, further consideration must now be given to clause 39 of Magna Carta.

The famous reference to *lex terrae* in clause 39 said nothing directly about intertemporal issues. It was an early example of a concern that there be no prose-

[3] AE Dick Howard *Magna Carta: Text and Commentary* (Revised edn University Press of Virginia 1998) 45. See also WS McKechnie *Magna Carta* (2nd edn Maclehose Glasgow 1914) 375: '*nisi per legale judicium parium suorum vel per legem terre.*'

[4] T Mommsen, P Krueger (eds) and A Watson (tr) *The Digest of Justinian* (University of Pennsylvania Press 1985) 845 (D 48 19 1): '*Quotiens de delicto quaeritur, placuit non eam poenam subire quem debere, quam condicio eius admittit eo tempore, quo sententia de eo fertur, sed eam, quam sustineret, si eo tempore esset sententiam passus, cum deliquisset.*'

[5] Translated from P Krueger (ed) *Codex Justinianus* (Berolini Apud Weidmannos 1877) 103 (C 1 14 7): '*Leges et constitutiones futuris certum est dare formam negotiis, non ad facta praeterita reuocari, nisi nominatim etiam de praeterito tempore adhuc pendentibus negotiis cautum sit.*' Contra the slightly different translation in SP Scott (tr and ed) *The Civil Law* (The Central Trust Company Cincinnati OH 1932) vol 12, 87.

[6] SE Thorne (tr) GE Woodbine (ed) *Bracton On the Laws and Customs of England* (Belknap Press Cambridge MA 1968) vol 3, 181 (f228): '*Item tempus spectandum erit cum omnis nova constitutio futuria formam imponere debeat et non praeteritis.*'

[7] *Taylor v The Queen* [1876–1877] 1 SCR 65, 109: '*Ce principe de la non-rétroactivité . . . est le même dans le droit Anglais que dans le droit Français, parcequ'il derive d'une même source, le droit Romain.*'

cution or conviction without law, but it did not stipulate, even impliedly, that the law must precede the events giving rise to the prosecution. The concern of this aspect of the Charter was to control the arbitrary exercise of monarchical executive power. It was not concerned with imposing temporal limits on legislative or judicial power. Though clause 39 included substantive as well as procedural guarantees limiting the royal prerogative,[8] a right to be free from retroactive law was not among those guarantees.

When Coke considered the question of retroactivity, it was to Bracton, not to Magna Carta, that he turned. Of the alienation of tenements Coke stated that the rule expressed in the Statute of Glocestor:

> extendeth to alienations made after the statute, and not before, for it is a rule and law of parliament, that regularly *nova constitutio futuris formam imponere debet, non praeteritis.*[9]

As Coke noted in his margin, the Latin component of that sentence was a quote from Bracton—which is the same as the translated extract above: 'every new enactment ought to impose a rule on future matters not on past'.[10] Coke's use of the word 'regularly' indicated his acknowledgment that the presumption could be rebutted. Smead attributed to Coke responsibility for giving the principle expressed in the *Corpus Juris Civilis* Code and received into English law by Bracton 'currency and acceptability'[11] and stated that 'its development as a part of present day jurisprudence begins with his writings'.[12]

Like clause 39 of Magna Carta, Coke too was concerned with controlling, through law, the monarch's power over both property and personal liberty.[13] Furthermore, Coke's statement of principle, drawing on Bracton, covered a broad range of retrospective effects. Its objection was not limited to retroactivity in the way that term is defined in Chapter one.[14]

Hobbes, on the other hand, cut to a core difficulty with retroactivity when he said that:

> harm inflicted for a fact done before there was a law that forbade it, is not punishment, but an act of hostility: for before the law, there is no transgression of the law.[15]

8 WS McKechnie *Magna Carta* (2nd edn Maclehose Glasgow 1914) 379, 380, 394; P Vinogradoff 'Magna Carta, C 39' in HE Malden (ed) *Magna Carta Commemoration Essays* (Royal Historical Society London 1917) 85.

9 E Coke *The Second Part of the Institutes of the Laws of England* (Brooke London 1797) vol 1, 292.

10 SE Thorne (tr) GE Woodbine (ed) *Bracton On the Laws and Customs of England* (Belknap Press Cambridge MA 1968) vol 3, 181 (f228).

11 EE Smead 'The Rule Against Retroactive Legislation: A Basic Principle of Jurisprudence' (1936) 20 Minnesota Law Review 775, 776.

12 *Ibid.*

13 E Coke as recorded in *Proceedings in Parliament Relating to Liberty of the Subject* (1628) 3 Howell's State Trials 78.

14 *Hough v Windus* (1884) 12 QBD 224, 227, 235 (CA); *Vansitart v Taylor* (1855) 4 El & Bl 910, 914; 119 ER 338, 340.

15 T Hobbes *Leviathan* (1651) JCA Gaskin (ed) (Oxford University Press 1996) ch 28, 207.

Hobbes' work will be returned to more fully in considering rationales for a general presumption against retroactivity in Chapter three.[16] It is noted briefly here only for the sake of completeness of this historical review.

The next significant argument against retroactive law making was made by Blackstone, who referred to the cruel Roman Emperor Caligula, who:

> wrote his laws in a very small character, and hung them up upon high pillars, the more effectually to ensnare the people.[17]

Blackstone then stated:

> There is still a more unreasonable method than this, which is called making of laws *ex post facto*: when *after* an action [indifferent in itself] is committed, the legislator then for the first time declares it to have been a crime, and inflicts a punishment upon the person who has committed it; here it is impossible that the party could foresee that an action, innocent when it was done, should be afterwards converted to guilt by a subsequent law; he had therefore no cause to abstain from it; and all punishment for not abstaining must of consequence be cruel and unjust. All laws should be therefore made to commence *in futuro*, and be notified before their commencement.[18]

The words in square brackets did not appear in Blackstone's first edition in 1765, but were included in parentheses in the second edition of the first volume of Blackstone's *Commentaries* in 1766,[19] and remained thereafter. The reference to an action 'indifferent in itself' is significant,[20] particularly given Blackstone's reliance on natural law.[21] Blackstone was dismissive of the role of municipal law in relation to actions that are 'naturally and intrinsically right or wrong',[22] or in other words acts '*mala in se*'.[23] He contrasted these with 'things in themselves indifferent',[24] or acts '*mala prohibita*',[25] which become right or wrong according to common law or legislation. Blackstone's antipathy for retroactive criminal legislation was limited to the criminalisation of acts that were not 'naturally and intrinsically' criminal. On this approach there was no objection to legislation retroactively criminalising an act that was 'naturally and intrinsically' wrong, on the basis that legislation was not necessary to establish the criminal nature of the act.

[16] Ch 3 Pts C(3) and C(4)(b).

[17] W Blackstone *Commentaries on the Laws of England* (Facsimile of the 1st edn (1765) University of Chicago Press 1979) vol 1, 46; (16th edn Cadell London 1825) vol 1, 45.

[18] *Ibid.*

[19] W Blackstone *Commentaries on the Laws of England* (2nd edn Clarendon Press Oxford 1766) vol 1, 46.

[20] Contra J Bentham *A Comment on the Commentaries: A Criticism of William Blackstone's Commentaries on the Laws of England* CW Everett (ed) (Clarendon Press Oxford 1928) 69–70 who stated that he did not know what Blackstone meant by this phrase.

[21] W Blackstone *Commentaries on the Laws of England* (Facsimile of the 1st edn (1765) University of Chicago Press 1979) eg vol 1, 42–3, 57 and especially 54–5; (16th edn Cadell London 1825) eg vol 1, 42, 57 and especially 53–4.

[22] *Ibid* 54; 54.

[23] *Ibid* 54; 53.

[24] *Ibid* 55; 54.

[25] *Ibid* 57; 57.

The French Declaration of the Rights of Man and Citizen of 1789 was the first modern constitutional expression of an insistence on punishment not just by laws rather than men, but more specifically by laws operative at the time of the commission of the offence said to justify the punishment. Article 8 provided that:

> no one may be punished except by virtue of a law passed and promulgated prior to the crime and applied in due legal form.[26]

Shortly afterwards, Feuerbach expressed aspects of the principle of legality in Latin: '*Nulla poena sine lege, nulla poena sine crimine, nullum crimen sine poena legali*',[27] from which the common contemporary expressions, used in civil law and common law systems, and in public international law, are derived: *nullum crimen sine lege* and *nulla poena sine lege.* Insofar as these maxims are taken to include a prohibition on retroactivity, emphasis on the need for the law to be *already existing* would be represented more accurately, though admittedly less neatly, by the expressions *nullum crimen sine lege antea exstanti* and *nulla poena sine lege antea exstanti.*

Purporting to favourably contrast the rule of law in England with continental European traditions,[28] one of Dicey's conceptions of the 'supremacy or the rule of law'[29] was that:

> no man is punishable or can be lawfully made to suffer in body or goods except for a distinct breach of law established in the ordinary legal manner before the ordinary courts of the land.[30]

Like clause 39 of Magna Carta and the maxims *nullum crimen sine lege* and *nulla poena sine lege,* the primary thrust of this passage was the control of executive power by precluding criminal liability or punishment except in accordance with law. Dicey did not expressly object to retroactive law making.

[26] '*Nul ne peut être puni qu'en vertu d'une loi etablie et promulguée antérieurement au délit et légalement appliquée.*'

[27] PJAR von Feuerbach *Lehrbuch des Peinlichen Rechts* (1801) [24], quoted in J Hall *General Principles of Criminal Law* (2nd edn Bobbs-Merrill Indianapolis IN 1960) 34 fn 34. Also referred to in G Hornung '*Nulla Poena Sine Lege* in German Law: A Reply to Cadoppi' [2002] Juridical Review 237, 238 fn 8. See, both on Feuerbach and more generally on this aspect of the history of the principle, Lord Rodger 'A Time for Everything under the Law: Some Reflections on Retrospectivity' (2005) 121 Law Quarterly Review 57, 65–6 and *R(Uttley) v Secretary of State for the Home Department* [2004] 1 WLR 2278, [39] (HL).

[28] Cf LE Irish *Time and Law: Retrospectivity and Prospectivity of Statutes and Judicial Decisions* (D Phil Thesis University of Oxford 1971) 65, who asserted that England was 'the first country in which the general condemnation of retrospective laws was widely observed'. For this proposition Irish cited J Hall *General Principles of Criminal Law* (2nd edn Bobbs-Merrill Indianapolis IN 1960) 27–35, who does not there make such a claim.

[29] AV Dicey *Lectures Introductory to the Study of the Law of the Constitution* (MacMillan London 1885) 172; *Introduction to the Study of the Law of the Constitution* (10th edn MacMillan London 1959) 187.

[30] *Ibid* 172; 188.

The rule of law was Dicey's second feature of English political institutions which he thought 'very closely connected'[31] to his first feature, which was the absolute sovereignty of parliament, meaning 'the right to make or unmake any law whatever'.[32] On that point Dicey[33] cited Blackstone who emphasized the 'sovereign and uncontroulable authority'[34] of parliament and who in turn[35] cited Coke, who referred to the 'transcendant and absolute power'[36] of parliament. This extremely strong view of parliamentary sovereignty might be thought by some to leave little room for an independent presumption against retroactivity[37] and is the basis of the traditionally accepted constitutional position that parliament may pass a retroactive law should it wish to do so.[38]

Parliament was, however, sensitive to the injustice that might be caused by the retroactive effect of its statutes. In 1793 parliament passed An Act to Prevent Acts of Parliament from Taking Effect from a Time Prior to the Passing Thereof,[39] which abolished the rule that a statute that did not make specific provision for its commencement took effect at the beginning of the parliamentary session during which it was passed. There is a view that executive discretion usually prevented injustices that otherwise might have occurred because of that rule.[40] However, the preamble to the statute that effected the change observed the 'great and manifest injustice' that could result from a law being deemed to commence at a date prior to its passage through parliament, and so it was enacted that any Act that did not contain a specific commencement date would commence on the date of royal assent.

This change removed issues of retroactivity of the kind that arose in the decision of the King's Bench in *R v Thurston*.[41] In that case a man killed a bailiff who had attempted to arrest him on the basis of a void warrant. Later in the same parliamentary term legislation was passed that had the effect of making good the warrant. If the legislation was deemed to take effect on the first day of the parliamentary session then the killing was murder. The precise nature of the arguments and decision is difficult to determine from the reports of the case, but it is tolerably clear that the statute validating the warrant was deemed to have applied at the time of the killing, prior to its passage through parliament, and that the defendant was guilty of murder.

[31] AV Dicey *Lectures Introductory to the Study of the Law of the Constitution* (MacMillan London 1885) 167. This was later reduced to 'closely connected': *Introduction to the Study of the Law of the Constitution* (3rd edn MacMillan London 1889) 171; and so it remained: *Introduction to the Study of the Law of the Constitution* (10th edn MacMillan London 1959) 184.

[32] AV Dicey *Lectures Introductory to the Study of the Law of the Constitution* (MacMillan London 1885) 36; *Introduction to the Study of the Law of the Constitution* (10th edn MacMillan London 1959) 40.

[33] *Ibid* 37–9; 41–2.

[34] W Blackstone *Commentaries on the Laws of England* (16th edn Cadell London 1825) vol 1, 160.

[35] *Ibid.*

[36] E Coke *The Fourth Part of the Institutes of the Laws of England* (Brooke London 1797) 36.

[37] Contra Ch 4 Pt B.

[38] Eg *Polyukhovich v The Commonwealth* (1991) 172 CLR 501, 534–5.

[39] (UK) 33 Geo III c 13.

[40] L Hall and SJ Seligman 'Mistake of Law and Mens Rea' (1941) 8 University of Chicago Law Review 641, 654–5.

[41] (1663) I Lev 91; 83 ER 312; 1 Keble 454; 83 ER 1049.

Although from 1793 parliament avoided the uniform retroactivity of statutes passed after the first day of a parliamentary session, occasionally it did pass explicitly retroactive individual pieces of legislation. Such a statute was considered in *Phillips v Eyre*.[42] Willes J stated that:

> Retrospective laws are, no doubt, prima facie of questionable policy, and contrary to the general principle that legislation by which the conduct of mankind is to be regulated ought, when introduced for the first time, to deal with future acts, and ought not to change the character of past transactions carried on upon the faith of the then existing law.[43]

He went on to state that:

> Accordingly, the Court will not ascribe retrospective force to new laws affecting rights, unless by express words or necessary implication it appears that such was the intention of the legislature. But to affirm that it is naturally or necessarily unjust to take away a vested right of action by act subsequent, is inconsistent both with the common law of England and the constant practice of legislation.[44]

In *Phillips v Eyre*, the reasoning in which is criticized in Chapter four,[45] the presumption against retroactivity was overcome, with the result that what was illegal at the time that it was done was later deemed to have been legal. There are, however, numerous cases in which arguments that an Act made lawful what was unlawful at the time that it occurred were unsuccessful in the face of the presumption against retroactivity.[46] In *Young v Adams* Lord Watson approved Erle CJ's statement in *Midland Railway Co v Pye* that retroactive operation is not to be granted:

> unless the intention of the legislature that it should be so construed is expressed in clear, plain and unambiguous language; because it manifestly shocks one's sense of justice that an act legal at the time of doing it should be made unlawful by some new enactment.[47]

Lord Watson continued:

> The ratio is equally apparent when a new enactment is said to convert an act wrongfully done at the time into a legal act, and to deprive the person injured of the remedy which the law then gave him.[48]

Similar antipathy towards retroactivity was apparent in *R v Griffiths*[49] in which the issue was whether a defence available at the time of the events giving rise to the

[42] (1870) LR 6 QB 1 (Exch).
[43] *Ibid* 23.
[44] *Ibid.*
[45] Ch 4 Pt F(2).
[46] Eg *Midland Railway Co v Pye* (1861) 10 CB (NS) 179; 142 ER 419; *Young v Adams* [1898] AC 469 (PC); *Re Chapman* [1896] 1 Ch 323.
[47] *Midland Railway Co v Pye* (1861) 10 CB (NS) 179, 191; 142 ER 419, 424, quoted in *Young v Adams* [1898] AC 469, 476 (PC).
[48] [1898] AC 469, 476 (PC).
[49] [1891] 2 QB 145.

litigation had been removed with retroactive effect by a subsequent statute. More precisely, the question was whether a provision of the Bankruptcy Act 1890,[50] amending the Debtors Act 1869,[51] applied to events completed before the coming into force of the 1890 Act. Five judges of the Queen's Bench on a case stated held that it did not. Lord Coleridge CJ delivered the leading judgment holding that the words 'shall have effect' appearing in the statute meant 'shall have effect from the date of entry into force of the statute'. Lord Coleridge CJ said:

> That conclusion is supported by the view that to give a retrospective effect to the statute would be to deprive the defendant of a defence upon which, at the time the acts complained of were committed, he was entitled to rely. It seems to me a very strong thing to hold that a defence which was open to a man at the time he did the act complained of has been taken away by the retrospective operation of a subsequent statute. No authority in support of such a construction has been cited to us. I think it is safer to hold that all the ingredients of the offence must have taken place before the Bankruptcy Act, 1890, came into operation, and I am therefore of opinion that this conviction cannot be sustained.[52]

A fairly stark example of a refusal to grant retroactive effect to a statute occurred in *Hickson v Darlow*.[53] The Bills of Sale Amendment Act 1882[54] enacted that a bill of sale had to be registered within seven days of its execution, failing which it would be void. It was held, applying the presumption against retroactivity, that this did not apply to bills of sale executed more than seven days prior to the commencement of the Act because, as Jessel MR said, such a reading would be making the statute 'enact an impossibility'.[55]

Attempts to deem lawful that which was unlawful, to nullify a defence that existed at the time of acting, and to interpret a statute so that it required an act to be done after the time for performing that act had passed, have all been assessed by the courts in light of the presumption against retroactivity. Those categories of case do not, however, represent the most common type of case in which arguments have arisen about whether a statute does or does not have retroactive effect. That distinction belongs to cases in which it was argued that a statute's effect was to deem that a legal right that in fact existed prior to the passage of that statute did not exist at that earlier time.

In *Gilmore v Shuter* although the plain words of the statute militated towards it having retroactive effect, the court refused so to construe it, because 'by an easy transposition of the words of the Act, a construction agreeable to justice may be made'.[56] This 'transposition' was made on the basis that it was 'usual . . . to make Acts of Parliament not repugnant to common justice'.[57] Similarly, in *Moon v*

[50] (Eng) 53 and 54 Vict c 71.
[51] (Eng) 32 and 33 Vict c 62.
[52] [1891] 2 QB 145, 148.
[53] (1883) 23 Ch D 690 (CA).
[54] (Eng) 45 and 46 Vict c 43 s 8.
[55] (1883) 23 Ch D 690, 694 (CA).
[56] (1678) T Jones 108, 109; 84 ER 1170, 1171.
[57] *Ibid.*

Durden[58] Parke B, before applying the presumption against retroactivity and holding that the Act did not have retroactive effect, expressly acknowledged that the ordinary meaning of the statute was to apply to transactions preceding the Act.[59]

The presumption against retroactivity was sometimes rebutted with the effect that a legal right that actually existed at an earlier time was deemed not to have existed at that time. *Towler v Chatterton*[60] was such a case. In *Towler v Chatterton* the fact that the statute provided for an eight month delay between its enactment and its commencement, allowing any outstanding actions to be brought on the basis of the law applicable at the time of the transactions to which they related, influenced the court in favour of granting the retroactive effect that was obviously parliament's design.

This review of learned authors, constitutional documents and decided cases indicates that the common law has long been cautious about statutes said to have some form of retrospective effect. At least since Hobbes and Blackstone that caution has included a specific objection to statutes with *retroactive* effect. Historically, common law judges have approached statutory construction from the perspective that granting retroactive effect to a statute is likely to cause injustice. The presumption against retroactivity has sometimes been rebutted by explicit language or other considerations, but such rebuttal does not diminish the fact that the starting point for common law judges in cases in which it is suggested that a statute has retroactive effect has long been that such effect should not ordinarily be found to exist.

C Adjudicative Retroactivity

Although the nature of the common law adjudicative process might be thought by some to limit the relevance of Roman law to consideration of adjudicative retroactivity in the common law,[61] Bracton stated, relevantly, that:

> If some new and unusual matters arise which have not previously been dealt with in the kingdom, if nevertheless similar matters have occurred, then let the new matters be decided by analogy, since the occasion is a good one for proceeding *a similibus ad similia*. But if nothing like these questions has ever occurred before, and deciding them is obscure and difficult, then let the matters be adjourned to the great court to be there determined by the council of the court.[62]

[58] (1848) 2 Ex 22, 42; 154 ER 389, 398.
[59] See also *Hitchcock v Way* (1837) 6 Ad & E 943, especially 951–2; 112 ER 360, especially 363–4.
[60] (1829) 6 Bing 258; 130 ER 1280.
[61] Eg CK Allen *Law in the Making* (7th edn Clarendon Press Oxford 1964) 202–3.
[62] This indicates that difficult questions were to be decided by a full bench. This translation differs from that provided in SE Thorne (tr) GE Woodbine (ed) *Bracton On the Laws and Customs of England* (Belknap Press Cambridge MA 1968) vol 2, 21 (f 1), where the original Latin is also provided: '*Si autem*

In the course of that passage, Bracton cited Roman law, in particular the statements in *The Digest of Justinian* that:

> It is not possible for every point to be specifically dealt with either in statutes or in *senatus consulta*; but whenever in any case their sense is clear, the president of the tribunal ought to proceed by analogical reasoning and declare the law accordingly.[63]

And that:

> whenever some particular thing or another has been brought within statute law, there is good ground for other things which further the same interest to be added in supplementation, whether this be done by juristic interpretation or *a fortiori* by judicial decision.[64]

At least since Bracton the approach of the common law to intertemporal issues has been starkly different according to whether a legislative enactment or a common law rule was under consideration. Bracton's insistence that enactments should apply to future events not to those past contrasted with his encouragement of reasoning by analogy in the adjudication of novel cases. This latter aspect was limited to the application (or perhaps modification) of existing principles to new but similar situations and, though the difference may be one of degree rather than of kind, it did not support the creation of new legal rules as circumstances demanded. The authority expressly to create a new legal rule and impose it on events already past was, however, later claimed by the courts.

Hudson described the jurisdiction of the Star Chamber (which was abolished in 1641):

> which, by the arm of sovereignty punisheth errors creeping into the Commonwealth, which otherwise might prove dangerous and infectious diseases . . . although no positive law or continued custom of common law giveth warrant to it.[65]

After quoting this passage from Hudson, Holdsworth noted that 'such powers could only be used for weighty causes'.[66] Hudson's account indicated that the Star Chamber did not, in the exercise of the power just described, even purport to rely on law, even retroactive law, as the basis of its actions, and so the more relevant enquiry is into the early cases of the Court of King's Bench.

aliqua nova et inconsueta emerserint et quae prius usitata non fuerint in regno, si tamen similia evenerint per simile iudicentur, cum bona sit occasio a similibus procedere ad similia. Si autem talia prius numquam evenerint, et obscurum et difficile sit eorum iudicium, tunc ponantur iudicia usque ad magnam curiam ut ibi per consilium curiae terminentur'. [Citations omitted]

[63] T Mommsen, P Krueger (eds) and A Watson (tr) *The Digest of Justinian* (University of Pennsylvania Press 1985) 845 (D 1 3 12): '*Non possunt omnes articuli singillatim aut legibus aut senatus consultis compraehendi: sed cum in aliqua causa sententia eorum manifesta est, is qui iurisdictioni praeest ad similia procedere atque ita ius dicere debet.*'

[64] *Ibid* (D 1 3 13): '*quotiens lege aliquid unum uel alterum introductum est, bona occassio est cetera, quae tendunt ad eandem utilitatem, uel interpretatione uel certe iurisdictione suppleri.*'

[65] W Hudson 'A Treatise of the Court of Star Chamber' in F Hargrave (ed) *Collectanea Juridica* (Brooke London 1792) vol 2, 107.

[66] WS Holdsworth *History of English Law* (7th edn Methuen London 1956) vol 1, 504.

Glanville Williams considered that the Court of King's Bench during the seventeenth century:

> asserted itself as the rival and later the heir of the Star Chamber by claiming an undefined discretion to punish wrongs.[67]

Lord Coke, sitting in the Court of King's Bench in *Bagg's Case*, claimed enormous discretion for the court and asserted that discretion to be an aspect of *law*, when he stated that to the Court of King's Bench belonged:

> authority, not only to correct errors in judicial proceedings, but other errors and misdemeanours extra-judicial, tending to the breach of peace, or oppression of the subjects, or to the raising of faction, controversy, debate, or to any manner of misgovernment; so that wrong or injury, either public or private, can be done, but that it shall (here) be reformed or punished by due course of law.[68]

A similar approach was evident in the same court more than 150 years later in *Millar v Taylor* in which Willes J, speaking about the law of copyright, referred to:

> principles of private justice, moral fitness, and public convenience; which, when applied to a new subject, make common law without a precedent.[69]

Another 85 years hence, in *Jefferys v Boosey*, also a copyright case, Pollock CB quoted that passage from *Millar v Taylor* and continued:

> I entirely agree with the spirit of this passage, so far as it regards the repressing what is a public evil, and preventing what would become a general mischief; but I think there is a wide difference between protecting the community against a new source of danger, and creating a new right. I think the Common Law is quite competent to pronounce anything to be illegal which is manifestly against the public good; but I think the Common Law cannot create new rights, and limit and define them, because, in the opinion of those who administer the Common Law, such rights ought to exist, according to their notions of what is just, right, and proper.[70]

Shortly after Willes J's statement in *Millar v Taylor*, which was simultaneously approved and limited by Pollock CB in *Jefferys v Boosey*, Lord Mansfield in *Jones v Randall*[71] also annunciated a role for the courts that included an ability to declare new specific legal rules on the basis of existing broad principles. In that case there was 'no positive law, nor any case in the books'[72] governing the case. Lord Mansfield agreed with counsel that 'if it is bad upon principle this is sufficient'.[73] Lord Mansfield thought that:

> The law would be a strange science if it rested solely upon cases; and if after so large an increase of commerce, arts and circumstances accruing, we must go to the time of Rich

[67] G Williams *Criminal Law: The General Part* (2nd edn Stevens London 1961) 593.
[68] (1615) 11 Co Rep 93b, 98a; 77 ER 1271, 1277–8.
[69] (1769) 4 Burr 2303, 2312; 98 ER 201, 206.
[70] (1854) 4 HLC 814, 936; 10 ER 681, 728–9.
[71] (1774) Lofft 383; 98 ER 706.
[72] *Ibid* 385; 707.
[73] *Ibid.*

1 to find a case, and see what is law. Precedent indeed may serve to fix principles, which for certainty's sake are not suffered to be shaken, whatever might be the weight of the principle, independent of precedent. But precedent, though it be evidence of law, is not law in itself; much less the whole of the law.[74]

Lord Mansfield then made an extremely wide claim:

Whatever is contrary, bonos mores est decorum,[75] the principles of our law prohibit, and the King's Court, as the general censor and guardian of the public manners, is bound to restrain and punish. [Footnote added][76]

110 years later, though only 30 years after Pollock CB's statement of a more confined creative role in *Jefferys v Boosey*, much greater restraint was exhibited by Stephen J in *The Queen v Price*:

upon the fullest examination of the authorities, I have, as the preceding review of them shews, been unable to discover any authority for the proposition that it is a misdemeanor to burn a dead body, and in the absence of such authority I feel that I have no right to declare it to be one.

There are some instances, no doubt, in which courts of justice have declared acts to be misdemeanors which had never previously been decided to be so, but I think it will be found that in every such case the act involved great public mischief or moral scandal. It is not my place to offer any opinion on the comparative merits of burning and burying corpses, but before I could hold that it must be a misdemeanor to burn a dead body, I must be satisfied not only that some people, or even that many people, object to the practice, but that it is, on plain, undeniable grounds, highly mischievous or grossly scandalous. Even then I should pause long before I held it to be a misdemeanor, for many acts involving the grossest indecency and grave public mischief—incest, for instance, and, where there is no conspiracy, seduction or adultery—are not misdemeanors, but I cannot take even the first step. . . . There are, no doubt, religious convictions and feelings connected with the subject which every one would wish to treat with respect and tenderness, and I suppose there is no doubt that as a matter of historical fact the disuse of burning bodies was due to the force of those sentiments. I do not think, however, that it can be said that every practice which startles and jars upon the religious sentiments of the majority of the population is for that reason a misdemeanor at common law. The statement of such a proposition, in plain words, is a sufficient refutation of it, but nothing short of this will support the conclusion that to burn a dead body must be a misdemeanor. . . . It may be that it would be well for Parliament to regulate or to forbid the burning of bodies, but the great leading rule of criminal law is that nothing is a crime unless it is plainly forbidden by law. This rule is no doubt subject to exceptions, but they are rare, narrow, and to be admitted with the greatest reluctance, and only upon the strongest reasons.[77]

[74] *Ibid.*

[75] This phrase does not make sense as reported. Lord Mansfield probably actually said '*contra bonos mores et decorum*', meaning 'against good manners and propriety'.

[76] (1774) Lofft 383, 385; 98 ER 706, 707. *R v Sidley* (1664) 1 Sid 168; 82 ER 1036, in which Sir Charles Sidley stood on a balcony above a large gathering of people and 'made water' on the people below, and *R v Delaval* (1763) 3 Burr 1434, 1438–9; 97 ER 913, 915 are authority for the same proposition.

[77] (1884) 12 QBD 247, 255–6. Contra *Shaw v DPP* [1962] AC 220 (HL), discussed in Ch 5 Pt G(1)(b).

This restraint led ATH Smith to opine that though historically common law judges:

> asserted extensive powers to add new crimes to the criminal calendar . . . it is clear that by the time Sir James Stephen wrote . . . the power had atrophied to the point of extinction.[78]

Perhaps the atrophy was not as large as Smith suggests, because in *The Queen v Stephenson*, decided later in the same year as *Price*, the question was whether it was:

> a misdemeanor to destroy a body upon which an inquisition is about to be properly held, with intent to prevent the holding of that inquest.[79]

There was some relevant authority. Nonetheless, in finding, as all five judges unanimously did, that such conduct amounted to a criminal offence, Stephen J said:

> This matter is not absolutely covered by authority. In one sense we do create new offences, that is to say, that as a Court we can and do define the law from time to time and apply it to the varying circumstances which arise.[80]

This contrasted not only with Stephen J's decision in *Price* but also with his extra-curial view of assertions of judicial power to create new common law offences, published just one year earlier, in 1883:

> Though the existence of this power as inherent in the judges has been asserted by several high authorities for a great length of time, it is hardly probable that any attempt would be made to exercise it at the present day; and any such attempt would be received with great opposition, and would place the bench in an invidious position. . . . I have given the history of this matter, and it is by no means favourable to the declaration by the bench of new offences.[81]

Although, as Lord Mansfield emphasized in *Jones v Randall*, the doctrine of precedent served to promote consistency,[82] where there was no relevant precedent, English courts have, with some exceptions, such as Stephen J's admirable decision in *Price*, historically not felt constrained by the absence of previous authority in finding conduct to be unlawful which could not have been so described at the time that it occurred.

Stephen J's reference in *Stephenson* to the judicial ability to 'define the law', and more directly, Lord Mansfield's statement in *Jones v Randall* that 'precedent, though it be evidence of law, is not law in itself' echoed the approach taken by Hale and Blackstone, which became popular bases for the declaratory theory.[83]

[78] ATH Smith 'Judicial Lawmaking in the Criminal Law' (1984) 100 Law Quarterly Review 46, 54–5.
[79] (1884) 13 QBD 331, 337.
[80] *Ibid.*
[81] JF Stephen *A History of the Criminal Law of England* (Reprint of the original 1883 edn Routledge/Thoemmes Press London 1996) vol 3, 359–60. Again, contra *Shaw v DPP* [1962] AC 220 (HL), discussed in Ch 5 Pt G(1)(b).
[82] See also *R v Dawes* (1767) 4 Burr 2120, 2121; 98 ER 106, 106.
[83] For a discussion of the declaratory theory see Ch 5 Pt B(2).

Hale sought to identify the 'formal constituents'[84] of the common law. Of his third constituent—judicial decisions—Hale wrote:

> It is true, the decisions of courts of justice, though by virtue of the laws of this realm they do bind, as a law between the parties thereto, as to the particular case in question, till reversed by error or attaint; yet they do not make a law, properly so called;—for that only the king and parliament can do; yet they have a great weight and authority in expounding, declaring, and publishing what the law of this kingdom is; especially when such decisions hold a consonancy and congruity with resolutions and decisions of former times. And though such decisions are less than a law, yet they are a greater evidence thereof than the opinion of any private persons.[85]

Explaining why judicial decisions were greater evidence of the law than the opinion of private persons, Hale said, inter alia, that:

> their judgments are strengthened and upheld by the laws of this kingdom, till they are by the same law reversed, or avoided.[86]

On the same theme Blackstone considered that:

> *the law*, and the *opinion of the judge*, are not always convertible terms, or one and the same thing; since it sometimes may happen that the judge may *mistake* the law. Upon the whole however, we may take it as a general rule, 'that the decisions of courts of justice are the evidence of what is common law:' in the same manner as, in the civil law, what the emperor had once determined was to serve as a guide for the future.[87]

Bentham wrote a memorandum about this passage, which his editor thought was 'apparently intended for further development'.[88] The memorandum was: 'Why contradictory Statutes do not do the mischief of contradictory decisions. Decisions retrospective.'[89] In a passage that his editor believed to be connected with that memorandum, Bentham wrote:

> The individual judicial decisions are acts of Judges; they are acts of authority. But the rules of law are general propositions: these general propositions are conclusions drawn from the above-mentioned individual acts: and these conclusions are what are formed by any one who happens to bestow his thoughts upon the subject. If he happens to be a judge, his conclusions will naturally carry more weight than those of a common man.[90]

Bentham did not object to Blackstone's view that judicial decisions are no more than evidence of the law, although elsewhere Bentham famously did object to the

[84] M Hale *The History and Analysis of the Common Law of England* (Walthoe London 1713) 66; *The History of the Common Law of England* (6th edn Butterworth London 1820) 88.

[85] *Ibid* 68; 89–90.

[86] *Ibid* 69; 90.

[87] W Blackstone *Commentaries on the Laws of England* (Facsimile of the 1st edn (1765) University of Chicago Press 1979) vol 1, 71; (16th edn Cadell London 1825) vol 1, 71.

[88] J Bentham *A Comment on the Commentaries: A Criticism of William Blackstone's Commentaries on the Laws of England* CW Everett (ed) (Clarendon Press Oxford 1928) 198.

[89] *Ibid.*

[90] *Ibid* 199.

very power of judges to make decisions not based on statute, in large part because of the potential retroactive effect of their doing so:

> It is the judges . . . that make the common law. Do you know how they make it? Just as a man makes laws for his dog. When your dog does anything you want to break him of, you wait till he does it, and then beat him for it. This is the way you make laws for your dog: and this is the way the judges make law for you and me. They won't tell a man beforehand what it is he *should not do* . . . they lie by till he has done something which they say he should not *have done*, and then they hang him for it.[91]

Despite the obviously creative role played by the courts from at least the beginning of the seventeenth century until at least the end of the nineteenth century, the theoretical view that judges' decisions were evidence of the law, rather than the law itself, was thought by many to support the view, expressed, for example, by Lord Esher MR, that:

> There is, in fact, no such thing as judge-made law, for the judges do not make the law, though they frequently have to apply existing law to circumstances as to which it has not previously been authoritatively laid down that such law is applicable.[92]

This was not, however, a uniform view. Mellish LJ, for example, observed that:

> the whole of the rules of equity, and nine tenths of the rules of common law, have in fact been made by the Judges.[93]

The belief that judges did not make law, but, in the sort of cases in which they might be thought by some to have been doing exactly that, only declared the application of existing common law principle to new situations, or corrected the mistaken approach of a previous court to existing principle, meant that, theoretically, problems of retroactivity never arose, because whatever was decided in a particular case, no matter how novel, was asserted to be merely the application of the existing common law.[94] Lord Mansfield and Lord Esher MR, as exemplars of this approach, were not suggesting that a pre-existing answer to any future legal question had been waiting since the beginning of the common law in Aladdin's cave, waiting to be discovered when the particular rule in storage was called forth by a judge confronted with novel facts that required its application.[95] Rather, they were suggesting the much more modest and more sensible position that within the common law lay principles of a general character, at a higher level of abstraction

[91] J Bentham 'Truth versus Ashhurst' in *The Works of Jeremy Bentham* J Bowring (ed) (William Tait Edinburgh 1843) vol 5, 235. See also J Bentham *A Comment on the Commentaries: A Criticism of William Blackstone's Commentaries on the Laws of England* CW Everett (ed) (Clarendon Press Oxford 1928) 67–70.

[92] *Willis v Baddeley* [1892] 2 QB 324, 326 (CA).

[93] *Allen v Jackson* (1875) 1 Ch D 399, 405 (CA).

[94] See further R Cross and J Harris *Precedent in English Law* (4th edn Clarendon Press Oxford 1991) 35–6 and the cases there cited.

[95] Contra J Austin *Lectures on Jurisprudence* R Campbell (ed) (5th edn Revised John Murray London 1911) vol 2, 634; Lord Reid 'The Judge as Lawmaker' (1972) 12 Journal of the Society of Public Teachers of Law 22, 22; *Jones v Secretary of State for Social Services* [1972] AC 944, 1026 (HL) (Lord Simon).

than rules that may be directly applicable in any given case, and that when decided cases did not provide an applicable rule, or provided a rule that was inconsistent with the broader principles of the common law, that those existing broad principles would point to an appropriate rule that had never previously been declared in specific form. Even this more modest position, however, because it allowed new specific rules to be applied to situations that arose when those rules did not exist, or at the very least were unknown, as though the new rules were applicable prior to their declaration, caused, in practice, retroactive effects.

What may otherwise have been rampant retroactivity caused by the declaratory theory was constrained by the emerging doctrine of precedent.[96] Notwithstanding that constraint, the willingness of common law judges to declare legal rules never before declared and to correct previous declarations of legal rules thought by them to be departures from existing common law principles, meant that the historical approach of the common law was to tolerate a high degree of adjudicative retroactivity.

D Conclusion

A clear historical pattern is apparent insofar as the construction of statutes is concerned. There is a longstanding and well recognized common law presumption against statutory retroactivity. As has been discussed, the common law's approach to adjudicative retroactivity is more complicated. The most important point is that, unlike its approach to the construction of statutes, the common law has traditionally been tolerant of the retroactive effects of judicial decisions developing or changing a common law rule.

[96] The relationship between the doctrine of precedent and the control of adjudicative retroactivity is discussed in Ch 5 Pt B.

3

Rationales for a General Presumption Against Retroactivity

A Introduction

The imposition of retroactive legal consequences is not self-evidently wrong. Before a value judgment can be made about retroactivity generally, and before decided cases that variously control or allow it can properly be considered, it is necessary to examine rationales that might underlie a general presumption against retroactivity. As a counterbalance to those values, it is appropriate also to identify some considerations that may, exceptionally, indicate the desirability of tolerating retroactivity. These considerations do not detract from the rationales for a general presumption against retroactivity, though they do justify the defeasible nature of that presumption.

Waldron thinks that the fact that there are only few and limited attempts at 'a full elaboration of the values underlying the principle of prospectivity' constitutes 'a pretty scandalous state of affairs'.[1] Similarly, Fuller thought that the 'literature of jurisprudence pays but scant attention to retroactive laws'.[2] This attempt is intended to be introductory rather than fulsome, because its purpose is not independent, but instead related to a broader consideration of how the common law, in practice, does or should deal with issues of retroactivity.

Because of its particular purpose, this enquiry into rationales does not extend to consideration of a normative principle of non-retroactivity of legislative action. The direct concern is with rationales that do or should underlie judicial decisions about the construction of statutes and about common law rules. However, some prescriptive accounts of the general undesirability of retroactive legislation rely on rationales that apply with equal force to judicial decisions and will therefore be drawn on to the extent that they so apply. This chapter seeks to establish rationales for a presumption against retroactivity, as well as to note circumstances in which that presumption is defeasible, at a level of generality that includes both judicial decisions about whether a statute has retroactive effect *and* judicial decisions about whether to develop or change a common law rule.

[1] J Waldron 'Retroactive Law: How Dodgy was Duynhoven?' (2004) 10 Otago Law Review 631, 640 fn 17.

[2] L Fuller *The Morality of Law* (Revised edn Yale University Press New Haven CT 1969) 52, fn 13.

B Certainty

1 The Meaning of Certainty

Because the meaning of a law may be contestable, a general presumption against retroactivity cannot realistically demand that the precise meaning of every law be known for certain and in advance of an event to which that law applies. Certainty, for present purposes, asks not that the meaning of all law be known in advance, but rather that when the meaning of a law is settled at the time of an event to which that law applies, that law should not later be altered in a way that vitiates the existing certainty about that law's application to that past event. In cases where the meaning of the law at the time of the relevant events was unclear, there is less certainty to protect. This type of case will be discussed more fully below.[3] It is sufficient to note at the moment that in such cases certainty requires that the ambiguity of legal meaning be resolved on the basis of legal materials and principles in existence at the time of the event giving rise to the litigation. This does not create certainty, but it does protect the limited degree of legal certainty that existed at the time of the event.

2 Certainty and Reliance

A consequence of this kind of certainty is that people can rely on the law as they find it at the time of their acts and omissions as being the law that is and will remain applicable to those acts and omissions. A key question is whether the relevant rationale for a general presumption against retroactivity is the protection of *actual reliance* or whether it is the protection of legal certainty, which creates an *ability to rely*, regardless of whether there is, in fact, reliance.

(a) The Case for Actual Reliance

One view is that people make decisions on the basis of predicted legal consequences and that a retroactive law is problematic because it means that a person who chooses her actions on the basis of predicted legal consequences will be affected not by those consequences, but by other unexpected consequences. She will have no control over the unexpected consequences because she has already performed the action that attracts the unpredicted, because retroactive, consequences.[4] This view assumes that the legal subject under consideration has, in predicting legal consequences, actually relied on the law at the time of acting.

[3] See Ch 3 Pt E(3).

[4] A Frandberg 'Retroactivity, Simulactivity, Infraactivity' in J Bjarup and M Blegvad *Time Law and Society* (Franz Steiner Stuttgart 1995) 70.

That Hart formulated a rationale for non-retroactivity based on actual reliance is apparent in his postscript responding to Dworkin, in which Hart argued that:

> the reason for regarding retrospective law-making as unjust is that it disappoints the justified expectations of those who, in acting, *have relied* on the assumption that the legal consequences of their acts will be determined by the known state of the law established at the time of their acts. [Emphasis added][5]

A similar emphasis on actual reliance is discernible in a number of judicial pronouncements. In *EWP v Moore* the question arose whether a common law rule should be changed. Staughton LJ stated that:

> one requirement of justice is that those who have arranged their affairs . . . in reliance on a decision of these courts which has stood for many years, should not find that their plans have been retrospectively upset.[6]

In the same case Bingham LJ thought that although the decision on the authority of which the case at hand was decided had not escaped criticism:

> it has been generally regarded as laying down the law. I do not doubt that it has been widely acted on, in good faith and on legal advice . . . I regard this as a paradigm situation in which it would be mischievous to disturb a settled rule on which parties have relied in organising their affairs.[7]

In *Phillips v Eyre* Willes J thought that legislation 'ought not to change the character of past transactions carried on upon the faith of the then existing law',[8] a statement that implies that the existence of actual reliance on the law was the operative rationale for the presumption against retroactivity.

(b) Evaluation of the Role of Actual Reliance

The potential unfairness of retroactive laws is probably most acute when there has been actual reliance on a law that is then retroactively altered. It does not, however, follow from this observation that actual reliance is an independent rationale for a general presumption against retroactivity. If actual reliance was an independent rationale, then, assuming the presumption against retroactivity to apply only when one of its rationales is engaged, the operation of the presumption against retroactivity in particular cases could be dependent upon demonstration of actual reliance. Before exploring the ramifications of such a result for the generality of the law, it should be asked whether the fact that actual reliance is a relevant or determinative factor in several other areas of the law indicates its desirability as a rationale for non-retroactivity.

5 HLA Hart *The Concept of Law* (2nd edn Clarendon Press Oxford 1994) 276.

6 [1992] QB 460, 474 (CA).

7 *Ibid* 475.

8 (1870) LR 6 QB 1, 23 (Exch). See also the explicit emphasis placed on the actual reliance of insurance companies in *Angus v Sun Alliance Insurance Co* [1988] 2 SCR 256, 268–9.

In private law, actual reliance on a representation is a precondition to the grant of a promissory estoppel.[9] So too, actual reliance on a representation is an element of the tort of negligent misstatement.[10] In public law, by contrast, the High Court of Australia held by majority in *Minister of State for Immigration and Ethnic Affairs v Teoh* that the existence of a procedural legitimate expectation about executive action does not depend on the state of mind of the individual alleging it.[11] Without explicitly disclaiming *Teoh*, more recent authority of that Court does, however, grant a greater role to actual reliance, for example in holding that the lack of subjective reliance meant that there was no practical unfairness involved in the disappointment of an expectation.[12] English authority on the question of whether the disappointment of a substantive legitimate expectation amounts to an abuse of power refers to actual reliance,[13] though strictly the position is that actual reliance is not necessary for the existence of a legitimate expectation.[14] Nonetheless, whether there has been actual reliance is usually relevant to the overall determination of the case.[15] The Court of Final Appeal of Hong Kong, without deciding whether actual reliance is necessary to establish a legitimate expectation, has been willing to *assume* the existence of reliance. That court considered in a case in which the relevant representations were 'calculated to induce reliance' that 'it is to be assumed in the circumstances that they had this effect'.[16]

These examples from private and public law involve reliance on a representation made by a private party or the executive government about factual matters such as whether something will or will not be done, is or is not relevant, or is or is not the case. The presumption against retroactivity does not, however, involve a representation of such a kind. It is directed to judicial choice of the applicable law. That choice may affect all those to whom the law applies, not just parties to litigation arising from a representation. Because of this fundamental difference, that actual reliance is an important concept in various areas of the law does not mean that it is an appropriate rationale for a general presumption against retroactivity.

If the operation of the presumption against retroactivity was to be conditional upon the factual question of whether a party seeking its protection had actually relied on the applicable law at the time of the event giving rise to the litigation, the

[9] *Waltons Stores (Interstate) v Maher* (1988) 164 CLR 387, 429; *Central London Property Trust v High Trees House* [1947] KB 130, 136.

[10] *Caparo Industries v Dickman* [1990] 2 AC 605, 638 (HL); *White v Jones* [1995] 2 AC 207, 272 (HL); *San Sebastian v The Minister Administering the Environmental Planning and Assessment Act* (1986) 162 CLR 341, 357.

[11] (1995) 183 CLR 273, 291, 301, contra 314. Cf the discussion of 'general reliance' in tort law in *Pyrenees Shire Council v Day* (1998) 192 CLR 330, [157]–[163].

[12] *Re Minister for Immigration and Multicultural Affairs, ex p Lam* (2003) 214 CLR 1, [35]–[37], and more generally, [62], [91]–[93], [145].

[13] *R v North and East Devon Health Authority, ex p Coughlan* [2001] QB 213, 244 (CA).

[14] *R v Education Secretary, ex p Begbie* [2000] 1 WLR 1115, 1124, 1133 (CA); *R(Bibi) v Newham LBC* [2002] 1 WLR 237, [31], [52]–[55] (CA); *R(Rashid) v Secretary of State for the Home Department* [2005] EWCA Civ 744, [25], [47]. See I Steele 'Substantive Legitimate Expectations: Striking The Right Balance?' (2005) 121 Law Quarterly Review 300, 308–10.

[15] *R v Education Secretary, ex p Begbie* [2000] 1 WLR 1115, 1124, 1131, 1133 (CA).

[16] *Ng Siu Tung v Director of Immigration* [2002] HKCFA 1, [110].

result would be that retroactivity would be considered acceptable in the absence of reliance but problematic in the face of reliance. This would lead ineluctably to the conclusion that the presumption against retroactivity protects those who know and rely on the law but is inapplicable to those who do not. Such a conclusion would be contrary to the principle of generality, which is an aspect of the rule of law.

Generality requires that laws are general in form and application; the latter aspect of which may be more specifically stated as requiring that a law applies to all those who come within its ambit. To allow the operation of the presumption against retroactivity to depend on whether a person had relied on the law at the time of the relevant event would mean that persons responsible for the same conduct at the same time would be subject to different laws on the basis of the subjective consideration of whether they relied on the law at the time of their conduct. Actual reliance cannot be countenanced as a rationale for a general presumption against retroactivity because it would protect from retroactivity those who knew and relied on the law, whilst allowing retroactivity affecting those ignorant or ambivalent about the applicable law or otherwise unable to demonstrate reliance.

There are at least two different ways in which the concept of actual reliance is discussed. The first is its straightforward description of situations in which at least one of the parties to litigation has in fact relied on a previous law applicable at the time of the event to which the litigation relates. The second way involves the less literal meaning that a judge *assumes* that because the law was settled at the time of the event to which the litigation relates, it was relied upon both by the parties to the litigation and by others. Bingham LJ's comment in *EWP v Moore*—'I do not doubt that it has been widely acted on'—lies within this second category.[17] This latter category does not, in truth, require that there has been actual reliance. It merely involves a willingness on the part of a judge to assume that people rely on the law in the absence of any evidence that anyone has actually done so. Accordingly, it is closer to a concentration on legal certainty, manifested in the protection of an ability to rely on the law, rather than insistence on the existence of actual reliance, as a rationale for a general presumption against retroactivity.

(c) Certainty and the Ability to Rely on the Law

The frustration of actual reliance is one possible result of a lack of certainty caused by retroactive law, but is not itself an independent rationale for a general presumption against retroactivity. An alternative candidate as a rationale for the presumption against retroactivity is the protection of an ability, or entitlement,[18] to rely on the law, regardless of whether such reliance actually occurred. The observation made by Lord Diplock in *Black-Clawson International v Papierwerke Waldhof-Aschaffenberg* that the:

[17] See also *O'Brien v Robinson* [1973] AC 912, 925 (HL); *Lynall v Inland Revenue Commissioners* [1972] AC 680, 696 (HL).

[18] *R v Griffiths* [1891] 2 QB 145, 148.

> acceptance of the rule of law as a constitutional principle requires that a citizen, before committing himself to any course of action, should be *able to know* in advance what are the legal consequences that will flow from it [emphasis added][19]

supports the contention that it is certainty, which enables actual reliance, but does not require it, that is a key rationale for a general presumption against retroactivity.

Certainty allows people to plan their affairs and know the legal ramifications of their plans but does not exclude from its concern those who cannot or do not make such calculations. This form of certainty, protected by the presumption against retroactivity, is an aspect of the rule of law, general in its application. Generality requires that the presumption against retroactivity is relevant to the determination of all cases involving potential retroactivity, not just those in which someone has actually relied on the law.

3 Certainty and Autonomy

Identifying certainty as a rationale for a general presumption against retroactivity may be thought by some to invite the further step of asking why legal certainty is a value worthy of protection. One possible answer to that question is that the protection of legal certainty is necessary to facilitate human autonomy. Autonomy, from the Greek *autos* meaning 'self' and *nomos* meaning 'rule', has been defined as:

> the capacity of a person critically to reflect upon, and then attempt to accept or change, his or her preferences, desires, values and ideals.[20]

In a criminal law context this has been expressed as:

> the desire to ensure that individuals are reasonably free to maintain control of their lives by choosing to avoid conduct which will attract criminal sanction; a choice made impossible if conduct is assessed by rules made in the future.[21]

The concept of autonomy is closely related to the concept of dignity. Raz considers that:

> Respecting human dignity entails treating humans as persons capable of planning and plotting their future. Thus, respecting people's dignity includes respecting their autonomy, their right to control their future.[22]

This concern with the *capability* to plan and the *right* to control one's own future is consistent with Hayek's concern that it be 'possible . . . to plan one's individual

[19] [1975] AC 591, 638 (HL). See also *R v Rimmington* [2006] 1 AC 459, [33] (HL).

[20] G Dworkin *The Theory and Practice of Autonomy* (Cambridge University Press 1988) 48. Cf J Rawls *A Theory of Justice* (Revised edn Oxford University Press 1999) 80.

[21] *Polyukhovich v The Commonwealth of Australia* (1991) 172 CLR 501, 688.

[22] J Raz 'The Rule of Law and its Virtue' (1977) 93 Law Quarterly Review 195, 204. See also J Griffin 'First Steps in an Account of Human Rights' (2001) 9 European Journal of Philosophy 306, 309–11, 319.

affairs',[23] and supports an account of legal certainty as *enabling* reliance and *facilitating* autonomy, regardless of whether a party to litigation has actually relied on the law to make any particular choice.

If someone has not made any conscious choice, even a choice not to act, on the basis of existing law, then it might be arguable that his personal autonomy cannot be impeded by a retroactive change to the applicable law. Whether that is true or not does not matter for present purposes as much as the point that the legal system should *allow* persons to make choices and respect their ability to do so, and should ensure that laws are general in their application. Thus it is appropriate to speak of *facilitating* autonomy, rather than of the protection of autonomy in any specific case, as a reason for the importance of the ability to rely on the law.

The relevance of autonomy to a general presumption against retroactivity lies in respect shown for choices that may already have been made. The right to control one's own future[24] does not involve, in the context of objections to retroactivity, people's plans and expectations actually coming to fruition. Non-retroactive laws and any number of non-legal factors may prevent that. Such a right means only that the range of possibilities open at the time choices may have been made should not afterwards be altered by deeming the law on the basis of which the choices may have been made to have been different to what it actually was at the time of those choices. To change the law retroactively is not just to prevent plans from coming to fruition but, more importantly, is to fail to respect the right to make plans at all. The *ability* to choose, which is a core component of autonomy, is deprived of its effectiveness by the retroactive alteration of the law on the basis of which the choice was entitled to be made. Furthermore, a retroactive law denies any opportunity to make different plans in response to the different legal framework.

Respect for autonomy involves respect for the *ability* to plan, which requires respect for the *ability to rely* on the law, all of which require restraint from deeming the law to have been something other than what it actually was at an earlier time. The aspect of restraining state power in this description of autonomy brings it close to a principle of negative liberty. It is the disrespect for plans already made and the deprivation of power to make different plans in response to different applicable laws that indicate that autonomy is truly the value here under consideration. Nonetheless, as negative liberty is related in this way, it is to negative liberty that attention should now be addressed.

[23] FA Hayek *The Road to Serfdom* (Routledge London 1944) 54, quoted by J Raz 'The Rule of Law and its Virtue' (1977) 93 Law Quarterly Review 195, 195.

[24] J Raz 'The Rule of Law and its Virtue' (1977) 93 Law Quarterly Review 195, 204. Cf G Dworkin *The Theory and Practice of Autonomy* (Cambridge University Press 1988) 17.

C Negative Liberty

1 Negative Liberty Generally

A correlative of the law's peculiar ability to change its own effect on the past is the desirability of limiting this extraordinary power. To some extent this desire for limitation rests on no deeper foundation than the philosophical belief that the state should be restrained from exercising extraordinary powers that impact on individual liberty except to the extent that such exercise can be satisfactorily justified in given circumstances. This type of belief underlay Hayek's view of the rule of law:

> the coercive power of the state can be used only in cases defined in advance by the law and in such a way that it can be foreseen how it will be used.[25]

It might be thought that the occurrence of retroactive laws decreases confidence in the legal system because people will be in fear of further retroactive laws. This still leaves the question: what is wrong with retroactive laws? At least two relevant underlying aspects of negative liberty can be identified: the deprivation of security relating to past events, and the removal of an actual freedom.

2 Deprivation of Security Relating to Past Events

The particular question that arises because of a concern that the state should not deprive legal subjects of security relating to the legal consequences of past events is whether the state, including its judicial branch, having made the law by which those subject to its jurisdiction are bound, should be entitled to subject people to the further intrusion of a retroactively altered law.

There is a sense of finality and security that comes with knowing how the law applied to past events—the impact of state regulation on that aspect of life is known and in the past. Entities other than the state certainly do not have the power to change retroactively the legal consequences of past events in which they were involved or which were otherwise of significance to them. They have no choice but to accept those consequences and get on with things. Having done this, and in the process of doing so, they should generally be entitled to feel, think and act as though the state will not alter the legal consequences of past events with that change being deemed to have been operative in the past. There should generally be no need to devote thought or resources to such past events. The sense of security that comes with knowing that the past cannot be altered should not lightly be displaced. It is clear that this application of liberty is closely related to the value of certainty. Indeed, certainty is a motivating value. Liberty is the value that requires

[25] FA Hayek *The Road to Serfdom* (Routledge London 1944) 62.

the legislative and judicial arms of the state not to interfere with certainty by exercising an exceptional legal power.

3 Removal of an Actual Freedom

Individual freedom is curtailed by retroactive laws not just in the sense that choices otherwise open to a legal subject are removed—which is also the case with many prospective laws—but also in the sense that a freedom to act that was not impeded, or was differently impeded, at the time of acting is subsequently removed or altered such that for legal purposes that freedom is deemed not to have existed or to have taken a different form at the time of acting. Furthermore, someone affected by the retroactive change cannot do anything to comply knowingly with the new law because the event to which it relates is in the past.[26] Further still, the retroactive removal of an actual freedom and retroactive imposition of a new rule may be accompanied by consequences such as pecuniary disadvantage or criminal penalty.

That removal of an actual freedom would have been the result of granting retroactive effect to a statute motivated judicial refusal to grant such effect in *Gardner v Cone*.[27] In that case a landlord was, at the time that his tenant requested permission to assign the lease, entitled, on any ground, to refuse that permission. The landlord refused permission to assign the lease. The tenant submitted that a statute[28] that commenced between the landlord's refusal to grant permission to assign and litigation to which that refusal was relevant, which provided that permission to assign must not be withheld unreasonably, was applicable to the refusal to assign that occurred prior to the commencement of the Act. Maugham J rejected that submission. To grant the statute retroactive effect would have been to deem nonexistent a freedom that the landlord lawfully enjoyed at the time of making his decision,[29] and to burden him with whatever remedy accompanied the new rule.

Whenever there is a retroactive law, *two different legal rules* are operative on *one period of time*, creating conflicting legal rules to which a person is subject.[30] The latter rule, and whatever consequences flow from its operation, are retroactively operative from the time that it comes into effect and ultimately will be the rule according to which the conduct in question will be judged. However, the person acting or choosing not to act was at the time of so choosing subject to only one

26 A Frandberg 'Retroactivity, Simulactivity, Infraactivity' in J Bjarup and M Blegvad *Time Law and Society* (Franz Steiner Stuttgart 1995) 70. Cf J Rawls *A Theory of Justice* (Revised edn Oxford University Press 1999) 208 who, discussing 'the precept that ought implies can', thought that a legal system 'must not impose a duty to do what cannot be done'.

27 [1928] Ch 955, discussed further in Ch 4 Pt C.

28 Landlord and Tenant Act 1927 (Eng) 17 & 18 Geo 5 c 36 s 19.

29 [1928] Ch 955, 967.

30 The potentially confusing consequences of which were discussed by Lord Mustill in *L'Office Cherifien des Phosphates v Yamashita-Shinnihon Steamship Co* [1994] 1 AC 486, 523–4 (HL).

relevant rule, which was not the one that is later deemed to have applied at that earlier time. However a person's freedom was in fact regulated by the law in existence at the time of the conduct under consideration, a retroactive law involves the state altering that freedom after the relevant conduct has occurred, with effect at the time of that conduct.

4 Negative Liberty and Criminal Law

(a) Nullum Crimen Sine Lege Antea Exstanti

Retroactive creation of a criminal offence is a particularly acute example of infraction by the state of individual liberty. Judicial disfavour for this kind of law making is well known and, on the whole, well understood. Hobbes put his objection thus: 'before the law, there is no transgression of the law'.[31] Holding a person criminally liable for doing what it was lawful to do at the time that he did it, is usually obviously wrong. The retroactive removal of an actual freedom coupled with the gravity of consequences that may accompany a breach of the criminal law mean that retroactive imposition of criminal liability is rarely justifiable.

(b) Nulla Poena Sine Lege Antea Exstanti

The relationship between liberty and retroactive alteration of criminal sentences is not as clearly stated or understood in existing literature. This relationship accordingly deserves detailed consideration. The crucial issue is whether the presumption against retroactivity militates against the imposition of a criminal sentence that is more severe than the sentence that was applicable at the time of the commission of the offence.

Hobbes' view was that:

> if a punishment be determined and prescribed in the law itself, and after the crime committed, there be a greater punishment inflicted, the excess is not punishment, but an act of hostility. For seeing the aim of punishment is not a revenge but terror; and the terror of a great punishment unknown, is taken away by the declaration of a less, the unexpected addition is no part of the punishment.[32]

A modern manifestation of this view is apparent in the opinion of Bray CJ in *Samuels v Songaila*:

> Penalties are imposed in order to deter the forbidden conduct and we have to assume that they have some deterrent effect. A man cannot be deterred from committing a forbidden act by fear of a sanction which is not in existence at the time he commits the act.[33]

[31] T Hobbes *Leviathan* (1651) JCA Gaskin (ed) (Oxford University Press 1996) ch 28, 207.

[32] *Ibid.* See also J Bentham 'Principles of Penal Law' in *The Works of Jeremy Bentham* J Bowring (ed) (William Tait Edinburgh 1843) vol 1, 396–7.

[33] (1977) 16 SASR 397. Cf *R v Kidman* (1915) 20 CLR 425, 450.

Such a view is dependent on a deterrent theory of punishment.[34] Theories of punishment typically deal with why and how punishment is imposed consequent to conviction of an offence. *Nulla poena sine lege antea exstanti* relates at a higher level of abstraction to the imposition of punishment than the discussion that occurs in the literature on theories of punishment. *Nulla poena sine lege antea exstanti* expresses the idea that there can be no sentence, of any kind or with any theoretical rationale, unless it is established by a law already in existence. As long as the sentence imposed is established by law in advance of the crime, the sentence's characteristics and justifying theory or theories are not matters to which the maxim relates or on which it depends.[35] The difficult matter is the identification of a rationale for the presumption against retroactive sentencing.

The readily acceptable view that it is inappropriate to think of criminal punishment as involving an agreement between society and an offender as to severity of the applicable punishment, led Waldron to the more controversial conclusion that the increase of the applicable punishment after the commission of the crime to which it relates is neither retroactive nor necessarily unjust or undesirable.[36] That such an increase does constitute retroactivity is proposed above.[37] That it is not unjust or undesirable might be a tenable position if the only rationale for the presumption against retroactivity was reliance, though even then, as Waldron acknowledges,[38] the nature of the crime under consideration may be relevant.

For some minor offences such as speeding and parking offences, there might be an understandable objection to retroactively increased punishment on the basis that, though no one is ever *entitled* to balance her desire to break the law with the severity of the punishment and rely on the balance struck at the time of committing the offence remaining accurate at the time of being sentenced for it, it is no secret that many people forgivably think that way about offences of this type. If someone was driving down a long straight well built road in good conditions with no other cars or people in the vicinity and deliberately chose to exceed a conservatively set speed limit on the basis that the penalty for doing so would be less of a bother to her than not driving at the higher speed that she thought to be safe, then there might be a reasonable objection to the retroactive imposition of a heavier fine because if the driver had been able to know the extent of her exposure to punishment at the time of driving, she may have chosen not to have exceeded the speed limit. The objection would be even stronger if the sentence changed not just

[34] Hobbes, Bentham and Bray CJ all relied on special deterrence, which focuses on the deterrent value to the particular offender, but objection to retroactive punishment has also been made on the basis of general deterrence, which focuses on the deterrent value to all potential offenders: EC Clark *An Analysis of Criminal Liability* (Cambridge University Press 1880) 7. See also G Williams *Criminal Law, The General Part* (2nd edn Stevens London 1961) 600–1, who relied on specific *and* general deterrence.

[35] Cf J Hall '*Nulla Poena Sine Lege*' (1937) 47 Yale Law Journal 165, 183.

[36] J Waldron 'Retroactive Law: How Dodgy was Duynhoven?' (2004) 10 Otago Law Review 631, 643: 'As for retrospective increases in sentencing, here I have to confess that I am unsure what exactly the objection is supposed to be.'

[37] Ch 1 Pt E(1).

[38] J Waldron 'Retroactive Law: How Dodgy was Duynhoven?' (2004) 10 Otago Law Review 631, 645.

in severity, but also in type, so that a sentence of imprisonment was retroactively imposed for exceeding the speed limit by a certain amount, or perhaps more realistically, that disqualification from driving would be the result.

Objection to retroactively increased sentences on the basis of reliance might be more strongly made in the case of criminalisation of morally controversial conduct such as euthanasia. If a husband assisted the suicide of his terminally ill wife after calculating that the criminal penalty for doing so was something that he was prepared to bear in order to end his wife's suffering, and the legislature subsequently retroactively changed the punishment for assisting suicide to match the punishment for murder, a reasonable objection might be made that the husband was wrongly deprived of his ability to know in advance the state sanction for acting in a way that he considered to be morally justifiable.

A final, practical, example of reliance militating against the retroactive increase of criminal punishment, at least in pending proceedings, is that if a decision by an accused not to plea bargain was made on the basis of the maximum punishment applicable at the time of the commission of the crime, it would seem unjust for the applicable punishment to then retroactively be increased when it was too late for that decision to be changed.[39]

Apart from these examples, and others like them that may be imagined, in which there may be a credible objection to retroactive punishment on the basis of the protection of an ability to rely on the law, it seems appropriate to think that an entitlement of someone who commits a criminal offence to be able to rely on being subjected only to the punishment that she bargained for, is not a defensible rationale for a general presumption against retroactive sentencing.[40] It seems intuitively unappealing to give credence to the complaint of someone who breaks the criminal law that she did not bargain on the punishment that she ultimately received.[41] Thus it is appropriate to turn to a consideration of individual liberty as a rationale for non-retroactivity of criminal punishment.

The maximum sentence applicable to a particular crime represents the limit of the state's penal response to the commission of that crime. The state does not issue divine utterances that 'thou shalt not' do something and then, if you do it, the state may impose whatever punishment it sees fit. By contravening a criminal law a person exposes himself, at the most, to the maximum punishment applicable to that offence at the time that it was committed. The state should ordinarily be restrained from retroactively increasing the applicable sentence not because of a bargain with potential offenders or because potential offenders were only given notice of, and

[39] S Atrill '*Nulla Poena Sine Lege* in Comparative Perspective: Retrospectivity under the ECHR and US Constitution' [2005] Public Law 107, 131; J Waldron 'Retroactive Law: How Dodgy was Duynhoven?' (2004) 10 Otago Law Review 631, 646.

[40] Contra S Atrill '*Nulla Poena Sine Lege* in Comparative Perspective: Retrospectivity under the ECHR and US Constitution' [2005] Public Law 107, 108.

[41] *R(Uttley) v Secretary of State for the Home Department* [2004] 1 WLR 2278, [40] (HL). As Lord Hope, dissenting, pointed out in *Flynn v HM Advocate* 2004 SCCR 281, [45] (PC), actual reliance is not relevant to the operation of the aspect of art 7 of the ECHR that prohibits retroactive punishments for criminal offences.

could only be deterred to the extent of, the lesser, known penalty; but because, however much the criminal conduct might be disapproved of, the liberty of the person responsible for it was constrained, both in terms of what he was prohibited from doing and what the maximum consequence for doing so would be, in a particular way at the time that he acted, so retroactively to increase the applicable punishment is retroactively to increase the interference with his liberty.

In defining retroactivity in Chapter one, an analogy was drawn between retroactive increase in tax rates and retroactive increase in criminal sentences.[42] It may be worthwhile to develop that comparison further in the context of the rationale for objecting to both. The objectionability of a law retroactively increasing the amount of tax liability might be thought to lie primarily in its disrespect for the ability of taxpayers to rely on the law. Taxpayers may have thought, on the basis of a law in force at the time the relevant income was earned, that a certain percentage of their income was theirs to keep, only to find, after a time during which they may have made decisions on that basis, that their reliance was frustrated by a law retroactively increasing their tax liability. It is not, however, only reliance that would be at stake in such a turn of events. The taxpayer's financial liberty was constrained in a particular way and is later deemed to have been more constrained than it in fact was. This focus on liberty is transferable to retroactive criminal sentencing.

If an offence is committed for which the maximum sentence at the time of commission was a fine, and the fine is later increased with effect for crimes already committed, the analogy is obvious. If a retroactively increased sentence of imprisonment is at issue, the objectionability that is common to such a case and the retroactive increase of tax liability, is that in both cases the state increases the magnitude of its incursion on individual liberty subsequent to the time at which the event justifying that incursion occurs, which is either the earning of income or the commission of a criminal offence, and deems the subsequent increase to have attached to that earlier justifying event.

Focusing on liberty as the rationale for *nulla poena sine lege antea exstanti* also means that although retroactive increases in punishment contravene the maxim, the enjoyment by an offender of a retroactive decrease in applicable punishment does not offend the rationale for the maxim. A retroactive decrease in punishment decreases interference with liberty and so the presumption against retroactivity may be rebutted.[43]

In case this exposition of the rationale for *nulla poena sine lege antea exstanti* is thought by some to be an unduly precious approach to liberty, a number of dangers of allowing the power to impose retroactive punishments should be identified. The first is that when it is decided that a law will operate retroactively, a fixed class of legal subjects exists to which the retroactive law applies. This class is constituted by all the people who have already committed the crime that brings

[42] Ch 1 Pt E.
[43] See Ch 4 Pt G(2)(c).

them within the scope of the retroactive sentencing law. The legislature is likely to have access to information about members of that class, although one would not expect a court to have information beyond the person before the court. Because a fixed class exists and its members may be knowable in advance of the law being determined, the law will not, insofar as its applicability to past events is concerned, be general in its application.[44]

This lack of generality leads to the second danger, which is the possibility of unfair discrimination in the law. The concern is that the law can be tailored to subject known individuals or groups to particular, and particularly harsh, penal consequences.[45] It is of course possible for there to be a lack of generality or unfair discrimination in prospective laws. However, the invariable existence of a fixed class to which a law with retroactive effect will apply means that retroactive laws *inherently* lack generality, which lack is accompanied by a greater risk of unfair discrimination.[46]

The imposition of a sentence determined according to a retroactive law means that the punishment that may be imposed is determined after the event that justifies it has already occurred. This runs contrary to the normal constitutional process of a general law existing in advance being applied to individual circumstances after the event triggering such application. Sentencing based on retroactive law means that the event does not trigger the specific application of a pre-existing general law but rather precedes (and perhaps triggers) the creation of a law applicable to a fixed and knowable class. Among other things, allowing this unusual process to occur creates the danger of a prosecutor who knows that the severity of a sentencing law is about to be increased with retroactive effect delaying the commencement of proceedings until such time as the more severe law has come into effect. Because of this contravention of normal constitutional processes, because of the dangers that it involves, and most fundamentally because retroactive sentencing constitutes an excessive use of state power, the principle of negative liberty militates against allowing retroactive sentencing as it militates against the imposition of retroactive criminal consequences more generally. Even for those who do not accept that increasing the sentence applicable to a crime that has already been committed constitutes retroactivity, most of the argument just expressed against such laws, even if characterised as retrospective but not retroactive, would be equally applicable.

[44] *R v Poumako* [2000] 2 NZLR 695, [76]–[77] (CA).

[45] *R(Uttley) v Secretary of State for the Home Department* [2004] 1 WLR 2278, [40] (HL); S Atrill '*Nulla Poena Sine Lege* in Comparative Perspective: Retrospectivity under the ECHR and US Constitution' [2005] Public Law 107, 108.

[46] Contra C Sampford *Retrospectivity and the Rule of Law* (Oxford University Press 2006) 77–9.

D Fair Warning

The value of certainty, in particular the ability to rely on the law, and a conception of negative liberty, have been established as rationales for a general presumption against retroactivity. Giving fair warning of legal consequences supports the fulfilment of the values of certainty and liberty and requires mention for that reason.

A basic statement of the importance and meaning of fair warning is that of Justice Holmes in *McBoyle v United States* that:

> it is reasonable that a fair warning should be given to the world in language that the common world will understand, of what the law intends to do if a certain line is passed.[47]

Exemplifying the negative impact on certainty that accompanies the absence of fair warning inherent in retroactive laws, Edinger quotes Wade:

> In all retroactive laws there must be an element of surprise, by which persons whose rights are affected are taken unawares. They are called upon to act in a manner different from what they had been led by the settled state of the law to anticipate.[48]

Related to the concept of fair warning is the idea of the law's role in guiding conduct.[49] Fuller was a notable adherent to this idea and expressed his objection to retroactive laws thus:

> Law has to do with the governance of human conduct by rules. To speak of governing or directing conduct today by rules that will be enacted tomorrow is to talk in blank prose.[50]

On the same theme, Fuller referred to 'the brutal absurdity of commanding a man today to do something yesterday'.[51] Austin took a different view of the role of law, but was, like Fuller, concerned by the inability of retroactive laws to influence conduct at the time of its commission. Austin said:

> the objection to laws *ex post facto*, is deducible from the general principle . . . that intention or inadvertence is necessary to constitute an injury. The law was not in existence at the time of the given act, forbearance, or omission: consequently the party did not, and could not know that he was violating a law. The sanction could not operate as a motive to obedience, inasmuch as there was nothing to obey.[52]

[47] 283 US 25, 27 (1931). See also *Polyukhovich v The Commonwealth of Australia* (1991) 172 CLR 501, 688.

[48] WP Wade *A Treatise on the Operation and Construction of Retroactive Laws* (FH Thomas St Louis MO 1880) 40–1, quoted by E Edinger 'Retrospectivity in Law' (1995) 29 University of British Columbia Law Review 5, 13.

[49] Further, and different, discussion of the role of guidance can be found in C Sampford *Retrospectivity and the Rule of Law* (Oxford University Press 2006) 82–8.

[50] LL Fuller *The Morality of Law* (Revised edn Yale University Press New Haven CT 1969) 53. Cf *Hickson v Darlow* (1883) 23 Ch D 690, 694 (CA).

[51] LL Fuller *The Morality of Law* (Revised edn Yale University Press New Haven CT 1969) 59.

[52] J Austin *Lectures on Jurisprudence* R Campbell (ed) (5th edn Revised John Murray London 1911) vol 1, 485–6.

As well as resulting in people *actually* being surprised, the absence of fair warning inherent in the retroactive application of law renders it impossible to rely on the law and make plans for the future even if no actual attempt was made to do so by a particular litigant. Fuller was concerned with the logical requirements of a rules based system, not with whether any particular party did or did not rely on a law. Similarly, Austin was as concerned that a party 'could not know' that a law was being violated as he was that any particular party 'did not' know that a law was being violated. These approaches to fair warning indicate its role in support of the value of legal certainty, manifested as an ability to rely on the law, and go beyond a concentration only on actual reliance.

Less has been written on the role of fair warning in protecting liberty, but the idea is simple: for people to be able knowingly to behave within the constraints on their liberty, fair warning of those constraints must be given. Comparably formulated, the role of fair warning in supporting certainty is that for people to be able to rely on the law, they must be able to know the applicable law. These ideas are commonly found in accounts of the rule of law and principle of legality and may also arise in assessing non-retroactive laws.[53] Their particular relevance to retroactivity is that a retroactive law, by definition, cannot be announced in advance to give those to whom it applies fair warning of its consequences. The only complication associated with fair warning that requires resolution arises from Kelsen's attempt to justify retroactive laws on the basis of the common law's insistence that ignorance of the law excuses no one.[54]

Kelsen noted that:

> Retroactive laws are considered to be objectionable and undesirable because it hurts our feeling of justice to inflict a sanction, especially a punishment, upon an individual because of an action or omission of which this individual could not know that it would entail this sanction.[55]

Taken on its own this statement would support the contentions here being made about fair warning. However, Kelsen went on to contrast this view with the principle that ignorance of the law excuses no one, stating that this principle justifies the position that the:

> fact that an individual does not know that the law attaches a sanction to his action or omission is no reason for not inflicting the sanction upon him.[56]

Kelsen observed that regardless of whether a person does or can know the applicable law there is an irrebuttable legal presumption that all the norms of a positive

[53] Eg J Raz 'The Rule of Law and its Virtue' (1977) 93 Law Quarterly Review 195, 198–9 on the rule of law and G Williams *Criminal Law, The General Part* (2nd edn Stevens London 1961) 582 on the principle of legality.

[54] *Ignorantia juris neminem excusat.*

[55] H Kelsen *General Theory of Law and State* (1945) A Wedberg (tr) (Russell and Russell New York 1961) 44.

[56] *Ibid.*

legal order *can* be known by the subjects of that order.[57] He asserted that it is 'obviously untrue' and a 'typical legal fiction' that all people *can* know the law applicable to them.[58] Kelsen concluded that:

> there is no essential difference between a retroactive law and many cases in which a non-retroactive law is not, and cannot, be known by the individual to whom this law has to be applied.[59]

It is indeed obviously untrue that all people *do* know the law applicable to them. Whether the law *can* be known is a more involved question, and is the more relevant question insofar as Kelsen's views are concerned. An unsupported assumption that people *cannot* know the law applicable to them, which Kelsen made, places the conclusions drawn on the basis of that assumption on precarious ground. More importantly, a law that was not *able* to be known would, for that reason alone, contravene the rule of law,[60] and, if it was a criminal law, the principle of legality.[61] A contravention of the rule of law cannot itself justify a retroactive law. To posit a justification of this kind is to attempt to build the legitimacy of one injustice on the assumed existence of another injustice. The fairness of the maxim on which Kelsen relied—that ignorance of the law excuses no one[62]—is itself dependent on the truth of the assumption that notice of the law is available. As Scott LJ said in *Blackpool Corporation v Locker* 'the very justification' for the maxim that ignorance of the law excuses no one 'is that the whole of our law, written or unwritten, is accessible to the public—in the sense, of course, that, at any rate, its legal advisers have access to it, at any moment, as of right'.[63] Were that not the case the law would be condoning its own secrecy. The operative legal presumption of the common law in any given case is that people *do* know the law.[64] This is in turn based on a wider systemic assumption that the law is *capable* of being known. To the extent that notice of laws is unavailable, that is a factual matter to be remedied to ensure compliance with the rule of law and the principle of legality. It is not a theoretical justification for retroactivity.[65]

Whilst Kelsen was primarily concerned with laws that *could* not be known; Gray was concerned with laws that *were* not known, even if knowable. Gray considered it a 'certain fact that courts are constantly making *ex post facto* Law'.[66] Gray did

[57] *Ibid.*
[58] *Ibid.*
[59] *Ibid.*
[60] J Raz 'The Rule of Law and its Virtue' (1977) 93 Law Quarterly Review 195, 198–9.
[61] G Williams *Criminal Law, The General Part* (2nd edn Stevens London 1961) 582. Cf *Christian v The Queen* [2007] 2 WLR 120, [24], [40]–[44], [84]–[85] (PC).
[62] On which see AP Simester and GR Sullivan *Criminal Law: Theory and Doctrine* (2nd edn Hart Publishing Oxford 2003) 555.
[63] [1948] 1 KB 349, 361 (CA).
[64] *R v Esop* (1836) 7 Car & P 456; 173 ER 203.
[65] AD Woozley 'What is Wrong with Retrospective Law?' (1968) 18 Philosophical Quarterly 41, 44–6 also objected to Kelsen's view on this topic, but for different reasons.
[66] JC Gray *The Nature and Sources of the Law* D Campbell and P Thomas (eds) (New edn Dartmouth Aldershot 1997) 63.

not, however, consider this problematic on the basis that in practical terms the law has retroactive application to most of 'the laity'[67] for the reason that most people do not know the legal consequences of their acts before they perform them. Gray concluded that 'the law of which a man has no knowledge is the same to him as if it did not exist'.[68] Gray's position is wrong because it depends on the type of individual involved and not on the type of law involved. A retroactive law is objectionable because it is usually not possible for *anyone* to know of it at the time of acting—by very nature of the law. A prospective law that binds someone who does not know about it is acceptable because the person *could* have availed himself of the requisite knowledge and as a practical matter failure to do so cannot be an excuse for non-compliance. Any other alternative would promote ignorance of the law.

Although Gray may have been correct that from an individual standpoint the impact of a law unknown is the same as the impact of a law unknowable, the important additional consideration is that when fair warning has been given of a law that remains unknown to the person to whom it applies, fault for the lack of knowledge can be attributed to the individual involved. If the law was actually not accessible or knowable, as Kelsen assumed, then it would be objectionable because the law *could not* be known. In such a situation, that a person *did not* know the law would be a consequence of the law being unknowable. That consequence does not provide a foundation for the tolerance of retroactivity on the ground that retroactivity is merely another way by which a person might not know the law. Rather, retroactivity is, like a law unknowable, objectionable because it deprives everyone of the *ability to know* the law in advance of making choices to which that law relates.

E Defeasibility

1 Introduction to Defeasibility

The values supporting the presumption against retroactivity are general in nature. There are competing considerations that may in some limited circumstances suggest retroactivity as the appropriate result, where, though retroactive, a law would be 'not offensively retroactive'.[69] Such considerations do not detract from the strength of the presumption against retroactivity, but rather indicate that the presumption is defeasible to countervailing reasons of sufficient strength. The circumstances in which the presumption will properly be rebutted are not possible to

[67] *Ibid.*
[68] *Ibid* 64.
[69] *Polyukhovich v The Commonwealth of Australia* (1991) 172 CLR 501, 690.

determine in advance by the specification of general rules. It is possible, however, to specify some considerations that may militate towards rebuttal of the general presumption against retroactivity. In at least one sense the position with respect to legislation is clear: when the legislature has left the courts no choice but to apply a statute retroactively, then the courts must give it retroactive effect. But the concern here is with underlying values that do or should inform judicial reasoning, not with unambiguous legislative commands.

2 A General Principle of Fairness

In *L'Office Cherifien des Phosphates v Yamashita-Shinnihon Steamship Co* Lord Mustill stated that 'the basis of the rule' requiring the courts to presume against a retroactive effect 'is no more than simple fairness, which ought to be the basis of every legal rule'.[70] He immediately observed that 'to change the legal character of a person's acts or omissions after the event will often be unfair'.[71] One difficulty with focusing on fairness as the test for retroactive application is that it asks a question—what is fair? It does not itself answer the question of whether a law does or should have retroactive effect, or offer any substantive assistance to how that question should be answered. As Lord Nicholls recently observed, fairness 'is an elusive concept. It is an instinctive response to a given set of facts.'[72] A further problem is that fairness has at least two guises. In one, it refers to the treatment of an individual, as an individual. In such cases it is better to focus on autonomy, liberty or whatever other value is actually at stake. A second guise incorporates consequentialist reasoning about broad social outcomes. In this vein, Isaacs J opined that Maxwell's famous statement that upon 'the presumption that the Legislature does not intend what is unjust rests the leaning against giving certain statutes a retrospective operation'[73]:

> is the universal touchstone for the Court to apply to any given case. But its application is not sure unless the whole circumstances are considered, that is to say, the whole of the circumstances which the Legislature may be assumed to have had before it. What may seem unjust when regarded from the standpoint of one person affected may be absolutely just when a broad view is taken of all who are affected.[74]

In either guise, fairness is a contestable conclusion, it is not itself a value pointing either towards or away from retroactivity. A conclusion that a particular result, either retroactive or not, is 'fair', may be justified, but that does not excuse the obligation to articulate the reasons that make it so. And it is the reasons that matter.

70 [1994] 1 AC 486, 525 (HL).

71 *Ibid.*

72 *Miller v Miller* [2006] 2 AC 618, [4] (HL).

73 P St J Langan (ed) *Maxwell on the Interpretation of Statutes* (12th edn Sweet and Maxwell London 1969) 215. Isaacs J quoted exactly the same passage from the 6th edn at 381.

74 *George Hudson v Australian Timber Workers' Union* (1923) 32 CLR 413, 434.

3 Where Uncertainty is Inevitable

As has been discussed, a key rationale for a general presumption against retroactivity is the protection of legal certainty. This rationale depends on the *possibility* of certainty. If there is little certainty to protect, for example because there is truly a lacuna in the law and a point is being decided for the first time, then it might be thought that the objection to retroactivity on the grounds of certainty largely falls away. Its residual component may be only that a dispute should be resolved consistently with relevant legal materials and principles in existence at the time of the events.

Hart thought that his objection to retroactive laws based on actual reliance was 'irrelevant' in cases of legal uncertainty.[75] In his postscript responding to Dworkin, Hart wrote:

> This objection, however, even if it has force against a court's retrospective change or overruling of clearly established law, seems quite irrelevant in hard cases since these are cases which the law has left incompletely regulated and where there is no known state of clearly established law to justify expectations.[76]

Such an absence of certainty precludes the ability to rely just as much as it precludes actual reliance.

For present purposes, there is no need to enter the apparently intractable jurisprudential debate about the nature of law. It is enough that it is sometimes not clear to people interested in the topic what the law is and that when a dispute arises that requires the law in such an area to be clarified, judges are imposing law that could not previously have been known by persons of ordinary intelligence and foresight enjoying competent legal advice. One could rationally go even further than Hart's comment above and adopt a position that where the law is uncertain, retroactivity, at least in its adjudicative form, is both desirable and inevitable. If the law does not provide a clear answer at the time of the relevant events and litigation ensues, the courts must determine the controversy according to law. If the pre-existing law is not clear, then the next best alternative is the imposition of retroactive law. Although such imposition may still have implications for the liberty of those affected by the retroactive law, such implications are materially different from a situation in which a certain law is retroactively changed. There the problematic incursion on liberty is solely a function of the retroactive law.

By contrast, where the law at the time of acting is uncertain, that uncertainty means that a person cannot know how her liberty is constrained. When it is later retroactively decided how her liberty was deemed to have been constrained, the pre-existing problem crystallises, because a person is actually subjected to a law that could not have been known in advance. The retroactive law avoids continued uncertainty and provides a legal answer to an issue previously ungoverned by a

[75] HLA Hart *The Concept of Law* (2nd edn Clarendon Press Oxford 1994) 276.

[76] *Ibid.* See also J Bell *Policy Arguments in Judicial Decisions* (Clarendon Press Oxford 1983) 234; A Palmer and C Sampford 'Judicial Retrospectivity in Australia' (1995) 4 Griffith Law Review 170, 174.

specific legal rule. Thus, in such a situation, a retroactive law is less of an affront to liberty than a retroactive law imposed on a situation where there is a pre-existing legal rule. When there is a pre-existing rule, the previous judicial decision or legislative enactment containing that rule provides the grounds for certainty and delimits the incursion on liberty. For retroactivity sensibly to be proposed in such cases, other reasons would be required.

4 The Exceptional Nature of Retroactivity

When judges should apply a law with retroactive effect is a question fraught with multifaceted difficulties. It is not amenable to general answers. The empiricist way of the common law has been to confront each difficulty in the precise circumstances in which it is raised. When this discussion shortly turns from general values to examination of particular cases, individual cases in which law was applied retroactively will be considered. The crucial general consideration is that the importance of the values that justify the presumption against retroactivity means that defeat of the presumption should be exceptional. As a prelude to later discussion of particular cases in which the presumption against retroactivity was justifiably overcome, some non-exhaustive categories of cases may be suggested.

First, the presumption against retroactivity may be defeated by matters specific to that presumption. For example, if a rule retroactively imposed relates to a matter on which no one could rely and which does not affect individual liberty, then the inapplicability of the rationales for the presumption might lead to its defeat.[77] Second, presumptive resistance to retroactivity might be trumped by factors not related to the presumption, such as disapproval (expressed other than by criminal sanction) of immoral even if strictly legal conduct,[78] a desire to punish heinous conduct by criminal sanction,[79] or an impetus to keep the law abreast of social or legal change.[80] Sometimes multiple factors will coalesce in one case. A possible subdivision within this second category is between factors that existed at the time of an initial rule that is later retroactively replaced,[81] and factors that arose after an initial rule and are said to justify its retroactive replacement.[82] This subdivision may be explored by reference to Kelsen's views.

Kelsen acknowledged that a norm cannot be 'efficacious' for those retroactively held to be subject to it, but considered this not to affect the 'validity' of a retroactive norm.[83] Kelsen thought that:

[77] Eg Ch 5 Pts E(1)(a), E(1)(b), F(2) and G(3). That the rationales for the presumption against retroactivity may actually militate *towards* retroactivity, rather than being irrelevant to it, is discussed in Ch 6 Pt C and, for example, in Ch 4 Pt G(2)(c).

[78] Eg Ch 5 Pt E(1)(d) and Ch 4 Pt F(3).

[79] Eg Ch 5 Pts C(3) and C(6) and Ch 4 Pt F(3); contra Ch 5 Pt G(1)(b).

[80] Eg Ch 5 Pts D(2), E(2)(c) and E(2)(d) and Ch 4 Pt F(3).

[81] Eg Ch 5 Pts E(2)(b), E(3) and G(2)(a).

[82] Eg Ch 5 Pts E(2)(c) and E(2)(d).

[83] H Kelsen *General Theory of Law and State* A Wedberg (tr) (Russell and Russell New York 1961) 43.

> Nothing prevents us from applying a norm as a scheme of interpretation, a standard of evaluation, to facts which occurred before the moment when the norm came into existence. What someone did in the past we may evaluate according to a norm which assumed validity only after it had been done. In the remote past it was a religious duty to sacrifice human beings to the gods, and slavery was a legal institution. Today we say that these human sacrifices *were* crimes and that slavery, as a legal institution, *was* immoral. We apply moral norms valid in our time to these facts, though the norms which forbid human sacrifices and slavery came into existence long after the facts occurred that we judge now, according to these new norms, as crimes and immoral. [Emphasis on past tense added][84]

A broad normative judgment about the morality, or even, in general terms, a judgment about the legality of past social practices is a different matter, however, to the imposition of specific legal liability on those individuals responsible for particular examples of such practices. Because neither of the former result in legal consequences for specific individuals they require less justification than the latter. Kelsen's statement lies within a category of laws that purport to impose retroactive adverse consequences on individuals who acted in accordance both with the specific applicable law and with generally accepted principles of morality applicable at the time of the relevant conduct. The retroactive law is said to be justified on the basis of subsequent moral, social or legal development the retroactive recognition of which is more important in a particular case than the values presumptively opposing retroactivity.

Retroactivity justified on a different basis occurs when generally accepted legal or moral principles applicable at the time of the relevant conduct, undermined, at the time of the conduct, the legitimacy of the conduct and the rule that allowed it. If those principles were apparent because the conduct constituted a crime under international law[85] or was criminal according to general principles of law recognized by the community of nations,[86] then the case for retroactivity within the domestic legal order may be overwhelming.[87]

Though these categories broadly represent many of the types of reasons that may justify retroactivity, whether retroactivity is justifiable in any particular case can only be decided by reference to the particular facts and circumstances of that case.

[84] *Ibid.*

[85] *Polyukhovich v The Commonwealth of Australia* (1991) 172 CLR 501.

[86] *R v C* [2004] 1 WLR 2098, [24] (CA).

[87] The wording in this sentence is based on art 11 (2) of the Universal Declaration of Human Rights, art 15 of the International Covenant on Civil and Political Rights and art 7 of the ECHR.

F Conclusion

Just as a general presumption against retroactivity is a component part of the rule of law[88] and, where criminal law is concerned, the principle of legality,[89] so too the rationales for a general presumption against retroactivity are in many ways specific applications of the rationales for the rule of law and principle of legality. Compelling as the values of certainty and liberty are, they do not justify an irrebuttable presumption against retroactivity. Rather, they support a general presumption against retroactivity that is, exceptionally, defeasible to strong reasons that may be established in particular cases.

[88] J Raz 'The Rule of Law and its Virtue' (1977) 93 Law Quarterly Review 195, 198–9.
[89] J Hall *General Principles of Criminal Law* (2nd edn Bobbs-Merrill Indianapolis IN 1960) 28, 58–9.

4

The Presumption Against Retroactivity in Statutory Construction

A Introduction

That there is a 'presumption against retrospectivity' is a frequently stated but rarely examined mantra in legal writing on the topic of statutory interpretation. Though the presumption against retrospectivity has numerous component parts, for example the presumption against interference with vested rights, this chapter seeks only to examine the presumption against *retroactivity*, as that term is explained in Chapter one. Nonetheless, some general statements of a 'presumption against retrospectivity' made in cases that do not involve actual or purported retroactivity are relevant to that examination. Subject to the constraint of article 7 of the ECHR, implemented by the mechanisms of the Human Rights Act 1998 (UK), on criminal laws in the United Kingdom, parliament is not, in English or Australian law, restricted from passing a statute with plainly retroactive effect.[1] However, in determining whether a statute has retroactive effect, courts will begin with a presumption against such a result.

Ultimately this chapter seeks not to review the presumption against retroactivity as it is applied in the field of statutory construction as an end in itself, but rather to examine an area of the law in which the presumption against retroactivity is undoubtedly embedded, as a platform for subsequent analysis, in Chapters five and seven, of whether a similar presumption against retroactivity, motivated by the same rationales of certainty and liberty, is or should be applicable to judicial decisions in which consideration is given to developing or changing a common law rule. A question crucial to this purpose is whether the presumption against retroactivity serves as a tool to divine and give effect to the intention of the legislature, or whether it is a common law principle to which courts will adhere independently of legislative intention, though which is defeasible to, amongst

[1] *Phillips v Eyre* (1870) LR 6 QB 1, 23 (Exch); *Polyukhovich v The Commonwealth of Australia* (1991) 172 CLR 501, 534–535, 649, 721. See also, for example, *British Columbia v Imperial Tobacco Canada* [2005] 2 SCR 473, [69]–[72]. However, if a statute is found to be inconsistent with the Australian Constitution, because it is the Constitution itself that renders the statute invalid, that statute cannot later retroactively be deemed by a new statute to have always had a different, and constitutionally acceptable, effect: *University of Wollongong v Metwally* (1984) 158 CLR 447, 457, 474–5, 478–9.

other things, statutory language of sufficient strength. If the presumption against retroactivity is no more than a tool to divine and give effect to legislative intention, then the presumption can have no role beyond the interpretation of statutes. If, however, it can be established that the presumption against retroactivity is a common law principle, based on the protection of certainty and liberty, then there is scope for viewing the presumption against retroactivity as having application beyond the process of construing statutes.

B The Nature of the Presumption Against Retroactivity

In a passage from *Maxwell on the Interpretation of Statutes* that Scarman J considered has been 'so frequently quoted with approval that it now itself enjoys almost judicial authority'[2] and that Isaacs J thought 'the universal touchstone for the Court to apply to any given case'[3] it was said that:

> Upon the presumption that the legislature does not intend what is unjust rests the leaning against giving certain statutes a retrospective operation. They are construed as operating only in cases or on facts which come into existence after the statutes were passed unless a retrospective effect is clearly intended. It is a fundamental rule of English law that no statute shall be construed to have a retrospective operation unless such a construction appears very clearly in the terms of the Act, or arises by necessary and distinct implication.[4]

The fame and influence of this passage justify closer examination than usually afforded to such general statements. The second of the three sentences from *Maxwell* goes well beyond, though includes, the concept of retroactivity here under discussion. More importantly, the first sentence contains a normative proposition that retroactivity is unjust. This judgment provides the basis for the courts' starting point to the construction of any legislation, which operates before the terms of that legislation are even considered. *Maxwell's* third sentence indicates that the presumption constitutes 'a fundamental rule of English law'. On this view of *Maxwell's* judicially accepted statement, the task for the courts is to begin with this 'fundamental rule', reflecting the courts' own view that retroactivity is usually unjust, and thus presumptively avoid retroactivity.[5] The task is not to approach a statute seeking to divine the legislative intention, using the presumption merely as an aid to interpretation. In addition to *Maxwell's* statement, it is necessary to consider whether this approach is apparent in judicial pronouncements of the presumption against retroactivity.

[2] *Carson v Carson* [1964] 1 WLR 511, 516 (P).
[3] *George Hudson v Australian Timber Workers' Union* (1923) 32 CLR 413, 434.
[4] P St J Langan *Maxwell on the Interpretation of Statutes* (12th edn Sweet and Maxwell London 1969) 215.
[5] Cf CK Allen *Law in the Making* (7th edn Clarendon Press Oxford 1964) 456.

A commonly cited judicial statement of the presumption is that of Wright J in *Re Athlumney*:

> Perhaps no rule of construction is more firmly established than this—that a retrospective operation is not to be given to a statute so as to impair an existing right or obligation, otherwise than as regards matters of procedure, unless that effect cannot be avoided without doing violence to the language of the enactment. If the enactment is expressed in language which is fairly capable of either interpretation, it ought to be construed as prospective only.[6]

Wright J was primarily concerned with the presumption against interference with vested rights, but his insistence that a 'retrospective operation is not to be given . . . unless that effect cannot be avoided' is of broader application insofar as it demonstrates both the strength of the presumption and the fact that the objective of the presumption is not to give effect to legislative intent but to avoid retroactivity unless that result is unavoidable.

Another well known statement of the presumption against retroactivity is that made by Willes J in *Phillips v Eyre*:

> Retrospective laws are, no doubt, prima facie of questionable policy, and contrary to the general principle that legislation by which the conduct of mankind is to be regulated ought, when introduced for the first time, to deal with future acts, and ought not to change the character of past transactions carried on upon the faith of the then existing law.[7]

Willes J went on to state that:

> Accordingly, the Court will not ascribe retrospective force to new laws affecting rights, unless by express words or necessary implication it appears that such was the intention of the legislature.[8]

Willes J expressed the view *held by the courts* that retroactive laws are 'prima facie of questionable policy' the result of which is the 'general principle' that laws will not be construed as having retroactive effect except in the circumstances he mentioned.

Lindley MR afforded the presumption the status of being a 'fundamental rule of English law' when he said that it is a:

> fundamental rule of English law that no statute should be construed so as to have a retrospective operation unless its language is such as plainly to require such a construction.[9]

Dixon CJ in *Maxwell v Murphy* was clear that the presumption constitutes a 'rule of the common law' that is brought to bear on the process of statutory construction when he said:

[6] [1898] 2 QB 547, 551–552.
[7] (1870) LR 6 QB 1, 23 (Exch).
[8] *Ibid.*
[9] *Lauri v Renad* [1892] 3 Ch 402, 421. See also *R v Lodhi* [2006] NSWCCA 121, [30]–[35].

> The general rule of the common law is that a statute changing the law ought not, unless the intention appears with reasonable certainty, to be understood as applying to facts or events that have already occurred in such a way as to confer or impose or otherwise affect rights or liabilities which the law had defined by reference to the past events.[10]

Lord Rodger thought that in this passage Dixon CJ 'conveniently stated' 'the essence of the core common law rule'.[11]

Constitutional significance was attributed to the presumption against retroactivity by Lord Wilberforce in *Black-Clawson International v Papierwerke Waldhof-Aschaffenburg*[12] where he made it clear that the courts' constitutional role is not simply to divine and give effect to parliament's intention, but to engage in a process of construction in which principles developed by the courts are brought to bear on the legislation in question. Lord Wilberforce said:

> Legislation in England is passed by Parliament, and put in the form of written words. This legislation is given legal effect upon subjects by virtue of judicial decision, and it is the function of the courts to say what the application of the words used to particular cases or individuals is to be. This power which has been devolved upon the judges from the earliest times is an essential part of the constitutional process by which subjects are brought under the rule of law—as distinct from the rule of the King or the rule of Parliament; and it would be a degradation of that process if the courts were to be merely a reflecting mirror of what some other interpretation agency might say. The saying that it is the function of the courts to ascertain the will or intention of Parliament is often enough repeated, so often indeed as to have become an incantation. If too often or unreflectingly stated, it leads to neglect of the important element of judicial construction; an element not confined to a mechanical analysis of today's words, but, if this task is to be properly done, related to such matters as intelligibility to the citizen, constitutional propriety, considerations of history, comity of nations, reasonable and non-retro-active effect and, no doubt, in some contexts, to social needs.[13]

For this reason it is appropriate, when assessing potential retroactivity, to refer to a process of statutory *construction* rather than interpretation. Of course members of parliament and legislative drafters are aware of the principles that the courts apply to the task of construing legislation. Indeed parliaments have enacted general guidance on the construction of statutes that attempt to codify or alter some of those principles.[14] However, the presumption against retroactivity is not,

[10] *Maxwell v Murphy* (1957) 96 CLR 261, 267. Applied, for example, in *Victrawl v Telstra Corporation* (1995) 183 CLR 595, 620–24.

[11] *Wilson v First County Trust (No 2)* [2004] 1 AC 816, [187] (HL).

[12] [1975] AC 591 (HL).

[13] *Ibid* 629–30. See also Lord Hoffmann's approach to the principle of legality, rather than specifically to the presumption against retroactivity, in *R v Home Secretary, ex p Simms* [2000] 2 AC 115, 131 (HL) and Gleeson CJ's approach to the general presumption against statutory modification or abrogation of fundamental rights in *Electrolux Home Products v Australian Workers' Union* (2004) 221 CLR 309, [21].

[14] Interpretation Act 1978 (UK), Acts Interpretation Act 1901 (Aus), Interpretation Act 1987 (NSW), Acts Interpretation Act 1954 (Qld), Acts Interpretation Act 1915 (SA), Acts Interpretation Act 1931 (Tas), Interpretation of Legislation Act 1984 (Vic), Interpretation Act 1984 (WA). Though provisions are made about the temporal effect of repealing a statute none of these statutes contains a general statement of the presumption against retroactivity.

except in criminal law,[15] usually the subject of such guidance. Independently of any statutory words, the courts will begin their task of statutory construction with the presumption against retroactivity. The nature of the presumption is such that it is a principle of the common law applied on the basis of a generally pejorative view of retroactive statutes held by the courts.

C Applications of the Presumption Against Retroactivity

Although *Gardner v Lucas*[16] is often cited as an application of the presumption against retroactivity, it is rarely considered in sufficient detail to reveal its significance for the question of whether the presumption against retroactivity is a common law principle of the kind described above.

A 1696 statute meant that an agreement made in 1873 was invalid for reason of form. The question was whether the agreement was saved by an 1874 statute which provided that no written agreement attested to by two witnesses 'shall be deemed invalid . . . because of any informality of execution'.[17] If it did save the agreement then the retroactive effect of the 1874 statute was that an agreement that was void for form in 1873 would, in 1875, be held to have been valid in 1873. Two of the Law Lords in *Gardner v Lucas* took differing views of the courts' role in cases in which the statutory language leaves room for doubt about the temporal effect of a statute. The Lord Chancellor, Lord Cairns, focused on the question of legislative intention:

> your Lordships have to examine the subject-matter of the enactment of the particular section which you have to construe, to bear in mind the effect of a construction which would make it retrospective, and to ask yourselves whether it is to be supposed that that construction was intended by the Legislature to be given to it.[18]

The Lord Chancellor's primary concern was the intention of the legislature, although he also referred to authority for the proposition that:

> any Court will be slow to construe an enactment as retrospective, and thereby as disturbing existing rights, unless Parliament has clearly said that the enactment is to be construed retrospectively.[19]

Lord Blackburn's speech favoured a stronger role for the courts in construing statutes according to the common law presumption against retroactivity rather

[15] As well as art 7 of the ECHR being incorporated into English law by force of the Human Rights Act, a similar prohibition appears in s 27 of the Charter of Human Rights and Responsibilities Act 2006 (Vic) and in s 11 of the Criminal Codes of Queensland and Western Australia.

[16] (1878) 3 App Cas 582 (HL).

[17] Conveyancing (Scotland) Act 1874 37 & 38 Vict c 94 s 39.

[18] (1878) 3 App Cas 582, 590 (HL).

[19] *Ibid.*

than, once the statutory language did not explicitly require a particular result, primarily being concerned with attempting to work out what the legislature intended. Lord Blackburn said:

> I think it extremely probable that of the lay members of the Legislature who passed the Act many might think they [the words of the provision] were retrospective; but we must construe the Act according to the legal rules of construction to see whether it expresses an intention of the Legislature that it should be retrospective.[20]

The expression of intention to which Lord Blackburn referred was not what the members of the legislature wanted or thought to be the temporal effect of the Act. Rather, it was an 'intention' construed by the court on the basis of pre-existing general rules of construction, including the presumption against retroactivity. This type of non-literal usage of the word 'intention'[21] has been characterized as 'an act of constitutional courtesy which the judiciary observes in its collective relationship with the Parliament'.[22] It is open to theoretical question whether a legislature, being a large group, the members of which have conflicting views and motivations, may form and act on one intention, and whether, in any event, courts are able to find and give effect to that intention.[23] What is important here, however, is that, on Lord Blackburn's approach, the courts will apply the presumption against retroactivity, as a common law principle, developed by the courts, which is defeasible only to strong reasons, such as inescapable statutory command, but typically not to lesser indications of legislative intention, howsoever such intention may be determined.

Further support for a conception of the presumption of retroactivity as a principle of the common law rather than a tool for the divination of legislative intention may be found in Lord O'Hagan's judgment in *Gardner v Lucas*. Lord O'Hagan thought that the retroactive application of the statute would be opposed to 'public policy and private interest'.[24] As the legislature had not made its views on what public policy and private interest required in terms of the temporal effect of the statute, Lord O'Hagan can only have been referring to the view of public policy and private interest held by the court. Lord O'Hagan was particularly concerned that if the statute had retroactive application anyone who had acted in reliance on the previous legal status of agreements could suffer serious adverse consequences, of which he gave examples.[25] Thus judicial concern for reliance,

[20] (1878) 3 App Cas 603.

[21] Cf *R(Wilkinson) v Inland Revenue Commissioners* (2005) 1 WLR 1718, [18] (HL).

[22] JJ Spigelman 'Principle of Legality and the Clear Statement Principle' (2005) 79 Australian Law Journal 769, 769. See also *R v Lodhi* [2006] NSWCCA 121, [40].

[23] R Ekins 'Legislative Intent and Group Action' (M Phil Thesis University of Oxford 2005), a precis of which is published as R Ekins 'The Relevance of the Rule of Recognition' (2006) 31 Australian Journal of Legal Philosophy 95; contra, eg, J Waldron *Law and Disagreement* (Clarendon Press Oxford 1999) Ch 6. Cf, for example, *R v Secretary of State for the Environment, Transport and the Regions, ex p Spath Holme* [2001] 2 AC 349, 396 (HL).

[24] (1878) 3 App Cas 582, 601 (HL).

[25] *Ibid.*

albeit actual reliance,[26] prompted both application of the presumption against retroactivity and a refusal for it to be rebutted by statutory words capable of being read other than as having retroactive effect.

In *Gardner v Lucas* the House of Lords was unanimous that the statute should not have retroactive application. It is apparent, however, that slightly differing views of the role of courts were at play. The Lord Chancellor, Lord Cairns, sought to search for the legislature's intention despite its ambiguity, whereas Lords Blackburn and O'Hagan construed the statute against the court's pejorative view of retroactivity, and did not seek to identify actual legislative intention in the absence of an inescapable legislative command of retroactivity. It is the latter approach that accords with a view of the presumption against retroactivity as a principle of the common law that gives effect to judicial concern about the protection of certainty and liberty. A similar standing judicial antipathy towards retroactivity was apparent in the judgment of Maugham J in *Gardner v Cone.*[27]

In that case Maugham J decided that, at the time that it occurred, an assignment of a lease without the licence of the lessor was a breach of a covenant contained in the lease. The next issue was the impact, if any, of a legislative provision that licence to assign not unreasonably be withheld, which took effect after the assignment but before the litigation.[28] The provision was explicitly applicable to leases made 'whether before or after the commencement of this Act'. The question was whether it was applicable to *breaches* occurring prior to the commencement of the Act. The plaintiff landlord sought relief for breach of the covenant disallowing assignment and the defendant tenant sought to assert that the new legislative provision was applicable and that consent to assign had unreasonably been withheld. Maugham J observed that 'it is clear that this Act is, in a loose sense, retrospective so far as it alters existing contracts'[29] but then found that although the legislature had quite clearly indicated its intention that the Act should apply to existing contracts:

> bearing in mind the principles applicable to the question of the construction of statutes, I have come to the conclusion that it is impossible for me to hold that that section has the effect of making something which was a breach of contract at the date when it was committed, a lawful act ex post facto.[30]

Having established that the Act did not unambiguously require retroactive effect, Maugham J was not concerned to attempt to divine what the legislature in fact intended on the subject of retroactivity. He was motivated, as discussed above,[31] by a concern not to abrogate the liberty that the lessor enjoyed at the time of deciding to refuse his licence to assign the lease. Just as *Gardner v Cone* demonstrates a court's protection of an actual liberty through its insistence on applying

26 Cf Ch 3 Pt B(2).
27 [1928] Ch 955.
28 Landlord and Tenant Act 1927 (Eng) 17 and 18 Geo V c 36 s 19.
29 [1928] Ch 955, 966.
30 *Ibid.*
31 See Ch 3 Pt C(3).

the presumption against retroactivity, so too *Noss Farm Products v Lilico*[32] demonstrates a court's concern, expressed through the presumption against retroactivity, that an act lawful when done should not later be deemed to have been unlawful.

In *Noss Farm Products v Lilico* the appellant defendants sold an article of food with a label attached to it and complied with all relevant laws at the time they did so. The person who bought the article of food then resold it, with the label unchanged, at a time after a change in the law relating to food labelling. The label did not comply with this new law. The relevant statute allowed the local authority to bring proceedings against a party not responsible for the sale giving rise to the offence, where the offence was due to that party's 'act or default'. Proceedings were brought against the original seller. The statute[33] made no mention of its temporal effect. On the face of the statute, the appellants might be thought to have been caught by its terms, the offence being due to their 'act' of labelling and there being no need for them to have committed a separate offence. However, the court was vehement that no such retroactive reading be given to the Act. Humphreys J, with whom Cassels J agreed, allowed the appeal against conviction stating:

> We are asked to say here that the meaning of that provision is, that if a man sells what is perfectly legal and proper according to law, nevertheless a year afterwards—and, it may be said, the law having in the meantime been altered—he is to be brought before a police court and, being a reputable person, is to be charged with a criminal offence. To my mind that is a monstrous proposition. I cannot conceive of any Act of Parliament being passed having such an effect.[34]

Thus a court's view of the inappropriateness of retroactivity, because of its incursion on individual liberty, was imposed on a statute which was silent on the matter and which could comfortably, so far as the language used goes, have been read to have retroactive effect.

Thus far the examples discussed have been cases where it was not clear whether the legislature intended retroactive effect or not. There are cases in which it is tolerably clear that the legislature did intend retroactivity and courts have nonetheless refused to give statutes such effect, finding that the legislature was not explicit enough in stating its intention. One such case is *Wijesuriya v Amit*,[35] a case decided by the Privy Council on appeal from the Supreme Court of Ceylon.

At issue in *Wijesuriya v Amit* was a tax ordinance which stated that it 'shall be deemed to have come into effect' on a date prior to the date on which the ordinance entered into force.[36] The judgment of the Privy Council was delivered by Lord Wilberforce who observed that it 'was conceded that the legislature has power both to impose a tax retrospectively, and retrospectively to make non-payment of the tax a penal offence. The question is whether the amending

32 [1945] 2 All ER 609 (KB).
33 Food and Drugs Act 1938 (Eng) 1 and 2 Geo VI c 56, in particular s 83.
34 [1945] 2 All ER 609, 610 (KB).
35 [1966] AC 372 (PC).
36 Heavy Oil Motor Vehicles Taxation (Amendment) Act 1961 (Ceylon) s 2(2).

ordinance has effectively done so.'[37] Deeming a provision to come into effect on a specified day prior to the entry into force of the enactment is a common way of the legislature unambiguously declaring its intention that the provision have retroactive effect. Even in the face of such an unambiguous statement, the Privy Council applied the presumption against retroactivity and, in the circumstances, found that the ordinance was not to be given retroactive effect.

The precise question was when the motor vehicle tax claimed by the government was due. The Privy Council was most concerned by the fact that at the date on which the government claimed that it was due, being a date prior to the entry into force of the ordinance, matters such as who was liable for the tax (the owner at the time of the passing of the ordinance or the owner at the time the provision might be deemed to have taken retroactive effect), under what conditions it was to be paid, and what the consequences of non-payment were to be, were unknown such that it could not be said that the tax was in fact due on such a date. Lord Wilberforce said:

> in order to enable tax to be collected it was not sufficient merely to date back the operation of the amendment; it was necessary expressly to adapt the existing scheme to the new conditions created by the amendment by specifying the date on which the past tax was to be due, who was to pay it, within what time and at what place, and stating clearly what consequences to what person would follow if payment was not made.[38]

In doing so, Lord Wilberforce applied to the particular circumstances of this case some of the inherent difficulties with retroactive law making and found that because those difficulties had not been addressed in the legislative scheme, the ordinance should not be construed as having retroactive effect. Thus a legislative provision was denied the retroactive effect that it was fairly obviously, though clumsily, intended by the legislature to have, because of the court's ingrained antipathy towards retroactivity. Similarly, in *R v Lodhi*[39] statutory provisions[40] that otherwise had expressly retroactive effect were denied application to pending proceedings because the court construed the statutes in the context of the court's respect for the common law principle of legality. In construing the statutes so as not to apply to pending proceedings, the court was concerned more with its own antipathy towards such statutes than with ascertaining legislative intention. The court was able to construe the statutes in this way because the statutes, whilst otherwise expressly retroactive, did not specifically provide for their application to pending proceedings.

[37] [1966] AC 372, 378 (PC).

[38] *Ibid* 380.

[39] [2006] NSWCCA 121, [22]–[50]. Contra *Zainal bin Hashim v Malaysia Government* [1980] AC 734 (PC), discussed in Ch 4 Pt F(1); *State of Victoria v Robertson* [2000] 1 VR 465, [17]–[21].

[40] Criminal Code Act 1995 (Aus) divs 101 and 106.3 as amended by the Anti-Terrorism Act 2005 (Aus) and the Anti-Terrorism Act (No 2) 2005 (Aus).

D Fairness as a Determinant of the Applicability of the Presumption

In some modern statements of the presumption against retroactivity there is an attempt to subordinate the presumption to a more general test of fairness. The most comprehensive statement of this approach, which for that reason is worth lengthy quotation, appears in *L'Office Cherifien des Phosphates v Yamashita-Shinnihon Steamship Co* in which Lord Mustill, who delivered the speech in the House of Lords with which all the other Law Lords agreed, said:

> My Lords, it would be impossible now to doubt that the court is required to approach questions of statutory interpretation with a disposition, and in some cases a very strong disposition, to assume that a statute is not intended to have retrospective effect. Nor indeed would I wish to cast any doubt on the validity of this approach for it ensures that the courts are constantly on the alert for the kind of unfairness which is found in, for example, the characterisation as criminal of past conduct which was lawful when it took place, or in alterations to the antecedent national, civil or familial status of individuals. Nevertheless, I must own up to reservations about the reliability of generalised presumptions and maxims when engaged in the task of finding out what Parliament intended by a particular form of words, for they too readily confine the court to a perspective which treats all statutes, and all situations to which they apply, as if they were the same. This is misleading, for the basis of the rule is no more than simple fairness, which ought to be the basis of every legal rule.[41]

Lord Mustill rightly acknowledged the role of the presumption against retroactivity in ensuring that the courts are constantly on the alert for the manifestations of retroactivity that he mentioned. Lord Mustill's reservations about the reliability of the presumption against retroactivity in 'finding out what Parliament intended' are no doubt well founded, but would not undermine the presumption if its purpose is accepted as being to give effect to a principle of the common law, developed by the courts, that involves courts in an exercise of *construing* a statute against the background of the presumption, rather than courts simply being engaged in a formalistic *interpretive* task of identifying then applying parliament's intention.[42] On this approach it is no criticism of the general applicability of the presumption against retroactivity to claim that it does not provide an accurate guide to 'finding out what Parliament intended'. The words of the statute and any permissible extrinsic materials do that. The presumption against retroactivity is instead directed towards the different goal of, wherever possible, construing statutes consistently with the common law's protection of certainty and liberty.

[41] [1994] 1 AC 486, 524–525 (HL).

[42] *Black-Clawson International v Papierwerke Waldhof-Aschaffenburg* [1975] AC 591, 629–30 (HL), quoted and discussed in Ch 4 Pt B.

The second aspect of Lord Mustill's speech in *Yamashita-Shinnihon Steamship* requiring comment is its concentration on the question of 'fairness'. Lord Mustill continued:

> True it is that to change the legal character of a person's acts or omissions after the event will very often be unfair; and since it is rightly taken for granted that Parliament will rarely wish to act in a way which seems unfair it is sensible to look very hard at a statute which appears to have this effect, to make sure that this is what Parliament really intended. This is, however, no more than common sense, the application of which may be impeded rather than helped by recourse to formulae which do not adapt themselves to individual circumstances, and which tend themselves to become the subject of minute analysis, whereas what ought to be analysed is the statute itself.
>
> . . . I do not find it necessary to cite and analyse the numerous authorities on retrospective effect, but prefer to proceed directly to the ascertainment of the intention which Parliament intended . . . by a reference to the following statement by Staughton LJ in *Secretary of State for Social Security v Tunnicliffe* [1991] 2 All ER 712, 724, quoted by Sir Thomas Bingham MR in the present case . . .:
>
> 'In my judgment the true principle is that Parliament is presumed not to have intended to alter the law applicable to past events and transactions in a manner which is unfair to those concerned in them, unless a contrary intention appears'.[43]

The passage from Staughton LJ's judgment in *Tunnicliffe* that Lord Mustill quoted in *Yamashita-Shinnihon Steamship* may be taken as the source of a movement towards the adoption of fairness as the touchstone for the application of the presumption against retroactivity.[44] That an undifferentiated test of fairness inherently causes unpredictable results is perhaps apparent from the fact that the decision of the House of Lords in *Plewa v Chief Adjudication Officer*[45] to overrule the Court of Appeal's decision in *Tunnicliffe* on the question of the temporal application of a particular statutory provision, adopted the Court of Appeal's approach of inquiring into the 'fairness' of particular temporal applications,[46] but differently weighed the same factors as considered by the Court of Appeal.[47]

Influenced by cases such as *Yamashita-Shinnihon Steamship*, *Tunnicliffe* and *Plewa*, the editors of Cross on *Statutory Interpretation* state that:

> The recent approach of the courts discussed here suggests that the courts operate a two-stage test. First, in the absence of inescapably clear words, they consider whether it would be unfair to apply the provision retrospectively. Second, if they conclude that to apply it would be unfair, this brings the presumption into play in its stronger form as requiring rebuttal by clear words or necessary implication. As *Plewa* illustrates, once the courts have concluded that it would be unfair to apply a provision retrospectively, they will rarely find themselves constrained to say that Parliament intended to act unfairly in that

[43] [1994] 1 AC 486, 525 (HL).

[44] See, eg, *A-G (NSW) v World Best Holdings* (2005) 63 NSWLR 557, [49]–[66], especially [59]. Contra *Re Barretto* [1994] QB 392, 401 (CA), discussed at Ch 4 Pt G(2)(a)(iii).

[45] [1995] 1 AC 249 (HL).

[46] *Ibid* 257, 258.

[47] *Ibid* 258.

way. Where the courts conclude that it would not be unfair, then they will give effect to the purpose of the provision which may lead to its retrospective application.[48]

This passage is of interest because it proposes that, where the statute does not inescapably require retroactive effect to be given, the courts make a decision about whether retroactivity would be unfair in the circumstances, this decision being made regardless of the words of the statute on the question of retroactivity, and, if retroactivity would be unfair, then the presumption is applied with the almost invariable result that the statute is not given retroactive effect. If, however, the courts consider that it would not be unfair to apply the statute retroactively, then they will be more concerned with giving effect to the statutory purpose rather than with the strict application of the presumption against retroactivity. On this approach it is clear that, leaving aside cases of retroactivity mandated by a statute either expressly or by necessary implication, the courts' primary consideration would be what fairness requires. The presumption against retroactivity would only be applied if fairness required its application.

Even if it is true that fairness 'ought to be the basis of every legal rule', that does not mean that a judge's perception of fairness should be the gateway to the application of the rule in each individual case. Over time, in response to long experience with a multitude of different cases, the common law has established rules designed to administer justice according to law in all cases that fall within their ambit. These rules, including, relevantly, the presumption against retroactivity, should be the starting point of judicial adjudication. The starting point should not be what a particular judge considers to be fair in a particular case.[49] If the application of a general rule is, in the first place, dependent on whether the judge considers that fairness requires such application, the rule will be deprived of its status as a rule, even a presumptive one. As Chapter three demonstrates, in the case of the presumption against retroactivity concern for certainty and liberty can more accurately be said to underlie the presumption than the amorphous concept of fairness.

Parliament may be expected to weigh competing considerations and arrive at statutory language that parliament considers to represent a fair result insofar as temporal application is concerned. There are unfortunately numerous examples of statutes in which parliament and its advisers have either not deliberated on, or have, deliberately or otherwise, not made clear the temporal effect of a statute. It falls to the courts to determine the temporal effect of statutes when litigation requires them to do so. They should not attempt to redo or do the job that parliament has or should have done—ie to consider what would generally be fair in all of the facts and circumstances. The court will ordinarily receive submissions only on the interests of the parties to the litigation, not on more general effects. A consideration of what fairness to the individual litigants requires may not accord with

[48] R Cross *Statutory Interpretation* J Bell and G Engle (eds) (3rd edn Butterworths London 1995) 189–90.

[49] *A-G (NSW) v World Best Holdings* (2005) 63 NSWLR 557, [153].

what a broader view of fairness may indicate.[50] As Lord Wilberforce stated in *Black-Clawson International v Papierwerke Waldhof-Aschaffenburg*, the courts' constitutional role includes the process of construing statutes against the background of fundamental common law principles, such as the presumption against retroactivity,[51] which is based at a high level of generality on a concern for the protection of certainty and liberty. If parliament leaves the temporal effect of a statute unclear, the presumption against retroactivity should ordinarily be decisive. The courts' constitutional role does not include general inquiries at the start of a process of judicial reasoning as to whether a particular application of a statute would or would not be 'fair'.

E A Presumption of Variable Strength?

In addition to difficulties associated with attempts to utilize 'fairness' as a test for determining the applicability of the presumption against retroactivity, a further and related difficulty lies in the idea that the presumption, even if applicable, is of variable strength. Using the word 'injustice' rather than 'unfairness', a judgment of Adam J in the Supreme Court of Victoria proposes this idea.

> The strength of the presumption against retrospectivity in any particular case, and accordingly the ease or difficulty with which it may be overcome, must, I would think, depend on the nature and degree of the injustice which would result from giving a statute a retrospective operation. Where a palpable injustice would result, the presumption should be given its fullest weight. In such a case it is but common sense to require the clearest indication of legislative intention that such an unjust result was intended. On the other hand, where to give retrospective operation to a statute might be considered to work some injustice to one party, but is clearly required to rectify a manifest injustice to others, there would, on principle, seem little reason for giving much weight to the presumption.[52]

Reliance on differing levels of 'injustice' as the determinant of the strength of the presumption against retroactivity suffers the same analytical difficulties as reliance on the concept of 'fairness' in *Tunnicliffe* and the cases that follow it which are discussed above.[53] Moreover, it is not clear how a presumption, by definition, could incorporate variability in its strength.

It is possible for different presumptions to be of different strengths, but not for the same presumption to be of variable strength. A presumption is a starting point.

[50] *George Hudson v Australian Timber Workers' Union* (1923) 32 CLR 413, 434; cf D Feldman 'Commencement, Transition and Retrospective Legislation' (1992) 108 Law Quarterly Review 212, 213.

[51] [1975] AC 591, 629–630 (HL).

[52] *Doro v Victorian Railways Commissioners* [1960] VR 84, 86, adopted by Dawson J in *Polyukhovich v The Commonwealth of Australia* (1991) 172 CLR 501, 642. See also *The Ironsides* (1862) Lush 458, 465; 167 ER 205, 209; and *Nicholas v Commissioner for Corporate Affairs* [1988] VR 289, 300–1.

[53] Ch 4 Pt D.

Once a presumption is found to be applicable, it applies regardless of the facts and circumstances of the case. Indeed it is through the prism of the presumption that decisions about the case are made. Once the facts and circumstances are considered, it may be that reasons for the rebuttal of the presumption can be established.[54] That is a different thing to the presumption being of variable strength. For a presumption to be of variable strength on the basis of the facts and circumstances of the case and/or what fairness or justice is thought to demand, would require the facts and circumstances of the case to determine the very presumption through which they are to be viewed. That would not be a presumption. The values of certainty and liberty justify a strong presumption against retroactivity. It is not the presumption against retroactivity that should vary in strength. It is the strength of the reasons said to rebut it that vary.

F Rebuttal of the Presumption Against Retroactivity

Beginning with a strong presumption against retroactivity as the 'touchstone'[55] and subsequently considering whether anything in 'the whole circumstances'[56] is sufficient to displace the presumption, gives full weight, in all circumstances, to the values protected by the presumption against retroactivity. If it can be shown in a particular case that retroactivity is consistent with those values or that in all the circumstances retroactivity is otherwise appropriate then the presumption may be successfully rebutted. This insistence on the application of a strong presumption combined with an acknowledgement of its defeasibility contrasts with the employment of 'fairness' as a test to establish the strength of the presumption in the first instance, and to claims that the presumption is of variable strength. Beyond statements of general approach, an inquiry into the rebuttal of the presumption against retroactivity can, because it is reliant on the facts and circumstances of particular cases, only proceed with reference to a sample of such cases.

1 Express Words or Necessary Intendment

A good example of a court finding that the express words of a statute required the court to apply that statute retroactively is the case of *Zainal bin Hashim v Malaysia Government*.[57] The plaintiff was dismissed from his office of constable in the Royal Malaysian Police force. At the time that it occurred the dismissal was contrary to

[54] See further Ch 3 Pt E.

[55] *George Hudson v Australian Timber Workers' Union* (1923) 32 CLR 413, 434. This approach, set out in full in Ch 3 Pt E(2), has been frequently cited, eg in *Wilson v First County Trust (No 2)* [2004] 1 AC 816, [215] (HL).

[56] *Ibid.*

[57] [1980] AC 734 (PC).

article 135(1) of the Federal Constitution of Malaysia.[58] After the first instance judgment finding in favour of the plaintiff the legislature passed a constitutional amendment which, if applicable to the plaintiff's case, would deem his dismissal to have been constitutionally valid. The amendment was by way of addition of a proviso to article 135(1) of the Federal Constitution of Malaysia which ended with the words 'and this proviso shall be deemed to have been an integral part of this clause as from Merdeka Day'.[59] Viscount Dilhorne, delivering the judgment of the Privy Council, said that:

> giving retrospective effect to this amendment made to the Constitution cannot be avoided without doing violence to the language of the amendment.[60]

Viscount Dilhorne concluded that in:

> their Lordships' view the conclusion is inescapable that the legislature intended to secure that no such actions started after Merdeka Day whether proceeding, or not started, when the amendment was made, should succeed on the ground that the power to dismiss had not been exercised by someone with the power to appoint.[61]

There would be little to be gained by discussion of numerous cases in which the language of the legislature was held to overcome the presumption against retroactivity.[62] Many turn on whether retroactivity 'cannot be avoided without doing violence to the language' of the statute.[63] This can occur either by force of the express words or by the necessary intendment of those words, a phrase which 'only means that the force of the language in its surroundings carries such strength of impression in one direction, that to entertain the opposite view appears wholly unreasonable'.[64]

The only other point of general application is that the presumption against retroactivity should provide the prism through which the words of the statute are read, even for the purpose of deciding whether the words *require* retroactive application. In this way the words of the statute may lead to the rebuttal of the presumption but they do not make the presumption inapplicable.

2 Validating Statutes

In *Phillips v Eyre* Willes J acknowledged the force of the general presumption against retroactivity[65] but also thought that:

[58] *Ibid* 740.

[59] Merdeka Day was when Malaysia's independence was proclaimed: 31 Aug 1957.

[60] [1980] AC 734, 741 (PC). See also *State of Victoria v Robertson* [2000] 1 VR 465, [20]–[21].

[61] *Ibid* 743.

[62] Other examples include *Millner v Raith* (1942) 66 CLR 1; *Taylor v Anstis* [1940] VLR 300; *A-G (NSW) v World Best Holdings* (2005) 63 NSWLR 557.

[63] Contra *A-G (NSW) v World Best Holdings* (2005) 63 NSWLR 557, [50]–[54].

[64] *Worrall v Commercial Banking Co of Sydney* (1917) 24 CLR 28, 32.

[65] See Ch 4 Pt B and Ch 3 Pt B(2).

> to affirm that it is naturally or necessarily unjust to take away a vested right of action by act subsequent, is inconsistent both with the common law of England and the constant practice of legislation.[66]

Willes J considered that some retroactive legislation was 'obviously just', particularly where its purpose was to 'render valid the acts of persons who had fallen honestly into error'.[67] As an example, Willes J discussed the retroactive statutes,[68] though not any judicial consideration of them, that followed a House of Lords' judicial decision in 1844 that declared null and void marriages celebrated in Ireland by ministers not episcopally ordained.[69] Willes J observed that by 'these beneficial and just statutes the past marriages were ratified and confirmed as from the beginning'.[70] However, the Act of indemnity before Willes J was not as benign as the example of 'just' retroactivity that he cited.

The Governor of Jamaica, Eyre, had Phillips imprisoned and flogged during the 1865 rebellion. The Jamaican Assembly then passed legislation indemnifying the Governor and those acting under his authority for acts done to suppress the rebellion. Furthermore, the Act provided that the Governor's declaration that such acts were done under his authority and for the purpose of suppressing the rebellion was conclusive evidence of the truth of such assertions. This statute was pleaded by the Governor in defence to Phillips' claim.

Willes J, delivering the judgment of a seven member Court of Exchequer, held that the statute successfully barred a plea alleging acts that were illegal at the time that they were committed. Willes J distinguished Acts of indemnity from retroactive criminalisation, saying:

> The retrospective Attainder Acts of earlier times, when the principles of law were not so well understood or so closely regarded as in the present day, and which are now looked upon as barbarous and loosely spoken of as ex post facto laws, were of a substantially different character. They did not confirm irregular acts, but voided and punished what had been lawful when done.[71]

The formal distinction made by Willes J between Acts of indemnity, which deem legal that which was illegal, and Acts that deem illegal that which was legal, is valid on its face. The more fundamental question, which requires further discussion, is whether, because of that distinction, Acts of indemnity, taken as a class, are inherently less objectionable than other forms of retroactive laws.

Dicey took a contrary view of Acts of indemnity than that taken by Willes J. Dicey thought that:

[66] (1870) LR 6 QB 1, 23 (Exch).

[67] *Ibid* 24.

[68] An Act for Confirmation of Certain Marriages in Ireland 1842 5 & 6 Vict c 113; An Act for Confirmation of Certain Marriages in Ireland 1843 6 & 7 Vict c 39; An Act for Marriages in Ireland 1844 7 & 8 Vict c 81 s 83.

[69] *The Queen v Millis* (1844) 10 Cl & F 534; 8 ER 844.

[70] (1870) LR 6 QB 1, 24 (Exch).

[71] *Ibid.*

> of all the laws which a Legislature can pass an Act of Indemnity is the most likely to produce injustice. It is on the face of it the legislation[72] of illegality; the hope of it encourages acts of vigour, but it also encourages violations of law and of humanity. The tale of Flogging Fitzgerald in Ireland,[73] or the history of Governor Eyre in Jamaica, is sufficient to remind us of the deeds of lawlessness and cruelty which in a period of civil conflict may be inspired by recklessness or panic, and may be pardoned by the retrospective sympathy or partisanship of a terror-stricken or vindictive Legislature. [Citations added][74]

This statement, seemingly critical of Acts of indemnity cannot, however, be accepted, as Irish apparently accepted it,[75] at face value. Dicey acknowledged that circumstances may arise:

> under which the maintenance of order or the protection of life may excuse or require deviation from the strict rules of legality[76]

and that an Act of indemnity would then be appropriate. His objection was not to Acts of indemnity per se but, in the course of a treatise devoted entirely to opposition to Irish home rule, to the passing of Acts of indemnity by an Irish Parliament rather than by the Parliament of the United Kingdom at Westminster. Dicey said, in words revealing his bias, that whether circumstances justifying an Act of indemnity had arisen:

> will always be decided far more justly by the Parliament at Westminster than it can be decided by the Parliament at Dublin. Can any one really maintain that a Parliament in which Mr Healy, or, for that matter, Col Saunderson, might be leader, would be as fair a tribunal as a Parliament under the guidance of Mr Gladstone or Lord Salisbury for determining whether an officer who, acting under the direction of the Irish Government and with a view to maintain order at Belfast or at Dublin, should have put an agitator or conspirator to death without due trial, had or had not done his duty.[77]

Acts of indemnity do not affect the liberty of defendants in the same way as retroactive laws that deem illegal that which was legal. Nonetheless, liberty concerns arise in a different way where Acts of indemnity are involved. In the case of a criminal law, prior to an Act of indemnity the liberty of all persons is protected, in part, by way of the State's prohibition of certain harmful conduct. If by way of its exceptional power to make retroactive laws the State deems that the prohibition that existed at the time of acting did not in fact exist, the liberty of all, protected by

[72] In the first edition, AV Dicey *A Leap in the Dark or Our New Constitution* (John Murray London 1893) 87, referred here to 'the legalisation of illegality' but changed this dramatic phrase to 'legislation of illegality' in the second edition.

[73] For details of which see *Wright v Fitzgerald* (1799) 27 Howell's State Trials 759 and P O'Higgins 'Wright v Fitzgerald Revisited' (1962) 25 Modern Law Review 413.

[74] AV Dicey *A Leap in the Dark: A Criticism of the Principles of Home Rule as Illustrated by the Bill of 1893* (2nd edn John Murray London 1911) 83–84.

[75] LE Irish *Time and Law: Retrospectivity and Prospectivity of Statutes and Judicial Decisions* (D Phil Thesis University of Oxford 1971) 419.

[76] AV Dicey *A Leap in the Dark: A Criticism of the Principles of Home Rule as Illustrated by the Bill of 1893* (2nd edn John Murray London 1911) 84.

[77] *Ibid.*

law at the time of the crime occurring, is removed with retroactive effect. This will be felt particularly acutely by those who suffer conduct illegal at the time that it occurred, but subsequently and retroactively legalized. To take the facts of *Phillips v Eyre*, Phillips was, at the time that he suffered such treatment, entitled to be free of arbitrary imprisonment and flogging and entitled to a remedy for breach of those rights. Phillips was, by the Act of indemnity, retroactively deprived of his rights and of his entitlement to a remedy.

Certainty is also affected by Acts of indemnity in the sense that conduct of which people were entitled to believe themselves to be free, a freedom protected by the criminal law, and which may have given rise to rights of self-defence, is subsequently deemed by an Act of indemnity to have been legal at the time at which it occurred. Presumably any exercise of a right of self-defence would correlatively be deemed to have been unlawful.[78] Added to these incursions on liberty and certainty is the related danger that concerned Dicey: abuse by the state of an exceptional legal power. Thus, Acts said to indemnify those guilty of acts unlawful at the time of their commission should be subject to the same presumption against retroactivity as is applicable more generally.

In *Phillips v Eyre* Willes J began his inquiry with the general presumption against retroactivity. He then appears to have considered the presumption rebutted because Acts of indemnity *as a class* indicated that result. A similar willingness to treat the presumption against retroactivity as weaker in the case of validating Acts is apparent in a comment made by Sugerman P in *Bawn v Metropolitan Meat Industry Board* that since validating Acts:

> are of necessity retrospective in their operation, it may be said that when it appears from the general scope and purview of a statute that it is intended to be validating in its operation, the presumption against retrospectivity is not so strong as in the case of other classes of statutes.[79]

This view was not apparent in the judgments of Asprey or Mason JJA in that case and all three judges rested their judgments on the basis that the statutory language used compelled a finding of retroactive effect.[80]

The language of the Act under consideration in *Phillips v Eyre* probably also compelled a finding of retroactivity. It should have been that factor alone, in both *Phillips v Eyre* and *Bawn v Metropolitan Meat Industry Board*, not any judicial sympathy for validating Acts as a class, that motivated those decisions.[81] That statutes passed by a legislature with the intention of altering the legal status of past events are likely to use language compelling the courts to give such statutes retroactive

[78] Cf *R v Thurston* (1663) I Lev 91; 83 ER 312; 1 Keble 454; 83 ER 1049, discussed in Ch 2 Pt B.

[79] (1970) 92 WN (NSW) 823, 827.

[80] *Ibid* 831, 840, 843.

[81] Similarly, the fact that the statutory language in *A-G (NSW) v World Best Holdings* (2005) 63 NSWLR 557, [43]–[66], [153] compelled the retroactive application to pending proceedings of the validating Act in that case, should have been the sole reason for that application, without reliance on the perceived 'fairness' of such retroactivity.

operation, is merely an explanation for why statutes passed with that intention are often granted retroactive effect. It may be that the label 'validating statute' or 'Act of indemnity' can only accurately be used once it is certain that the statute does indeed have retroactive effect. The mere assertion of such labels is not, however, a reason for courts to weaken the presumption against retroactivity. Rather, courts should, as usual, be circumspect about granting retroactive application to any statute regardless of whether some might consider it to be intended by the legislature to validate or indemnify acts illegal when they occurred.[82] This preferable approach is apparent in the speech of Lord Reid in *Starkowski v A-G*.[83] Understanding the approach adopted in *Starkowski* requires attention to its facts.

A child was born in England in 1949. His parents were not married at the time of his birth. They purported to marry in an English registry office in 1950. The child sought a declaration that his parents were lawfully married and that he was legitimated by that marriage. The difficulty was that his mother had been married to a man other than his father in a religious ceremony in Austria in May 1945. At that time in that country the German marriage law was in force, which provided that a valid marriage could only be concluded before civil authorities. After Austria's liberation the Provisional Government issued an order providing for the validation by registration of marriages such as the one in question, such validation being deemed to have been effective from the time of the religious ceremony. In 1949, prior to the purported marriage in England, and without the mother's knowledge or consent, her marriage in Austria was registered and therefore validated under Austrian law. The question for the English courts was whether to recognize the retroactive Austrian Act, or to refuse to do so on the ground that its recognition would be contrary to English public policy.

Lord Reid said:

> there is at first sight compelling force in the appellant's argument that a person ought at any time to be able to find out with certainty whether he or she is married or not, and that the law of England ought not to recognize a principle which may result in a person being for the moment unmarried in law but knowing that he is liable to become married retrospectively.[84]

He was ultimately of the opinion, however, that:

> the balance of justice and convenience is clearly in favour of recognizing the validity of such retrospective legislation (subject, it may be, to some exceptions), and the objections to doing so are not substantial and are not founded on any compelling principle. Once it is settled that the formal validity of a marriage is to be determined by reference to the law of the place of celebration, there is no compelling reason why the reference should not be to that law as it is when the question arises for decision.[85]

82 *Young v Adams* [1898] AC 469, 476 (PC), discussed in Ch 2 Pt B.
83 [1954] AC 155 (HL).
84 *Ibid* 172.
85 *Ibid*. Cf FA Mann 'The Time Element in the Conflict of Laws' (1954) 31 British Year Book of International Law 217, 235–6, 243–4, contra JK Grodecki 'Conflicts of Laws in Time' (1959) 35 British Year Book of International Law 58, 75–6.

Lord Reid began his consideration concerned with certainty of legal status. Once satisfied that certainty was not unduly threatened by the retroactive legislation,[86] he concluded that 'the balance of justice and convenience' lay with following the normal rule of English private international law that the formal validity of a marriage is determined by the *lex celebrationis*, taken at the time of the litigation, even though that law was retroactive. The result was that the child was found to be the illegitimate son of a bigamist.

It must be acknowledged that because it was deciding whether or not to *recognize* a foreign law, the court had more discretion in this case to apply its own view of justice than it would have done had the statute before it been an English one. The overarching question was whether the effect of the foreign statute was consistent with English public policy, and, in general, if not in *Starkowski*,[87] this turns more on a statute's substantive content than its temporal application.[88] *Starkowski* nonetheless provides an example of an approach to Acts of validation that rightly begins with a presumption against retroactivity, which may be rebutted if the particular circumstances justify it.

3 Importance of Subject Matter

In addition to 'validating statutes', there have been other attempts to categorize types of Acts that may more readily be granted retroactive effect. Examples include 'beneficial statutes'[89] and statutes directed to 'public protection'.[90] The nomenclature of these suggested categories is broad and their contents contestable. Legislatures presumably consider all of their statutes, on balance, to be beneficial and many of them to be directed towards public protection. That does not mean that particular individuals are not disadvantaged by them so that such a statute is not beneficial or protective insofar as particular litigants are concerned. It is better to acknowledge this complexity at the outset, avoid ambiguous and overly broad categorization, and proceed to consideration of the facts, circumstances and subject matter of each case, which is required to determine whether a court should construe a statute as having retroactive effect.

In *Barber v Pigden*[91] the question was whether a husband was liable for his wife's tort. At the time the tort was committed (1934 and early 1935), the common law

[86] [1954] AC 155, 172 (HL).

[87] FA Mann 'The Time Element in the Conflict of Laws' (1954) 31 British Year Book of International Law 217, 245.

[88] *Ibid* 240.

[89] Eg *Brousseau v Alberta Securities Commission* [1989] 1 SCR 301, 318–319; E Edinger 'Retrospectivity in Law' (1995) 29 University of British Columbia Law Review 5, 14; JF Burrows *Statute Law in New Zealand* (3rd edn Lexis Nexis Wellington 2003) 406.

[90] Eg *Dental Council of New Zealand v Bell* [1992] 1 NZLR 438, 445 (HC); *Brousseau v Alberta Securities Commission* [1989] 1 SCR 301, 318–19; E Edinger 'Retrospectivity in Law' (1995) 29 University of British Columbia Law Review 5, 14. Contra JP Salembier 'Understanding Retroactivity: When the Past Just Ain't What it Used to Be' (2003) 33 Hong Kong Law Journal 99, 130–33.

[91] [1937] 1 KB 664 (CA).

rule was that he was so liable. On 2 August 1935 the Law Reform (Married Women and Tortfeasors) Act 1935[92] came into force and abolished that common law rule. On 16 August 1935 the writ in the action was issued. The question was which rule applied to the case.

Greer LJ decided, based on the statutory language alone, that the Act had retroactive effect.[93] In addition to the statutory language Scott LJ was concerned with the nature of the subject matter. He said:

> The language of Part I discloses an intention to make a clean sweep of the old legal fiction of our common law that a woman on marrying became merged in the personality of her husband, and ceased to be a fully qualified and separate human person.[94]

Scott LJ continued:

> as far as the present case is concerned, the dominant intention of the Act is clear beyond all doubt: it is to effect a drastic reform of our law in a branch where there has been too much legal fiction and too much technicality of legal procedure; and I do not think the rule against retrospective interpretation . . . is properly applicable to such a statute abolishing legal fictions any more than to a merely procedural statute. The purpose of Part I of the Act is to give back to a woman, though married, the full human status allowed by the common law to a man, a maiden or a widow, of which the common law had robbed her; in short, it restores to her her natural status and capacity. It does it by sweeping away a host of legal fictions—fictions which in origin were inextricably mixed up with old procedural law. It is well recognized that the canon against retrospective interpretation does not apply to a statute dealing with adjective law, ie, procedure, and I think that a statute abolishing old legal fictions is so nearly akin to a procedural statute that the canon can have little, if any, application. After all, the canon expresses no rigid or absolute rule. It rests on a presumption of common-sense in a well-ordered and civilized society; and that presumption does not seem germane to the root-and-branch view Parliament was obviously taking when it passed this Act, of the historical interferences by lawyers with the natural rights of woman. Anyhow, the inhibition of the rule is a matter of degree, and must vary secundum materiam. A little consideration of this statute in my view suffices to exclude the presumption altogether.[95]

Scott LJ was concerned with limiting the *application* of the presumption, in a similar way to which the presumption is generally inapplicable to cases involving procedure.[96] The difficulty with this approach is that statutes dealing with procedure, although they usually apply to litigation involving facts occurring prior to the commencement of the procedural change, because they are typically

[92] (Eng) 25 and 26 Geo V c 30.

[93] [1937] 1 KB 664, 672–3 (CA).

[94] *Ibid* 677.

[95] *Ibid* 678.

[96] As to which see P St J Langan *Maxwell on the Interpretation of Statutes* (12th edn Sweet and Maxwell London 1969) 222; *Maxwell v Murphy* (1957) 96 CLR 261, 267; *Rodway v The Queen* (1990) 169 CLR 515, 518; *R v Chandra Dharma* [1905] 2 KB 335, 339; *Blyth v Blyth* [1966] AC 643, 656–7, 666, 670, 675 (HL); DC Pearce and RS Geddes *Statutory Interpretation in Australia* (6th edn Lexis Nexis Australia 2006) 320–329; C Sampford *Retrospectivity and the Rule of Law* (Oxford University Press 2006) 122–32.

'concerned only with the way in which certain rights are to be enforced'[97] do not have the effect of deeming a new law to apply to a past event as though it was the law at the time of that event and so, typically, are not retroactive.[98] It is because procedural statutes do not purport to have retroactive effect that the presumption against retroactivity is generally inapplicable to them. By contrast, in *Barber v Pigden*, the law relating to who was liable for the tort changed between commission of the tort and the accompanying litigation. The decision to apply the later law regarding liability, to facts that occurred when the law was otherwise, granted retroactive effect to the later law. Scott LJ's view that the presumption was *inapplicable* is therefore unconvincing.

Scott LJ's judgment was more soundly based on his view that the statute in question involved 'drastic reform of our law', that the presumption against retroactivity 'expresses no rigid or absolute rule' and that the presumption should be considered to be rebutted in light of 'the root-and-branch view Parliament was obviously taking when it passed this Act, of the historical interferences by lawyers with the natural rights of woman'. On this approach the presumption against retroactivity was, as usual, applicable; but the language of the statute combined with the fact that the Act sought to effect fundamental change to an area of the law founded on a view of the status of women that was no longer considered to be acceptable, exceptionally justified retroactivity. Sweeping away a legal fiction would not, of itself, necessarily justify retroactivity, but sweeping away a legal fiction as offensive as the subsumption of a woman's legal identity by her husband's did justify retroactive effect. The retroactive application by the courts of the legislative reform indicates a view shared by both of these branches of government that a law fusing a woman's legal identity with that of her husband's was not only unacceptable for the future but was also unacceptable in the past—so unacceptable that it should no longer be applied by the courts, even to causes of action arising prior to the legislative reform. A similar approach was evident in the judgment of Dawson J in *Polyukhovich v The Commonwealth of Australia.*[99]

In *Polyukhovich* the statute in question retroactively made criminal in Australia war crimes committed in Europe during the Second World War. Dawson J stated the presumption against retroactivity before adding: 'However, the injustice which might be inflicted by construing an enactment so as to give it a retrospective operation may vary according to its subject matter.'[100] Applying this approach Dawson J held that:

> the ex post facto creation of war crimes may be seen to be justifiable in a way that is not possible with other ex post facto criminal laws, particularly where the conduct proscribed

[97] DC Pearce and RS Geddes *Statutory Interpretation in Australia* (6th edn Lexis Nexis Australia 2006) 321.

[98] *Wright v Hale* (1860) 6 H & N 227, 231; 158 ER 94, 95; *R v Chandra Dharma* [1905] 2 KB 335, 339; *Bank of Athens v Royal Exchange Assurance* [1938] 1 KB 771, 773; *Rodway v The Queen* (1990) 169 CLR 515, 518.

[99] (1991) 172 CLR 501.

[100] *Ibid* 642.

> would have been criminal conduct had it occurred within Australia. The wrongful nature of the conduct ought to have been apparent to those who engaged in it even if, because of the circumstances in which the conduct took place, there was no offence against domestic law. And, of course, if the conduct amounted to genocide or a crime against humanity, that comment would be the stronger.[101]

Dawson J referred to, but did not reach any conclusions about issues of international criminal law.[102] He concluded that aside from whether the actions were criminal under international law prior to 1945:

> the wrongful nature of the conduct would . . . have been plainly evident. War crimes of the kind created by the Act simply could not, in any civilized community, have been described as innocent or blameless conduct merely because of the absence of proscription by law.[103]

Dawson J considered that the heinous nature of the conduct in question overcame the presumption against retroactivity. This is consistent with Kelsen's view on a related issue:

> Justice required the punishment of these men, in spite of the fact that under positive law they were not punishable at the time they performed the acts made punishable with retroactive force. In case two postulates of justice are in conflict with each other, the higher one prevails; and to punish those who were morally responsible for the international crime of the Second World War may certainly be considered as more important than to comply with the rather relative rule against ex post facto laws, open to so many exceptions.[104]

This type of reasoning indicates a willingness to override the presumption against retroactivity in a case where, regardless of whether the acts committed were legal at the time of their commission, those acts are, and more importantly *were*, so heinous as to justify or even, on Kelsen's approach, require, the imposition of retroactive liability. The liberty of those responsible for such acts, and the presumption against retroactivity that would ordinarily protect that liberty, are subordinated to the community's interest in the punishment of heinous conduct.

An additional justification would have been that the conduct in question was, at the time of the Second World War, criminal under international law, as was held by the International Military Tribunal at Nuremberg.[105] Conduct being, at the time of its occurrence, criminal under international law, satisfies the exception to the prohibition on retroactive criminal liability under article 7 of the ECHR and article 15 of the International Covenant on Civil and Political Rights. This was not,

[101] *Ibid.*
[102] *Ibid.*
[103] *Ibid.*
[104] H Kelsen 'Will the Judgment in the Nuremberg Trial Constitute a Precedent in International Law?' (1947) 1 International Law Quarterly 153, 165. See also H Kelsen 'Collective and Individual Responsibility in International Law with Particular Regard to the Punishment of War Criminals' (1943) California Law Review 530, 544.
[105] (1947) 41 American Journal of International Law 172.

however, determinative in *Polyukhovich*, where the emphasis was on the heinousness of the conduct. Placing conduct amounting to war crimes in this exceptional category is not especially difficult. Statutes dealing with conduct of a lower level of obnoxiousness create harder cases.[106]

In *Lord Howard de Walden v Inland Revenue Commissioners*[107] legislation directed towards restricting tax evasion was at issue.[108] Lord Greene MR said for the Court of Appeal:

> The fact that the section has to some extent a retroactive effect appears to us of no importance when it is realised that the legislation is a move in a long and fiercely contested battle with individuals who well understand the rigour of the contest.[109]

This comment led the editor of the seventh edition of *Craies on Statute Law* to assert that a:

> new class of legislation in the later Finance Acts directed against tax evasion is free from any presumption against a retrospective effect.[110]

Lord Greene was apparently of the view that concern for the ability to rely on the law was inapplicable to the game of cat and mouse played between tax authorities and tax avoiders. This is not, however, a uniformly held judicial view.[111]

The circumstances in which a court will find the presumption against retroactivity to be rebutted are not susceptible to accurate generalisation beyond noting their exceptional nature and that strong reasons will be required. There are examples, such as the cases dealing with tax statutes, in which this framework does not yield a clear result. It is better openly to grapple with the competing factors in

[106] Cf J Stone *Human Law and Human Justice* (Stevens and Sons London 1965) 250–1.

[107] [1942] 1 KB 389 (CA).

[108] The presumption against retroactivity in the context of tax statutes is discussed in more detail by GT Loomer 'Taxing Out of Time: Parliamentary Supremacy and Retroactive Tax Legislation' [2006] British Tax Review 64; and P Baker 'Retrospective Tax Legislation and the European Convention on Human Rights' [2005] British Tax Review 1.

[109] [1942] 1 KB 389, 398 (CA).

[110] SGG Edgar *Craies on Statute Law* (7th edn Sweet and Maxwell London 1971) 404. This passage does not appear in the 8th edn. By contrast, the editor of the 8th edn states that in 'the context of expropriating the private property of the citizen for the purposes of the state it requires absolutely clear words to make a provision of legislation retrospective', citing *Wijesureya v Amit* [1966] AC 372 (PC) and *Greenberg v Inland Revenue Commissioners* [1972] AC 109, 145 (HL). He nonetheless suggests that retroactive tax legislation need not involve any unfairness if it is preceded by a duly publicised executive announcement of the pending retroactive change and if the retroactivity is only to the date of that announcement: D Greenberg (ed) *Craies on Legislation* (8th edn Sweet and Maxwell London 2004) 395–6. This idea involves a threat to the separation of powers, examination of which is beyond the present discussion. Some of the relevant arguments appear in C Sampford *Retrospectivity and the Rule of Law* (Oxford University Press 2006) 156–14. See also *Inland Revenue Commissioners v Joiner* [1975] 1 WLR 1701, 1714 (HL).

[111] *A-G v Richmond* [1909] AC 466, 475 (HL); *Commissioner of Stamp Duties v Byrnes* [1911] AC 386, 392 (PC); *Inland Revenue Commissioners v Joiner* [1975] 1 WLR 1701, 1714 (HL); *Re The Estate of William Vicars* (1944) 45 SR (NSW) 85, 93. And cf the discussion of *Wijesureya v Amit* [1966] AC 372 (PC) in Ch 4 Pt C. Cf the change, by way of adjudicative retroactivity, from *Inland Revenue Commissioners v Duke of Westminster* [1936] AC 1 (HL) to *Furniss v Dawson* [1984] 1 AC 474 (HL).

such cases than to pretend that the result is clear by unconvincing assertions of what 'fairness' requires.[112] The presumption creates an onus on a party advocating retroactivity, so that if in a close case reasons of sufficient strength favouring retroactivity cannot be established, then retroactivity will not be justified.

G Detailed Studies

1 The Intertemporal Effect of the Human Rights Act 1998 (UK)

After the Human Rights Act entered into force there was a series of decisions on the question of whether the Act was applicable to events occurring prior to the Act's commencement that were the subject of litigation occurring after that date. The first question for present purposes is whether such application would involve true retroactivity.

(a) Was Retroactivity in Issue?

In *R v Lambert* the Court of Appeal certified questions to the House of Lords, the relevant one of which was:

> Is a defendant whose trial took place before the coming into force of sections 6 and 7(1)(b) of the Human Rights Act 1998 entitled, after they come into force, to rely, in the course of an appeal, on an alleged breach of his Convention rights by the trial court or an investigating or prosecuting authority?[113]

Lord Steyn was the only member of the House in *Lambert* willing to answer that question in the affirmative. Indicating that he did not consider retroactive effect to be in issue, Lord Steyn said of section 6(1) of the Human Rights Act:[114]

> It binds the House. It will be noted that the effect of section 6(1) is to provide that it *is unlawful* for the House *to act* in a way which is incompatible with a Convention right. The question is whether this provision applies to the appeal before the House. Given that it is expressed to limit the way in which a court may act, it is difficult to escape the conclusion that in the relevant sense no appellate court may act incompatibly with a Convention right. Surely, for an appellate court to uphold a conviction obtained in breach of a Convention right must be to act incompatibly with a Convention right. It is unlawful for it to do so. So interpreted no true retrospectivity is involved. Section 6(1) regulates the conduct of appellate courts de futuro.[115]

[112] Fairness is discussed at Ch 3 Pt E(2) and Ch 4 Pts D and E.
[113] [2002] 2 AC 545, [24] (HL).
[114] Which provides that it 'is unlawful for a public authority to act in a way which is incompatible with a Convention right'. See also s 6(3)(a) which provides that a court is a public authority.
[115] [2002] 2 AC 545, [28] (HL).

The key part of that passage is Lord Steyn's assertion that:

> for an appellate court to uphold a conviction obtained in breach of a Convention right must be to act incompatibly with a Convention right.

That statement is accurate as far as it goes, but it does not answer the crucial question, which is whether the conviction was 'obtained in breach of a Convention right'. Because such rights were only granted direct force in domestic law by the Human Rights Act after the conviction occurred, the conviction could not, at the time that it occurred, as a matter of domestic law, have been obtained in breach of a Convention right.[116]

Explaining that if the Human Rights Act did apply in *Lambert*, that its effect would be retroactive, Lord Hutton said:

> In my opinion an Act has a retrospective effect if it operates to make unlawful or unsafe a conviction which was lawful and safe at the time it was imposed. This is the result for which the appellant contends. Before the commencement of the 1998 Act he had been lawfully convicted and his conviction was safe. But he submits that the effect of section 6 of the 1998 Act, coming into operation after his conviction, is to make the conviction unlawful and unsafe. In my opinion it is no answer for the appellant to maintain that he is only concerned with the lawfulness of a decision taken by the Appellate Committee on a date after 2 October 2000. I consider that this argument does not alter the reality that if the House were to quash the conviction it would be giving a retrospective effect to section 6.[117]

The temporal effect for which the appellant in *Lambert* contended constitutes retroactivity because there was no real question about whether the House of Lords was required to comply with Convention rights after the entry into force of the Human Rights Act. Of course it was. The question was whether such compliance required the House to find an earlier decision to have been wrong in law when at the time that it was decided it was right in law. If that was required, section 6 of the Human Rights Act would have retroactive effect.

Lambert was a criminal case in which the temporal effect of section 6 of the Human Rights Act was at issue. By contrast, in *Wilson v First County Trust (No 2)*[118] the primary question was whether section 3 of the Human Rights Act 1998[119] applied to the construction of the Consumer Credit Act 1974 (UK). It is clear that section 3 of the Human Rights Act may serve to alter the construction given to statutes already in force at the time of the commencement of the Human Rights Act.[120] Paragraph (a) of section 3(2) of the Human Rights Act expressly states that

[116] *Re McKerr* [2004] 1 WLR 807, [62]–[63] (HL).

[117] *Ibid* [169].

[118] [2004] 1 AC 816 (HL).

[119] Which provides in sub-section (1) that: 'So far as it is possible to do so, primary legislation and subordinate legislation must be read and given effect in a way which is compatible with the Convention rights.'

[120] As done, eg, in *Ghaidan v Godin-Mendoza* [2004] 2 AC 557 (HL). For a similar approach to the Canadian Charter of Rights and Freedoms, which is Pt 1 of The Constitution Act 1982 (Can), see, eg, *Benner v Canada (Secretary of State)* [1997] 1 SCR 358, [44]–[45].

section 3 applies to primary legislation and subordinate legislation 'whenever enacted'. The question in *Wilson* was whether section 3 of the Human Rights Act could apply to the construction of existing legislation in circumstances where the cause of action arose prior to the commencement of the Human Rights Act.[121] As Lord Hope put it:

> The question in this case is whether the rights and obligations of parties to an agreement made before 2 October 2000 are, as a result of the coming into force of the relevant provisions of the 1998 Act, different now from what they were when the agreement was entered into.[122]

Lord Nicholls observed that if that question were answered in the affirmative it 'would mean that parties' rights under existing legislation in respect of a transaction completed before the Act came into force could be changed overnight, to the benefit of one party and the prejudice of the other'.[123] Moreover, it would involve deeming the parties' rights at the time that the cause of action arose, which was the time of the agreement being made, being deemed after the entry into force of the Human Rights Act, to have been different to what they actually were at the earlier time. Such a result would amount to retroactive application of section 3 of the Human Rights Act.

(b) Treatment of the Presumption Against Retroactivity

The Law Lords in *Lambert* who declined to find that the Human Rights Act had retroactive effect applied the presumption against retroactivity to their construction of that Act. Lord Hutton said: 'It is a well established principle that no statute should be construed so as to have a retrospective operation unless its language is such as plainly to require such a construction.'[124] This statement of the presumption is consistent with the view that the presumption is a common law principle independent of legislative intent. That the Human Rights Act might be thought to be a 'beneficial' statute did not alter the presumption against retroactivity. Lord Slynn, after referring to the presumption, said that 'it is not to be assumed a priori

[121] In this respect *Wilson* is materially different from *Ghaidan v Godin-Mendoza* [2004] 2 AC 557 (HL), in which para 2(1) of sch 1 to the Rent Act 1977 (Eng), which provided that the surviving spouse of a deceased statutory tenant 'shall after the death be the statutory tenant', was interpreted consistently with arts 8 and 14 of the ECHR to include a same sex partner in the definition of 'spouse'. Because the surviving spouse accrued the right to tenancy only on the death of the original tenant, it was at the date of that death, which was after the commencement of the Human Rights Act, at which the Human Rights Act was held to apply. Thus, although the interpretive command of s (3)(2)(a) of the Human Rights Act meant that a 1977 Act was interpreted in accordance with the Human Rights Act 1998, the event giving rise to the cause of action occurred after the commencement of the Human Rights Act, which accordingly did not have retroactive effect. Contra D Mead 'Rights, Relationships and Retrospectivity: The Impact of Convention Rights on Pre-Existing Private Relationships following *Wilson* and *Ghaidan*' [2005] Public Law 459.

[122] [2004] 1 AC 816, [92] (HL).

[123] *Ibid* [18].

[124] [2002] 2 AC 545, [169] (HL), see also [143] (Lord Clyde).

that Convention rights, however commendable, are to be enforceable in national courts in respect of past events'.[125]

The decision of the House in *Lambert* was challenged shortly afterwards in *R v Kansal (No 2)*.[126] The House reaffirmed its earlier decision, but only after 'a very public wobble'.[127] In *Kansal* Lord Lloyd took the place of Lord Clyde in a Judicial Committee otherwise congruently constituted to that in *Lambert.* Lord Lloyd thought the decision in *Lambert* 'plainly erroneous'[128] and adopted the reasons of Lord Hope in *Kansal.* However, Lord Lloyd,[129] like Lord Steyn,[130] did not share Lord Hope's view that the House sitting with five members should depart from the decision in *Lambert.* Lord Hope reviewed the relevant statutory provisions and thought them retroactive. In doing so, he was concerned only with the statutory words and showed no sign of beginning with a presumption against retroactivity.[131] Conversely, Lord Hutton, like Lord Slynn, thought *Lambert* was correctly decided and emphasised that:

> there are strong reasons of policy, grounded in the need for certainty in the law and finality in litigation, why a conviction which was valid and lawful at the time it took place should not be set aside because of a change in the substantive law brought about by legislation.[132]

A similar focus on the presumption against retroactivity and its rationales was evident in the speeches in *Wilson.* Lord Scott considered that 'to legislate so as to alter the legal consequences of events that have already taken place is likely to produce unfair or unjust results' for which reason there is a 'common law presumption' against retroactivity.[133] Lord Rodger applied the 'powerful presumption against retroactivity', referring to 'the obvious, and potentially far-reaching, unfairness of unsettling the law relating to past events and transactions'.[134]

(c) Applicability of the Presumption Against Retroactivity

As demonstrated by the fact that three of the Law Lords in *Kansal* thought that *Lambert* was wrongly decided, the decisions that the Human Rights Act does not have retroactive effect have not uniformly been acknowledged as correct. As mentioned above, Lord Hope's reasoning in *Kansal* did not reveal a concern for the presumption against retroactivity as a common law principle. Beyleveld, Kirkham and Townend, in an article written after *Kansal* but before *Wilson,* go further and openly

125 *Ibid* [6].
126 [2002] 2 AC 69 (HL).
127 Lord Rodger 'A Time for Everything under the Law: Some Reflections on Retrospectivity' (2005) 121 Law Quarterly Review 57, 58.
128 [2002] 2 AC 69, [17] (HL).
129 *Ibid* [20]–[21].
130 *Ibid* [27].
131 *Ibid* [57]–[88].
132 *Ibid* [103].
133 [2004] 1 AC 816, [153] (HL).
134 *Ibid* [212].

question the applicability of the presumption to the Human Rights Act. They refer to Lord Slynn's comment in *Lambert* that it might be thought undesirable that:

> convictions lawful when made should have to be set aside as a result of considering Convention rights only subsequently enforceable in national courts[135]

and suggest that, instead, the general rule that lawful convictions not be set aside should be inapplicable where international human rights law is being implemented and in light of the 'general constitutional principle'[136] expressed in *X(Minors) v Bedfordshire County Council* that:

> the public policy consideration which has first claim on the loyalty of the law is that wrongs should be remedied and that very potent counter considerations are required to override that policy.[137]

But reliance on this general statement in this particular context, like Lord Steyn's judgment in *Lambert*, overlooks the very question at hand—whether there is a wrong in the relevant sense if it only becomes a wrong in domestic law subsequent to the original decision being made.

Beyleveld, Kirkham and Townend go on to argue that there is or should be a presumption *of* retroactivity when questions of human rights violations arise.[138] They refer to this as 'retrospectivity to protect fairness' and object to 'a context-insensitive general presumption against retrospective legislation even in criminal law'.[139] They advocate retroactivity 'to correct or mitigate human rights wrongs'.[140] There are two different ideas here, which require treatment in turn. First, that there should be a presumption *of* retroactivity in human rights matters. Second, the objection to a 'context-insensitive' presumption against retroactivity.

The suggestion that there should be a presumption *of* retroactivity in human rights matters is relatively easy to make when the only case considered is a criminal case in which the standards applied at trial might be thought to be below what is required by human rights standards subsequently applicable in domestic law. When other types of case are considered one could just as easily say, as Lord Nicholls did in *Wilson*, that 'One would not expect a statute promoting human rights values to render unlawful acts which were lawful when done.'[141]

Even in criminal cases the suggestion that the presumption against retroactivity should be inapplicable and replaced by a presumption *of* retroactivity confronts weighty competing considerations that were expressed in *Minto v Police.*[142] That case involved convictions occurring prior to the New Zealand Bill of Rights Act

135 [2002] 2 AC 545, [10] (HL).

136 D Beyleveld R Kirkham and D Townend 'Which Presumption? A Critique of the House of Lords Reasoning on Retrospectivity and the Human Rights Act' (2002) 22 Legal Studies 185, 187.

137 [1995] 2 AC 633, 749 (HL).

138 D Beyleveld R Kirkham and D Townend 'Which Presumption? A Critique of the House of Lords Reasoning on Retrospectivity and the Human Rights Act' (2002) 22 Legal Studies 185, 190 et seq.

139 *Ibid* 191.

140 *Ibid.*

141 [2004] 1 AC 816, [12] (HL).

142 [1990–1992] 1 NZBORR 208, which assisted Lord Clyde in *Lambert* [2002] 2 AC 545, [147] (HL).

1990, being appealed after the entry into force of that Act. The attempt to rely on the retroactive application of a right to peaceful assembly as protected in section 16 of the Act, as a ground of appeal against convictions for breaching the peace resulting from staging a demonstration prior to the entry into force of the Act, was unsuccessful. Robertson J said that the appellants' counsel:

> argued that the 'beneficial' effect of such a retrospective interpretation should overwhelm the presumption against the retrospective effect of statutes. Certainly it would be beneficial from his clients' point of view to have their misdemeanour undone in this fashion. But I do not accept that it would be 'beneficial' for the law or society at large if a court were to declare invalid that which was valid at the time it was done.[143]

Considerations of the kinds mentioned in *Wilson* and in *Minto* indicate that the suggestion that there should be a general presumption *of* retroactivity in cases involving human rights is ill-conceived. Many other objections could be made to carving out 'human rights matters' from the otherwise general applicability of the presumption of retroactivity, but the suggestion worthy of more serious discussion is that the presumption against retroactivity should not be applied in a 'context insensitive' manner in cases relating to human rights standards.

(d) Fairness and a Presumption of Variable Strength

There is some support in the cases addressing the temporal effect of the Human Rights Act, particularly *Wilson*, for an approach to the presumption against retroactivity that alters the strength of the presumption according to what fairness is deemed to require in a particular case. In *Wilson* Lord Nicholls, citing Lord Mustill's speech in *L'Office Cherifien des Phosphates v Yamashita-Shinnihon Steamship Co*, stated his view that 'the subject matter of statutes is so varied' that 'generalised maxims are not a reliable guide'.[144] Thus, continued Lord Nicholls, 'the underlying rationale should be sought'.[145] Lord Nicholls thought[146] that this rationale was expressed by Staughton LJ in *Tunnicliffe*: that parliament is presumed not to alter the law applicable to past events in a way that is unfair.[147] Lord Nicholls' application of this 'statement of principle'[148] consisted of no more than his assertion that 'the principle of interpretation set out in section 3(1)' of the Human Rights Act does not apply to 'causes of action accruing before the section came into force':

> because to apply it in such cases, and thereby change the construction and effect of existing legislation, might well produce an unfair result for one party or the other. The Human Rights Act was not intended to have this effect.[149]

[143] [1990–1992] 1 NZBORR 208, 214.
[144] [2004] 1 AC 816, [19] (HL).
[145] *Ibid.*
[146] *Ibid.*
[147] [1991] 2 All ER 712, 724 (CA).
[148] [2004] 1 AC 816, [19] (HL). Contra the more sceptical view of 'fairness' expressed by Lord Nicholls in *Miller v Miller* [2006] 2 AC 618, [4].
[149] [2004] 1 AC 816, [20] (HL).

Lord Nicholls' discussion of fairness was predicated on his observation that granting retroactive effect to section 3 of the Human Rights Act in all circumstances:

> would operate capriciously, with the outcome depending on whether the parties' rights were determined by a court before or after 2 October 2000. The outcome in one case involving pre-Act happenings could differ from the outcome in another comparable case depending solely on when the cases were heard by a court. Parliament cannot have intended section 3(1) should operate in this unfair and arbitrary fashion.[150]

Lord Hope indicated in *Wilson* that he was willing to take 'a more relaxed approach'[151] to finding that section 3 of the Human Rights Act had retroactive effect because its 'purpose is to ensure that legislation is read and given effect in a way that is compatible with Convention rights, so far as it is possible to do so, whenever the legislation was enacted'.[152] This did not amount to a presumption *of* retroactivity, but it did demonstrate a weakening of the presumption against retroactivity because a human rights statute was under consideration. This apparent willingness to find retroactivity was, however, overcome by the fact that construing section 3 of the Human Rights Act as having retroactive effect would have retroactively removed from Mrs Wilson statutory protections that she enjoyed at the time of reaching her agreement with First County Trust. Lord Hope said:

> It seems to me that the presumption against the retrospective effect of legislation ought to be given its full weight in these circumstances.[153]

Lord Hope considered that:

> There is an obvious attraction in a solution to the application of the presumption to the obligation in section 3(1) which depends on clear, bright line rules which do not admit of any exceptions. But rules of that kind would be bound to lead to unfairness in some cases or to have consequences that could not have been intended for other reasons. So I would prefer to base my decision in this case on the particular facts and circumstances.[154]

This raises the question of the level of generality at which *Wilson* was decided. On the most general available reading, Lord Hope limited his decision to a holding that section 3 of the Human Rights Act is not available for the construction of the sections of the Consumer Credit Act that were raised in *Wilson*.[155] Lord Hope's judgment appears also to be open to the reading that section 3 of the Human Rights Act could apply retroactively even to the same provisions of the Consumer Credit Act if that would create a fair result in the facts and circumstances of a different case. Lord Nicholls emphasised that he was not deciding that section 3 of the Human Rights Act never applies to events occurring prior to its entry into force[156] and said:

150 *Ibid* [18].
151 *Ibid* [99].
152 *Ibid.*
153 *Ibid* [101].
154 *Ibid.*
155 *Ibid.*
156 *Ibid* [21].

> Whether section 3 applies to pre-Act events depends upon the application of the principle identified by Staughton LJ in the context of the particular issues before the court.[157]

Again, though one might assume that this judgment was intended to apply more generally than to the specific facts of the case at hand, there is nothing in the reasoning that made this explicit. Instead there is only Lord Nicholls' insistence that a test of fairness must be applied to the facts and circumstances before the court to determine whether retroactive effect should be granted in a particular case.

The determination of Lords Nicholls and Hope, on this issue, to deliver judgments of narrow application is difficult to reconcile with the fact that neither of the two parties to the case were represented before the House of Lords yet the House obviously considered the case to be of sufficient general importance to hear submissions on behalf of the Secretary of State for Trade and Industry, the Finance and Leasing Association, four major insurance companies and the Speaker of the House of Commons. More fundamentally, if the retroactive effect of the Human Rights Act would have favoured Mrs Wilson rather than the pawnbroking corporation with which she entered into a loan agreement containing an extortionate rate of interest, one could imagine a greater degree of judicial sympathy for the argument in favour of retroactivity. If the application of a Convention right were to protect rather than disadvantage a customer of an unscrupulous pawnbroker, what was thought to be 'fair' in the particular facts of a case may well point in favour of retroactivity rather than against it. This type of approach treats retroactive legal effect as a consequence to be manipulated in favour of the particular judicial view of fairness adopted in the case, not as an unusual legal consequence to be presumptively resisted and found to exist only if strong reasons in favour of it can be established by arguments of general application.

Lord Rodger was the only member of the House to address the issue of generality at any length and took the broadest view of the application of the decision. Lord Rodger thought that the:

> operative provisions of the 1998 Act must all apply in the same way when used to give effect to the same Convention right. But they may apply differently when used to give effect to different Convention rights.[158]

Lord Rodger continued:

> It is crucially important to bear in mind that this is not a question about the application of section 127(3) of the 1974 Act, as potentially modified by section 3 of the 1998 Act, so as to affect vested rights or pending actions. Rather, it is a general question about the application of the operative provisions of the 1998 Act, when used to give effect to the article 1 right, so as to affect vested rights or pending proceedings. That question admits of only a single answer in regard to vested rights and pending proceedings respectively. And that answer cannot be found by examining the circumstances of particular cases and then applying a more or less flexible test in the light of those circumstances. This is just

[157] [2004] 1 AC 816, [21].
[158] *Ibid* [209].

> an aspect of the point emphasised by Lord Mustill in *L'Office Cherifien des Phosphates v Yamashita-Shinnihon Steamship Co Ltd* [1994] 1 AC 486, 528c, when he said that a court which sets out to apply the test of fairness is concerned 'not with the merits of the particular case, but with the generality of rights which Parliament must have contemplated would suffer if the section took effect retrospectively.'
>
> . . .
>
> So in this case the single answer to the broadly conceived question is to be found by considering how Parliament intended the operative provisions of the 1998 Act to apply in relation to the generality of vested rights or pending proceedings—not in relation to vested rights or pending proceedings under the 1974 Act, far less in relation to the individual plight of Mrs Wilson and First County. To descend to those levels of particularity would not only result in a myriad of single decisions but would be to attribute to Parliament the implausible intention that the meticulously drawn 1998 Act, embodying a landmark reform, was to apply in a piecemeal and haphazard fashion.[159]

Unlike the judgments of Lords Nicholls and Hope, Lord Rodger's judgment in *Wilson* exhibited an appreciation that the case was about whether section 3 of the Human Rights Act, when combined with article 1 of the First Protocol to the ECHR, did or did not apply to events occurring prior to the passage of the Human Rights Act; and, just as importantly, that in order to respect the generality of the law, that there is only one answer to that question which is applicable to all cases that raise the same legal question.

This approach appears to have been accepted in *Re McKerr*,[160] in which the question was whether section 6 of the Human Rights Act was applicable to events occurring prior to its entry into force, where the European Court of Human Rights in Strasbourg had already found the events to constitute a violation of article 2 of the ECHR.[161] The House of Lords acted on the basis that the Human Rights Act was, in general, not retroactive.[162] So did the Court of Appeal in dismissing a claim that section 6 of the Human Rights Act applied retroactively to a breach of article 5[163] of the ECHR.[164] There now seems to be sufficient evidence to conclude that the Human Rights Act does not, except insofar as it expressly provides, have retroactive effect, regardless of which section of the Act or which article of the ECHR is in issue.[165] Because an approach that respects the importance of generality has ultimately been adopted, that is all that need be said on the question of generality; but more discussion is needed of the related question of the use of fairness as a primary determinant of retroactivity. As the facts were said to be so important to the decision in *Wilson*, more attention to those facts is necessary.

159 *Ibid* [215].
160 [2004] 1 WLR 807 (HL).
161 Which protects the 'right to life'.
162 [2004] 1 WLR 807, [17], [20]–[21], [48], [66]–[67], [80], [89] (HL).
163 Which relates to liberty of the person.
164 *R(Wright) v Secretary of State for the Home Department* [2006] EWCA Civ 67, [22]–[23], [35]–[36], [51].
165 *Chief Constable of West Yorkshire Police v A* [2005] 1 AC 51, [13], [53] (HL).

Mrs Wilson and First County Trust struck a pawning agreement the subject of which was Mrs Wilson's car. The 'document fee' of 250 pounds was added to the loan amount of 5000 pounds and the 'credit' of the agreement was stated as 5250 pounds. By way of context, the agreed annual percentage interest was 94.78 per cent, which was halved at first instance as being an extortionate credit bargain. The Court of Appeal held that the document fee did not constitute part of the credit, thus the credit was inaccurately stated on the agreement. The consequence of this, by force of the Consumer Credit Act, was that the agreement could not be enforced by the court. As Lord Nicholls observed, the 'overall result was that Mrs Wilson was entitled to keep the amount of her loan, pay no interest and recover her car'.[166] For this reason there was a suggestion in the Court of Appeal that the basis on which the agreement was not enforced contravened the right enjoyed by all natural and legal persons, and so by First County Trust, to enjoyment of its possessions, which is guaranteed by article 1 of the First Protocol to the ECHR. The question was whether, via section 3 of the Human Rights Act, which did not come into force until after the first instance decision had been made, article 1 of the First Protocol was applicable to the case.

In reaching their conclusions on the basis of fairness, Lords Nicholls and Hope did not explain which particular aspects of the facts and circumstances justified their opinions that 'fairness' militated against retroactivity. Consideration of the facts indicates that reasonable minds could consider that 'fairness' would require that as a result of mistaking the amount of 'credit' with the total amount owed, First County Trust not be completely deprived of the court's assistance in enforcing any part of its agreement and should be able to pray in aid article 1 of the First Protocol to the ECHR. This may be thought to be particularly so in light of the fact that Mrs Wilson signed the agreement with the total amount owed listed as the amount of credit and that the judge at first instance thought that the total amount owed, including the document fee, did indeed constitute the 'credit' amount. It could coherently be argued that fairness did not require that as a result of this mistake Mrs Wilson be entitled to keep her car as well as the money that she borrowed without any obligation to repay it or to pay any interest on it. The inherent contestability of 'fairness' means that individual perceptions of fairness stated in a conclusory manner were inappropriate grounds for a decision about whether section 3 of the Human Rights Act is retroactive, even if that decision were to be limited to that section's relationship with a particular statute or even particular sections within a statute.

If, as Lord Rodger thought, and as is the better view, the relevant issue was whether section 3 of the Human Rights Act, in conjunction with article 1 of the First Protocol, is always retroactive or always not retroactive, then relying on views of fairness in the particular facts and circumstances of this one case was inappropriate not only because of the inherent contestability of the concept of fairness but also because the court was involved in a decision about the temporal effect of a

[166] [2004] 1 AC 816, [6] (HL).

statutory provision that is of significance far beyond the particular circumstances of the one factual scenario before the court. A decision of this breadth must consider principles of broad application, not just what would be the fairest outcome in one particular case.

An example of the principles relevant to the question of whether section 3 of the Human Rights Act coupled with article 1 of the First Protocol should apply retroactively is that people should be able to rely on the legal rules that were applicable to the creation of their bargains. The provisions of the Consumer Credit Act relevant in *Wilson* were intended to provide consumer protection. Consumers were entitled to rely on those protections at the time that they entered into transactions. Retroactively to remove those protections would be retroactively to remove the ability of consumers so to rely.

Because reasonable minds often may differ on what fairness would require, the application of a generally applicable and uniformly strong, though defeasible, presumption, is a preferable means to determine whether a statute should be construed as having retroactive effect. The very nature of a presumption, which presumptively protects particular values, is that it is not sensitive to context. It represents what the legal system ordinarily considers to be fair at a level of generality beyond any particular case. It is a starting point for any matter to which it is applicable. It may be rebutted where necessary, and it is in the assessment of whether the presumption should be rebutted that sensitivity to context is important. There is nothing in *Wilson* or the issues to which it gives rise that indicates at a high level of generality that the construction of section 3 of the Human Rights Act in conjunction with article 1 of the First Protocol should not conform to the presumption against retroactivity. On the contrary, the relevance of certainty to this type of case affirms conformity to the presumption.

(e) Statutory Language

The provision of the Human Rights Act that was most influential in the cases considering whether sections 3 and 6 of the Human Rights Act have retroactive effect was section 22(4), which provides that:

> Paragraph (b) of subsection (1) of section 7 applies to proceedings brought by or at the instigation of a public authority *whenever the act in question took place*; but otherwise that subsection does not apply to an act taking place before the coming into force of that section. [Emphasis added]

The provision referred to, section 7(1)(b) of the Human Rights Act, provides that:

> A person who claims that a public authority has acted (or proposes to act) in a way which is made unlawful by section 6(1) may rely on the Convention right or rights concerned in any legal proceedings, but only if he is (or would be) a victim of the unlawful act.

A number of the Law Lords who found in *Lambert*, *Kansal* and *Wilson* that the Human Rights Act does not have retroactive effect reasoned that as parliament expressly provided for retroactive effect in this one respect, if it had intended any additional retroactive effect, it would similarly have provided for it. In the absence of such express provision, the presumption against retroactivity was not rebutted and the statutes were construed to find that the Human Rights Act had no retroactive effect beyond that which was provided in sections 22(4) and 7(1)(b).[167]

2 Retroactive Sentencing

Attention has already been paid to the question of whether the imposition of a sentence on the basis of a law passed subsequently to the commission of the crime for which the sentence is imposed constitutes retroactivity,[168] and to the explication of rationales for a presumption against retroactive sentencing.[169] The present focus is on applications of and deviations from the presumption against retroactivity in the field of sentencing. Recent English cases on this subject have concentrated on article 7 of the ECHR, which relevantly provides that:

> a heavier penalty [shall not] be imposed than the one that was applicable at the time the criminal offence was committed.

But there may be reason to think that the common law presumption should not be forgotten.

(a) Article 7 of the ECHR and the Common Law Presumption Against Retroactivity

(i) The 'Applicable' Sentence One area in which the difference between article 7 of the ECHR and the common law presumption against retroactivity can be seen is the focus on the word 'applicable' in article 7. This was the core issue in *R(Uttley) v Secretary of State for the Home Department.*[170] Uttley committed numerous sexual offences, including rape, the latest of which was in 1983. He was not convicted of those offences until 1995. He was sentenced to twelve years imprisonment. In both 1983 and 1995 the maximum sentence for rape was life imprisonment. From 1983 until 1991, the applicable sentencing regime was such that, if sentenced at that time, subject to his good behaviour in prison, Uttley would have served two thirds of the sentence imposed on him and then been released at which time the sentence would have expired. In 1991 the law changed so that the applicable sentencing regime in 1995, when Uttley was convicted, and at the time of his release in 2003, was that subject to good behaviour Uttley was eligible for release after serving two thirds of his sentence but release was on a licence placing him under supervision and imposing certain restrictions on his liberty.

[167] Eg *Lambert* [2002] 2 AC 545, [144] (HL); *Kansal* [2002] 2 AC 69, [104] (HL); *Wilson* [2004] 1 AC 816, [160], [212] (HL). See also *Wainwright v Home Office* [2002] QB 1334, [29] (CA).

[168] Ch 1 Pt E(1).

[169] Ch 3 Pt C(4)(b).

[170] [2004] 1 WLR 2278 (HL).

Failure to comply with the conditions of the licence would place Uttley at risk of recall to serve the remainder of his sentence. The licence would last until three quarters of the sentence imposed elapsed. If Uttley were to commit an imprisonable offence before the full twelve year term of his sentence expired, all or part of the outstanding term could be added to the sentence for that subsequent offence. The question that attracted attention was whether Uttley's subjection to this new post-imprisonment regime constituted the imposition of 'a heavier penalty than the one that was applicable at the time the criminal offence was committed'.

The House of Lords concentrated on the existence and meaning of the word 'applicable' in article 7[171] and held unanimously that it refers to the maximum sentence that *could* have been imposed for an offence at the time of its commission, not the sentence that *would* have been imposed at that time. Thus, on the reasoning in *Uttley*, the comparison is between the maximum sentence that could have been imposed at the time of commission of the offence and the actual sentence that *was* imposed at the time of sentencing.[172] So long as the latter is not heavier than the former, article 7 is not contravened.

Lord Rodger said in *Uttley* that article 7:

> does not envisage . . . speculative excursions into the realm of the counter-factual. Its purpose is not to ensure that the offender is punished in exactly the same way as he would have been punished at the time of the offence, but to ensure that he is not punished more heavily than the relevant law passed by the legislature would have permitted at that time. So long as the court keeps within the range laid down by the legislature at the time of the offence, it can choose the sentence which it considers most appropriate.[173]

Atrill objects to the decision in *Uttley* and takes a very different view on the appropriateness of engaging in 'counterfactual' exercises. He considers that a sentencing judge in the position of the judge in *Uttley* should predict 'the likely sentence that a fellow member of the judiciary would have viewed as appropriate, bearing in mind sentencing guidelines in place at the relevant point in history: an exercise that ought to be easy to undertake'.[174] Atrill continues:

> the judiciary are constantly involved in such counterfactuals: such counterfactuals are the basis of tort and contract law inquiries into the position of the claimant if the tort had not been committed or if the contract had not been breached.[175]

The decisions in *Uttley* and *Flynn* are consistent with the judgment of the Strasbourg Court in *Coeme v Belgium*,[176] which is relied on in both of those judgments. According to *Coeme* it must only be verified:

[171] *Ibid* [18], [42], [45], [58]. See also *Flynn v HM Advocate* 2004 SCCR 281, [41], [109] (PC).

[172] [2004] 1 WLR 2278, [21], [38], [42], [45], [58], [85], [109] (HL).

[173] *Ibid* [42].

[174] S Atrill '*Nulla Poena Sine Lege* in Comparative Perspective: Retrospectivity under the ECHR and US Constitution' [2005] Public Law 107, 129.

[175] *Ibid.*

[176] ECtHR 2000-VII 75.

> that at the time when an accused person performed the act which led to his being prosecuted and convicted there was in force a legal provision which made that punishable, and that the punishment imposed did not exceed the limits fixed by that provision.[177]

Atrill's objection to this approach may not be the most appealing. The view taken by the Strasbourg Court, the Privy Council and the House of Lords of the meaning of the word 'applicable' in article 7 certainly seems open on the language of the article. Possibly a more effective criticism of *Uttley* is that in focusing on the text of article 7 and being concerned with the appropriate comparators to be used in determining compliance with article 7, the judgments and the submissions on which they were based all overlooked the applicability and content of the common law presumption against retroactivity. In case it might be thought that there is no meaningful difference between the two, it may be useful to consider a hypothetical example demonstrating at least one of the differences.

That example is the introduction of a minimum sentence after the commission of a crime but prior to sentencing for it. If a crime was committed in 2006 for which the maximum sentence was five years imprisonment and there were relevant sentencing guidelines indicating that a sentence of about two years would have been appropriate, but by 2008 when the person responsible for the crime was sentenced there was a new statutory sentencing regime in place, pursuant to which the maximum sentence was increased to ten years imprisonment and a mandatory minimum sentence of five years imprisonment was introduced; according to the reasoning in *Coeme*, *Uttley* and *Flynn*, the application of the 2008 sentencing regime to a crime committed in 2006, resulting in the mandatory imposition of a sentence of five years imprisonment would not contravene article 7. This example would, however, constitute retroactive sentencing.

At the time of the commission of the crime the defendant was exposed to a sentencing law representing the limit and form of state incursion into his liberty in response to his crime. To allow retroactive change to the punishment imposed by the state creates the risks of lack of generality and discrimination discussed in Chapter three.[178] Furthermore, insofar as pending proceedings are concerned, a person charged with a crime may have made important decisions such as whether to plead guilty on the basis of the law in force at the time of that decision. If he decided not to plead guilty, for the law later to be altered with retroactive effect would deprive him of the ability to make a decision at an early stage of the case against him, on the basis of the sentencing regime to which he would ultimately be exposed. Because of this retroactive effect, the statutory language and other facts and circumstances would need to be considered for the purpose of determining whether the presumption against retroactivity was rebutted.

The maxim *nulla poena sine lege antea exstanti* includes the requirement that punishment be based on a law already in existence. Accordingly the question for the common law is not whether the punishment is heavier than the applicable

[177] ECtHR 2000-VII 75 [145].
[178] Ch 3 Pt C(4)(b).

maximum at the time of commission of the crime. The question is whether the sentence is imposed on the basis of a law applicable at the time of the commission of the crime. This fairly simple question removes the relevance of the sort of 'counterfactual' exercise dismissed by the House of Lords in *Uttley*[179] and advocated by Atrill. Changes in patterns of exercise of judicial sentencing discretion should not be caught by the presumption against retroactivity so understood,[180] but variation of the applicable law should be so caught. Although the better view may be that the circumstances in *Uttley* did not contravene article 7 of the ECHR, that should not have been the end of the argument. The application of the common law presumption against retroactivity may have led to a different result in the case.

(ii) Whether the Legal Consequence Imposed Constitutes a 'Penalty' A further distinction between article 7 of the ECHR and the common law presumption against retroactive sentencing may be made. Article 7 is only applicable if the legal consequence imposed upon a person can be characterised as a penalty. The common law presumption against retroactivity is concerned primarily with the temporal effect of a legal provision, not, in the first instance, its subject matter.[181] Whether a legal consequence imposed following the commission of a crime can properly be characterised as a penalty is not relevant to the determination of whether the common law presumption is applicable, though it may be one consideration in the analysis of whether the presumption is rebutted. Some of these issues were evident in *R v Field*.[182]

In *Field* the question was whether an order could be made under section 28 of the Criminal Justice and Court Services Act 2000 (Eng) disqualifying an adult from working with children, based on an offence committed prior to the entry into force of that Act. The case turned on whether the disqualification order was a penalty for the purposes of article 7.[183] The Court of Appeal's decision was summarised by Kay LJ:

> It seems to us of considerable importance that a conviction is not a necessary condition for the making of such an order. When one considers the nature and purpose of such an order it points overwhelmingly to this being for preventative rather than punitive effect. Precisely the same order is made whether a person is convicted or not and the making of the order has no regard to the extent or seriousness of the offending but rather to whether a repetition of the conduct is likely.[184]

179 [2004] 1 WLR 2278, [42], [45], [64] (HL).

180 *Flynn v HM Advocate* 2004 SCCR 281, [45], [100] (PC). Contra *R v MJR* (2002) 54 NSWLR 368; cf *R v WJM* (2005) 92 SASR 371, [30]–[47]; *R v Green* [2006] NTCCA 22, [26]–[47], [89-[97].

181 Contra *Wilson v First County Trust (No 2)* [2004] 1 AC 816, [98] (HL).

182 [2003] 1 WLR 882 (CA), applied in *R v G* [2005] EWCA Crim 1300, [22]–[23].

183 [2003] 1 WLR 882, [19] (CA).

184 *Ibid* [58]. See also *R v R* [2004] 1 WLR 490 (CA), *R v Carlisle* [2005] EWCA Crim 469 and *R v B* [2006] EWCA Crim 2966 on the characterisation of a court order imposing an extended licence as preventive rather than punitive, rendering the presumption against retroactivity inapplicable, largely on the basis of the *purpose* of that order. Contra *R v T* [2003] 4 All ER 877 (CA).

All of the offences committed by the two appellants in *Field* were committed prior to the entry into force of the Human Rights Act, yet apparently the issue of whether section 3 of the Human Rights Act in conjunction with article 7 of the ECHR was applicable to those events was not raised. This may have been because the court accepted the submission made on behalf of the Secretary of State for the Home Department that the disqualification order depended for its future application on conduct that occurred in the past but was not retroactive.[185] Thus it may have been assumed that the relevant event for the application of the Human Rights Act was the imposition of the disqualification order, which did occur after the commencement of the Human Rights Act. That prejudges the ultimate question raised by the case. If the disqualification order was a penalty flowing from the criminal event, then it would be the criminal event that would locate in time the applicable law. If that were so, then on the reasoning in *Wilson,* section 3 of the Human Rights Act, and as a matter of domestic law article 7, would not have been temporally applicable to the facts in *Field* at all. Because the court ultimately held that the disqualification order was not a penalty for the purposes of article 7 this oversight made no difference to the result in the case.

The same result would also have been reached by application of the common law presumption, but again by a different path. The crucial matter is the causal severance between the past conduct and the disqualification order. The disqualification order did not flow from the criminal conduct in the same way that a criminal sentence would. Although being charged with a criminal act was a pre-condition for the disqualification order, neither the severity of the criminal conduct or even conviction of a criminal offence on the basis of that conduct were necessary determinants of the disqualification order, which was imposed on the basis of a prediction about future conduct and for the purpose of public protection. Though reliance on the 'purpose' of the order to distinguish it from a criminal sentence is fraught with difficulties, not least because of the various rationales for criminal punishment that may be put forward,[186] the nature of the disqualification order in *Field* was, particularly because it did not depend on a conviction, not sufficiently closely attached to events already past to constitute retroactivity. It was directed towards protection of the public in the future. The presumption against retroactivity would have been inapplicable not because the disqualification order was not a 'penalty' but rather because it was not a legal consequence of the criminal conduct and so involved no retroactivity. In this respect it is similar to the decision of *Re a Solicitor's Clerk*, which was discussed in Chapter one.[187]

[185] [2003] 1 WLR 882, [60]–[61] (CA).

[186] Eg s 142 of the Criminal Justice Act 2003 (UK) provides that in dealing with an offender a court *must* 'have regard to the following purposes of sentencing': '(a) the punishment of offenders, (b) the reduction of crime (including its reduction by deterrence), (c) the reform and rehabilitation of offenders, (d) the protection of the public, and (e) the making of reparation by offenders to persons affected by their offences.'

[187] [1957] 1 WLR 1219 (QB), discussed in Ch 1 Pt G(2).

(iii) Imposition of a Different Type of Penalty In *Coeme, Uttley* and *Flynn*[188] it was held that so long as the sentence actually imposed was not as heavy as the maximum penalty applicable at the time of the commission of the offence, then even though the law on the basis of which the sentence was imposed was a different law to that applicable at the time of the offence, there was no breach of article 7. In *Welch v United Kingdom*,[189] in which the Strasbourg Court found a violation of article 7, the applicable maximum sentence at the time of commission of the drug trafficking offences of which Welch was convicted was life imprisonment and he was sentenced to 22 years imprisonment and a confiscation order. It is not immediately apparent that the sentence imposed was, in the words of article 7, 'a heavier penalty' than life imprisonment. The Strasbourg Court did not address this question and was apparently content to hold that the imposition of a different *type* of penalty to that which was applicable at the time of commission of the relevant crime constituted a breach of article 7.[190] As Lord Phillips observed in *Uttley*, of *Welch*: 'The confiscation order was considered in isolation as a discrete penalty.'[191] There was no attempt by the Strasbourg Court to ground this approach in the language of article 7.

The imposition of a type of penalty not available at the time of the commission of the offence for which it is imposed will always be retroactive. That characterisation will not necessarily engage article 7 of the ECHR, but it should always engage the common law presumption against retroactivity. Indeed the Court of Appeal applied the presumption against retroactivity in a case similar to *Welch*.

In *Re Barretto*[192] a confiscation order pursuant to the Drug Trafficking Offences Act 1986 (Eng), which was the same Act in question in *Welch*, was imposed. Under that Act a person convicted of drug trafficking who had realisable assets less than the amount of financial benefit gained from that trafficking, could be made the subject of a confiscation order that represented his realisable assets rather than his ill gotten gains. The application of this Act in *Barretto* was not, as it was in *Welch*, retroactive. However, after that order had been made, but before it had been satisfied in full, section 16 of the Criminal Justice (International Co-operation) Act 1990 (UK) created a mechanism whereby if after the making of a confiscation order of the kind made against Barretto the court was satisfied that a greater amount could be realised from the convicted person's assets than was taken into account in the making of the original order, then that greater amount could be realized. Non-compliance with such an order could result in imprisonment. After the making of the original confiscation order the police became aware of additional assets under Barretto's control. When the receiver appointed under the 1986 Act sought to enforce the court's order, the receiver sought to take advantage of section 16 of the 1990 Act which was by then in force.

188 All discussed in Ch 4 Pt G(2)(a)(i).
189 (1995) 20 EHRR 247.
190 Cf *R(Uttley) v Secretary of State for the Home Department* [2004] 1 WLR 2278, [46] (HL).
191 *Ibid* [26].
192 [1994] QB 392 (CA).

Sir Thomas Bingham MR stated:

> To permit this obligation to be increased and the penalty strengthened by means of a law enacted subsequently would in my view contravene the presumption against retroactivity as this has, I think, been understood in English law: see *L'Office Cherifien des Phosphates v Yamashita-Shinnihon Steamship Co Ltd* [1994] 1 AC 486, 494–496.[193]

This reference to *Yamashita-Shinnihon Steamship* is significant. It raises the issue of 'fairness' discussed above.[194] It is particularly significant because also sitting in *Barretto* was Staughton LJ, the author of the much cited passage in *Tunnicliffe* that was relied on by Lord Mustill in *Yamashita-Shinnihon Steamship*. In *Barretto* Staughton LJ referred to his judgment in *Tunnicliffe* and then said that counsel for the receiver submitted:

> that there is nothing unfair in requiring a drug trafficker to surrender gains which he has made in the past and concealed from the court on a previous occasion.[195]

Staughton LJ responded:

> But I do not think that one should go into detail to that extent. It will generally be unfair to increase the penalty for any past conduct however disreputable. So the presumption applies and that by itself could well be enough to dismiss this appeal.[196]

Staughton LJ went on to consider the terms of the statute, holding that it should not be construed as having retroactive effect.

It is clear that Staughton LJ did not mean by his usage of the word 'fairness' in *Tunnicliffe* that judges should make decisions about the temporal application of statutes based on their view of what would be fair in the precise facts at hand.[197] He evidently meant fairness at a higher level of abstraction: in the case of sentencing, that it 'will generally be unfair to increase the penalty for any past conduct however disreputable'.

Justification of the presumption against retroactivity on the basis of fairness, which is a different thing to determining the applicability or strength of the presumption in specific cases on the basis of fairness, was also the basis of Sir Thomas Bingham MR's conclusion in *Barretto*:

> Many would think that on the present facts there would be nothing unfair in stripping Mr Barretto of the fruits of his criminal activity which he did not disclose in January 1990 even if this means relying on a law enacted later. But the court is here concerned with fairness in a more particular sense. A defendant is not to be substantially prejudiced by laws construed as having retroactive effect unless Parliament's intention that they should have that effect is plain. The blackest malefactor is as much entitled to the benefit of that presumption as anyone else. Parliament has not displaced the presumption in this case

[193] *Ibid* 400.

[194] Ch 4 Pt D and Ch 4 Pt G(1)(d).

[195] [1994] QB 392, 401 (CA).

[196] *Ibid.*

[197] Cf Ch 4 Pt D and, especially, *Wilson v First County Trust (No 2)* [2004] 1 AC 816, [215] (HL), quoted in Ch 4 Pt G(1)(d).

> and it would not be fair to treat it as having done so however strong one's disapproval of Mr Barretto's conduct.[198]

Unfortunately the reasoning in *Barretto* appears to have been overlooked in subsequent cases.

For the common law the primary consideration is whether the sentencing measure in question was in force at the time of the commission of the crime, not whether it involves the imposition of a heavier sentence than that applicable at the time of the commission of the crime, whether the measure imposed can be characterised as a penalty or whether the new law involves the imposition of a sentence of a different type. Those matters may become relevant, along with the statutory language used, to the question of whether the common law presumption against retroactivity has been rebutted, but they do not affect the question of whether the common law presumption against retroactivity is applicable. It is applicable in all cases in which it is argued that a sentence should be imposed on the basis of a law that was not in force at the time that the relevant crime was committed. Despite its breadth, the common law presumption against retroactivity appears to have been overlooked in the cases discussed above in favour of an approach focused narrowly on the words of article 7 of the ECHR.

The common law's protection of traditional rights should not be ignored by slavish adherence to perceived limits of the ECHR. The ECHR represents minimum standards of human rights for 47 countries. Pursuant to the provisions of the Human Rights Act, the common law must change if the common law does not protect Convention rights, but the ECHR does not require that the common law be ignored if the common law provides additional protection or that it not be developed in order to do so. In some cases the mechanisms of the Human Rights Act combined with article 7 of the ECHR will provide stronger protection than the traditional common law presumption, but in cases where the common law presumption is applicable, but article 7 is not, the presumption should still operate. There is no reason why English law should not exceed the minimum guarantees of the Convention, and, in the case of retroactivity, every reason why it should.

(iv) Recidivism The discussion of retroactive sentencing thus far has not involved an argument that any of the relevant article 7 jurisprudence is wrong; only that the terms of article 7 of the ECHR are more limited than the common law presumption against retroactivity and that, accordingly, the common law presumption should not be overlooked. There is at least one aspect of the Strasbourg Court's article 7 jurisprudence on sentencing which is, however, open to question. Consideration of that aspect requires close examination of the facts in the relevant case: *Achour v France*.[199]

A man was convicted of a drug offence in France in 1984 and served a sentence of imprisonment ending in 1986. The legislation applicable to sentencing recidivists

[198] [1994] QB 392, 400–1 (CA).
[199] (2005) 41 EHRR 751.

then in force was such that if convicted again within five years of the expiry of the sentence served for his first offence he would, as a recidivist, be subject to greater punishment for a second offence than if it was his first. Thus in 1991 he ceased to be liable to punishment as a recidivist. In 1994 the law relating to sentencing recidivists was changed so that the period beyond the expiry of the first sentence during which one would in the event of a second offence be considered a recidivist was extended to ten years. In 1995, which was less than ten years from the expiry of his first sentence, the man committed a second drug offence of which he was convicted in 1997. The French Court, applying the new law, sentenced him as a recidivist.

By a four to three majority the Strasbourg Court found that this constituted a breach of article 7 of the ECHR. The majority was particularly influenced by the fact that in 1991 the man ceased to be liable to punishment as a recidivist and the application to him of the 1994 law served to deprive him of that status.[200] The majority thought that recidivism is comprised of both the first and second offences, which are 'an indivisible whole'.[201]

The majority judgment was further based on two unexplained propositions. First, that as 'a corollary of the principle that only the law can define a crime and prescribe a penalty, the provisions of the criminal law are to be strictly construed',[202] which, though a well established principle, is difficult to detect in the text of article 7 of the ECHR. Second, that provisions of the criminal law 'are subject to the rule that new, more severe legislation cannot be applied to an ongoing situation that arose before it came into force'.[203] This extremely wide and vague assertion is not justified by article 7 of the ECHR and it is not clear on what else it might have been based. It goes well beyond a prohibition on retroactivity and purports to preclude the application of a new criminal law which is more severe than its predecessor to an 'ongoing situation'. No attempt was made to define an 'ongoing situation' though it must be assumed to include the facts of *Achour*. It may not include a situation in which the new statute entered into force prior to the expiry of the time period under the first statute. The majority expressly refused to decide whether such a situation would contravene article 7.[204]

The dissent focused, as did the French Government's argument,[205] on the fact that recidivism is an aggravating factor in sentencing for the second offence, not punishment for the first offence.[206] The dissent stated starkly that 'it is the second offence which makes a person a recidivist'.[207] Following this logic, the dissent argued that a sentence, aggravated by recidivism, imposed for the second offence, 'will not be heavier than the one applicable at the time when the second offence

[200] *Ibid* [40]–[41], [43].
[201] *Ibid* [36].
[202] *Ibid* [37].
[203] *Ibid.*
[204] *Ibid* [42].
[205] *Ibid* [22], [25]–[26].
[206] *Ibid* [10], [12], of the dissenting judgment.
[207] *Ibid* [12].

was committed, since by definition that time will be after the date on which the new law came into force'.[208]

The dissent recognised the force of the majority's concern that after the expiry of the five year period under the old statute the man would not have been subject to sentencing as a recidivist.[209] However, once it is appreciated that recidivism is a matter to be taken into account in sentencing for the second offence, it is clear that the law on the basis of which the sentence was passed was in force at the time of the commission of that offence. Thus the new law on recidivism did not have retroactive effect. This view is consistent with longstanding case law of the Criminal Division of the French Court of Cassation, which was applied by that Court in *Achour* and was quoted, though not accepted, in the judgment of the majority of the Strasbourg Court:

> the increase in the sentence in the event of recidivism amounts to an additional penalty not for the first offence but for the second, which the offender may choose to commit or not to commit. Accordingly, new legislation may, without having retrospective effect, lay down the penalties that may be imposed in future for offences committed while it is in force; the offender cannot request the application of the penalties under the previous legislation for an offence committed since the new legislation has been in force, his status as a recidivist being determined by the new legislation.[210]

The key question is whether the punishment is for the first offence. If it is not, then there is no retroactivity. Taking into account a person's criminal record is an ordinary part of sentencing. It may be done without a specific statutory framework. In *Achour* there was a specific statutory framework, but it remains the case that the framework was applicable to sentencing for the second offence, even though that process of sentencing took into account matters that occurred previously.

It might be thought that to change a statutory framework under which a person, if convicted, would not have a previous offence taken into account, to a framework under which that same previous conviction would be relevant, would be a harsh legislative policy. Considerations of finality may support that view, though it is difficult to imagine anyone proposing that a person had a vested right for a previous conviction not to be taken into account. Whatever the merits of those views, the fact that consideration of previous convictions is a matter to be taken into account in sentencing for the second conviction means that the facts in *Achour* did not involve any retroactivity. In the words of article 7(1) of the ECHR, taking into account the previous conviction in sentencing for the second offence did not mean that a 'heavier penalty' was 'imposed' *for the first offence* 'than the one that was applicable at the time the criminal offence was committed'. If the law on recidivism changed after the commission of the second offence and was made applicable to sentencing for that offence then there would be retroactivity in the normal way. But that was not this case.

[208] *Ibid* [13].
[209] *Ibid* [14].
[210] Cass Crim 31 Aug 1893 D 1896.1.137 quoted in (2005) 41 EHRR 751, [17].

Although the facts and applicable law were different and the ECHR did not exist at the time, the same conceptual point arose in the English case of *R v Austin*.[211] The appellant in *Austin* was convicted on indictment of knowingly living on the earnings of prostitution. The law on the basis of which he was sentenced provided that in addition to a term of imprisonment:

> in the case of a second or subsequent conviction, such second or subsequent conviction being a conviction on indictment, the Court may sentence a male offender to be . . . whipped.[212]

The appellant had previously been convicted of the same offence, though before the Act under which he was sentenced for his subsequent offence entered into force. The question was whether the appellant could be whipped. Phillimore J concluded:

> It is said that a retrospective effect must not be given to a penal statute. No doubt; one can hardly imagine the Legislature punishing a man for having done an act which at the time of its commission was a perfectly innocent act. But to prescribe punishment for an old offender in case in the future he persists in his crime is quite another matter. The offence in question was committed since the Act. The Act says that a man guilty in the future may, if he has already been guilty in the past, be punished as he could not have been before the Act. There is nothing wrong in that. No man has such a vested interest in his past crimes and their consequences as would entitle him to insist that in no future legislation shall any regard whatever be had to his previous history.

The appellant was sentenced to be whipped on the basis that his previous convictions satisfied the precondition for such a sentence, which was established, non-retroactively, by the new Act.

When the point next arises in an English court, that court will be faced with contradictory authorities in the form of the Strasbourg Court's decision in *Achour* and the Court of Criminal Appeal's decision in *Austin*. The underlying basis of the difference in those cases is different approaches to the concept of retroactivity.[213] Although the Strasbourg Court's decision must be taken into account,[214] the Court of Criminal Appeal's decision is based on sounder logic which is applicable both to the common law presumption against retroactivity and to article 7 of the ECHR.

(b) The Common Law Presumption Against Retroactive Sentencing

There are three categories of case that require mention. First, cases that viewed the presumption as inapplicable. Second, cases that acknowledged that the presumption was applicable but found it to be rebutted. Third, cases in which the presumption against retroactivity was applied to the construction of a sentencing statute to preclude it from having retroactive effect.

211 [1913] 1 KB 551 (CCA).
212 Criminal Law Amendment Act 1912 (UK) 2 and 3 Geo V c 20 s 7(5).
213 On which see Ch 1 Pt B.
214 Human Rights Act 1998 (UK) s 2(1)(a).

(i) Inapplicability of the Presumption Against Retroactivity Numerous cases of retroactive sentencing that declared the presumption against retroactivity to be *inapplicable* followed the 'very short route'[215] that the sentencing judges 'had . . . [the subsequent legislation] before them'[216] and that the subsequent legislation spoke 'from the date of its coming into operation in respect of all proceedings thereafter determined by the court'[217] such that the presumption against retroactivity had 'no relevance'.[218] This sort of reasoning has been considered and criticised above[219] and will not be repeated here. The more pertinent cases for this discussion are those in which it was accepted that the presumption applied.

(ii) Rebuttal of the Presumption Against Retroactivity In the wartime case of *DPP v Lamb*[220] offences were committed against the Defence (Finance) Regulations 1939 between September 1939 and May 1940. At that time the applicable maximum pecuniary penalty was a fine of 100 pounds. In June 1940 an Order in Council created an alternative pecuniary penalty, which was the imposition of a fine not more than three times the value of the amount involved in the breach of the Regulation. Whichever amount was the larger was to be the applicable maximum. The relevant informations were laid in August 1940 and came before the magistrate for sentencing in September 1940, the truth of the informations having been admitted. The question raised in the case stated by the magistrate was whether the newer alternative penalty was applicable. He had formed the view that it was not. The Court of King's Bench held that he was wrong. Tucker J, after emphasising that the increase in punishment was retroactive,[221] said:

> Although I do not, I confess, like the idea of punishments being increased after the offences have been completed, none the less, the language is clear, and I think it is impossible to escape from its consequences.[222]

Those consequences were that 'the order is applicable to an offence which has already been committed'.[223] The language of the Order in Council on which the judgment turned was '[w]here any person is convicted', which was the opening phrase of the sentencing provision. The decision in *Lamb* that these general words, unsupported by any more explicit or powerful direction in favour of retroactivity, constituted a command to apply the order retroactively, from which it was 'impossible to escape', is a decision that affords no strength to the presumption against retroactivity.

215 *O'Neill v Reid* [1959] NZLR 331, 336 (SC).
216 *Buckman v Button* [1943] KB 405, 411. See also *DPP v Lamb* [1941] 2 KB 89, 101.
217 *Maher v Hamilton* [1990] Tas R 199, 204. See also *Arnold v Neilsen* (1976) 9 ALR 191, 193.
218 *Lewis v French* [1962] Tas SR 138, 140. Contra *Worsley v Crawford* (1994) 4 Tas R 78.
219 Ch 1 Pt E(1) and Ch 3 Pt C(4)(b).
220 [1941] 2 KB 89.
221 Noted in Ch 1 Pt B.
222 [1941] 2 KB 89, 105.
223 *Ibid.*

Lamb was followed in two subsequent wartime cases, *Buckman v Button*[224] and *R v Oliver*.[225] In *Oliver* the relevant statutory words were that '[a]ny person guilty of an offence against this regulation . . . shall be liable'[226] to the increased penalty, which far exceeded[227] the penalty applicable at the time of the offences. As in *Lamb*, reference was made to the presumption against retroactivity, but it was held that these general words overcame the presumption. *Lamb* and the decisions that followed it acknowledged the applicability of the presumption but were then prepared for it to be defeated by extremely general statutory words. The status of the presumption against retroactivity as a principle of the common law to which courts will give effect independently of legislative intention is not apparent in such decisions. Accordingly *Lamb* has been doubted in more recent cases.

Sir Thomas Bingham MR and Staughton LJ expressed their reservations about *Lamb* in *Barretto*.[228] In the decision of the Full Court of the Supreme Court of South Australia in *Samuels v Songaila*[229] Bray CJ attempted to distinguish the triumvirate of wartime cases beginning with *Lamb*, before adding that if no valid distinction could be made he could only say that he did not agree with them. In the same case Zelling J thought that *Lamb* could be distinguished but that *Buckman v Button* and *Oliver* were 'clearly wrong'.[230] King J thought that none of these three cases could be distinguished on their face but thought that they 'must be explained' by a greater judicial willingness to impose retroactive penalties in time of war for 'offences of a type which are likely to impair the war effort' such that they could not be regarded as general authorities.[231] In *Barretto* and *Samuels v Songaila* the respective courts made decisions that are consistent with the existence of a common law presumption against retroactivity that is strong enough not to be defeated by general statutory words, and for that reason it is those decisions, not *Lamb* or cases relying on it, that should be followed. In addition to *Barretto* and *Samuels v Songaila*, there are further cases worthy of discussion in which the common law presumption against retroactivity operated to preclude the application of a sentencing law that entered into force after the relevant crime had been committed.

(iii) Applications of the Presumption Against Retroactivity The strength of the presumption against retroactivity as a common law principle, operative in the face of legislative intent that was very likely to have been in favour of the immediate application of the new legislative measure to all crimes whensoever committed, was apparent in the decision of the Victorian Supreme Court in *Bakker v*

224 [1943] KB 405.
225 [1944] KB 68 (CCA).
226 *Ibid* 75.
227 *Ibid.*
228 [1994] QB 392, 400, 402 (CA).
229 (1977) 16 SASR 397.
230 *Ibid* 415–16.
231 *Ibid* 420.

Stewart.[232] That case raised the issue of whether a statutory provision that removed the court's power in certain drink driving offences to adjourn an information without proceeding to conviction,[233] was applicable to offences committed prior to that change in the law. Adjournment without conviction had been the method used by judges to avoid imposing mandatory penalties, a practice that the legislature was apparently eager to stop. Lush J, influenced by *Samuels v Songaila*, held that the new statutory provision:

> cannot be classed as a procedural section, nor can it be classed as merely operating *in futuro* upon situations originating in the past. In effect, it increases the penalties for the relevant offences by terminating the only known method of avoiding an imposition of the mandatory penalties and, accordingly, in my opinion, it deals with both liability and penalty. It is, therefore, not to be applied to offences committed before it came into operation.[234]

Another application of the presumption was apparent in the decision of the Chief Justice of Western Australia in *Richardson v Brennan.*[235] In that case the statutory minimum penalty was increased between commission of the offence and conviction for it. The sentencing magistrate imposed the later and more severe minimum penalty. Wolff CJ applied the presumption against retroactivity, with its concomitant protection against arbitrary results and against the spectre of government abuse of retroactive sentencing laws, and allowed the appeal, observing that:

> The fallacy of applying the new and increased monetary penalty is forcefully illustrated by considering the hypothesis that the charge was heard, the conviction recorded and the fine imposed on the day before . . . [the date of commencement of the new legislation]. . . . Clearly it should not depend on the fortuitous circumstance of when the charge was heard, the conviction recorded or the penalty imposed.[236]

These cases represent applications of the common law presumption to reject submissions that a sentencing statute was retroactive. In the absence of an inescapable statutory command of retroactivity, the courts did not seek to ascertain legislative intention on the question of temporal effect, but rather construed legislation in accordance with the common law presumption against retroactivity to avoid the exercise by the legislature of an unusual power to the detriment of criminal defendants.

(c) Retroactive Changes in Favour of the Defendant

If a defendant is sentenced on the basis of a statute that entered into force after he committed the relevant offence, then, regardless of whether the sentence is more

232 [1980] VR 17.
233 Motor Car Act 1958 (Vic) s 89A.
234 [1980] VR 17, 23.
235 [1966] WAR 159.
236 *Ibid* 160.

or less severe than that to which he was exposed under the law in force at the time of his crime, the relevant statute may be said to have retroactive effect. The presumption against retroactivity is a starting point applicable in all cases where retroactivity is said to exist and so is not dependent on a view of the beneficence or otherwise of that retroactivity. What may vary, however, is the strength of the reasons said to rebut the presumption. In cases involving increased penalties judicial concern about limiting state power over individual liberty underlies the courts' unwillingness to construe legislation as having rebutted the presumption. By contrast, where the legislature has decreased the severity of the sentence that may be applied and so 'mollifies the rigor of the criminal law'[237] there is less reason to fear abuse of state power. Rather, as mentioned in Chapter three,[238] the state has reduced its incursion on individual liberty and so the courts will be very likely to find the presumption rebutted. An example of this approach is the case of *R v Morton* in which the Full Court of the Supreme Court of Victoria stated that the conferral of a benefit on the defendant 'outweighs the presumption against retrospectivity'.[239]

The rebuttal of the presumption against retroactivity where the applicable sentence has decreased between commission of an offence and sentencing for it, is mandated by various statutes in Australia and Canada. These general statutes typically state that if, subsequent to the commission of an offence but prior to sentencing for it, the sentence for that offence is increased by statute, that increase shall not apply to those who have already committed the offence; but go on to provide that if, subsequent to the commission of an offence, the applicable sentence is reduced, the defendant is to benefit from the reduction.[240]

This approach is consistent with article 15(1) of the International Covenant on Civil and Political Rights which, after prohibiting the imposition of a sentence heavier than the applicable sentence at the time of commission of the offence, states that if 'subsequent to the commission of the offence, provision is made by law for the imposition of the lighter penalty, the offender shall benefit thereby'.[241] A similar provision does not appear in article 7 of the ECHR, which is otherwise substantially similar. Neither article prohibits retroactivity *per se*, but only the imposition of 'a heavier penalty . . . than the one that was applicable at the time the criminal offence was committed'. Accordingly neither article prohibits the retroactive reduction of a penalty, and article 15, as well as statutes applicable in Australia and Canada, actually require that reductions in sentence be granted retroactive effect. Although article 7 does not contain the same requirement, it

[237] *Calder v Bull* 3 US (Dallas) 386, 391 (1798).

[238] Ch 3 Pt C(4)(b).

[239] [1986] VR 863, 867.

[240] Eg Crimes Act 1914 (Aus) s 4F; Crimes (Sentencing Procedure) Act 1999 (NSW) s 19; Criminal Code 1899 (Qld) s 11(2); Sentencing Act 1991 (Vic) s 114; cf Sentencing Act 1995 (WA) s 10; Canadian Charter of Rights and Freedoms s 11(i), discussed in *R v Johnson* [2003] 2 SCR 357 [41]–[46].

[241] A difficulty with this provision was resolved in *Chan Chi-hung v The Queen* [1996] AC 442, 450–53 (PC).

may be expected that the common law presumption against retroactivity would be rebutted in such circumstances.

Any apparent asymmetry[242] by which increases in sentence typically are not retroactive, whilst decreases in sentence typically are retroactive, is an asymmetry of result only. When the reasons for each result are considered, consistency is apparent. The reason that applies in both cases is that the courts, in some cases with additional direction by the legislature, are concerned to protect individual liberty. That concern means that any retroactive change to the amount of punishment to which a defendant has exposed himself by committing a crime is presumptively resisted. If exposure to criminal punishment is increased, then it is difficult to see how, in the absence of inescapable statutory command, the presumption against retroactivity would be rebutted. However, if the change decreases the magnitude of exposure to a criminal sentence, then furtherance of individual liberty may ordinarily be expected to lead to the rebuttal of the presumption against retroactivity. This is encapsulated in section 11(i) of the Canadian Charter of Rights and Freedoms, which succinctly states that if there is any variation in sentence between the time of commission and the time of sentencing, the defendant is entitled 'to the benefit of the lesser punishment'.

Related reasons for a willingness to overcome the presumption against retroactivity in cases of ameliorative sentencing statutes were suggested by King J in *Samuels v Songaila*:

> If Parliament were to reduce a penalty, it might appear that Parliament had judged the former penalty to be harsh or unjust and therefore intended that the harshness or injustice should not be continued even in relation to offences already committed. Similarly, where Parliament abolishes a particular type of punishment, such as capital or corporal punishment, it might be easy to find a legislative intention that the type of punishment which has been abolished should not be imposed in future, even in relation to offences committed before its abolition.[243]

Such reasoning exhibits courts' concern for individual liberty by expressing an inclination to find the presumption against retroactivity rebutted in the case of statutory changes that benefit a defendant.

It is not necessarily the case, however, that it will always be appropriate for the presumption against retroactivity to be rebutted when the applicable sentence is reduced between commission of the offence and sentencing for it. One example where this might not be appropriate would be if the reduction of sentence was specifically tailored to benefit a particular group of people who had already offended and were improperly favoured by the legislature, perhaps because of their political affiliation. In such a case rule of law considerations, and more specifically the importance of generality in the law,[244] would arise and may lead the

242 Cf *R v MJR* (2002) 54 NSWLR 368, [14]–[16], [19].

243 (1977) 16 SASR 397, 421.

244 See the discussion of generality in Ch 3 Pt C(4)(b).

courts properly to resist any purported retroactivity unless compelled by inescapable statutory command to do otherwise.

Whatever issues may be relevant in a particular case, the structure of reasoning should remain the same. The presumption against retroactivity is applicable in all cases in which a party contends for retroactive effect, but in the case of statutes reducing the severity of sentences, it is likely that reasons will exist in most cases that are strong enough for a court to overcome the presumption.

H Conclusion

This chapter has sought to examine the presumption against retroactivity in the construction of statutes. Three themes can be identified. First, the presumption against retroactivity is a principle of the common law against which courts will construe statutes. It is not a tool for the divination and implementation of legislative intention. Second, 'fairness' is not an appropriate test for determining the applicability or strength of the presumption. Third, the presumption against retroactivity should not vary in strength. Motivated by the common law's concern for certainty and liberty, it should be of constant strength in all cases, though in particular cases strong reasons may rebut it.

5

Adjudicative Retroactivity

A Introductory Matters

1 What is Adjudicative Retroactivity?

When a judge expresses a common law rule that is contrary to or not based on existing authority and makes a decision based on that rule, the newly expressed rule is applied to facts that predate the expression of the rule. Such a decision also supplies a new rule for future cases even where the facts giving rise to those cases occurred prior to the formation of the rule. In these ways a rule formed at a later time is applied to facts arising prior to that formation as though the rule was operative at the time of those facts occurring. This outcome satisfies the definition of retroactivity: the application of a new law to a past event as though it was the law at the time of that event.

2 The Declaratory Theory

Some theorists consider that common law adjudication never decides a new rule, although it may declare a rule that was previously undeclared, and apply it to facts predating that declaration as though it was always applicable. In the view of such theorists the rule was always applicable even if that applicability was unknown to everyone and there was a longstanding judicial precedent of the highest authority indicating that the law was otherwise. This contrivance is not just of historical interest.[1] Despite frequent derogatory remarks made about the declaratory theory,[2] it continues to influence judges and academics,[3] sometimes in modified form.[4] This

[1] For the historical position see Ch 2 Pt C.

[2] Eg *Skelton v Collins* (1966) 115 CLR 94, 134–5; Lord Reid 'The Judge as Lawmaker' (1972) 12 Journal of the Society of Public Teachers of Law 22, 22; J Stone *Precedent and Law* (Butterworths Sydney 1985) 189; M McHugh 'The Law-making Function of the Judicial Process—Part I' (1988) 62 Australian Law Journal 15, 16–18; R Cross and J Harris *Precedent in English Law* (4th edn Clarendon Press Oxford 1991) 26–33; Lord Bingham 'The Judge as Lawmaker: An English Perspective' in T Bingham *The Business of Judging: Selected Essays and Speeches* (Oxford University Press 2000) 28–30; *A v Secretary of State for the Home Department* [2006] 2 AC 221, [152] (HL).

discussion need not and will not enter in any depth the apparently intractable debate about whether the common law is made or found.

Whether the law deemed to apply to facts which precede that deeming is declared by a judge who reveals a rule that is said to have always existed even though no one else knew about it, or is announced by a judge engaged in the task of making or changing the law, does not affect the fact that the ability to rely on the law and the knowable parameters of a person's liberty are determined by the law as it apparently (according, for example, to binding judicial authority) was at the time of the relevant event. A judicial decision declaring the law has just as much retroactive *effect* as a judicial decision or retroactive statute making or changing the law. The important matter under discussion is the retroactive *effect* of judicial decisions that depart from existing precedent or decide a matter on which there was no existing authority.[5] Whether those decisions are retroactive by *nature* is not under discussion.

Even the most devout declaratory theorist would accept that a disappointed litigant who relied on an existing precedent only to discover that his case was to become the vehicle for the court to depart from that precedent and declare the law to be otherwise suffers retroactive *effects*, though such a theorist would reject the proposition that there is anything retroactive about the *nature* of the process, particularly if viewed from a systemic level rather than from the perspective of the individual litigants and the particular rule that is held to apply to them. Finnis takes a systemic view in his comment[6] on *Kleinwort Benson v Lincoln City Council.*[7] Finnis thinks that a 'higher tribunal', 'considering our law as a principled and lasting whole', could 'declare' a rule contrary to the one previously accepted:

> and apply it to the parties, their transactions, and their supporting beliefs, as having been at all relevant times legally correct and an authentic legal rule. From this highest-level view of our law as a justifying because justified whole, the newly declared rule would not, in the last analysis, be retroactive—would, in the last analysis, abrogate no part of our law's substantive content. The judicial reasoning towards, and act of declaring, the rule would be fundamentally different from the enactment of new statutory provisions; only in result would it coincide with that rare form of legislative action which, sometimes reasonably, makes new statutory provisions retroactive.[8]

Finnis's position seems to be that the common law, as a coherent body of prin-

[3] *Re Spectrum Plus (in liquidation)* [2005] 2 AC 680, [34] (HL); *R v Governor of Brockhill Prison, ex p Evans (No 2)* [2001] 2 AC 19, 45 (HL); S Atrill '*Nulla Poena Sine Lege* in Comparative Perspective: Retrospectivity under the ECHR and US Constitution' [2005] Public Law 107, 130.

[4] *Giannarelli v Wraith* (1988) 165 CLR 543, 584–6; *Kleinwort Benson v Lincoln City Council* [1999] 2 AC 349, 377–9, 381 (HL); JM Finnis 'The Fairy Tale's Moral' (1999) 115 Law Quarterly Review 170.

[5] Cf *Re Spectrum Plus (in liquidation)* [2005] 2 AC 680, [34]–[35] (HL).

[6] JM Finnis 'The Fairy Tale's Moral' (1999) 115 Law Quarterly Review 170. Contra P Cane 'The Temporal Element in Law' (2001) 117 Law Quarterly Review 5.

[7] [1999] 2 AC 349 (HL).

[8] JM Finnis 'The Fairy Tale's Moral' (1999) 115 Law Quarterly Review 170, 174–5.

ciples, is not retroactive.[9] Assuming that the common law is a coherent body of principles, then it is not really controversial that a coherent system of law is not, as a system, retroactive. The more contentious question is whether a particular rule within that system is, or can be, retroactive. An appellate court that makes a decision contrary to prior authority may well be making the legal system, viewed as a whole, more coherent, as the majority in *Kleinwort Benson* believed themselves to be doing. But that does not mean that departing from existing authority on a particular rule in question does not have retroactive effect. The decision in *Kleinwort Benson* to allow recovery of money paid under a mistake of law was contrary to what the courts at the time of the mistake had consistently held the law to be. That the House of Lords' decision may have increased the overall coherence of the law when viewed at the 'highest level', or at least when viewed at the level of the law relating to unjust enrichment generally, does not alter the retroactive effect of changing the particular rule about recovery of money paid under a mistake of law.

Furthermore, the values of certainty and liberty are affected just as much if a decision on a common law rule departs from existing authority as if a retroactive statute is passed that changes a statutory rule. It is of course true, as Finnis emphasizes, that the judicial and legislative *processes* are different. The difference in process does not, as Finnis acknowledges, alter the fact that changes in the judicial view of a common law rule has the same retroactive effect as a retroactive statutory change. The difference in process might be thought to be particularly unimportant to those affected by the judicial exposition of a common law rule to which at the time of their decisions they could not know that they were subject.

3 The Scope of this Chapter

This chapter is not concerned with whether any actual or proposed creation of or change to a common law rule was or would have been desirable when considered in isolation from the retroactive effect of the judicial decision in which the rule was announced. As Julius Stone wrote:

> Questions of justice or policy arising from the temporal dimension of law are distinct from (though ancillary to) those concerning the substantive rule governing the instant facts.[10]

Nor is this chapter concerned with the broad debate about whether or to what extent judges do or should have a creative or 'activist' role in developing or reforming the law. The more confined scope of this chapter is to consider the extent to which retroactive consequences that accompany judicial creation of or changes to a common law rule are or should be taken into account by courts. For the sake of simplicity, the terms 'making law' and 'changing law' and equivalents

[9] See also the view of 'law as integrity' expressed by R Dworkin *Law's Empire* (Hart Publishing Oxford 1998) ch 7, summarised at 167 and 225 and exemplified at 228 and 245.

[10] J Stone *Precedent and Law* (Butterworths Sydney 1985) 186.

to them will be used in circumstances where they describe the results of adjudication accurately enough for the meaning to be clear, even though some would object to the theoretical assumption that such terms contain. It would be close to impossible to collect and discuss all cases decided in which consideration was given to judicially making or changing a legal rule. That would be a history of the development of the common law. Rather, cases illustrative of issues of retroactivity, which often constitute landmarks in the common law, will be selected.

Enough has been written previously in this book on the meaning of retroactivity generally, but some further comments are necessary about the application of this relatively strict definition to the delimitation of the types of cases under discussion in this chapter. There are some categories of case that might at first glance be thought to involve issues of retroactivity, but on closer analysis, though they may generally be classed as falling within the bounds of intertemporal law or involving a degree of retrospectivity, they do not involve true retroactivity.

One example of such an excluded category is the unsettled area of deciding the consequences, if any, of an act of the executive government, such as promulgating a subordinate statutory instrument or making an administrative decision, on which people have relied but which is later found by the courts to be ultra vires the statute thought by some to enable it. In this type of case, which was discussed, for example, in *Boddington v British Transport Police*,[11] there is no prior judicial decision indicating that a byelaw promulgated or decision made by an administrative authority is valid and capable of being acted on. The presumption of legality is involved, in the sense that people may be entitled to assume that byelaws and decisions made by the executive are lawful, but in the absence of a previous judicial decision indicating that a particular byelaw or decision of an administrative authority is intra vires, there is no change in the law and so there is no retroactivity.[12] People understandably rely on byelaws and decisions of administrative authorities, and the legal effects, if any, of a byelaw or decision declared void is a serious question that continues to excite debate.[13] The issue would come within a subject described as intertemporal law and may justify the generic label of retrospectivity, but it is not a question involving either statutory or adjudicative retroactivity.

A similar example is the legal consequence, if any, of a statute declared by a

[11] [1999] 2 AC 143 (HL). Insistence that a byelaw declared void can never have had any legal effect is apparent, eg, in *Boddington* [1999] 2 AC 143, 155–156 (HL) and *Hoffmann-La Roche v Secretary of State for Trade and Industry* [1975] AC 295, 365 (HL). Views that some legal consequences may attach to a byelaw held to be void are apparent, eg, in *Boddington* [1999] 2 AC 143, 164, 165, 172 (HL) and *Percy v Hall* [1997] QB 924, 947–8, 951–2 (CA).

[12] Contra *R v Unger* [1977] 2 NSWLR 990, 995 and E Campbell 'The Retrospectivity of Judicial Decisions and the Legality of Governmental Acts' (2003) 29 Monash University Law Review 49, 61, 83.

[13] The literature is vast. One useful entry point is C Forsyth ' "The Metaphysic of Nullity" Invalidity, Conceptual Reasoning and the Rule of Law' in *The Golden Metwand and the Crooked Cord: Essays on Public Law in Honour of Sir William Wade QC* C Forsyth and I Hare (eds) (Clarendon Press Oxford 1998) 141.

court to be void for incompatibility with a written constitution in circumstances where the presumption of constitutionality may have enabled people to rely on a statute later held to be unconstitutional.[14] The presumption of constitutionality cannot itself make a statute constitutional, and a judicial decision that a statute is not and never was constitutional may upset those who relied on that statute, but it does not change the law and so is not retroactive.[15] A judicial decision that particular legislation is beyond the competence of a devolved legislature within the United Kingdom falls into the same category.[16]

A different example of an intertemporal issue that may look like it involves retroactivity, but in truth does not, is the ratification by a principal of his agent's act that, when it occurred, exceeded the scope of authority conferred on the agent. The consequence of the principal's ratification is that the agent's act is deemed to have been authorised at the time of the action.[17] The law of agency engages in an intertemporal sleight of hand, but there is no change to that law and so no retroactivity. A conceptually similar example is that at common law a foetus does not have rights,[18] but if born, a minor can sue on the basis of a wrong done while that minor was in utero,[19] or perhaps even prior to conception.[20] In such a case either a wrong exists from the time of its occurrence but can only become the subject of a legal action once the party harmed gains legal personality, ie is born; or, and this is the alternative that involves intertemporal trickery, there was no wrong committed to the foetus at the time of the event held after birth to cause harm, but after birth, that prior event is found to have been wrongful at the time that it occurred. Furthermore, in some circumstances when it is to a minor's advantage, she may be deemed to have been born at a time when she was actually in utero, but such

[14] Discussed, eg, in *Ha v New South Wales* (1997) 189 CLR 465, 503–4, 515 contra the approach of the Canadian Supreme Court in *Re Manitoba Language Rights* [1985] 1 SCR 721 and s 172(1) of the Constitution of the Republic of South Africa. See Ch 6 of this book for discussion of 'prospective overruling'.

[15] Cf *A-G (Australia) v The Queen* (1957) 95 CLR 529, 546–8 (PC) (*The Boilermakers' Case*). The High Court had in previous litigation presumed constitutional the statute later held to be unconstitutional by the High Court and then by the Privy Council in *The Boilermakers' Case*. The previous litigation did not actually decide the statute to be constitutional and so there was no actual retroactivity involved when it was held to be unconstitutional in *The Boilermakers' Case*. All that happened was that an 'invalidity' that existed from the passage of the statute had, until *The Boilermakers' Case*, been 'disregarded': (1957) 95 CLR 529, 548 (PC).

[16] See the powers to control the intertemporal effects of their decisions conferred on courts by the Scotland Act 1998 (UK) s 102, the Government of Wales Act 1998 (UK) s 110 and the Northern Ireland Act 1998 (UK) s 81.

[17] *Wilson v Tumman* (1843) 6 Man & G 236, 242; 134 ER 879, 882; *Bolton Partners v Lambert* (1889) 41 Ch D 295 (CA).

[18] *Paton v British Pregnancy Advisory Service Trustees* [1979] QB 276, 279.

[19] *Watt v Rama* [1972] VR 353; *X and Y v Pal* (1991) 23 NSWLR 26, 30, 37–45; *Burton v Islington Health Authority* [1993] QB 204 (CA); *Harriton v Stephens* [2006] HCA 15; *McKay v Essex Area Health Authority* [1982] QB 1166 (CA), though as the latter two cases, which deal with 'wrongful life' claims, demonstrate, whether such an action will be successful is a different matter.

[20] *Kosky v The Trustees of The Sisters of Charity* [1982] VR 961, 969–970; *Waller v James* [2006] HCA 16.

deeming can occur only after birth.[21] Despite the intertemporal fiction, in all of these types of case, there is no change in the law, and so no retroactivity.

There is a long tradition of consideration of intertemporal issues in private international law.[22] That consideration is primarily focused on the question of, when choosing which law, in the sense of the law of which place, to apply, also choosing the time at which the law of the place chosen is to be taken. If the *lex causae* is retroactive, there will for that reason be an issue of retroactivity,[23] but though there may be parallels between the two ideas,[24] choice of the time of law as part of the choice of law exercise within private international law, whatever its intertemporal complexities, does not inherently involve any retroactivity.

This chapter will consider, across private, public and criminal law, (without treating those as hermetically sealed categories) significant cases in which a common law rule was expounded where there was no prior rule on the point, in which a common law rule was expounded that was inconsistent with previous authority, and in which a judicial decision interpreting a statutory provision departed from a previous judicial decision on that same provision. This chapter will not discuss judicial decisions about the meaning of a statutory provision that are inconsistent with what many people, prior to a judicial decision on the point, may have assumed the statute to mean. Such decisions do not change the law[25] and so, like the other examples discussed above, do not involve true retroactivity.

[21] *Villar v Gilbey* [1907] AC 139, 144–5, 151 (HL); *Williams v Ocean Coal Company Limited* [1907] 2 KB 422, 429 (CA); *Schofield v Orrell Colliery Company Limited* [1909] 1 KB 178, 181, 182 (CA). This approach is derived from Roman Law: T Mommsen, P Krueger (eds) and A Watson (tr) *The Digest of Justinian* (University of Pennsylvania Press Philadelphia PA 1985) 15 (D 1 5 7): 'The fetus in the womb is deemed to be fully a human being, whenever the question concerns advantages accruing to him when born, even though before birth his existence is never assumed in favor of anyone else.'; 'Qui in utero est, perinde ac si in rebus humanis esset custoditur, quotiens de commodis ipsius partus quaeritur: quamquam alii antequam nascatur nequaquam prosit.'

[22] Eg JHC Morris 'The Time Factor in the Conflict of Laws' (1966) International and Comparative Law Quarterly 422; E Spiro 'The Incidence of Time in the Conflict of Laws' (1960) 9 International and Comparative Law Quarterly 357; JK Grodecki 'Conflicts of Laws in Time' (1959) 35 British Year Book of International Law 58; FA Mann 'The Time Element in the Conflict of Laws' (1954) 31 British Year Book of International Law 217; FC von Savigny *Private International Law and the Retrospective Operation of Statutes: A Treatise on the Conflict of Laws and the Limits of their Operation in Respect of Place and Time* W Guthrie (tr) (2nd edn T&T Clark Edinburgh 1880) ch 2.

[23] *Starkowski v A-G* [1954] AC 155 (HL); *Phillips v Eyre* (1870) LR 6 QB 1 (Exch).

[24] *Wilson v First County Trust (No 2)* [2004] 1 AC 816, [131] (HL); Lord Rodger 'A Time for Everything under the Law: Some Reflections on Retrospectivity' (2005) 121 Law Quarterly Review 57, 61; *James B Beam Distilling Co v Georgia* 501 US 529, 534–5 (1991).

[25] Contra *Re Spectrum Plus (in liquidation)* [2005] 2 AC 680, [6] (HL).

B The Doctrine of Precedent and Judicial Attachment to Existing Principle in Novel Cases

The doctrine of precedent is an entire subject, which has been afforded detailed treatment by many judges and academics.[26] A recent description of the doctrine of precedent was given by Lord Nicholls in *Re Spectrum Plus (in liquidation)*:

> To promote a desirable degree of consistency and certainty about the present state of 'the law', courts in this country have long adopted the practice of treating decisions on a point of law as precedents for the future. If the same point of law arises in another case at a later date a court will treat a previous decision as binding or persuasive, depending upon the well-known hierarchical principles of 'stare decisis'.[27]

Numerous interrelated rationales for the doctrine of precedent exist.[28] For present purposes the relevant rationale, or if not rationale then at least effect, is that the doctrine of precedent controls the occurrence of adjudicative retroactivity. A doctrine that confines the circumstances in which courts may depart from previous decisions requires, as a general rule, that where an applicable legal rule was operative at the time of an event giving rise to litigation, that it will be applied to that litigation. Thus the doctrine of precedent correlatively confines the opportunities for new rules to be applied as though they were the rules operative at the time of the relevant events.

Sometimes cases arise in which there is no existing legal rule applicable to the circumstances. When such cases are decided a degree of adjudicative retroactivity is inevitable because a new rule is created to deal with the situation and is applied to facts arising at a time when no authoritative rule existed, as though it was the law at that time. The severity of this retroactivity is limited by judicial attachment to existing principle. McHugh J has referred in this connection to the 'essential unity' of the common law, by virtue of which: 'New ground can only be claimed if it can be joined to the old.'[29] This point has proved especially fertile ground for analogies. Lord Goff referred to Maitland's reference to a 'seamless web' and his own reference to a 'mosaic'.[30] Lord Wright mentioned the traditional approach of common law judges who developed the law 'from case to case, like the ancient Mediterranean mariners, hugging the coast from point to point',[31] before expressing his own view that:

[26] Perhaps the most famous of which is R Cross and J Harris *Precedent in English Law* (4th edn Clarendon Press Oxford 1991).

[27] [2005] 2 AC 680, [5] (HL). See also JD Heydon 'Limits to the Powers of Ultimate Appellate Courts' (2006) 122 Law Quarterly Review 399, 403.

[28] Many of which are discussed by JD Heydon 'Limits to the Powers of Ultimate Appellate Courts' (2006) 122 Law Quarterly Review 399, 403–5.

[29] M McHugh 'The Law-making Function of the Judicial Process—Part II' (1988) 62 Australian Law Journal 116, 120.

[30] *Kleinwort Benson v Lincoln County Council* [1999] 2 AC 349, 378 (HL).

[31] Lord Wright 'The Study of Law' (1938) 54 Law Quarterly Review 185, 186.

> the law is a living organism, constantly growing, expanding, adapting itself, like a tree, which maintains its identity all the time, though in its full growth it looks very different from what it was when a sapling.[32]

Perhaps the most famous, useful, and non-analogical description of the process of gradual development of the law by judges was offered by Justice Holmes when he said that they do so 'only interstitially',[33] though even he could not resist the metaphorical urge, following that comment with the expression that judges are 'confined from molar to molecular motions'.[34] This cautious approach, like the doctrine of precedent, serves to control adjudicative retroactivity by limiting the number of cases in which a new rule is created and, where a new rule is created and applied to old facts as though it was the rule applicable at the time of those facts, this approach requires that new rule to be grounded in existing principle, which reduces the degree of surprise that retroactivity may otherwise cause.

This brief discussion of the doctrine of precedent and judicial attachment to existing principle in novel cases suffices to launch the claim that although when the common law is changed by development or overruling the process of common law adjudication is such that the change has retroactive effect, the occasions on which this occurs are limited by the operation of the doctrine of precedent and judicial attachment to existing principles in novel cases, which, in this respect, presumptively oppose retroactivity in common law adjudication. The evidence for that claim lies in the multitude of cases that are decided every day in which the result is governed by existing authority or, in the absence of precisely applicable authority, existing principle. The more interesting issue, and the one to which this chapter is devoted, is an examination of the grounds on which this presumption is or should be overcome. The contention will be that in common law cases that make law by developing a new rule or changing an existing rule, the potential retroactive effects of doing so should always be considered, though the presumption against retroactivity may ultimately be defeated by countervailing considerations of sufficient strength.

Perhaps the two most significant cases in which the House of Lords departed from previous authority with fairly dramatic retroactive effect are *R v R*,[35] in which the marital immunity to a charge of rape was finally abolished, and *Kleinwort Benson v Lincoln County Council*,[36] which overturned the rule that money paid under a mistake of law could not be the subject of a claim for restitution. The issues arising from these cases deserve detailed treatment as archetypes of adjudicative retroactivity, before embarking on a more general discussion.

[32] Lord Wright 'The Study of Law' (1938) 54 Law Quarterly Review 194.

[33] *Southern Pacific Co v Jensen* 244 US 205, 221 (1917), a term also favoured by HLA Hart *The Concept of Law* (2nd edn Clarendon Press Oxford 1994) 273, 274. See also *Re Spectrum Plus (in liquidation)* [2005] 2 AC 680, [33] (HL).

[34] *Southern Pacific Co v Jensen* 244 US 205, 221 (1917). For those not familiar with scientific measurement, this is explained by JD Heydon 'Limits to the Powers of Ultimate Appellate Courts' (2006) 122 Law Quarterly Review 399, 400 fn 6.

[35] [1992] 1 AC 599 (HL).

[36] [1999] 2 AC 349 (HL).

C The Marital Rape Cases

1 Outline of the Facts, Decisions and Issues

R v R was the case that finally and completely abolished in England the marital immunity to a charge of rape. In 1989 the appellant attempted to have non-consensual sex with his wife, who had left the matrimonial home and given notice to her husband of her intention to petition for divorce. He was convicted in 1990 of attempted rape as well as assault occasioning bodily harm, the trial judge having rejected a submission that despite her refusal to engage in sexual intercourse the wife must be deemed to have consented by virtue of the marriage. That submission, and the husband's unsuccessful appeals to the Court of Appeal and then to the House of Lords, were based on a line of authority[37] commencing with Hale's assertion that a:

> husband cannot be guilty of a rape committed by himself upon his lawful wife, for by their mutual matrimonial consent and contract the wife hath given up herself in this kind unto her husband, which she cannot retract.[38]

A number of exceptions to and doubts about this view had been expressed,[39] but it had never authoritatively been held to be wrong. In *R v R* Lord Lane CJ, in the Court of Appeal, observed that:

> courts have been paying lip service to the Hale proposition, whilst at the same time increasing the number of exceptions, the number of situations to which it does not apply. This is a legitimate use of the flexibility of the common law which can and should adapt itself to changing social attitudes.
>
> There comes a time when the changes are so great that it is no longer enough to create further exceptions restricting the effect of the proposition, a time when the proposition itself requires examination to see whether its terms are in accord with what is generally regarded today as acceptable behaviour.
>
> . . . the idea that a wife by marriage consents in advance to her husband having sexual intercourse with her whatever her state of health or however proper her objections (if that is what Hale meant), is no longer acceptable. It can never have been other than a fiction, and fiction is a poor basis for the criminal law. The extent to which events have overtaken Hale's proposition is well illustrated by his last four words, 'which she cannot retract.'
>
> It seems to us that where the common law rule no longer even remotely represents what is the true position of a wife in present day society, the duty of the court is to take

[37] Including *R v Miller* [1954] 2 QB 282 (Assizes); *R v J* [1991] 1 All ER 759 (CC); *R v S* (Crown Court at Stafford, 15 Jan 1991, Swinton-Thomas J).

[38] M Hale *History of the Pleas of the Crown* (New edn S Emlyn London 1800) vol 1 ch 58, 629.

[39] Including in *Popkin v Popkin* (Consistory Court, Hilary Term Second Session 1794, Lord Stowell) noted at 1 Hag Ecc 765 fn (b); 162 ER 745 fn (b); *The Queen v Clarence* (1889) 22 QBD 23, 33, 57–8; *R v Clarke* [1949] 2 All ER 448, 449 (Assizes); *R v O'Brien* [1974] 3 All ER 663, 665 (CC); *R v Steele* (1976) 65 Cr App R 22, 25 (CA); *R v Roberts* [1986] Crim L R 188 (CA); *R v C* [1991] 1 All ER 755, 758 (CC).

steps to alter the rule if it can legitimately do so in the light of any relevant Parliamentary enactment.[40]

Having decided that there was no statutory impediment to alteration of the common law, Lord Lane CJ concluded that:

This is not the creation of a new offence, it is the removal of a common law fiction which has become anachronistic and offensive and we consider that it is our duty having reached that conclusion to act upon it.[41]

Lord Keith, who spoke for the House of Lords, expressly agreed with this observation.[42] Lord Keith considered that Hale's

proposition was generally regarded as an accurate statement of the common law of England. The common law is, however, capable of evolving in the light of changing social, economic and cultural developments. Hale's proposition reflected the state of affairs in these respects at the time it was enunciated. Since then the status of women, and particularly of married women, has changed out of all recognition in various ways which are very familiar and upon which it is unnecessary to go into detail. Apart from property matters and the availability of matrimonial remedies, one of the most important changes is that marriage is in modern times regarded as a partnership of equals, and no longer one in which the wife must be the subservient chattel of the husband. Hale's proposition involves that by marriage a wife gives her irrevocable consent to sexual intercourse with her husband under all circumstances and irrespective of the state of her health or how she happens to be feeling at the time. In modern times any reasonable person must regard that conception as quite unacceptable.[43]

Like Lord Lane CJ, Lord Keith was heavily influenced by Lord Emslie's judgment in *S v HM Advocate*, which stated that:

A live system of law will always have regard to changing circumstances to test the justification for any exception to the application of a general rule. Nowadays it cannot seriously be maintained that by marriage a wife submits herself irrevocably to sexual intercourse in all circumstances. It cannot be affirmed nowadays, whatever the position may have been in earlier centuries, that it is an incident of modern marriage that a wife consents to intercourse in all circumstances, including sexual intercourse obtained only by force. There is no doubt that a wife does not consent to assault upon her person and there is no plausible justification for saying today that she nevertheless is to be taken to consent to intercourse by assault.[44]

Throughout the judgments of both Lord Lane CJ and Lord Keith their primary concern was to examine what would be the best rule. There was no explicit consideration of the retroactive effect on the defendant of the final abolition of the immunity. Similarly, the majority of the High Court of Australia was content to

40 [1992] 1 AC 599, 610 (CA).
41 *Ibid* 611.
42 [1992] 1 AC 599, 623 (HL).
43 *Ibid* 616.
44 1989 SLT 469, 473.

reject a submission that an obligation to submit to sexual intercourse is a legal consequence of marriage simply by holding that:

> if it was ever the common law that by marriage a wife gave irrevocable consent to sexual intercourse by her husband, it is no longer the common law.[45]

By contrast, in *R v J*, an earlier Crown Court case in which the marital immunity to a charge of rape was applied, Rougier J recognized the potential adjudicative retroactivity of not applying the historical immunity:

> I am mindful that there is an important general principle to be considered here, and that is that the law, especially the criminal law, should be clear so that a man may know where he stands in relation to it. I am not being so fanciful as to suppose that this defendant carefully considered the authorities and took counsel's advice before behaving as is alleged, but the basic principle extends a long way beyond the bounds of this case and should operate to prevent a man being convicted by means of decisions on the law ex post facto.[46]

At the time that the defendant in *R v R* attempted to force himself upon his wife, subject to some exceptions, and despite a judicial trend away from the marital immunity to rape, decided cases indicated that, if none of those exceptions applied, a husband could not, as a matter of law, be convicted of raping his wife, and so R was, at the time that he acted, at liberty to do so.[47] R may or may not have known of this disturbing legal rule but, like everyone, he was prima facie entitled to the ability to rely on the law as it was at the time of his actions. The Court of Appeal and the House of Lords were not, however, concerned with whether R's conduct was within the law at the time of the conduct but rather with the question of whether the law should be changed and thus render his conduct criminal at the time that the conduct occurred. Once that decision was made, the law as decided in *R v R* also applied to cases decided after *R v R* that involved facts that arose before *R v R*.[48]

After the House of Lords' decision in *R v R* that the law should be changed, the compatibility of that change with article 7 of the ECHR, and the application of the changed rule to cases in which the facts arose prior to the change, was tested before the Strasbourg Court in the companion cases of *SW v United Kingdom*[49] and *CR v United Kingdom*.[50] Article 7 of the ECHR, which does not distinguish between statutory and common law crimes, provides, relevantly, that:

45 *The Queen v L* (1991) 174 CLR 379, 390, see also 405.

46 [1991] 1 All ER 759, 768 (CC).

47 Contra Brennan J's view in *The Queen v L* (1991) 174 CLR 379, 391–402 that Hale's statement of the immunity was mistaken when it was made and that the law of marriage was never that a wife's irrevocable standing consent to sexual intercourse with her husband was an incident of marriage. Thus, according to Brennan J at 402, the 'common law fiction' that developed on the basis of Hale's erroneous statement 'has always been offensive to human dignity and incompatible with the legal status of a spouse'. That a right to non-consensual forced intercourse within marriage ever existed was also doubted by Lord Emslie in *S v HM Advocate* 1989 SLT 469, 473.

48 *R v Graham L* [2003] EWCA Crim 1512, [20]; *R v C* [2004] 1 WLR 2098, [22], [25] (CA).

49 (1996) 21 EHRR 363.

50 *Ibid.*

> No one shall be held guilty of any criminal offence on account of any act or omission which did not constitute a criminal offence under national or international law at the time when it was committed.

2 Foreseeability of Legal Change

In determining whether an act or omission constituted a criminal offence at the time of its occurrence, the Strasbourg Court has usually given prominence to 'qualitative requirements, notably those of accessibility and foreseeability'.[51] That court does not object to the progressive interpretation of the law, recognising that there 'will always be a need for elucidation of doubtful points and for adaption to changing circumstances'.[52] Consistently with this flexibility, the court accepts that 'consequences need not be foreseeable with absolute certainty' and applies the lower requirement that a person must be able 'to foresee, to a degree that is reasonable in the circumstances, the consequences which a given action may entail'.[53] In *SW and CR v United Kingdom* the Strasbourg Court held that the English courts' gradual erosion of the marital immunity to a charge of rape made the complete abolition of that immunity foreseeable.[54] Whether the particular defendants actually foresaw the retroactive change was not a question asked by the Strasbourg Court, which was instead rightly concerned with whether the retroactive change was objectively foreseeable.[55] Just as it is the ability to rely on the law, not actual reliance, that militates against retroactivity,[56] so it is the ability to foresee retroactive legal change, rather than actual foresight, that may militate towards overcoming objections to retroactivity.

There is confusion in the authorities about whether foreseeability, to a degree reasonable in the circumstances, may be satisfied with the 'assistance of the [domestic] courts' interpretation'[57] or whether the content of hypothetical legal advice given prior to a court's decision is a surer guide to the reasonable foreseeability of a particular legal consequence.[58]

The decision of the court in criminal proceedings is the consequence that must be foreseeable. To suggest that the court may itself provide interpretive assistance and thereby fulfil the requirement of foreseeability substitutes hindsight for fore-

[51] *SW v United Kingdom* (1996) 21 EHRR 363, [35] citing *Tolstoy Miloslavsky v United Kingdom* (1995) 20 EHRR 442, [37]. The same point is also made in *Cantoni v France* ECtHR (1996) Series A No 20, 1614, [29], *Baskaya v Turkey* (2001) 31 EHRR 10, [36], *Coeme v Belgium* ECtHR 2000-VII 75, [145], *Streletz v Germany* (2001) 33 EHRR 31, [50]–[51], *K-HW v Germany* (2003) 36 EHRR 59, [45], and *Veeber v Estonia (No 2)* (2004) 39 EHRR 6, [33].

[52] *Baskaya v Turkey* (2001) 31 EHRR 10, [39].

[53] *Sunday Times v United Kingdom* (1979) 2 EHRR 245, [49].

[54] *SW v United Kingdom* (1996) 21 EHRR 363, [43].

[55] R Higgins 'Time and Law' (1997) 46 International and Comparative Law Quarterly 501, 508.

[56] Ch 3 Pt B(2).

[57] *Kokkinakis v Greece* (1994) 17 EHRR 397, [52]; *SW v United Kingdom* (1996) 21 EHRR 363, [35]; *Baskaya v Turkey* (2001) 31 EHRR 10, [36]; *Veeber v Estonia (No 2)* (2004) 39 EHRR 6, [30].

[58] *Cantoni v France* ECtHR (1996) Series A No 20, 1614, [35]; *Baskaya v Turkey* (2001) 31 EHRR 10, [37].

seeability and thereby defeats its very purpose: to analyse whether what happened could have been foreseen, to an extent reasonable in the circumstances, before it did happen. An interpretation of a criminal provision by a court at the time of conviction in no way provides interpretive 'assistance' to the accused person.

Notwithstanding some confusion on matters of detail, it is clear that the Strasbourg Court intends the requirements of accessibility and foreseeability 'to enable the applicant to regulate his conduct'.[59] Although the deployment of the concept of foreseeability in this context is said to pursue this laudable aim, it is open to question whether such deployment is consistent with the plain terms of article 7. Even if a changed interpretation of the law is foreseeable, the effect of that change may be that an act which, in the words of article 7, 'did not constitute a criminal offence under national or international law at the time when it was committed' is found at a later time to have been criminal at the time that it was committed. Foreseeable retroactivity is still retroactivity.

Because the terms of article 7 do not, on their face, admit of any exception to the prohibition on retroactive criminal liability other than the conduct being a crime under international law or, pursuant to paragraph 2 of article 7, 'criminal according to the general principles of law recognised by civilised nations' at the time of the conduct,[60] the Strasbourg Court's willingness to allow retroactive criminal liability that was reasonably foreseeable at the time of the conduct later deemed to have been criminal must be examined more closely.

The foundation for the prominence afforded by that court to accessibility and foreseeability in article 7 cases is the case of *Sunday Times v United Kingdom*,[61] the relevant aspect of which was about article 10(2) of the ECHR. Article 10(2) provides that particular legal requirements or consequences must be 'prescribed by law'. To interpret this phrase the court drew on earlier cases interpreting the phrase 'in accordance with the law' contained in article 8(2).[62] To satisfy article 10(2), the law in question must be:

> accessible to the persons concerned and formulated with sufficient precision to enable them—if need be, with appropriate legal advice—to foresee, to a degree that is reasonable in the circumstances, the consequences that a given action may entail.[63]

The Strasbourg Court attaches the same meaning and requirements to the word 'law' wherever that word appears throughout the Convention,[64] and so the

[59] *Rekvenyi v Hungary* ECtHR 1999-III 423, [60].

[60] In s 27(4) of the Charter of Human Rights and Responsibilities Act 2006 (Vic) the only exception is that the conduct constituted a crime under international law at the time that it was committed. There is no reference to general principles of law recognized by the community of nations.

[61] (1979) 2 EHRR 245, [48]–[49]. See also *Tolstoy Miloslavsky v United Kingdom* (1995) 20 EHRR 442, [37].

[62] *Tolstoy Miloslavsky v United Kingdom* (1995) 20 EHRR 442, [37].

[63] *Ibid.* See also *Sunday Times v United Kingdom* (1979) 2 EHRR 245, [49] and *Hashman v United Kingdom* (2000) 30 EHRR 241, [31].

[64] *Coeme v Belgium* ECtHR 2000-VII 75, [145]; *Baskaya v Turkey* (2001) 31 EHRR 10, [36]. The same meaning has also been adopted for the expressions 'lawful' and 'in accordance with a procedure prescribed by law' in art 5(1): eg *Steel v United Kingdom* (1999) 28 EHRR 603, [54].

requirements of accessibility and foreseeability have been attached to the consideration of the 'law' in article 7 cases.

Though it may be superficially appealing, this transplant to article 7 cases of the concept of foreseeability deployed in other parts of the Convention may be inappropriate, at least without modification. The concern in cases other than those turning on article 7 is that a:

> norm cannot be regarded as a 'law' unless it is formulated with sufficient precision to enable the citizen to regulate his conduct.[65]

To qualify as a 'law' for Convention purposes, a norm, to repeat part of the passage from *Tolstoy Miloslavsky* set out above, must be 'formulated with sufficient precision' to enable a person to foresee 'the consequences that a given action may entail'. In such cases there is no question of the law changing, the concern is only whether the constant law is sufficiently clear for a person to foresee the consequences of her conduct.

If the test for 'law' applicable elsewhere in the Convention was strictly applied to article 7 cases then no retroactive law could pass it, because at the time that foreseeability is to be measured, ie the time of the relevant conduct, the rule later held to be retroactively applicable would never have been formulated, let alone 'formulated with sufficient precision' to meet the requirements of foreseeability. Nor could a rule not yet in existence be 'accessible' at the time of the conduct to which it is later applied.

It would be possible to frame an overarching question applicable both to cases that involve retroactivity and cases that do not: whether the law, considered in general terms rather than only as a specific legal rule, is such that a person can foresee the legal consequences of her conduct. In the case of retroactive legal consequences an additional layer to be considered, which is not present in the absence of retroactivity, is whether the retroactive change to the specific rule in question was reasonably foreseeable.[66] Without making this distinction explicit, this may be the overarching question that the Strasbourg Court asked in *SW and CR v United Kingdom*. The answer given was that the gradual change in the common law meant that the retroactive judicial abolition of the marital immunity to a charge of rape was reasonably foreseeable by a person enjoying competent legal advice. This foreseeability of retroactive legal change was one factor that points towards the departure from the plain terms of article 7 being justifiable, but, in part because an oppressive or discriminatory law may be foreseeable, foreseeability alone is insufficient for such a conclusion to be warranted.

[65] *Hashman v United Kingdom* (2000) 30 EHRR 241, [31].

[66] Cf J Austin *Lectures on Jurisprudence* R Campbell (ed) (5th edn Revised John Murray London 1911) vol 2, 651–2.

3 Heinous Conduct

In the context of noting the Strasbourg Court's view that legal change with retroactive effect was foreseeable in the case of the abolition of the marital immunity to a charge of rape, Waldron[67] quotes Blackstone's view on ex post facto statutes that:

> it is impossible that the party could foresee that an action, innocent when it was done, should be afterwards converted to guilt by a subsequent law.[68]

In a preceding passage, Blackstone indicated that his objection was only to retroactive criminalisation of an act that is 'indifferent in itself'.[69] Blackstone had no objection to the retroactive imposition of criminal liability for acts that are, to use Blackstone's language, 'naturally and intrinsically' wrong.[70] On this approach, in addition to the foreseeability of retroactive legal change, the nature of the conduct retroactively criminalised is crucial.[71]

In *SW and CR v United Kingdom* the Strasbourg Court, after concentrating on the foreseeability of the change of law, also referred to the 'essentially debasing character of rape' which 'is so manifest that the result' produced by the decision of the House of Lords in *R v R* 'cannot be said to be at variance with the object and purpose of Art 7'.[72] Moreover, the court held, the abandonment with retroactive effect of the marital immunity to a charge of rape:

> was in conformity not only with a civilised concept of marriage but also, and above all, with the fundamental objectives of the Convention, the very essence of which is respect for human dignity and human freedom.[73]

Consideration of the gravity of the conduct deemed criminal was even more evident in the Strasbourg Court's judgment in *Streletz v Germany*.[74] The court held that the convictions in unified Germany of border guards of the former German Democratic Republic and their superiors for the manslaughter of persons attempting to cross the border between the German Democratic Republic and the Federal Republic of Germany did not contravene the prohibition on retroactive criminal punishment in article 7. The reasoning in that case has been criticised elsewhere.[75] The important point for present purposes is that in considering whether article 7 was breached, the Strasbourg Court strongly emphasised the

[67] J Waldron 'Retroactive Law: How Dodgy was Duynhoven?' (2004) 10 Otago Law Review 631, 643.

[68] W Blackstone *Commentaries on the Laws of England* (16th edn Cadell London 1825) vol 1, 45.

[69] *Ibid.*

[70] *Ibid* 54. This rests on Blackstone's distinction between acts *mala in se* and acts *mala prohibita*, which is discussed in Ch 2 Pt B. Cf *Christian v The Queen* [2007] 2 WLR 120, [84]–[85].

[71] Cf Ch 4 Pt F(3).

[72] *SW v United Kingdom* (1996) 21 EHRR 363, [44].

[73] *Ibid.*

[74] (2001) 33 EHRR 31; *K-HW v Germany* (2003) 36 EHRR 59.

[75] B Juratowitch 'Retroactive Criminal Liability and International Human Rights Law' (2004) 75 British Year Book of International Law 337.

nature of the conduct in question and, in particular, the fact that it was contrary to provisions of international human rights law such as the right to life and the right to leave any country.

If the conduct retroactively deemed to have been criminal was heinous, then regardless of its precise legal status at the time of its occurrence, *SW and CR v United Kingdom* and *Streletz* indicate that the Strasbourg Court will be more amenable to finding that article 7 has not been breached. Although the Strasbourg Court does not, because of the absolute language of article 7 and its non-derogable status,[76] openly admit it, what is actually happening in such cases is that the general prohibition on the imposition of retroactive criminal liability is defeated by a desire to punish heinous conduct.

A dual focus on foreseeability of the retroactive change and the gravity of the conduct retroactively deemed criminal is also apparent in the subsequent decision of the English Court of Appeal in *R v C.*[77] In that case the appellant was convicted in 2002 of raping his wife in 1970. The appellant argued, relying on article 7(1) of the ECHR, that the prosecution on that count was an abuse of process because the events in issue occurred prior to the Court of Appeal's decision in *R v R*, at which time the law did not recognise that a man could rape his wife. The appellant sought to distinguish *SW and CR v United Kingdom* on the basis that in those cases the events occurred in 1989 at which time the change in the law could have been foreseen with reasonable certainty, whereas there was no such foreseeability in 1970. Judge LJ, for the Court of Appeal, observed that 'a number of exceptions were grafted onto the principle for which Hale provided the untested authority'[78] and proceeded to disagree with the submission made by counsel for the appellant that the content of hypothetical legal advice given in 1970 would have been that while it was morally wrong for the defendant to force himself on his wife he would not be committing a criminal offence in doing so. Judge LJ did not, however, disagree with the concept that the content of hypothetical legal advice at the time of the relevant event is an appropriate mechanism for testing whether the change in the law was foreseeable. Indeed, Judge LJ set out at length what the content of appropriate advice would have been:

> The solicitor would have started by pointing out to his client that to rape his wife would be barbaric, and that he would not condone it. He would then have told his client that the courts had developed and could be expected to continue to develop exceptions to the supposed rule of irrevocable consent, and that if ever the issue were considered in this court, the supposed immunity of a husband from a successful prosecution for rape of his wife might be recognised for what it was, a legal fiction. He would in any event also have told his client that depending on the circumstances he might be convicted of indecent assault on his wife, punishable with imprisonment, and would be liable to be convicted of offences of violence ranging from common assault, by putting her in fear of violence, up to and including wounding or causing grievous bodily harm if he injured her in order

[76] ECHR art 15(2).
[77] [2004] 1 WLR 2098 (CA).
[78] *Ibid* [15].

to force her to have sexual intercourse . . . notwithstanding the repetition of Hale's principle in the authorities, he might be liable for rape, probably liable for indecent assault, and certainly liable for the appropriate offence of violence. On this view therefore he would have been told that he could not rape his wife with complete impunity.[79]

On this approach both the foreseeability of retroactive legal change, which was satisfied by the gradual erosion by judicial decision of the immunity such that it should have been expected that the immunity would eventually be abolished with retroactive effect, and the barbaric nature of rape, including as committed by a husband against his wife, were important factors in the assessment of whether article 7 of the ECHR was breached. Judge LJ quoted the Strasbourg Court's comments on the debasing character of rape and the importance of human dignity and freedom, partly on the basis of which the retroactive effects of the abolition of the marital immunity were held not to be contrary to article 7.[80] Judge LJ, unlike the Strasbourg Court, additionally asserted reliance on article 7(2) of the ECHR,[81] holding that:

Article 7(2) provides ample justification for a husband's trial and punishment for the rape of his wife, according to the general principles recognised by civilised nations. Indeed, as it seems to us, it would be surprising to discover that the law in any civilised country protected a woman from rape, with the solitary and glaring exception of rape by the man who had promised to love and comfort her.[82]

Although there was no attempt actually to identify the relevant laws in other legal systems,[83] article 7(2) was used by the Court of Appeal, in combination with its emphasis on the barbaric nature of rape, to conclude that even though judicial decisions indicated the existence of legal immunity to a charge of rape at the time that the appellant acted:

This appellant knew perfectly well that to rape his wife was wrong, and that his marriage certificate did not entitle him to force his unwanted sexual attentions on her, nor did he suggest that he believed that he would be immune from prosecution if he did so.[84]

This sensible approach to the issue is not universally accepted. Of *SW and CR v United Kingdom* it has been commented that the Strasbourg Court:

[79] *Ibid* [19].

[80] *Ibid* [23].

[81] Which provides that art 7 'shall not prejudice the trial and punishment of a person for any act or ommission which at the time when it was committed, was criminal according to the general principles of law recognised by civilised nations'.

[82] *Ibid* [24]; contra *SW v United Kingdom* (1996) 21 EHRR 363, 381 (European Commission of Human Rights) Dissenting opinion of L Loucaides, joined by S Trechsel, MA Nowicki and I Cabral Barreto; R Beddard 'Retrospective Crime' (1995) 145 New Law Journal 663, 664–5.

[83] Such an endeavour is not within the scope of this book, but, eg, Cadoppi reports that the Italian Corte di Cassazione in 1976 deemed rape to be a crime that was possible within marriage: A Cadoppi '*Nulla Poena Sine Lege* and Scots Criminal Law: A Continental Perspective' [1998] Juridical Review 73, 81–2.

[84] [2004] 1 WLR 2098, [26] (CA).

> has approved a radical reversal of the previous law, out of social and moral concerns. Judicial legislation of this kind, in the light of changing perceptions, is the very problem against which Article 7 is directed.[85]

It is true that the type of legal change that occurred in the marital rape cases engages the terms of article 7 of the ECHR. The pressing question is whether the heinous nature of the conduct under consideration, combined with the foreseeability of retroactive change, justified departure from the plain terms of article 7. There are two more matters briefly to be considered before answering that question.

4 Changed Status of Women

Judicial objection to the barbarity of rape committed within marriage was set in the context of the empowerment of women within marriage. At the time that Hale asserted the existence of the immunity and Hume proposed a similar rule in Scotland: 'a married woman could be said', according to the Scottish High Court of Justiciary, 'to have subjected herself to her husband's dominion in all things. She was required to obey him in all things.'[86] At the time of the abolition of any immunity that may have existed in Scots law, the court observed, by contrast, that a 'husband and wife are now for all practical purposes equal partners in marriage'.[87] This change in the social and legal incidents of marriage motivated abolition with retroactive effect of a husband's immunity to a charge of raping his wife.

5 An Illogical Immunity

A final consideration is that the historical immunity was not only morally but also logically unattractive. As mentioned by Judge LJ, a husband who forced himself upon his wife could be guilty of criminal offences of violence committed in the course of doing so, but could not be guilty of the actual act of non-consensual intercourse. In 1954 *R v Miller*[88] established the incongruous position that although a man could not be liable for the rape of his wife he could be found guilty of assault occasioning actual bodily harm for causing injury to his wife's state of mind by roughly forcing intercourse with her. Of this case, Lord Keith said in *R v R* that it:

[85] C Osborne 'Does the End Justify the Means? Retrospectivity, Article 7, and the Marital Rape Exemption' [1996] European Human Rights Law Review 406, 416.

[86] *S v HM Advocate* 1989 SLT 469, 473.

[87] *Ibid.*

[88] [1954] 2 QB 282, 292 (Assizes).

> is unrealistic to sort out the sexual intercourse from the other acts involved in the assault and to allow the wife to complain of the minor acts but not of the major and most unpleasant one.[89]

It might have been thought by men responsible for the law in centuries, or even decades, gone by that rape was entirely a sexual matter and not, in itself, a matter of violence. It is now appreciated that rape is and always has been a sexual crime *and* an inherently violent crime, so to criminalise a husband's battery against his wife but not his rape of his wife was anomalous.

6 Conclusions on the Marital Rape Cases

The marital rape cases present a difficult problem. Conduct that did not expose a man responsible for it to criminal liability at the time of that conduct was the basis of a subsequent conviction, thus prima facie contravening the prohibition on retroactive criminal laws. Yet there are strong reasons to think that criminal liability, even retroactively imposed, was appropriate. In exceptional cases like *SW and CR v United Kingdom* and *Streletz*, the Strasbourg Court has, because the terms of article 7 allow exceptions only in very restricted circumstances, pretended that there has been no retroactivity. This approach merits criticism for its unwillingness to acknowledge that retroactive criminal liability has occurred and for its refusal openly to grapple with the problem. However, the very concerns that cumulatively motivated the English courts and the Strasbourg Court in the marital rape cases to find as they did, provide strong reasons to think that the prohibition expressed in article 7 should be interpreted as being defeasible in exceptional circumstances.

There were four considerations in the marital rape cases that militated towards the defeat of the prohibition on retroactive criminal liability. First, the gradual erosion of the immunity by a series of judicial decisions made it reasonably foreseeable that the immunity would be abolished with retroactive effect. Second, the conduct involved was so heinous and inconsistent with respect for human dignity and freedom that its punishment was a greater imperative than adherence to a strict prohibition on retroactive criminal liability. Third, women had become significantly more empowered within marriage since the assertion of the immunity. Fourth, the law was not only unjust, but also illogical insofar as criminal liability existed for acts associated with rape within marriage but not for rape itself.

Objections to the suggestion that article 7 should be interpreted as being defeasible in circumstances other than those mentioned in the article itself can be imagined, not least that the very purpose of the prohibition may be undermined by an admission of its defeasibility in circumstances not identified in advance. It should be remembered, however, that article 7(2), which permits conviction for conduct that was not criminal in the domestic legal system at the time of the conduct if that

[89] [1992] 1 AC 599, 619 (HL).

conduct was 'criminal according to the general principles of law recognised by civilised nations', was included to emphasise that article 7(1):

> did not affect laws which, under the very exceptional circumstances at the end of the Second World War, were passed in order to suppress war-crimes, treason and collaboration with the enemy, and did not aim at any legal or moral condemnation of these laws.[90]

Of retroactive liability for the war crime of aggression, the International Military Tribunal at Nuremberg thought that:

> To assert that it is unjust to punish those who in defiance of treaties and assurances have attacked neighbouring states without warning is obviously untrue, for in such circumstances the attacker must know that he is doing wrong, and so far from it being unjust to punish him, it would be unjust if his wrong were allowed to go unpunished.[91]

Thus, from its inception, article 7 has envisaged the possibility of exceptions to the prohibition on retroactive criminal liability, including on the basis of an imperative to punish heinous conduct. Subsequent experience has revealed that justice requires that article 7 should be read so that those exceptions are not limited only to the plain terms of that article, though they should remain truly exceptional. The marital rape cases were exceptional. The legal rule that granted immunity to a man who raped his wife was so abhorrent that no court committed to justice should ever have applied it[92] and, when this was finally realized, it was better to give that realisation retroactive force than to allow an unjust immunity to shield from punishment a person responsible for such heinous conduct.

D Restitution of Money Paid under a Mistake of Law

1 The Facts and Issues in *Kleinwort Benson v Lincoln County Council*

Kleinwort Benson v Lincoln County Council[93] has stimulated a glut of commentary. The present objective is not to review existing commentary, or to evaluate the soundness of the decision from the point of view of the law of unjust enrichment, but only to examine the intertemporal issues in the case. A basic account of the factual background is a necessary precursor to this undertaking.

[90] Report of the Committee of Experts CM/WP 1 (50) 15 (16 March 1950): TP iii, 485, quoted in JES Fawcett *The Application of the European Convention on Human Rights* (2nd edn Clarendon Press Oxford 1987) 201.

[91] (1947) 41 American Journal of International Law 172, 217. See also Lord Rodger 'A Time for Everything under the Law: Some Reflections on Retrospectivity' (2005) 121 Law Quarterly Review 57, 66.

[92] Contra the disturbing assertions made in defence of the rule by G Williams 'The Problem of Domestic Rape' (1991) 141 New Law Journal 205–7, 246–7.

[93] [1999] 2 AC 349 (HL).

Following the decision of the House of Lords in *Hazell v Hammersmith and Fulham London Borough Council*[94] that interest rate swap agreements entered into by local authorities were void for being ultra vires the Local Government Act 1972 (Eng), Kleinwort Benson, a bank, sought restitution of the sums that it paid to local authorities under such agreements. At the time of the transactions all parties were operating under the mistaken belief that the transactions were intra vires the local authorities' statutory foundation. The bank thought that other causes of action that may have been open to it were barred by lapse of time, but that time for bringing a claim based on mistake would only run from the date of the decision in *Hazell* when the mistake became discoverable, and so a claim of mistake would be within time. Thus the bank submitted that the 'long-established rule'[95] that did not allow restitution of money paid under a mistake of law,[96] which had never enjoyed the authority of the House of Lords, 'should no longer form part of the English law of restitution'.[97]

A majority of the House of Lords held that restitution of money paid under a mistake of law should be available and that Kleinwort Benson was entitled to restitution because it paid the money under a mistake of law constituted by the belief that the local authorities could lawfully enter into the transactions and were therefore legally entitled to the payments. Lords Browne-Wilkinson and Lloyd dissented. The relevant aspect of dissent for present purposes was Lord Browne-Wilkinson's view that 'at the time of the payment, the payer was not labouring under any mistake'.[98] Lord Browne-Wilkinson accepted that judicial decisions have retrospective effect, but added:

> retrospection cannot falsify history: if at the date of each payment it was settled law that local authorities had capacity to enter into swap contracts, the bank were not labouring under any mistake of law at that date. The subsequent decision in Hazell could not create a mistake where no mistake existed at the time.[99]

This approach highlights the crux of the intertemporal issues in the case.

In seeking to understand *Kleinwort Benson* it is important to separate the two different decisions that were involved. The first decision, *Hazell*, decided that local authorities could not lawfully engage in interest rate swap transactions. Such transactions were ultra vires and were ultra vires when they occurred. There was no prior judicial decision indicating otherwise, though there was no doubt a practical assumption that such transactions were permissible, supported in theoretical terms by a presumption of legality of acts of public authorities. *Hazell* did not deem the law to be otherwise than it in fact was, it simply decided a point for the first time and did so contrary to what many people apparently believed the law

[94] [1992] 2 AC 1 (HL).

[95] [1999] 2 AC 349, 366 (HL).

[96] *Bilbie v Lumley* (1802) 2 East 469; 102 ER 448. The High Court of Australia rejected that rule in *David Securities v Commonwealth Bank of Australia* (1992) 175 CLR 353, 370–76, 401–2.

[97] [1999] 2 AC 349, 366 (HL).

[98] *Ibid* 357.

[99] *Ibid* 358.

to be.[100] Thus it involved no retroactivity in the sense explained in the first chapter.[101]

By contrast, *Kleinwort Benson* did make a retroactive change to the law insofar as it held that money paid under a mistake of law may be recoverable. There was prior judicial authority to the contrary, which was overruled, with retroactive effect, by *Kleinwort Benson*. From the time of the decision in *Kleinwort Benson* onwards, subject to statutes of limitation, issue estoppel, res judicata and the doctrine of merger, it has been possible to claim restitution of money paid under a mistake of law whensoever the payment was made and whensoever the mistake was discoverable. With that important distinction between *Hazell* and *Kleinwort Benson* established, the next question, and the basis of Lord Browne-Wilkinson's dissent, is the time at which the mistake of law is to be assessed.

A mistake is where someone believes one thing when something else is actually the case. It is a dissonance between belief and reality. A mistake can occur only if these two things are compared at the same point in time; but to say that the inquiry is into the *actual* position at the time of the payment being made on the basis of the *belief* that there was a legal obligation to pay, does not mean that the *assessment* of the actual and supposed positions cannot occur at a later time. Indeed, the nature of adjudication is such that the assessment can only occur at a later date. *Hazell* decided that that there was no legal obligation to pay at the time of the payments being made. In *Kleinwort Benson* it was held that because the bank thought it was obliged to pay, but at the time of the payment it was actually not obliged to pay, that it had made a mistake of law and was entitled to restitution on that ground.[102]

Kleinwort Benson was not as complicated as it might have been, because *Hazell* did not involve any retroactivity. *Hazell* was just a decision made in 1991 that when the transactions occurred between 1982 and 1985 that they were, in 1982 to 1985, beyond the statutory power of the local authorities. Presumably a case will one day arise where the judicial decision that reveals that a payment was made under a mistake of law will involve retroactivity. It will hold that a payment made in accordance with binding judicial authority was mistaken because the court now takes a different view of the law and overrules that prior decision with retroactive effect. If that had occurred in *Kleinwort Benson* there would have been two examples of retroactivity in the same case: the decision retroactively creating a mistake of law and the retroactive decision that restitution of a payment made under a mistake of law may be available. Fortunately, as the latter position is now settled, when the case arises in which the mistake of law is retroactively created by a judicial decision overruling a prior judicial decision, there will only be one retroactive issue to deal with in the case. When it arises, the majority's logic in *Kleinwort Benson* will be applicable.

[100] *Ibid* 411.
[101] See also Ch 5 Pt A(3).
[102] [1999] 2 AC 349, 379, 400, 411 (HL).

The mistake must occur at the time of the payment, but as the existence of that mistake will be assessed at a later point in time, if at that later point in time the law is changed with retroactive effect then one of those retroactive effects will be to deem that a mistake existed at the earlier time.[103] Such is the power of retroactivity. It can, at a later time, deem something to have been the law at an earlier time, which was not actually the law at that earlier time. It is true that if a person pays money in accordance with a binding precedent of the highest court then, at the time of payment, he is not acting under a mistake of law. However, if at the time of the case being determined the law relevant to the question of whether the money was paid under a mistake of law is changed with retroactive effect, meaning that the law at the earlier time is deemed to have been something that it was not, then in assessing whether it should at the later time be held that payment was made at the earlier time under a mistake of law, it is the retroactively effective later law under which that decision should be made. A retroactively created mistake of law is still a mistake of law. This hypothetical case contrasts with what actually happened in *Kleinwort Benson* in which the bank was actually mistaken at the time of the payment, not retroactively deemed to have been mistaken, though the mistake did not become known until the decision in *Hazell*. However the approach just outlined should also have traction for those who think that the bank and the local authorities were acting in accordance with the law applicable at the time that they acted, and that the law was retroactively changed in *Hazell*.

A major concern arising from the decision of the House of Lords in *Kleinwort Benson* was its potential to disturb settled transactions. *Kleinwort Benson* itself involved recovery of money paid more than six years prior to the commencement of proceedings and was decided on the basis that section 32(1)(c) of the Limitation Act 1980 (Eng), which provided that in actions for relief from the consequences of a mistake the period of limitation shall not run until the plaintiff had discovered the mistake or with reasonable diligence could have discovered it, was operative on the basis that the mistake of law was not discoverable until the decision of the House of Lords in *Hazell*.[104] In a case involving a prior judicial decision being overruled with retroactive effect and so retroactively creating a mistake of law deemed to have existed at the time of an earlier payment, the date of discoverability of the mistake may not be for a very long time after the relevant transaction occurred. Lord Goff recognized that the period was potentially 'indefinite' and accordingly recommended urgent legislative change.[105] The Law Commission's sensible proposal is that a three year time limit should begin to run from the date of discoverability[106] but that, in any event, a claim may not be brought more than ten years after the mistake was deemed to have been made.[107]

[103] Cf *Deutsche Morgan Grenfell v Inland Revenue Commissioners* [2006] 3 WLR 781, [23] (HL).

[104] Contra *Torrens Aloha v Citibank* (1997) 72 FCR 581, 593–9.

[105] [1999] 2 AC 349, 389 (HL).

[106] Law Commission of England and Wales *Limitation of Actions* (Law Com No 270, 2001) [3.7], [3.39], [3.98].

[107] *Ibid* [3.101], [3.113], [4.77]–[4.78].

2 Reasons for Retroactivity

Because the only retroactivity involved in *Kleinwort Benson* was the change in the law to allow recovery of money paid under a mistake of law, it is only that change that requires evaluation for whether it appropriately overcame a presumptive judicial reluctance to alter established legal rules.

At first glance it might seem that reliance considerations have no place in an area of the law dealing with mistake. A claim of mistake of law can only arise if the law was not known and so it could not be relied upon. This approach confuses, however, the two rules under consideration. The first was the rule about which the payer was mistaken, in *Kleinwort Benson*, whether the Local Government Act empowered the local authorities to enter into the transactions and thus whether the bank was obliged to pay what it owed pursuant to those transactions. The second rule was that payments made under a mistake about *any* law are not recoverable. This second rule was knowable at the time of making the mistake about the first rule and could conceivably have been relied on by the local authorities for general risk assessments about the certainty of transactions. Such an assessment could have included the fact that it was a known legal rule that if it turned out that the bank paid money to the local authorities under a mistake of law, including the mistake that was in fact subsequently found to exist, that such money would not be recoverable by the bank in restitution.

Framed in this way, reliance on a blanket refusal to allow restitution of money received by a person not entitled to it, who only received it because some other person wrongly believed that there was a legal obligation to pay it, is not a form of reliance deserving of protection. Things would be different if, the payment having been made, the recipient actually relied in good faith on its apparent entitlement to the payment. In such circumstances, the defence of change of position may be operative. Lord Goff,[108] in making the change to allow recovery of payments made under a mistake of law, emphasised that the recognition of a defence of change of position within a coherent law of restitution founded upon the principle of unjust enrichment, in 1991,[109] was a fundamental development in the law since the creation, in 1802,[110] of the rule that payments made under a mistake of law were not recoverable, which made the change in the law effected by *Kleinwort Benson* 'inevitable'.[111] Lord Goff held that:

> a blanket rule of non-recovery, irrespective of the justice of the case, cannot sensibly survive in a rubric of the law based on the principle of unjust enrichment; and because recognition of a defence of change of position demonstrates that this must be proved in

[108] [1999] 2 AC 349, 373 (HL). See also *David Securities v Commonwealth Bank of Australia* (1992) 175 CLR 353, 384–6.

[109] *Lipkin Gorman v Karpnale* [1991] 2 AC 548 (HL).

[110] *Bilbie v Lumley* (1802) 2 East 469; 102 ER 448.

[111] [1999] 2 AC 349, 373 (HL).

> fact if it is to justify retention, in whole or in part, of money which would otherwise be repayable on the ground that the payee was unjustly enriched by its receipt.[112]

Since the recognition of the defence of change of position, the law of unjust enrichment has a mechanism for dealing with particular cases of actual reliance, which means that there was no obstacle on the grounds of reliance to abolishing with retroactive effect the rule that there could never be restitution of a payment made under mistake of law. Because it would involve relying on keeping, in all circumstances, money to which there was no entitlement, the ability to rely on that rule was not worth protecting.

A further reason that the retroactivity in *Kleinwort Benson* was not objectionable was that the respondent local authorities did not seek to defend the rule that money paid under a mistake of law was not recoverable. There had been 'prolonged criticism of the rule by scholars',[113] recent decisions of courts in other major common law jurisdictions had abrogated the rule, the civil law did not apply a blanket exclusion of recovery of money paid under a mistake of law, and the point had never been determined by the House of Lords.[114] All of these additional factors added to the force of the argument that a principled approach to the law of unjust enrichment as it had developed, required that the rule be changed. The fact that any potential reliance considerations were not worth protecting because, in the absence of the defence of change of position being made out, such reliance would have been on a supposed entitlement to retain a payment to which a party was not entitled in the first place, means that there is no convincing objection to the change in the law being made retroactively by way of judicial decision.

E Private Law

Private law, or at least certain parts of it, is generally thought to be an area in which caution must be exercised before effecting retroactive change. In its 1966 Practice Statement in which it announced its intention to depart from its previous decisions when it appears right to do so, the House of Lords assured that it would:

> bear in mind the danger of disturbing retrospectively the basis on which contracts, settlements of property and fiscal arrangements have been entered into.[115]

Judicial expressions of reluctance to change the law affecting contracts, property settlements and other areas in which existing commercial arrangements may be

[112] *Ibid.*
[113] *Ibid* 368.
[114] *Ibid* 368–75.
[115] *Practice Statement (Judicial Precedent)* [1966] 1 WLR 1234 (HL).

upset are plentiful, both before and since that Practice Statement.[116] However, often the very case in which such a cautionary statement is made is one in which the common law is changed in an area of private law.[117] In such cases the caution may serve as a judicial acknowledgement of the seriousness of what is about to be done, but it does not prevent it from being done. The present task is to examine cases in which private law rules have been created or changed that demonstrate issues of retroactivity.

1 The Creation of New Law without Overruling Prior Authority

(a) Existing Authorities in Disarray Making a Degree of Retroactivity Inevitable

The most famous common law case in this category, if not the most famous common law case, is *Donoghue v Stevenson*,[118] in which the minority and majority were agreed that the existing authorities were not in a coherent state. Lord Macmillan, for example, observed that 'the current of authority has by no means always set in the same direction'.[119] The House of Lords had not previously ruled on the matter in question. All of the Law Lords in the case were concerned both with attempting to discern the existing law and, because of its uncertain state, with what, as a matter of principle, rooted in the existing authorities, the law should be held to be for application in the case before them.[120] The House, by a three to two decision, held that the manufacturer of a bottled drink owed a duty of care to those intended by the manufacturer to consume the drink to take care to avoid injuring them. Lord Atkin emphasised that his famous statement of general principle[121] was deduced from previous cases. He further indicated that even if decided cases did not explicitly support his decision, that none could be found to dispute it and reasons of principle and justice required that there be a legal remedy for so obvious a social wrong.[122]

The uniform concern in all of the judgments in *Donoghue v Stevenson* was with identifying the best legal rule, not with its retroactive impact on manufacturers who had already produced and sold things under the previous law without the ability to know about the duty of care to end users that would subsequently be imposed upon them with retroactive effect. Because the judgments indicate that the previous legal position was unclear, and probably in no fit state to be relied upon, the case is in the

[116] Eg *Bourne v Keane* [1919] AC 815, 860, 874 (HL); *Geelong Harbour Trust Commissioners v Gibbs Bright* (1970) 122 CLR 504, 518; Lord Reid 'The Judge as Lawmaker' (1972) 12 Journal of the Society of Public Teachers of Law 22, 23; *The Hannah Blumenthal* [1983] 1 AC 854, 913, 922 (HL); *Re Spectrum Plus (in liquidation)* [2005] 2 AC 680, [63]–[64] (HL).

[117] Eg *Bourne v Keane* [1919] AC 815 (HL); *Re Spectrum Plus (in liquidation)* [2005] 2 AC 680 (HL).

[118] [1932] AC 562 (HL).

[119] *Ibid* 612.

[120] *Ibid* 577–8, 582–3, 618.

[121] *Ibid* 580.

[122] *Ibid* 583.

category of 'hard cases' discussed by Hart, 'which the law has left incompletely regulated and where there is no known state of clear law to justify expectations'.[123] In such cases objections to retroactivity fade away because, in the absence of an applicable rule knowable in advance, whatever decision is reached about the applicable law, it will, from the perspective of the litigants, have retroactive effect and at least one of them will be prejudiced by that retroactivity.[124]

Assuming that the duty of care found to exist in *Donoghue v Stevenson* did not exist prior to its formulation in that case, it is, apart from the issue of insurance, nonetheless:

> difficult to believe . . . that the manufacturers in *Donoghue v Stevenson* would have conducted themselves differently had they known that the law was what the House of Lords later declared it to be.[125]

If, contrary to this view, manufacturers relied upon the absence of a duty of care to end users and therefore adopted careless practices in disregard of the harm that might be caused to people within their contemplation, it would be difficult to have any sympathy for the protection of an ability to engage in such reliance. Manufacturers were not previously at liberty to produce defective goods. They were undoubtedly under obligations to those to whom they sold the goods. The only question was whether their liability extended to damage caused to other people. Although the retroactive effect of the decision did not play any explicit role in the reasoning of any of the Law Lords who decided *Donoghue v Stevenson*, no strong objection to the decision could be mounted on the grounds of its retroactivity. The uncertain state of the law had already negated any ability to rely on the law, including for insurance purposes. Furthermore, any reliance that there might have been on the absence of a duty of care to end users was not a form of reliance worthy of protection, and there was no liberty interest at stake.

(b) Ability to Rely on the Law not in Issue

Given that the desirability of an ability to rely on the law is a crucial rationale of the presumption against retroactivity, if that rationale is inapplicable in a particular case, a substantial objection to the retroactive effect of a decision creating new law will be removed. *Donoghue v Stevenson* is one example of such a case.[126] *The Wagon Mound No 2*[127] is another. That for liability in negligence to exist the damage caused must have been reasonably foreseeable was established, both by the Privy Council in *The Wagon Mound No 1*[128] and by the House of Lords in *Hughes v Lord Advocate*.[129] The issue in *The Wagon Mound No 2* was the application of

[123] HLA Hart *The Concept of Law* (2nd edn Clarendon Press Oxford 1994) 276.
[124] See also Ch 3 Pt E(3).
[125] R Cross and J Harris *Precedent in English Law* (4th edn Clarendon Press Oxford 1991) 32.
[126] See also C Sampford *Retrospectivity and the Rule of Law* (Oxford University Press 2006) 86–7.
[127] [1967] 1 AC 617 (PC).
[128] [1961] AC 388 (PC), discussed in Ch 5 Pt E(2)(b).
[129] [1963] AC 837 (HL).

that test in cases in which the risk of the damage occurring could be described as 'remote'. Lord Reid, delivering the advice of the Privy Council, held that Walsh J's decision in the Supreme Court of New South Wales, from which the appeal lay directly, that 'if a real risk can properly be described as remote it must then be held to be not reasonably foreseeable'[130] was, although a view open on the authorities at the time of Walsh J's decision, not a view with which the Privy Council agreed as a matter of principle.

Instead, Lord Reid held that if:

> it is clear that the reasonable man would have realised or foreseen and prevented the risk, then it must follow that the appellant is liable in damages

even if the risk could properly be described as 'remote' so long as the risk was not one that a reasonable man would 'brush aside as far-fetched' and 'if action to eliminate it presented no difficulty, involved no disadvantage, and required no expense'.[131] This is not the place to add to the extensive criticism that has been directed at the advice of the Privy Council on the ground that it involved an unwarranted and dramatic expansion of the risks for which defendants are liable. The only point sought to be made here is that the conduct that gave rise to the case would probably not have been any different if the law at the time of that conduct was then as it was later held by the Privy Council to have been. Thus, whatever complaints might be made about the decision on other grounds, subject to the issue of insurance, none can sensibly be made on the ground of its retroactive effects.

(c) Gradual Development of New Law

The development in English law of the doctrine of *forum non conveniens*, 'one of the most civilised of legal principles',[132] illustrates the gradual adoption of a legal rule the retroactive effects of which did not provide any compelling reason against its adoption. The law prior to the majority decision of the House of Lords in *The Atlantic Star*[133] was, broadly, that if a plaintiff could establish the jurisdiction of the English courts over a defendant then he could pursue the action in England so long as he was not acting vexatiously or oppressively or in abuse of the processes of the English court.[134] This was largely on the ground that the 'right of access to the King's court must not be lightly refused,'[135] a position that Lord Reid thought rooted in:

[130] [1967] 1 AC 617, 643 (PC).

[131] *Ibid* 643–4.

[132] *Airbus Industrie v Patel* [1999] 1 AC 119, 141 (HL).

[133] [1974] AC 436 (HL).

[134] *St Pierre v South American Stores (Gath and Chaves)* [1936] 1 KB 382 (CA), especially 398 and see the discussions in *The Atlantic Star* [1974] AC 436, 453 (HL) and *The Abidin Daver* [1984] 1 AC 398, 417–18 (HL). The law in Australia remains closer to this position: *Oceanic Sun Line v Fay* (1988) 165 CLR 197; *Voth v Manildra* (1991) 171 CLR 538.

[135] *St Pierre v South American Stores (Gath and Chaves)* [1936] 1 KB 382, 398 (CA).

> the good old days, the passing of which many may regret, when inhabitants of this island felt an innate superiority over those unfortunate enough to belong to other races.[136]

As Lord Reid observed in *The Atlantic Star*, this situation meant that jurisdiction could be established in England where:

> Neither the parties nor the subject matter of the action need have any connection with England. There may be proceedings on the same subject matter in a foreign court. It may be a far more appropriate forum. The defendant may have to suffer great expense and inconvenience in coming here. In the end the decisions of the English and foreign courts may conflict.[137]

In *The Atlantic Star* Lord Reid thought it time for a re-examination of this 'rather insular doctrine'[138] and its consequences. A 'liberal' reading was given to 'vexatious' and 'oppressive' to expand the range of circumstances in which proceedings commenced in England as of right could be stayed by the exercise of a discretion of the English court.[139]

The next developmental step was taken in *MacShannon v Rockware Glass*[140] in which the tests of oppression and vexation were discarded entirely and replaced with a focus on the defendant seeking a stay of English proceedings established as of right needing to satisfy the English court that there is:

> another forum to whose jurisdiction he is amenable in which justice can be done between the parties at substantially less inconvenience or expense

and that:

> the stay must not deprive the plaintiff of a legitimate personal or juridical advantage which would be available to him if he invoked the jurisdiction of the English court.[141]

In sum, because the law developed to focus on whether justice required that the jurisdiction of the English court be stayed,[142] it became easier for a defendant to convince an English court to decline jurisdiction, though this was still done within the analytical framework that had survived from Scott LJ's judgment in *St Pierre v South American Stores.*[143]

In the *Abidin Daver* Lord Diplock noted that although the opinion of the narrow majority in *The Atlantic Star* was 'initially accepted with reluctance' and 'treated at first as having been decided on its own special facts rather than being of wider import', looked at ten years after the decision, it had 'become readily identifiable not as a mere decision upon its own exceptional facts but as a landmark case'.[144] This

136 *The Atlantic Star* [1974] AC 436, 453 (HL).
137 *Ibid.*
138 *Ibid.*
139 *Ibid* 454, 468, 477.
140 [1978] AC 795 (HL).
141 *Ibid* 812, see also 819 but cf 828–9.
142 *Ibid* 819.
143 [1936] 1 KB 382, 398 (CA).
144 [1984] 1 AC 398, 407 (HL).

landmark ultimately led Lord Diplock to be able to say by the time of *The Abidin Daver* that 'judicial chauvinism has been replaced by judicial comity'[145] and that English law had become indistinguishable from the Scottish doctrine of *forum non conveniens*. This process of development culminated in the authoritative statement of English law relating to *forum non conveniens* made by Lord Goff in *Spiliada Maritime Corp v Cansulex*,[146] which was, in raw terms, that if jurisdiction is established as of right in England, a stay will be granted on the grounds of *forum non conveniens* if the defendant can satisfy the court that there is another forum that is 'clearly or distinctly more appropriate than the English forum'.[147] If that is established by the defendant a stay will be granted unless the plaintiff can satisfy the court that 'there are special circumstances by reason of which justice requires that the trial should nevertheless take place' in England.[148]

This is a substantially different position from the law as stated in *St Pierre v South American Stores*, yet it was formed gradually over the course of a number of decisions and without ever moving too far from the previous decision on the point. Lord Wright might have said that the fully grown tree of the doctrine of *forum non conveniens* as expressed in *Spiliada* was unrecognisable from the sapling represented by *St Pierre v South American Stores*, but that at all steps between those two points, the identity of English law on the staying of jurisdiction established as of right was, though gradually changing, coherently maintained.[149] This carefully constructed doctrine was brusquely swept aside by the decision of the European Court of Justice in *Owusu v Jackson*[150] that, because of the European Union Judgments Regulation,[151] any proceedings commenced in the English jurisdiction cannot be stayed on grounds of *forum non conveniens*.

At no point in the judgments in any of the English cases was explicit consideration given to the retroactive effect of the changes in the law that were being made. The concern throughout was with the best formulation of the legal rule and with its application. On one view decisions made by plaintiffs to, for example, allow to lapse the time in which foreign proceedings must be brought, or to go to the trouble and expense of arresting a ship and initiating proceedings in England in the knowledge that the ship would provide security for a potential judgment in their favour, in reliance on the view of the law judicially accepted as authoritative at the time of those practical decisions being made, demanded, but were not afforded, judicial respect in considering whether to change the law to the detriment of plaintiffs' ability to choose to litigate in England regardless of the contacts of the litigation to England, so long as jurisdiction could be established. However, the better

[145] *Ibid* 411.

[146] [1987] 1 AC 460, 476–8 (HL).

[147] *Ibid* 477.

[148] *Ibid* 476.

[149] Cf Lord Wright 'The Study of Law' (1938) 54 Law Quarterly Review 185, 194, discussed in Ch 5 Pt B.

[150] [2005] ECR I-1383.

[151] Council Reg 44/2001 EC on jurisdiction and the recognition and enforcement of judgments in civil and commercial matters.

view is that the area of law being changed and the nature of the change made to it were such that the very focus of the judicial decisions changing the law was on what was most just between the parties and what was in the interests of justice generally.

Any specific disadvantage suffered by the plaintiff, including because of a change in the law, could be taken account of in the exercise of judicial discretion, for example by the English court requiring an undertaking from a defendant that it would waive an otherwise applicable time bar in the foreign natural forum as a condition to the English court declining to exercise its own jurisdiction.[152] In all cases, the application of the doctrine of *forum non conveniens* was not intended to affect a party's substantive rights or to prevent the adjudication of those rights. It was directed only towards where that adjudication took place. Just as the right to a fair trial does not dictate where that fair trial occurs,[153] nor can a concern about the retroactive effects of judicial decisions incorporate too much concern for one of those effects being a different forum for the determination of substantive rights rather than actual alteration of substantive rights themselves.

An area in which there is greater potential for reliance interests to be affected by retroactive change to the law is the gradual development of the legal protection of privacy. No general tort of invasion of privacy has been recognized in England or Australia,[154] but a right to privacy is a value underlying more specific causes of action.[155] Existing causes of action such as trespass to land[156] and breach of confidence[157] protect privacy interests. The extent of that protection has grown, but a consistent skeleton of principle is apparent.[158] Perhaps the most notable development is that the action for breach of confidence has outgrown its attachment to the existence of a confidential relationship and now rests on the nature of the information.[159] In English law the development of the action for breach of confidence has been significantly influenced by article 8 of the ECHR.[160] The incorporation of article 8, which provides for a right to private and family life, into the domestic law of the United Kingdom means that the 'legal landscape has altered'.[161] The legal protection of privacy continues to develop.[162] Indeed the

[152] *Spiliada Maritime Corp v Cansulex* [1987] 1 AC 460, 486–8 (HL).

[153] *OT Africa Line v Hijazy* [2001] 1 Lloyd's Rep 76, [42] (QB).

[154] *Wainwright v Home Office* [2004] 2 AC 406 (HL); *ABC v Lenah Game Meats* (2001) 208 CLR 199.

[155] *Campbell v MGN* [2004] 2 AC 457, [43] (HL).

[156] *Entick v Carrington* (1765) 2 Wils KB 275, 291; 95 ER 807, 817–818; *TCN Channel Nine v Anning* (2002) 54 NSWLR 333, [52]–[54].

[157] *Prince Albert v Strange* (1849) 1 Mac & G 25, especially 47; 41 ER 1171, especially 1179: 'where privacy is the right invaded'; *Douglas v Hello!* [2001] QB 967, [65]–[73] (CA); *Campbell v MGN* [2004] 2 AC 457 (HL).

[158] Eg *A v B* [2003] QB 195, [5] (CA).

[159] *Campbell v MGN* [2004] 2 AC 457, [13]–[14], [43]–[48], [85] (HL); *Douglas v Hello!* [2001] QB 967, [126] (CA); *A-G v Guardian Newspapers (No 2)* [1990] 1 AC 109, 281 (HL); *ABC v Lenah Game Meats* (2001) 208 CLR 199, [39].

[160] *A v B* [2003] QB 195, [4] (CA); *Douglas v Hello!* [2001] QB 967, [111], [166]–[167] (CA); *Campbell v MGN* [2004] 2 AC 457, [16]–[17], [49]–[52], [86], [103]–[124], [132]–[141], [167] (HL).

[161] *Douglas v Hello!* [2001] QB 967, [116] (CA). See also Ch 5 Pt C(2)(c).

[162] *Campbell v MGN* [2004] 2 AC 457, [11] (HL); *Wainwright v United Kingdom* (ECtHR, 26 Sep 2006), [55].

High Court of Australia has said that it has not ruled out the future recognition of a freestanding tort of invasion of privacy.[163]

Media proprietors and others justifiably claim an interest in knowing the scope of the law's protection of privacy so that they can know the lawful bounds within which they can obtain and publish information. Unfortunately, that scope is presently unclear. If a radical step is taken by judicial decision, then there may be cause for complaint on the basis of the retroactive effect of that step. So far, however, the advances have been gradual, based on longstanding causes of action that have always protected privacy interests, and, to the extent that there has been any dynamism, it has been prompted by the change to the legal landscape effected by the incorporation in the domestic law of the United Kingdom of article 8 of the ECHR, a change not lacking in advance warning or publicity. These reasons mean that the development of the legal protection of privacy that has so far occurred is not objectionable on the basis of retroactivity.

(d) Moral Obloquy

The relationship between law and morality is notoriously thorny. The present objective is not to make any general contribution to debates about that relationship, but only to support the relatively modest proposition that when a case comes to be adjudicated and there is no clear existing legal authority on the point, and judges take into account widely held views of morality to inform their decision about how to develop the law in the case before them, that any objections to the retroactivity of such decisions that may otherwise exist are reduced by the adherence of the retroactive law to pre-existing widely accepted morality. There can be no reliance on a particular law, because in this area the law is by definition unclear. Given that whatever decision is made will have retroactive effect, the least surprising of those decisions will be the one that accords with popular morality. *Wilson v Glossop*[164] fits this pattern.

The undoubted law in 1888 was that if a woman committed adultery, her husband was no longer liable for her maintenance. There was no authority on the precise issue in *Wilson v Glossop*, which was whether a man who connived at the adultery of his wife was liable for her maintenance. The report of the case is discreetly lacking in any more precise factual details of the nature of this connivance. Lord Esher MR thought:

> That a husband even after his wife has committed adultery should turn her out without means of support is harsh, but to say that a man who has been an accomplice can do so is degrading. There is not and there could not be a symptom of authority in support of such a proposition.[165]

[163] *ABC v Lenah Game Meats* (2001) 208 CLR 199, [132], [185]–[189].
[164] (1888) 20 QBD 354 (CA).
[165] *Ibid* 356.

After noting that there was 'no direct authority' Fry LJ opined that:

> to say that such circumstances justify the husband in turning his wife out of doors would be morally and socially wrong.[166]

Lopes LJ rhetorically asked of the husband, what 'right has he to complain of that to which he has been a willing party?'[167] For these reasons, the law was developed to preclude the husband from denying his liability to maintain his wife on the basis of an event at which he connived.

It is not clear from the report of the case whether the husband connived at his wife's adultery expressly for the purpose of furnishing him with what he thought would be a legal justification for dissolution of the marriage and the alleviation of his duty of maintenance. In any case the relevant question is whether someone would be entitled to calculate his actions in reliance on that view of the law, rather than whether the defendant in *Wilson v Glossop* actually so relied. There are two reasons to think that no such ability to rely should have existed and thus that there is little objection to the retroactive effect of the Court of Appeal's decision in the case. First, there was no existing precedent precisely establishing such a proposition on which reliance could safely be placed. This form of extreme cynicism had not previously fallen to be adjudicated. Second, to the extent that the existing law might have given such cynical husbands hope of the result sought by the defendant husband in *Wilson v Glossop*, the degree of moral obloquy in the course adopted by the husband, including the fact that he was a willing party to the event on the basis of which he later claimed to be entitled to turn out his wife and avoid his obligation to maintain her, was sufficient to demand that the law refuse to allow him to shirk his obligations.

(e) Use of Obiter Dicta to Signal a Change in the Law

Discussion so far in this chapter has centred on cases that changed the law and applied that changed law to the facts in the case in which the change was made. Where judges are convinced that a change in the law is desirable and a suitable factual vehicle presents itself for them to make that view known, they have on occasion heralded that change by way of obiter dicta. In such cases the law is effectively changed, without retroactive effect on the case before the court. Because statements made by way of obiter dicta are not binding and so do not actually change the law, there is no prospect of true retroactivity in a case of this kind and so, strictly, it is outside the scope of this book. Nonetheless, there is one case that merits mention because of its signal use of this judicial technique to effectively change the law whilst avoiding retroactivity.

[166] *Ibid* 357.
[167] *Ibid* 358.

In *Hedley Byrne v Heller*[168] the House of Lords addressed the question:

> whether and in what circumstances a person can recover damages for loss suffered by reason of his having relied on an innocent but negligent misrepresentation.[169]

In previous cases attempts to establish this kind of liability had failed. Though the House of Lords gave, at considerable length, the answer that such a form of liability did exist, largely for reasons of 'logic' and 'common sense',[170] and began to sketch its contours, it was inapplicable in the case at hand because the respondents 'effectively disclaimed any assumption of a duty of care'.[171] There was no retroactivity because the law did not change with any effect on the case before the court.

Lord Rodger thinks that this technique means that 'a court may go a long way towards giving what is, in substance, a prospective ruling'.[172] However, the statement of the new legal rule could well have severely and retroactively affected other cases the facts of which arose prior to the decision in *Hedley Byrne v Heller*. No consideration was given in the case to this fact. Such consideration would only have become necessary in a case in which the new rule expressed as obiter dicta in *Hedley Byrne v Heller* was sought to be applied as the ratio decidendi of a subsequent case, the facts of which arose prior to the decision in *Hedley Byrne v Heller*. In any case in which the facts arose after the elaborate obiter dicta of *Hedley Byrne v Heller* were laid down, fair warning of the pending change would have been given. Lord Devlin's words would be applicable. The change would not have come:

> out of a blue sky. Rumblings from Olympus in the form of obiter dicta will give warning of unsettled weather. Unsettled weather is itself of course bound to cause uncertainty, but inevitably it precedes the solution of every difficult question of law.[173]

Perhaps inspired by this statement, Lord Nicholls recently said that:

> development of the common law, as a response to changed conditions, does not come like a bolt out of a clear sky. Invariably the clouds gather first, often from different quarters, indicating with increasing obviousness what is coming.[174]

The utterance of extended obiter dicta may be undesirable for other reasons,[175] but the use of obiter dicta to announce a change in the law does not have retroactive effect on the case in which the announcement is made and alleviates the need for there to be any retroactive surprise when the change in law is actually applied in a case, so long as the facts of that case arose after the announcement of the change by way of obiter dicta.

[168] [1964] AC 465 (HL).

[169] *Ibid* 480.

[170] *Ibid* 517.

[171] *Ibid* 504, see also 492–3, 533, 540.

[172] Lord Rodger 'A Time for Everything under the Law: Some Reflections on Retrospectivity' (2005) 121 Law Quarterly Review 57, 78.

[173] Lord Devlin 'Judges and Lawmakers' (1976) Modern Law Review 1, 10.

[174] *Re Spectrum Plus (in liquidation)* [2005] 2 AC 680, [33] (HL).

[175] Such as those discussed by JD Heydon 'Limits to the Powers of Ultimate Appellate Courts' (2006) 122 Law Quarterly Review 399, 416–17.

2 The Creation of New Law by Overruling a Prior Authority

(a) Ability to Rely on the Law not in Issue

An area in which the ability to rely on the existing law has not arisen as a concern in judicial decisions about whether to change the law is the law relating to divorce. In *Indyka v Indyka*[176] the existing authority under review was *Le Mesurier v Le Mesurier*,[177] in which the Privy Council in 1895 held the law to be that only the courts of the place of the husband's (and therefore the wife's) domicile had jurisdiction to pronounce a divorce, whatever other contacts, such as the presence of the marital home, connected the issue with another jurisdiction. Although that view was followed in the Commonwealth, it was not consonant with the private international law of other countries.[178] It was a decision that had 'most unfortunate consequences',[179] for example that if a husband and wife were married and had spent all of their lives in a country other than England, that if the husband abandoned his wife and moved permanently to England she could not obtain a divorce recognized under English law without doing so in an English court, because, in the eyes of English law, when her husband's domicile switched to England, hers followed.[180] The rule had frequently been modified by parliament[181] such that the common law rule's 'essence' had 'been permanently destroyed'.[182] The Law Lords were unanimous in *Indyka* that the rule in *Le Mesurier* should be departed from but were less than unanimous about the reasons for that departure and what rule should replace it.

Lord Reid, who was in favour of recognising a rule that the courts of the place of the matrimonial home have jurisdiction to dissolve a marriage,[183] said that:

> it is well recognised that we ought not to alter what is presently understood to be the law if that involves any real likelihood of injustice to people who have relied on the present position in arranging their affairs. But I have been unable to think of any case and counsel have been unable to suggest any case where such injustice would result from what I have invited your Lordships to accept.[184]

Although Lord Pearce acknowledged two related issues of potential retroactivity,[185] other than Lord Reid, none of the Lords who decided *Indyka* gave explicit consideration to the retroactive effect of their departure from *Le Mesurier*.[186]

176 [1969] 1 AC 33 (HL).
177 [1895] AC 517 (PC).
178 [1969] 1 AC 33, 64 (HL).
179 *Ibid* 64.
180 *Ibid* 92.
181 *Ibid* 65–6, 73, 98–9, 102–3, 108–9.
182 *Ibid* 66.
183 *Ibid* 68.
184 *Ibid* 69. See also *Ross Smith v Ross Smith* [1963] AC 280, 304, 307–8 (HL). Cf *Hindcastle v Barbara Attenborough* [1997] AC 70, 95 (HL).
185 *Ibid* 86, 91.
186 Although see *Re Edward and Edward* (1987) 39 DLR (4th) 654, 660–64 in which the Saskatchewan Court of Appeal did discuss the retroactivity created by applying *Indyka* to the recognition of a foreign divorce that occurred prior to *Indyka* being decided.

The view expressed in *Indyka* that the law of divorce is not something on which people do or, more importantly, should be able to rely requires re-examination in light of the frequent impermanence of marriage and modern legal developments. The comparatively recent acceptance in Australia and England of the validity and significance of prenuptial agreements about the division of assets upon the breakdown of a marriage[187] indicates both that people do consider the law relating to divorce at the time of marriage and that the legal system protects their entitlement to do so. It does not require any imagination to realise that the ability to rely on the law of divorce is important to people who are already married who are considering whether to seek a divorce. Thus the assumption made in *Indyka* that the law on jurisdiction to grant a divorce is not something on which people would or should be able to rely, if it was ever sound, is sound no longer. That does not mean, however, that *Indyka* should have been decided differently.

As was manifest from the judgments, there were strong reasons to change the common law from its inflexible position that only the courts of the husband's domicile had jurisdiction to dissolve a marriage. A rule that allowed a husband permanently to flee the jurisdiction in which he married and lived with his wife and in which his wife still lived, in reliance on the legal effect of that flight being that his wife could not seek dissolution of the marriage and accompanying orders with respect to maintenance and division of property in the courts of her permanent place of residence that would be recognised or enforced by an English court, was so neglectful of the wife's position as to be wrong in principle and to require overruling notwithstanding the retroactivity. A husband's reliance on such a rule would not, because of the moral obloquy that it would reveal, be worthy of protection.

(b) Prior Authority Wrong in Principle

When a court of ultimate appeal comes to reconsider one of its own decisions it is often said that the prior decision being incorrectly decided is insufficient to justify overruling it.[188] That is particularly so if the question may be said to be a finely balanced one about which the highest court has already expressed its view.[189] Where, however, the question may be characterised as one in which the answer previously given is wrong in principle, for example because it was inconsistent with a funda-

[187] In Australia, by force of Pt VIIIA of the Family Law Act 1975 (Aus), inserted by the Family Law Amendment Act 2000 (Aus); and in England as held, eg, in *K v K* (2003) 1 FLR 120 (Fam).

[188] *Geelong Harbor Trust Commissioners v Gibbs Bright* [1974] AC 810, 818 (PC); *Miliangos v George Frank (Textiles)* [1976] AC 443, 496 (HL); *Jones v Secretary of State for Social Services* [1972] AC 944, 966, 996, 1023–1025 (HL); *Queensland v The Commonwealth of Australia* (1977) 139 CLR 585, 599–600, 603–604. Cf *Brodie v Singleton Shire Council* (2001) 206 CLR 512, [212]. Contra BV Harris 'Final Appellate Courts Overruling Their Own "Wrong" Precedents: The Ongoing Search for Principle' (2002) 118 Law Quarterly Review 408.

[189] *Jones v Secretary of State for Social Services* [1972] AC 944, 966, 996, 1024 (HL); *Fitzleet Estates v Cherry* [1977] 1 WLR 1345, 1349 (HL); *The Hannah Blumenthal* [1983] 1 AC 854, 912, 913 (HL); *A-G (NSW) v Perpetual Trustee Co* (1952) 85 CLR 237, 244; *Queensland v The Commonwealth of Australia* (1977) 139 CLR 585, 603; *Babaniaris v Lutony Fashions* (1987) 163 CLR 1, 14.

mental principle of the common law,[190] inconsistent with the plain meaning of a statute,[191] productive of uncertainty and potentially arbitrary results,[192] or otherwise *patently* wrong,[193] there may be greater willingness to overrule the decision. If the decision of which overruling is sought was decided by a court other than the ultimate appellate court, there will be less objection to it being overruled on the basis of it being incorrectly decided, and particularly if it can be said to be wrong in principle, since the hierarchy of courts means that it is never entirely safe to rely on a decision of a court below the ultimate appellate court.[194] This is not without difficulty, however, because the retroactive effects of overruling may be just as great regardless of the position in the hierarchy of courts at which an overruled decision was decided. The first case to be discussed in this section is one that has been described as 'perhaps the most dramatic (some would say revolutionary) reversal of a legal principle in modern times'.[195]

The issue in *The Wagon Mound*[196] was whether the Privy Council should overrule the decision of the Court of Appeal in *Re Polemis and Furness Withy*[197] that if a defendant is negligent then he is responsible for all of the direct consequences of that negligence, whether reasonably foreseeable or not. Applications of *Polemis* were reviewed at length by Viscount Simonds, delivering the advice of the Privy Council, who observed that 'the authority of *Polemis* has been severely shaken though lip-service has from time to time been paid to it',[198] before opining that *Polemis*:

> should no longer be regarded as good law. . . . For it does not seem consonant with current ideas of justice or morality that for an act of negligence, however slight or venial, which results in some trivial foreseeable damage the actor should be liable for all consequences however unforeseeable and however grave, so long as they can be said to be 'direct.'[199]

A test of reasonable foreseeability, held the Privy Council, 'corresponds with the common conscience of mankind' whereas the directness test in *Polemis* led 'nowhere but the never-ending and insoluble problems of causation'.[200] The Privy

[190] *R v Howe* [1987] 1 AC 417 (HL), discussed at Ch 5 Pt G(2)(a).

[191] Cf *Babaniaris v Lutony Fashions* (1987) 163 CLR 1, discussed at Ch 5 Pt E(3).

[192] *The Johanna Oldendorff* [1974] AC 479, 533–6, 551–5, 561 (HL).

[193] Eg *Re Spectrum Plus (in liquidation)* [2005] 2 AC 680 (HL), discussed in this Pt.

[194] *Ibid* [43], [64]. See *Babaniaris v Lutony Fashions* (1987) 163 CLR 1, 14, 22–4 on overruling the longstanding interpretation of a statute given by a lower court.

[195] CK Allen *Law in the Making* (7th edn Clarendon Press Oxford 1964) 343.

[196] [1961] AC 388 (PC). See also *Hughes v Lord Advocate* [1963] AC 837 (HL).

[197] [1921] 3 KB 560 (CA).

[198] [1961] AC 388, 422 (PC).

[199] *Ibid.* Cf *Herrington v British Railways Board* [1972] AC 877, 931 contra 897 (HL), in which Lord Diplock expressed the view that the rule in *Robert Addie & Sons (Collieries) v Dumbreck* [1929] AC 358 (HL) that an occupier owed no duty to take reasonable care to any trespasser was wrong when it was decided. Cf *Commissioner for Railways v Cardy* (1960) 104 CLR 274, 285–6, 291–2, 318–19 and *Hackshaw v Shaw* (1984) 155 CLR 614, eg 654–62 where *Robert Addie v Dumbreck* was thought to be inconsistent with general principles of the law of negligence developed since it was decided.

[200] [1961] AC 388, 423 (PC).

Council sought to root the new legal rule that it created in principle discernible from existing authority by insisting that the view 'that the essential factor in determining liability is whether the damage is of such a kind as the reasonable man should have foreseen'[201] accorded with the approach of Lord Atkin in *Donoghue v Stevenson* that 'liability for negligence' is 'based upon a general public sentiment of moral wrongdoing for which the offender must pay'.[202] In *The Wagon Mound* the Privy Council considered it to be:

> a departure from this sovereign principle if liability is made to depend solely on the damage being the 'direct' or 'natural' consequence of the precedent act.[203]

The deviations that had occurred from *Polemis* prior to the Privy Council's decision in *The Wagon Mound* meant, according to the Privy Council, that it was 'not probable that many cases' would 'have a different result' on the basis of whether they were decided before or after *The Wagon Mound*, though it was 'hoped that the law will be thereby simplified, and that in some cases, at least, palpable injustice will be avoided'.[204]

As in *The Wagon Mound No 2*, discussed above,[205] the rule overturned in *The Wagon Mound* was not one on which anyone could have relied in making a decision about conduct giving rise to litigation. Moreover, the decision in *The Wagon Mound* was in favour of the defendant and so concerns about the insurance arrangements of potential defendants that often accompany retroactive changes to the law of negligence were less applicable in this case. As a conceptual matter the change in the law effected by *The Wagon Mound* was not, however, necessarily in favour of defendants in general. Although defendants could no longer, as a result of *The Wagon Mound*, be held liable for damage caused that was not foreseeable, even if it was a direct result of a defendant's act or omission; defendants could be liable for reasonably foreseeable damage that was not a direct result of a defendant's act or omission.[206] This represented a potentially new basis for liability. Correlatively, plaintiffs could no longer rely on recovering any loss caused by others so long as the relationship between the defendant's act and the plaintiff's loss was a direct one. If the loss suffered in *The Wagon Mound* was direct but not reasonably foreseeable then the plaintiff in *The Wagon Mound* was affected in this way. Plaintiffs potentially benefited, however, from the rule that reasonably foreseeable damage was recoverable even if it was not directly caused.

The fact that the change effected by *The Wagon Mound* did not give rise to reliance concerns and was designed to bring into effect a new rule anchored in existing principle, and replace a rule with potentially arbitrary consequences that was not being faithfully applied; and that the change did not inherently favour

[201] *Ibid* 426.
[202] [1932] AC 562, 580 (HL).
[203] [1961] AC 388, 426 (PC).
[204] *Ibid* 422.
[205] Ch 5 Pt E(1)(b).
[206] [1961] AC 388, 426 (PC).

either plaintiffs or defendants, meant that the potentially retroactive effect on the plaintiff in the case and in other potential cases in which the facts arose prior to the Privy Council's decision in *The Wagon Mound*, was not of sufficient concern, particularly given the Privy Council's view that the practical outcome of cases would probably not be much affected, to outweigh the replacement of a rule that was thought to be wrong in principle.

The probable absence of prejudicial retroactive effects was more explicitly considered by the House of Lords in its decision to change the common law in *Bourne v Keane*.[207] In that case a Roman Catholic testator left money so that masses would be said for his soul. The question was whether the bequests were void for being superstitious. At first instance and in the Court of Appeal existing authorities were applied to hold that the bequests were void for that reason. The House of Lords, by majority, overruled those authorities, which were not binding on the House, and held the bequests to be valid.

Lord Buckmaster laid down a number of principles about overruling existing authority, including the proposition that a decision 'upon which title to property depends', 'once laid down and accepted for a long period of time, ought not to be altered unless your Lordships could say positively that it was wrong and productive of inconvenience'.[208] The principles laid down by Lord Buckmaster to control the occasions on which prior authority may be overruled did not, however, prevent him from overruling the relevant existing authority in the case at hand. Of the principles that he had just expressed, Lord Buckmaster said:

> I cannot find, however, that they compel acceptance as accurate of a doctrine plainly outside a statute and outside the common law, when no title and no contract will be shaken, no person can complain, and no general course of dealing be altered by the remedy of a mistake. For over eighty years Roman Catholics have been unlawfully restricted in the disposal of their property; that seems to me no reason why the restrictions should continue to be imposed.[209]

No one was significantly disadvantaged by the retroactive effect of the overruling that occurred in *Bourne v Keane*. That effect was that dispositions that were void at the time that they were made were retroactively deemed to have been effective at the time that they were made. A class of persons defined by their desire to act on a particular religious belief were deemed to have been entitled to do what they were previously not entitled to do. The only potential interest affected was the financial interest of surviving family members in the estate, a point made by Lord Wrenbury in dissent.[210] There are and were any number of uses beyond the financial betterment of surviving family members to which a deceased's estate could lawfully be put, so to reinstate one more such use when it was the wish of the testator seems not to damage the interests of family members too much, particularly

[207] [1919] AC 815 (HL).
[208] *Ibid* 874, see also 860.
[209] *Ibid*.
[210] *Ibid* 917.

when it is borne in mind that, as with any other disposition, a bequest to say masses, even if retroactively deemed to have been effective, would still be subject to rules of succession law under which wills may be challenged. If the family's legitimate interests really were unfairly prejudiced, this more general remedy would be available, which seems eminently more suitable than refusing in all circumstances to legalise a use that the testator thought to be important for the treatment of his soul in the afterlife.

Despite the caution about overruling expressed by the House of Lords in *Bourne v Keane* it was willing to overrule existing authority in that case for two good reasons. The first was that the existing rule was wrong in principle and the second was that no significant prejudice would be caused to anyone by the retroactive change to the law. The first of those two reasons was also apparent in *Re Spectrum Plus (in liquidation)*.[211] In *Spectrum*, unlike either *The Wagon Mound* or *Bourne v Keane*, there were significant reliance interests at stake. Thus a crucial issue in *Spectrum* was whether a previous decision being wrong in principle was itself sufficient to justify overruling it. The most illustrative discussion of this point was in the judgment of Lord Hope, who noted that:

> Lord Phillips of Worth Matravers MR said that, even if Slade J's construction of the debenture in *Siebe Gorman v Barclays Bank*[212] had appeared to him to be erroneous, he would have been inclined to hold that the form of the debenture had, by custom and usage, acquired the meaning and effect that he had attributed to it.[213] This was because the form had been used for 25 years under the understanding that this was its meaning and effect. Banks had relied upon this understanding, and individuals had guaranteed the liabilities of companies to banks on the understanding that the banks would be entitled to look first to their charges on book debts unaffected by the claims of preferred creditors. The respondents say that this is the course that ought now to be followed in the interests of commercial certainty.[214]

Having noted this view, Lord Hope observed the following 'powerful considerations':[215]

> It is hard to think of an area of the law where the need for certainty is more important than that with which your Lordships are concerned in this case. The commercial life of this country depends to a large extent on the reliability of the security arrangements that are entered into between debtors and their creditors. The law provides the context in which these arrangements are entered into, and it lays down the rules that have to be applied when the arrangements break down. Mistakes as to the law can make all the difference between success and failure when the creditor seeks to realise his security.[216]

211 [2005] 2 AC 680 (HL).
212 [1979] 2 Lloyd's Rep 142 (Ch).
213 [2004] Ch 337, 383, [97] (CA).
214 [2005] 2 AC 680, [62] (HL).
215 *Ibid* [64].
216 *Ibid* [63].

Nonetheless, Lord Hope, like all of their Lordships, thought that the 'proper course'[217] was for the decision of Slade J in *Siebe Gorman v Barclays Bank* to be overruled. It:

> was a decision that was taken at first instance, and it has now been conclusively demonstrated that the construction which he placed on the debenture was wrong. This is not one of those cases where there are respectable arguments either way. With regret, the conclusion has to be that it is not possible to defend the decision on any rational basis. It is not enough to say that it has stood for more than 25 years. The fact is that, like any other first instance decision, it was always open to correction if the country's highest appellate court was persuaded that there was something wrong with it. Those who relied upon it must be taken to have been aware of this. It provided guidance, and no criticism can reasonably be levelled at those who felt that it was proper to rely on it. But it was no more immune from review by the ultimate appellate court than any other decision which has been taken at first instance.[218]

The competing interests in *Spectrum* were both of a high order of magnitude. The reliance interests were strong. The decision on which reliance was placed was thought to be clearly wrong in principle. These factors pointed in opposite directions on the question of whether the existing rule should be changed with retroactive effect. The fact that the earlier decision was made by a judge at first instance[219] was a key factor in deciding to overrule it.[220] That would not ease the justifiable frustration of those who relied on the existing law, but from a broader perspective it was a credible basis on which to choose between competing interests.

(c) Response to Changed Legal Circumstances

An obvious example of a judicial decision in which the law was changed because related legal developments made that change desirable is *Kleinwort Benson*, which is discussed fully above[221] and in which Lord Goff indicated that the development of a coherent law of restitution founded on the principle of unjust enrichment that included a defence of change of position made a change in the law to allow recovery for a mistake of law 'inevitable'.[222] This may be likened to the majority of the High Court of Australia in *Brodie v Singleton Shire Council*, who thought that the emergence of a coherent tort of negligence meant that the immunity of highway authorities for nonfeasance could not rationally be maintained.[223] The immunity was abolished, but only marginal consideration was given to the retroactive effect of doing so.[224] Similarly, the emergence of a coherent tort of negligence was

217 *Ibid* [64].

218 *Ibid.*

219 As it was in *R v R* [1992] 1 AC 599 (HL), discussed in Ch 5 Pt C, and *R v Governor of Brockhill Prison, ex p Evans (No 2)* [2001] 2 AC 19 (HL), discussed in Ch 5 Pt F(3).

220 *Ibid* [43], [64].

221 Ch 5 Pt D.

222 [1999] 2 AC 349, 373 (HL). See also *The Despina R* [1979] AC 685 (HL), discussed in Ch 5 Pt E(2)(d).

223 (2001) 206 CLR 512, [110]–[129], [194]–[195], [209].

224 *Ibid* [215]–[217], [229]–[230], [317].

thought by a majority of the High Court of Australia in *Burnie Port Authority v General Jones*[225] to have absorbed the rule in *Rylands v Fletcher*.[226] In *Burnie*, in contrast to *Kleinwort Benson* and *Brodie*, the change in law had no impact on the result of the particular litigation and it was thought 'highly unlikely' that liability would ever exist under the principles of negligence where it would not have existed under *Rylands v Fletcher*.[227] Arguably, in cases where broader legal developments render the maintenance of a specific rule unsustainable, general principles of law, which had emerged at the time of the facts giving rise to the particular dispute, even then outflanked a narrower rule, which did not sit conformably with the newer, broader, principles, such that even at the time of the relevant facts, the legal position was unclear, making retroactively imposed clarity necessary, or at least less objectionable than retroactivity in cases where a rule operative at the time of the relevant events was undoubtedly good law.

Indyka, which is also discussed above,[228] is evidence that statutory changes to the same field of law may form a basis for retroactive judicial change of the common law.[229] Changing a common law rule because of a change in legal circumstances parallels the process of gradual development of new common law rules, without overruling any existing authority, motivated by a change in legal circumstances. A notable example, discussed above,[230] is the development of the law of privacy, partly in response to the incorporation into the English legal order of article 8 of the ECHR.[231]

Without explicit adoption into the Australian legal order of international instruments expressing universal human rights, the High Court of Australia was, influenced by the modern recognition of those rights, willing to change the common law on the question of native title because the previous rule was unjustly discriminatory against indigenous people.[232] The court was also influenced by improved understandings of the social organisation of indigenous communities at the time of settlement.[233]

[225] (1994) 179 CLR 520.

[226] (1866) LR 1 Exch 265 and (1868) LR 3 HL 330. In *Transco v Stockport Metropolitan Borough Council* [2004] 2 AC 1 (HL) the House of Lords declined to adopt the approach in *Burnie Port Authority v General Jones*.

[227] (1994) 179 CLR 520, 555 contra 591–4.

[228] Ch 5 Pt E(2)(a).

[229] [1969] 1 AC 33, 96–103 (HL).

[230] Ch 5 Pt E(1)(c).

[231] An example, in the sphere of public housing, of the change in legal landscape caused by the Human Rights Act 1998 (UK) providing a basis for the House of Lords to depart from a previous decision is *Ghaidan v Godin-Mendoza* [2004] 2 AC 557 (HL), also discussed in Ch 4 Pt G(1)(a), in which, because of the interpretive command in s 3 of the Human Rights Act, the word 'spouse' in the Rent Act 1977 (Eng) was interpreted to include a same sex partner, contrary to the earlier decision of the House in *Fitzpatrick v Sterling Housing Association* [2001] 1 AC 27 (HL). Cf *Dyson Holdings v Fox* [1976] 1 QB 503 (CA) where, because of changed social, rather than legal, conditions, and contrary to prior authority, a common law wife was found by the court to be included by the statutory term 'family'.

[232] *Mabo v Queensland (No 2)* (1992) 175 CLR 1, 42.

[233] *Ibid* 38–40.

(d) Response to Changed Factual Circumstances

Judges are able to change the law without criticising their predecessors if the reason for the change in law is a change of factual conditions to which the law should respond. One example of this type of case is the decision of the House of Lords in *Perrin v Morgan*[234] that 'money' could mean something other than cash, which was a departure from the position established in 1725.[235] A second example is *MT v MT*[236] in which the question was whether a child born 340 days after the last opportunity for intercourse between spouses could be regarded as legitimate. Previous authority, including a recent decision of the Court of Appeal,[237] had declined to hold so long a period of gestation to be a medical impossibility. However, in *MT* the medical evidence persuaded Ormerod J that advances in gynaecological knowledge in recent years justified him refusing to follow previous cases, which were based on imperfect scientific knowledge. A third example is Lord Pearson's view in *Herrington v British Railways Board*[238] that changed urban conditions provided a justification for overruling the rule that an occupier owed no duty to take reasonable care to any trespasser,[239] although from an empirical perspective it is doubtful that the behaviour of children in urban environments had changed in a material way. A fourth example is the reliance in *Hall v Simons*[240] on changes to the legal profession, its regulation, and the expectations of those who seek its services, as justification for departing from the rule that in certain circumstances conferred immunity from suit on advocates.[241] Although illustrating the point that changed factual circumstances may motivate courts to change the law,[242] none of these examples demonstrate the point as clearly as *Miliangos v George Frank (Textiles)*.[243]

In *Miliangos* English purchasers contracted with a Swiss seller for the purchase of polyester yarn. The proper law of the contract was Swiss and the contract expressed the price in Swiss francs. The yarn was delivered and the price was not paid. The Swiss seller instituted proceedings in England and the question was in

234 [1943] AC 399 (HL).

235 *Shelmer's Case* (1725) Gilb 200, 202; 25 ER 139, 141.

236 [1949] P 331. Cf *Preston-Jones v Preston-Jones* [1951] AC 391 (HL).

237 *Hadlum v Hadlum* [1949] P 197 (CA).

238 [1972] AC 877, 929 (HL).

239 *Robert Addie & Sons (Collieries) v Dumbreck* [1929] AC 358 (HL).

240 [2002] 1 AC 615, 682–683, 704, 709–710, 736–737 (HL), discussed further in Ch 5 Pt E(2)(e). Cf *D'Orta-Ekenaike v Victoria Legal Aid* [2005] HCA 12, [146].

241 *Rondel v Worsley* [1969] 1 AC 191 (HL). In public law, changed factual circumstances have also motivated retroactive changes to the common law. The replacement by the High Court of Australia in *Bropho v Western Australia* (1990) 171 CLR 1, 19 of a rigid presumption that general words of a statute do not bind the Crown, with an approach concerned more with the legislature's intention about whether a particular statute binds the Crown, in part because of the burgeoning growth of 'the myriad of governmental commercial and industrial instrumentalities covered by the shield of the Crown', is one example. *Birmingham Corporation v West Midland Baptist (Trust) Association* [1970] AC 874, 898–9 (HL) is another.

242 Caution about which was expressed in *State Government Insurance Commission v Trigwell* (1979) 142 CLR 617, 633.

243 [1976] AC 443 (HL).

what currency the judgment order should be made. *Re United Railways of Havana and Regla Warehouse*[244] was authority for the rule that English courts could only give judgment in pounds sterling, to which a foreign currency claim had to be converted at the date when the debt giving rise to the judgment became due. The Court of Appeal, by majority, did not follow this decision in *Schorsch Meier v Hennin*,[245] holding instead that an English court could give judgment in a foreign currency where that currency was the currency of the contract. The point came before the House of Lords for resolution in *Miliangos*. Variation in the relative values of the two currencies between the date of the debt falling due and the time of the litigation meant that the answer mattered.

After reaffirming:

> that the only judicial means by which decisions of this House can be reviewed is by this House itself, under the declaration of 1966,[246]

Lord Wilberforce said this of the House's previous decision in *Re United Railways of Havana and Regla Warehouse*:

> My Lords, even if I were inclined to question some of the arguments used in the speeches, I should find it inappropriate and unnecessary to say that, in the circumstances of the time and on the arguments and authorities presented, the decision was wrong or is open to distinction or explanation.
>
> What we can do, and what is our responsibility, is to consider whether this decision, clear and comparatively recent, should be regarded as a binding precedent in today's circumstances. For that purpose it is permissible to examine the speeches in order to understand the considerations upon which the opinions there reached were based, for the ultimate purpose of seeing whether there have emerged fresh considerations which might have appealed to those who gave those opinions and so may appeal to their successors.[247]

Lord Wilberforce and Lord Cross both emphasized that since 1961 when the existing authority under consideration was decided, many of the major currencies had floated, and that commercial experience made it plain that the law required changing.[248] Ultimately, the law was changed because 'justice demands that the creditor should not suffer from fluctuations in the value of sterling'.[249]

Lord Simon was the sole dissentient in *Miliangos*. He observed that beyond some consideration of the Rules of Court, there had been:

> no consideration of what consequences the retrospective alteration of the law (for, let us face it, that is the reality) may have.[250]

This concern was surely misplaced because though the decision did retroactively change the law, it did so to ensure that debts were paid in the currency in

244 [1961] AC 1007 (HL).
245 [1975] QB 416 (CA).
246 [1976] AC 443, 459 (HL).
247 *Ibid* 460.
248 *Ibid* 463–4, 497.
249 *Ibid* 465.
250 *Ibid* 490.

which they were agreed, rather than the value of the debt in the agreed currency fluctuating with the value of the British pound. This retroactive change improved certainty by granting judgment on the basis of what was agreed in the contract, something on which both parties could rely, and discarding a parochial rule which, because of changed factual conditions, had become a potential cause of injustice.

Miliangos left open the questions of whether a judgment for damages in tort or for breach of contract could be awarded in a currency other than sterling, which were answered in *The Despina R*.[251] The previous authorities on these issues,[252] which held that judgment could only be in sterling, were based on the view that English courts lacked jurisdiction to award damages in a foreign currency.[253] When the law changed in *Miliangos*, this assumption was so undermined as to require reconsideration.[254]

The decision in *The Despina R* that, in tort and for breach of contract, the plaintiff may be awarded damages in the currency in which she suffered her loss, was based on the principle of *restitutio in integrum*.[255] This corrective principle is primarily backward looking. The defendant was never entitled to cause the damage, and was asked to do no more than to restore the plaintiff to the position the plaintiff was in prior to the defendant causing the damage. The retroactive effect of *The Despina R* was a new rule that payment of damages in the currency in which the loss was suffered could be ordered because a plaintiff should be put in as close a position to that in which she would have been in the absence of the tortious wrong or breach of contract. This contrasts to the old rule, that damages could be awarded only in sterling, under which no account could be taken of currency fluctuations that could arbitrarily hamper any attempt to achieve *restitutio in integrum*. Having a restorative obligation alleviated in the event of a particular kind of currency fluctuation is hardly something on which anyone could rely. In *Miliangos* changed factual conditions motivated retroactive change to the law. In *The Despina R* changed legal circumstances coupled with the inapplicability of reliance justified further change.

(e) Absence of Effect on Litigants before the Court

Just as the decision in *Hedley Byrne v Heller*[256] effectively changed the law without affecting the litigants in the case, so too did the decision of the House of Lords in *Hall v Simons*.[257] These two cases are related in terms of substantive law as well as

251 [1979] AC 685 (HL).

252 *The Volturno* [1921] 2 AC 544 (HL) on damages in tort and *Di Ferdinando v Simon, Smits & Co* [1920] 3 KB 409 (CA) on damages for breach of contract.

253 [1979] AC 685, 696 (HL).

254 J Harris 'Towards Principles of Overruling—When Should a Final Court of Appeal Second Guess?' (1990) 10 Oxford Journal of Legal Studies 135, 140 fn 26.

255 [1979] AC 685, 696–7, 701, 705 (HL).

256 *Hedley Byrne v Heller* [1964] AC 465 (HL), discussed in Ch 5 Pt E(1)(e).

257 [2002] 1 AC 615 (HL).

their intertemporal effect. *Hedley Byrne v Heller* meant that liability for negligent misrepresentation could arise independently of a contract.[258] The traditional advocates' immunity rested on the basis that there was no contract between a barrister and his client and so there could be no negligence.[259] When this foundation for advocates' immunity was removed, the justifications for the immunity were recrafted in *Rondel v Worsley*.[260] The question in *Hall v Simons* was whether the House of Lords should depart from *Rondel v Worsley*. The facts of the case were outside the scope of the existing immunity.[261] Nonetheless, the House of Lords took the opportunity to abolish all forms of advocates' immunity.[262] The result for the litigants in the case would have been the same whether the House adopted this broader ground of decision or not and so they did not suffer any retroactive effects.[263]

Only Lord Hope expressly considered the potential retroactive effect of the abolition of the immunity on persons other than litigants before the court,[264] and the lack of support from other members of the House for his proposal that the ruling have prospective effect only, means that the abolition of the immunity has retroactive effect in the ordinary way. The abolition of the immunity has subsequently been applied with retroactive effect. However, in that case the retroactive accrual of the cause of action was held to mean that the claim was time barred.[265]

Even if a case arises in which the abolition of the immunity actually results in a finding of retroactive liability, there is an argument that the retroactivity caused by the abolition was justified. Before *Hall v Simons* was decided advocates' immunity had been subject to criticism by judges, academics and practitioners, with a constant theme that reexamination of the immunity was necessary.[266] The absence of the immunity in Canada had not given rise to any of the problems feared by those who opposed its abolition in England.[267] Alternative means were available to deal with the fear of collateral attacks on existing judgments, a fear said by some to justify the immunity.[268] Crucially, and for which reasons any retroactivity would probably be justifiable, the existence of the immunity was, at least since *Rondel v Worsley*, only for the purported public benefit, not for the personal protection of

[258] [1964] AC 465, 502–3 (HL).

[259] See the discussion in *Hall v Simons* [2002] 1 AC 615, 676, 685–6 (HL).

[260] [1969] 1 AC 191 (HL). See also *Saif Ali v Sydney Mitchell* [1980] AC 198 (HL).

[261] [2002] 1 AC 615, 688, 709 (HL).

[262] Contra *D'Orta-Ekenaike v Victoria Legal Aid* [2005] HCA 12, in which the majority of the High Court of Australia declined such an invitation, though not because of any potential retroactive effect on those who enjoyed the immunity (contra [342]).

[263] Contra *Chamberlains v Sun Poi Lai* [2006] NZSC 70, in which the New Zealand Supreme Court abolished advocates' immunity in a case that did have retroactive effect on the litigants.

[264] [2002] 1 AC 615, 710, 726 (HL). Cf *Re Spectrum Plus (in liquidation)* [2005] 2 AC 680, [72]–[73] (HL); *Chamberlains v Sun Poi Lai* [2006] NZSC 70, [95], [129]–[154], [205].

[265] *Awoyomi v Radford* [2007] EWHC 1671, [18]–[20] (QB).

[266] [2002] 1 AC 615, 677–8 (HL).

[267] *Ibid* 681, 695 contra 722. Cf *D'Orta-Ekenaike v Victoria Legal Aid* [2005] HCA 12, [61]–[63].

[268] [2002] 1 AC 615, 679–80, 685, 699–703, 705–7 contra 722–3, 742–3, 750–2; *D'Orta-Ekenaike v Victoria Legal Aid* [2005] HCA 12, [43]–[46].

individual advocates, who were never entitled to act negligently. The recognition that public policy no longer required the immunity[269] meant that the House could, with retroactive effect, 'bring to an end an anomalous exception to the basic premise that there should be a remedy for a wrong'.[270]

(f) Refusal to Overrule a Decision because of Potential Retroactive Effects

The daily application of the common law involves almost unceasing refusal to overrule prior authority, by courts that have the power to do so, sometimes on the basis of the potential retroactive effects of overruling. Usually, such refusal calls for little or no comment. The existing authority is just followed. Occasionally, for example when a specific invitation to overrule existing authority is declined, more comment is made about the reasons for refusing to do so. In private law cases, certainty, and more precisely the reliance that certainty enables, often provides the reason for such refusal. One notable example of such a case was the refusal of the House of Lords in *The Hannah Blumenthal*[271] to overrule its own decision made two years earlier in *The Bremer Vulcan*[272] that inordinate and inexcusable delay by a claimant under an arbitration agreement did not entitle the respondent to treat the arbitration agreement as repudiated, because of the mutual obligation to apply to the arbitral tribunal for directions to prevent delay as part of a broader mutual obligation to ensure that disputes between the agreeing parties be resolved on their merits and with reasonable speed. The decision in *The Bremer Vulcan* was later described as creating 'serious disquiet among the whole commercial community'[273] and provoked the suggestion that it bore 'no relation to commercial reality'.[274] Nonetheless, the case was thought by the House of Lords in *The Hannah Blumenthal* to be one in which the House resolved a doubtful point on which differing rational views were possible, and in light of Lord Brandon's:

> stress on what is generally accepted to be the special need for certainty, consistency and continuity in the field of commercial law[275]

the earlier decision was not disturbed.

The commitment of the House of Lords to respect for existing authority in this aspect of commercial law was called into question by its decision five years later in *The Antclizo* in which Lord Goff, with whom the other Law Lords (including Lords Brandon and Brightman who sat in *The Hannah Blumenthal*) agreed, stated his strong inclination to accept the invitation to review the whole area of law in which *The Bremer Vulcan* and *The Hannah Blumenthal* fell, and declined to do so only on the grounds that the case at hand presented an inadequate factual vehicle for such

269 See Ch 5 Pt E(2)(d).
270 [2002] 1 AC 615, 681 (HL), see also 688, 710–11, 727.
271 [1983] 1 AC 854 (HL).
272 [1981] AC 909 (HL).
273 *The Antclizo* [1988] 1 WLR 603, 606 (HL).
274 *Ibid.*
275 [1983] 1 AC 854, 913 (HL), see also 922.

an undertaking. Criticism should not be too quickly made of this, partly because it is not known whether their Lordships would have judicially altered the law after such a review[276] and, perhaps more importantly, because greater experience with the decision and the intensity of criticism in both commercial and legal circles may have revealed it to be wrong in principle rather than merely an unpopular resolution of a question that could properly have been decided either way.

3 Overruling a Prior Judicial Interpretation of a Statute

When a judicial decision overrules a prior judicial decision on the meaning of a statutory provision, the statute itself obviously is not and could not be changed. Nonetheless, as Lord Diplock said, when a court:

> interprets a written law as bearing one of two or more possible meanings . . . the effect of the exercise of its interpretative role is to make law.[277]

The law, constituted by a statute interpreted and applied by a court, may be one thing at the time of events giving rise to litigation and, in that litigation, be deemed to have been something else at the time of those events. Thus when the perspective of a litigant is adopted, and the concern is solely with adjudicative retroactivity rather than the separation of powers[278] or the magnitude of the proper judicial role more generally,[279] then overruling a previous judicial decision about the meaning of a statutory provision is equivalent to overruling a previous judicial decision about a common law rule. The interpretation of the statute adopted may, for the purposes of a concern with retroactivity, be considered as amounting to a common law rule. From the perspective of a litigant, both change the law retroactively. Three illustrative cases in this area will be discussed. In the first the absence of reliance interests and the requirements of justice meant that the existing authority was overruled. In the second the presence of potential reliance meant that the existing authority was followed despite doubts about its merits as a legal rule. The third is a case in which potential reliance should have motivated the court not to overrule a previous decision, but did not.

In *R v Bow Road Justices, ex p Adedigba*[280] the question for the Court of Appeal was whether to follow existing authority, which was not binding on it, commencing in 1849 with *R v Blane*,[281] which held that the English 'bastardy laws' were inapplicable to children born outside England, even when a child and both of his

[276] Even without such a review their Lordships recommended legislative change on the subject, which would have allowed the legislature the opportunity to consider the question of the temporal application of any amendment.

[277] *Geelong Harbour Trust Commissioners v Gibbs Bright* [1974] AC 810, 820 (PC).

[278] *Ogden Industries v Lucas* [1970] AC 113, 127 (PC).

[279] JD Heydon 'Limits to the Powers of Ultimate Appellate Courts' (2006) 122 Law Quarterly Review 399, 407–8.

[280] [1968] 2 QB 572 (CA).

[281] (1849) 13 QB 769; 116 ER 1458.

parents lived in England. The Affiliation Proceedings Act 1957,[282] under which the applicant mother in *Adedigba* applied for an order that the father of her two children pay maintenance to her, was not different in any material respect to the 1844 Act[283] considered in *R v Blane.* Three categories of reasons for the Court of Appeal's unanimous decision to overrule existing authority are discernible. First, the area of law was not one in which potential reliance was a concern. Lord Denning was not:

> troubled by the fact that R v Blane has stood for 120 years. It is not a property or commercial case. It has not formed the basis of titles or commercial dealings. It is the sort of precedent which we can and should overrule when it is seen to be wrong.[284]

Salmon LJ said he 'should have no qualms about upsetting'[285] the reliance of a putative father who had arranged his affairs on the basis of the existing rule that although a father, his children and his children's mother were all in England, the father would not be liable for maintenance. The moral obloquy of such reliance would well justify upsetting it. This should be further understood in light of the second basis for the decision: that the existing rule was wrong in principle, and wrong when it was decided. It was said to be 'contrary alike to justice, humanity and common sense and had no foundation of any kind in law'[286] and productive of decisions that were 'both unjust to the private citizen and inimical to the public weal'.[287] Once an existing rule is held to be wrong in principle it is hardly necessary for it also to be characterised as out of date with changed social conditions, but presumably for an abundance of caution, as a third reason for its decision, the Court of Appeal so characterised it.[288] Before leaving *Adedigba* it is worth noting that Lord Denning regarded retroactive application of the new rule as a *desirable* rather than merely an *inevitable* consequence of overruling the existing rule. He observed that if the court followed the existing rule then prospective statutory change would be likely, which would leave the deserving applicant in the case before the court without a remedy.[289] The reasons for overruling the existing rule meant that the application of the old rule to the case, even though all relevant facts occurred while the old rule was operative, would have produced an unjust result.[290]

Also meriting discussion are the decisions of the High Court of Australia and of the Privy Council in *Geelong Harbour Trust Commissioners v Gibbs Bright.*[291]

[282] (Eng) 5 and 6 Eliz II c 55.

[283] An Act for the further Amendment of the Laws Relating to the Poor in England 1844 (Eng) 7 and 8 Vict c 101.

[284] [1968] 2 QB 572, 579 (CA), see also 582–3, 585.

[285] *Ibid* 583.

[286] *Ibid* 580.

[287] *Ibid* 586.

[288] *Ibid* 579, 582, 586.

[289] *Ibid* 579. Cf *Jones v Secretary of State for Social Services* [1972] AC 944, 1015 (HL).

[290] Cf *Abbott v The Queen* [1977] AC 755, 769 (PC) (Lords Wilberforce and Edmund-Davies, dissenting); *R v Knuller* [1973] AC 435, 479 (HL) (Lord Diplock, dissenting).

[291] (1970) 122 CLR 504; [1974] AC 810 (PC).

Pursuant to the applicable statute the Harbour Trust could recover damages from the agent of any vessel 'for any injury caused by such vessel'.[292] Previous authority of the High Court of Australia held that a similar statutory section only imposed liability of the kind that would be imposed under the common law,[293] ie not strict liability as the plain words of the statute might be thought to suggest. Barwick CJ, with whom Owen J agreed, dissenting, thought the plain meaning was indeed to impose liability regardless of fault and saw 'no reason why we should perpetuate error, rather than declare what we consider is the meaning of the statute'.[294] He observed that the meaning of the statute 'did not affect the title to property or any matter of conveyancing' and that 'conduct in the handling of ships could not be affected by the reasoning of the Justices of this Court'.[295] Barwick CJ thought that the only potential reliance on the existing rule could be 'the insurance of marine risks', which he thought:

> is in general an annual affair and the negotiation of such contracts of insurance can scarce found a claim to the continuance of an insupportable construction of such plain words as those of the statute here under consideration.[296]

McTiernan and Menzies JJ, who along with Kitto J formed the majority emphasized that:

> a decision of this Court has stood without question for over fifty years and has, inevitably, been present to the minds of those responsible for legislation made during this time, including the Act now under consideration. Moreover, commerce has, no doubt, been conducted on the footing of the correctness of what this Court has decided.[297]

The majority, and the Privy Council, which dismissed the appeal, did not examine the substance of the question of statutory interpretation and so failed to engage with Barwick CJ's view that the existing rule was wrong in principle and so should have been overturned where the only countervailing factor was insurance arrangements. Instead, the majority apparently thought that, regardless of the merits of the existing rule,[298] if any change were to be effected to the meaning previously given by the High Court to the statutory provision, then it should be done by parliament with prospective effect. The Privy Council decided not to interfere with the High Court's view that certainty was more important than correctness in the particular case. In doing so, Lord Diplock, who delivered the advice of the Privy Council, emphasised the adjudicative retroactivity that would result from chang-

[292] Geelong Harbour Trust Act 1928–1951 (Vic) s 110.

[293] *Townsville Harbour Board v Scottish Shire Line* (1914) 18 CLR 306, eg 314–15.

[294] (1970) 122 CLR 504, 516–17. Cf *Australian Agricultural Co v Federated Engine Drivers and Firemen's Association of Australasia* (1913) 17 CLR 261, 278–9.

[295] (1970) 122 CLR 504, 515.

[296] *Ibid.*

[297] *Ibid* 518. Cf *The Jordan II* [2005] 1 WLR 1363, [16], [28] (HL). Contra *Re Spectrum Plus (in liquidation)* [2005] 2 AC 680, [62]–[64] (HL), discussed in Ch 5 Pt E(2)(b).

[298] J Harris 'Towards Principles of Overruling—When Should a Final Court of Appeal Second Guess?' (1990) 10 Oxford Journal of Legal Studies 135, 147–9.

ing the law as suggested by Barwick CJ. Lord Diplock observed that Barwick CJ's approach:

> would indubitably change the law to impose upon owners, masters and agents of vessels in Australian ports a more onerous liability than they or the harbour authorities or their respective insurers had any previous ground for thinking might be incurred by them. No doubt, as the Chief Justice pointed out, it would not be difficult to deal with the extended liability as respects future damage, by appropriate adjustments in the insurance policies of those concerned; but any change made by judicial decision would be also retrospective. It would create in harbour authorities new rights of action in respect of collisions which had resulted from act of God at any time within the six year limitation period before the High Court's decision altered the law, though no such right of action had existed at the time of the collision.[299]

The particular question of statutory interpretation is not presently important, but the fact that the majority of the High Court, undisturbed by the Privy Council, was prepared to follow an existing interpretation without even considering whether it was satisfactory[300] deserves critical note. The prevailing view in *Geelong Harbour* was that because commercial, or more precisely, insurance arrangements were assumed to be made on the basis of the existing interpretation, whether that interpretation was true to the statute was not a question even worth discussing because of the adjudicative retroactivity that changing the interpretation would involve. This was so even where the existing interpretation was, on its face, inconsistent with the plain words of the statute. The willingness to consider commercial certainty as a potentially superior value to abstract legal 'correctness' is commendable, but in *Geelong Harbour* there was no explicit discussion by the majority of the competing values at stake because the question of whether the existing approach was consistent with the plain terms of the statute was ignored.

It would be preferable if the merits of the existing interpretation are openly considered. If the interpretation is still thought to be the best interpretation, then no further question will arise. If the interpretation is open to question, then the factors militating against changing the law with retroactive effect, such as commercial reliance, should be considered and weighed against the interest in reopening the question of the interpretation to be given to the statute. Where the existing rule may confidently be said to be wrong in principle, in the sense that it cannot be reconciled with the plain terms of the statute, then the impetus judicially to change the law, with the inevitable retroactive effect of doing so, will be strong, even in the face of commercial reliance on the existing rule.

The third case is one in which the majority of the High Court of Australia overruled existing authority on the basis of their view that it was clearly wrong.[301] This contrasted with the minority view that the existing decision was not one about which one could say that it was 'wrong and productive of inconvenience'.

299 [1974] AC 810, 819 (PC). See also *Launchbury v Morgans* [1973] AC 127, 137 (HL).
300 Contra *The Jordan II* [2005] 1 WLR 1363, [29] (HL).
301 *Babaniaris v Lutony Fashions* (1987) 163 CLR 1, 14, 22–4.

Because that threshold was not reached, the minority was able to take the view that potential reliance on the existing law provided a reason not to overturn a decision that might otherwise be thought to be wrong.[302] The question in the case, *Babaniaris v Lutony Fashions*, was whether a woman who performed sewing work in her own home pursuant to a contract for services with a garment manufacturer was an 'outworker' within the meaning of section 3(1) of the Workers Compensation Act 1958 (Vic) and thus disentitled to compensation under that Act. Previous authority indicated that a person in her situation was entitled to compensation but the Full Court of the Supreme Court of Victoria overruled that interpretation of the Act and the High Court of Australia, by a majority of three to two, dismissed the appeal.

The High Court did not divide on the issue of when, in general, it is appropriate to reconsider the interpretation given to a statute. Indeed it was Mason J, a member of the majority, who provided the statement of principle that overruling is less likely where the issue decided in the earlier case was:

> finely balanced, involving a difficult choice between strongly competing considerations. . . . In such a situation a lack of clarity in the expression of the legislative intention makes it legitimate for the court to regard the injustice or inconvenience which would flow from overruling the earlier decision as having an influential effect on the outcome.[303]

The division was over whether the existing authority was or was not wrong in principle. That question usually cannot be approached at a high level of abstraction. If a construction is inconsistent with the plain terms of the statute one would expect the decision to be held to be wrong in principle, but that statement in turn opens similarly difficult questions about when something is inconsistent with the plain terms of a statute. However each of those questions is answered in a particular case, it would be unfortunate if such a malleable standard was to provide an immutable threshold beyond which the retroactive effects of a decision changing the law are not relevant. Such an approach would make too much turn on whether the existing interpretation could or could not be characterized as wrong in principle. Instead, even if an existing decision might be thought to be wrong in principle, and so more amenable to retroactive change, room should be allowed for cases in which the retroactive effects of correcting the existing interpretation may motivate a judicial decision not to change the law. In such a case the legislature, assuming it shared the court's view about the law being wrong in principle, might be expected to change the law non-retroactively, as the minority in *Babaniaris v Lutony Fashions* thought was the appropriate course.

The result of the adjudicative retroactivity in that case was that a woman who should have been able to rely on the existing law, that she was entitled to workers'

[302] *Babaniaris v Lutony Fashions* (1987) 163 CLR 27, 30–1.

[303] *Ibid* 14. See also *Jones v Secretary of State for Social Services* [1972] AC 944, 996–7 (HL) and *D'Orta-Ekenaike v Victoria Legal Aid* [2005] HCA 12, [24]: 'chief significance must be attached to the fact that a disputed question of construction was finally resolved. . . . This Court should not depart from that decision without powerful reasons to do so. A mere preference for one construction over the other would not suffice.'

compensation, in making decisions about the terms of her contract for services and her own financial and health, including insurance arrangements, was retroactively deprived of her entitlement to workers' compensation after she had suffered an injury. Industrial relations is not a field in which legislatures are known for inactivity, and prospective legislative change could have occurred if the existing interpretation was thought by the legislature, perhaps prompted by judicial utterances, to require change. The willingness of the majority in *Babaniaris* to change the interpretation of the statute because the existing interpretation was thought to be wrong in principle rightly recognised that whether an existing interpretation is or is not inconsistent with the plain terms of the statute is a question that should be asked regardless of the reliance considerations at stake—a step that the majority in *Geelong Harbour* was not, in deference to commercial insurance arrangements, prepared to take. But unfortunately the majority in *Babaniaris* was not then willing to give proper consideration to the entitlement of a seamstress to rely on the law. This should have been done by asking the further question of whether, notwithstanding the apparent inconsistency of the earlier decision with the plain terms of the statute, that interpretation should remain unaltered by the judiciary because of the significance of the potential reliance on that decision.

4 Conclusions on Private Law

The ability to rely on an existing legal rule will often be in issue in private law cases and, when it is, it will militate against retroactive legal change. The ability to rely on the law is not, however, at issue in all private law matters. It is more likely, for example, to be relevant in cases involving contractual agreements, property settlements and personal status than in cases involving restoration of harm done or the return of a benefit to which a person was never entitled, which arise under the law of tort or unjust enrichment. Because the ability to rely on the law is a key rationale for presuming against retroactivity, the absence of legitimate reliance interests, or their defeasibility to more compelling competing interests, may result in the rebuttal of the presumption in particular cases. Where the existing law is unclear or where change to the law occurs gradually over a number of cases, then the accompanying retroactive effects may be justifiable because they are unavoidable, slight or predictable. Adjudicative retroactivity may also be justifiable if, for example, existing authority permits moral obloquy, is out of line with changed legal or factual circumstances or is wrong in principle.

Whether, in private law matters, competing interests trump the common law's presumptive resistance to retroactivity should not be determined by whether the case involves commercial dealings, including insurance arrangements.[304] The ability to rely on the law, to which all legal persons are equally entitled, though which may often be acutely relevant in many commercial settings, and may

[304] For further discussion of the relevance of insurance see C Sampford *Retrospectivity and the Rule of Law* (Oxford University Press 2006) 182.

include insurance arrangements, is what requires protection. Weighing interests competing with the ability to rely on the law is a task that judges should confront openly and, consistently with the doctrine of precedent and attachment to existing principle in novel cases,[305] is a task that judges should commence with a presumption against retroactivity defeasible only in compelling circumstances.

F Public Law

1 The Creation of New Law without Overruling Prior Authority

In *Conway v Rimmer*[306] the House of Lords created a new rule affecting the Crown's immunity from producing in litigation certain types of document, which differed from the expression of the rule by the House in *Duncan v Cammell Laird*.[307] It is generally thought that this new rule was created by confining the decision in *Duncan v Cammell Laird* to a special category of facts, rather than overruling it.[308] After *Duncan v Cammell Laird* the rule was accepted as being that if the Crown claimed privilege over a document, the court would consider that claim to be final and conclusive on the matter and would not determine for itself whether the claim of privilege was justified.[309] The rule established by *Conway v Rimmer* is that if the Crown claims public interest immunity, it is ultimately for the court to decide whether that claim should be successful.[310] In changing the law in this way the House of Lords emphasised that judicial experience since the decision in *Duncan v Cammell Laird* revealed that the broad rule for which that case came to be thought of as authority was unsatisfactory in practice.[311]

One concern about this change that was discussed in *Conway v Rimmer* was the Crown's submission that the risk of later production in civil litigation may cause a lack of candour in documents created by Crown officers.[312] Their Lordships were confident that their decision would have no impact on the candour of officers of the Crown, particularly because the immunity would continue to exist for those cases in which the court was satisfied that the public interest required non-disclosure.[313] This was discussed as a prospective matter: whether the candour of

[305] Cf *Mabo v Queensland (No 2)* (1992) 175 CLR 1, 30.

[306] [1968] AC 910 (HL).

[307] [1942] AC 624 (HL).

[308] [1968] AC 910, 938–9, 990 (HL); J Harris 'Towards Principles of Overruling—When Should a Final Court of Appeal Second Guess?' (1990) 10 Oxford Journal of Legal Studies 135, 141; LV Prott 'When Will a Superior Court Overrule Its Own Decision?' (1978) 52 Australian Law Journal 304, 305; contra [1968] AC 910, 958 (HL).

[309] [1968] AC 910, 938, 958, 973 (HL); cf the actual content of the decision in *Duncan v Cammell Laird* [1942] AC 624, 642 (HL).

[310] [1968] AC 910, 971, 988, 992 (HL).

[311] *Ibid* 937, 970–1, 984, 985.

[312] *Ibid* 957, 972, 976, 988–9, 992.

[313] *Ibid* 957, 976, 988–9.

reports written in the future would be affected. There was no discussion in the judgments of whether it was appropriate for documents written in the past, potentially in reliance on the existence of a broad Crown privilege which, in practice, lay within the grant of the Crown itself, to be exposed to a new rule according to which it is for the court to determine whether the document should be produced. This retroactive effect of the decision probably caused consternation amongst some authors of Crown documents who wrote those documents believing that production could never be required in civil litigation.

The approach of the House of Lords to future documents can also be applied to documents already written: those documents that were required to be immune from production for the protection of the public interest would be granted immunity and those that were not, would be documents that the public interest (admittedly as determined by the court rather than the executive), which was always the rationale for the privilege, never required to be immune.[314] If as a result of the retroactive change candid statements were revealed to people who were not intended by their authors ever to see them, then the court's approach rightly assumed that transparent candour, rather than secretive candour, is, except within a confined class of information that the change to the rule would not affect, a positive attribute of public affairs. To the extent that potential reliance of Crown officials was upset by the retroactive change, that must be contrasted to the public interest, and the interest of individual litigants, in the fair conduct of litigation on the basis of all relevant information.[315] It may be that potential reliance of the executive government, defeat of which involves greater accountability and transparency of government and greater equality of arms before the courts, is less worthy of protection than the ability of private individuals to rely on the law. Similarly, in *R v North and East Devon Health Authority, ex p Coughlan*,[316] any difficulties for the health authority caused by the retroactivity involved in developing the law to intensify judicial review of a decision of the executive government to renege on a promise made to a specific individual that she would enjoy a substantive benefit, were implicitly subordinated to the desirability of protecting the substantive legitimate expectations of vulnerable private citizens.

Miss Coughlan, who was severely disabled, was promised by the health authority, which had a statutory obligation for her care, that she could remain living at a particular National Health Service facility so long as she chose to do so. The health authority later decided to close that facility for financial reasons without identifying alternative accommodation for Miss Coughlan. The Court of Appeal observed that:

> In the past it would have been argued that the promise was to be ignored since it could not have any effect on how the public body exercised its judgment in what it thought was the public interest. Today such an argument would have no prospect of success. . . .[317]

[314] Cf *A-G (Northern Territory) v Kearney* (1985) 158 CLR 500, 515–16, 522–5.

[315] [1968] AC 910, 985, 988–9, 992 (HL).

[316] [2001] QB 213 (CA).

[317] *Ibid* [55].

It was common ground between the parties that the promise could be broken 'if, and only if, an overriding public interest required it'.[318] An important development in the law apparent in *Coughlan*, which contrasts sharply to the traditional principles of *Associated Provincial Picture Houses Ltd v Wednesbury Corporation*,[319] was that it was held to be *for the court to decide* 'whether there is a sufficient overriding interest to justify a departure from what has been previously promised'.[320] Another development was the explicit categorisation of cases involving 'a legitimate expectation of a *benefit which is substantive*', [321] combined with judicial willingness to protect such expectations if their disappointment is thought by the court to amount to an abuse of power.

The court was at pains to establish that its decision was rooted in existing authority, whilst also acknowledging that this was 'still a developing field of law'[322] and that the role of the courts in protecting substantive legitimate expectations 'is still controversial'.[323] The retroactivity involved in continuing the development of the law in this area included that the health authority was deemed to have been required to pay greater regard to its promise to Mrs Coughlan than, in fact, was legally required of the health authority at the time that it decided to renege on its promise in favour of other valid considerations.[324] The reason that, on balance, the retroactivity in *Coughlan* is tolerable is that, although the health authority was subjected to more intensive judicial review than it might have expected, and was held to a promise that it previously might have expected legally to depart from, it was ultimately not required to do anything other than comply with an express promise made by it on a number of occasions in precise terms to a small group of severely disabled individuals for whose care it was, by statute, responsible.[325]

The court did not hold that a public authority could never depart from a substantive legitimate expectation to which it had given rise. If proper consideration is given to the departure from a promise and powerful counterveiling factors are present, the court may judge that disappointing a substantive legitimate expectation does not constitute an abuse of power and is therefore lawful.[326] In *Coughlan*, however, the fact that when the health authority decided to break its promise, it made no alternative arrangements for those for whose care it was responsible, made it justifiable for the court to find that the disappointment of the promise was unlawful.

[318] *Ibid* [52].
[319] [1948] 1 KB 223 (CA)
[320] [2001] QB 213, [58] (CA). See also [52] and [81]–[83].
[321] *Ibid* [57].
[322] *Ibid* [59].
[323] *Ibid*. See also [71].
[324] Cf *ibid* [65].
[325] *Ibid* [86].
[326] *R(Bibi) v Newham LBC* [2002] 1 WLR 237, [41], [43], [49]–[51] (CA); PP Craig *Administrative Law* (5th edn Sweet and Maxwell London 2003) 652–6; and I Steele 'Substantive Legitimate Expectations: Striking The Right Balance?' (2005) 121 Law Quarterly Review 300, 314 et seq.

2 The Creation of New Law by Overruling Prior Authority

(a) Judicial Review of Questions of Law

Lord Bingham has said that the pre-eminent judge-made changes in the law in recent times have occurred in the area of judicial review of administrative action.[327] That description includes the process of change that began in *Anisminic v Foreign Compensation Commission*[328] and culminated with *R v Hull University Visitor, ex p Page*.[329] *Anisminic* began the departure from the doctrine represented by *R v Bolton*[330] that jurisdictional error was reviewable but an error within jurisdiction, including one of law, was not reviewable. The significance of *Anisminic* is that, whilst retaining the nomenclature, it dispensed with any meaningful distinction between a jurisdictional error of law (an error of law going to the jurisdiction of an administrative authority) and a non-jurisdictional error of law (an error of law made by an administrative authority within its lawful jurisdiction).[331] The abandonment of the distinction between these traditional categories was explicitly recognised by the time of *O'Reilly v Mackman*, in which it was forthrightly stated that if an administrative tribunal made any error of law, it must have deviated from the scope of its lawful authority.[332] The rationale for and implication of this change were fully spelt out in *Page*. The rationale was that parliament only conferred on an administrative authority the power to act within the law, and the courts, so it was assumed, are the arbiters of the correct view of the law,[333] so by substituting their own view on legal questions, the courts keep administrative authorities within the bounds of the law, as parliament is presumed to intend.[334] The implication was that any error of law held by a reviewing court to have been made by an administrative authority may be quashed and the court's view of the law substituted.[335]

The statement of principle in *Page* that completed the departure, that began in *Anisminic*, from reliance on the 'esoteric'[336] distinction between jurisdictional and non-jurisdictional errors of law was, for the majority of the House, obiter dicta. The majority perpetuated the distinction between jurisdictional and

[327] Lord Bingham 'The Judge as Lawmaker: An English Perspective' in T Bingham *The Business of Judging: Selected Essays and Speeches* (Oxford University Press 2000) 29. See also the comment by Lord Goff in *Kleinwort Benson v Lincoln County Council* [1999] 2 AC 349, 378 (HL) that '[p]erhaps the most remarkable example' of a 'major departure' from 'established principle' was 'the decisions of this House in the middle of this century which led to the creation of our modern system of administrative law'.

[328] [1969] 2 AC 147 (HL).

[329] [1993] AC 682 (HL).

[330] (1841) 1 QB 66, 72–5; 113 ER 1054, 1057–8.

[331] [1969] 2 AC 147, 174, 194–5, 207–8, contra 181–2 (HL).

[332] [1983] 2 AC 237, 278, 283 (HL).

[333] Cf *R v Monopolies Commission, ex p South Yorkshire Transport* [1993] 1 WLR 23, 32 (HL).

[334] [1993] AC 682, 701–2, 705–6 (HL); *Anisminic* [1969] 2 AC 147, 195, 207 (HL).

[335] [1993] AC 682, 702, 706 (HL).

[336] *O'Reilly v Mackman* [1983] 2 AC 237, 278 (HL).

non-jurisdictional error in the particular field of university visitors, and held that the visitor's decision was within jurisdiction and so not amenable to judicial review.[337] As in *Hedley Byrne v Heller*,[338] a major restatement of the law was issued by way of obiter dicta, thus confining its retroactive effect. In any case, the general statement made in *Page* was the culmination of a long and gradual process of change towards the position that courts may substitute their own judgment for any question of law on which they think an administrative authority has erred. This gradualness reduced the retroactive effect of each decision in this series, particularly after *Anisminic* broke the initial ground. None of these are, however, the strongest reason not to object to the retroactive effect of decisions in this series.

The strongest reason is that the law by which the administrative authority and those subject to its powers were bound and on the basis of which the administrative authority made a substantive determination, was not changed by a decision about whether all determinations of law were judicially reviewable. The practical consequence of deciding that all questions of law were judicially reviewable may well have been, as it was in *Anisminic* and in *O'Reilly v Mackman*, that the court then had an opportunity to take, and did take, a different view from the administrative authority on the substantive legal question in issue. This is a similar result to what may occur in an appeal on a question of law. If the decision of the court on the substantive question changed the law from what it previously was on that topic, then an issue of retroactivity would arise independently of the change to the law of judicial review. But it is only the retroactivity of changing the law of judicial review that is here under discussion. That change had no direct impact on the answer to the issue of law decided by the authority and subject to judicial review. The retroactive impact was only on the matter of whether the court could subject the determination of the authority to review, not on what the result of that review would be.

Even if the retroactively changed answer to the question of whether judicial review of all errors of law was available could have been known by the parties prior to the events giving rise to the dispute, it is difficult to see how their actions might have been different in light of that knowledge or that they were, by virtue of that change in the law alone, deprived of some liberty or entitlement that they otherwise would have enjoyed. An administrative authority could suggest that its liberty to make its own determinations on questions of law within its jurisdiction was retroactively removed. Indeed that liberty was at the heart of these cases, and on balance the courts concluded that making unreviewable determinations of law was not a liberty that should be, or should have been, enjoyed by administrative authorities. It may be assumed that administrative authorities do not make decisions that they think are unlawful, so knowledge of the retroactive change would presumably not change any determinations that an administrative authority might make. Accordingly, neither the ability to rely on the law, nor the law's

[337] [1993] AC 682, 704 (HL).
[338] [1964] AC 465 (HL), discussed in Ch 5 Pt E(1)(e).

delineation of *individual* liberty was directly affected by the change in law on the topic of whether all questions of law decided by administrative authorities are judicially reviewable.

To the extent that a practical consequence of the change in the law of judicial review was that the determinations of the authority were then found, on review, to be incorrect on a question of law, it may be noted in passing that in both *Anisminic* and *O'Reilly v Mackman* the decisions on the issues of law reviewed, as distinct from the decisions to review them, were favourable to the private entity or persons rather than to the relevant administrative authority.[339] This adds some support to the claim that, in public law, retroactivity is less likely to be objectionable where the decision with retroactive effect favours the private person or entity rather than the executive government.

(b) Judicial Review of Questions of Fact

The law relating to judicial review of questions of fact is fraught with difficulties.[340] The present discussion is limited to one illustrative example. *R v Secretary of State for the Home Department, ex p Zamir* held that the standard of review to be applied by a court on an application for judicial review of a decision to detain and remove from the United Kingdom a non-national on the basis of an immigration officer's determination that the person was an 'illegal entrant' under section 33(1) of the Immigration Act 1971 (UK), was that the decision would be left undisturbed unless it was one for which there were 'no grounds' or it was a decision that 'no reasonable person' could have made.[341] Less than three years later the House of Lords departed from that view and held in *R v Secretary of State for the Home Department, ex p Khawaja*[342] that because whether a person was an illegal entrant was a condition precedent to the lawful exercise of the relevant powers conferred by statute on the executive government, the court must appraise for itself the evidence gathered by administrative officers and the court must satisfy itself on the civil standard of proof, appropriately calibrated for the fact that individual liberty was at stake, that the conclusion that someone was an illegal entrant was justified by the evidence. The importance of *Khawaja* is that it changed the standard of review applicable to questions of fact on which the lawful exercise of executive power depends.

Like the cases that changed the law on whether any error of law was reviewable by a court, *Khawaja* did not involve any change to what was to be decided. It changed the law only on the question of who, ultimately, was responsible for deciding it. The law to be applied by the primary decision maker was not changed.

339 Cf the minority view in *Page* [1993] AC 682, 709–712 (HL), which was that judicial review should be available on all questions of law decided by a university visitor, but that in the case at hand there was no error of law.

340 See PP Craig *Administrative Law* (5th edn Sweet and Maxwell London 2003) 502–10.

341 [1980] AC 930, 948–9 (HL); and see the discussion of *Zamir* in *R v Secretary of State for the Home Department, ex p Khawaja* [1984] 1 AC 74, 108 (HL).

342 [1984] 1 AC 74 (HL).

Thus the ability of individuals to rely on the substantive law could not have been in issue.[343] The fact that individual liberty was at stake in *Khawaja*, in the sense that those found to be illegal entrants could be detained and removed, motivated the court both to adopt the more intensive standard of review and the higher standard of proof.[344]

The report of *Khawaja* includes two joined appeals, both by persons who had been found by immigration officers to be illegal entrants. The change in law effected in *Khawaja* favoured them both in the sense that they both enjoyed the opportunity to have the court determine for itself whether they were illegal entrants, with the accompanying chance that they would be found not to be. As demonstrated by the fact that one of them was found by the court to be an illegal entrant and one of them was found by the court not to be an illegal entrant, the alteration of the standard of review, because it did not alter the law on the substantive question of whether they were or were not illegal entrants, did not necessarily, in the end, favour applicants for review.

3 Overruling a Prior Judicial Interpretation of a Statute

Naturally, many cases in the field of public law turn on the interpretation of statutes. The issue in such cases is, as in the judicial review cases discussed above, typically whether the executive has exceeded the limits of the power conferred on it by parliament. For the reasons discussed above, in many cases reliance will not be in issue and the court will, unencumbered by concerns about retroactivity, adopt what it considers to be the best view of the scope of the statutory power. It is worth discussing, however, two cases in which the executive did rely on the existing judicial interpretation of a statute only to discover that the courts later overruled the existing view with retroactive effect.

The first case is *Vestey v Inland Revenue Commissioners*,[345] in which the interpretation of section 412 of the Income Tax Act 1952[346] was in question. That provision aimed to prevent the avoidance by persons ordinarily resident in the United Kingdom of their tax obligations by the transfer of assets to persons abroad. It did so by providing, inter alia, that if 'an individual' resident in the United Kingdom had, after assets had been transferred abroad, a 'power to enjoy' the income from those assets, then that income would be deemed to be the taxable income of that individual in the United Kingdom. In *Congreve v Inland Revenue Commissioners*[347] the House of Lords had held that this provision covered a person who did not

[343] Contra J Harris 'Towards Principles of Overruling—When Should a Final Court of Appeal Second Guess?' (1990) 10 Oxford Journal of Legal Studies 135, 169–70.

[344] [1984] 1 AC 74, 97, 109–11, 113–4, 125 (HL).

[345] [1980] AC 1148 (HL).

[346] (UK) 15 and 16 Geo VI and 1 Eliz II c 10.

[347] [1948] 1 All ER 948 (HL).

transfer the assets but nonetheless had a power to enjoy income from them after they were transferred. The question in *Vestey* was whether that interpretation should be overruled and replaced by a rule that the statutory provision in question applied only to the transferor. *Vestey* involved a discretionary trust settled on foreign trustees for the benefit of the descendants, who lived in the United Kingdom, of the settlors. If the ratio decidendi of *Congreve* was applied to these facts then each beneficiary could theoretically have been liable for taxation on the entire income of the trust. The Revenue submitted that it could not tax, across all of the beneficiaries, more than the total amount applicable to the total income, but that within that limit it could apportion the tax liability among the beneficiaries as the Revenue, in its discretion, saw fit. The House of Lords was less comfortable with the idea that the Revenue could decide whom to tax and how much to tax them than the Revenue was.

Lord Wilberforce emphasised that the imposition of liability for income tax and the magnitude of that tax are matters for parliament and that it would be 'a radical departure from constitutional principle' for it to be otherwise.[348] If *Congreve* was correct then it would have produced a result in the case of a discretionary trust with multiple beneficiaries resident in the United Kingdom that was 'arbitrary, potentially unjust, and fundamentally unconstitutional'.[349]

Lord Wilberforce acknowledged that 'no doubt many persons have been taxed on the basis'[350] of the interpretation in *Congreve*, but there was otherwise no serious consideration of the Revenue's reliance on *Congreve* in collecting tax and estimating its future receipts. The House was more concerned with the principle that 'a taxpayer is entitled to know what tax is claimed against him',[351] which was violated by a legal rule that allowed the Revenue to determine which beneficiaries of a discretionary trust would be liable for taxation and for how much each would be liable. The interest of the public at large, through the Revenue, in being able to rely on the existing tax law for the purpose of collecting tax and estimating future receipts should not be overlooked. However, in *Vestey*, the confinement of the executive to its lawful authority and the protection of the ability of individuals to know in advance the basis on which they would be taxed were more compelling interests.

There was no mention in *Vestey* of the instruction in the Practice Statement on Judicial Precedent of the danger of retroactively disturbing 'the basis on which settlements of property and fiscal arrangements have been entered into'.[352] Harris suggested that this may have been because the decision was in favour of private citizens, rather than the executive.[353] Presumably a 'fiscal arrangement' can only

348 [1980] AC 1148, 1172 (HL).
349 *Ibid* 1176, see also 1174, 1196–7, 1198.
350 *Ibid* 1175.
351 *Ibid* 1172.
352 *Practice Statement (Judicial Precedent)* [1966] 1 WLR 1234 (HL).
353 J Harris 'Towards Principles of Overruling—When Should a Final Court of Appeal Second Guess?' (1990) 10 Oxford Journal of Legal Studies 135, 171 fn 15.

be entered into by a private entity rather than the Revenue. To build on the explanation given by Harris, the law represented in *Congreve* was not something on which private citizens could rely. The essence of the problem with the rule in *Congreve*, for the sort of case that arose in *Vestey*, was that tax liability of particular individuals lay in the discretion of the Revenue. Because individuals *could not* make arrangements on the basis of the existing law, the general caution about fiscal arrangements counselled by the Practice Statement was overcome by judicial eagerness to alter a rule that disrespected taxpayer's right to be taxed by parliament in the form of laws on which taxpayers could rely.

The view taken of the statute in *Congreve*, that it covered all those with a power to enjoy the income of the transferred assets regardless of whether they were responsible for the transfer, was, on its face, a tenable one,[354] a characteristic that might ordinarily protect a decision on the meaning of a statute from overruling.[355] However, as was emphasised in *Vestey*,[356] the consequences of the rule in *Congreve* for a discretionary trust with multiple beneficiaries were not contemplated in *Congreve* itself. When the House of Lords realized that in such circumstances the rule in *Congreve* allowed the executive to exceed the constitutional limits of its tax collection powers and undermined the ability of private entities to know the extent of their tax obligations, the case for overruling it and holding that the statutory provision was only applicable to transferors, was overwhelming.

The second case in this category, and perhaps the case that best illustrates adjudicative retroactivity in the area of public law, is *R v Governor of Brockhill Prison, ex p Evans (No 2)*.[357] Ms Evans was sentenced to two years in prison. She was entitled by statute to a reduction in the period to be served after her conviction because of time spent in prison prior to trial.[358] The amount of that reduction, and hence her release date, were calculated by the governor of the prison in accordance with several decisions of the Divisional Court that interpreted the relevant statutory provision.[359] Those authorities were overruled by the Divisional Court upon Ms Evans' application, with the result that her release occurred 59 days after the date on which, according to the new interpretation of the statute, she was entitled to have been released.[360] Ms Evans brought an application against the prison governor for damages for false imprisonment on the basis of her detention

[354] [1980] AC 1148, 1174, 1198 (HL). Cf *Westminster Council v Southern Railway Co* [1936] AC 511, 563–5 (HL) where existing authority was overruled as wrong in principle.

[355] *Jones v Secretary of State for Social Services* [1972] AC 944, 996–7 (HL); *Lancashire and Yorkshire Railway Co v Mayor of Borough of Bury* (1889) 14 App Cas 417, 419–20 (HL).

[356] [1980] AC 1148, 1176, 1178, 1187, 1196, 1198 (HL). See also *West Ham Union v Edmonton Union* [1908] AC 1, 4–5 (HL).

[357] [2001] 2 AC 19 (HL), noted by P Cane 'The Temporal Element in Law' (2001) 117 Law Quarterly Review 5.

[358] Criminal Justice Act 1967 (Eng) s 67.

[359] Including *R v Governor of Blundeston Prison, ex p Gaffney* [1982] 1 WLR 696 (QB); *R v Secretary of State for the Home Office, ex p Read* (1987) 9 Cr App R(S) 206 (QB); *R v Governor of Styal Prison, ex p Mooney* [1996] 1 Cr App R(S) 74 (QB).

[360] *R v Governor of Brockhill Prison, ex p Evans* [1997] QB 443.

after the date on which she was ultimately held to have been entitled to release.[361] There was no change to the law of false imprisonment. The question was whether judicial alteration of the meaning of a statute could have the retroactive effect of deeming imprisonment that was consistent with the judicial view of that statute at the time of the imprisonment to have been unlawful and so to have constituted false imprisonment.

It was accepted before the House of Lords that false imprisonment is a tort of strict liability.[362] Thus the governor's state of mind about what the law obliged him to do was not a relevant factor in the assessment of whether what he did actually was consistent with the law. The new interpretation of the statute was deemed to have been the law at the time that, under the new interpretation, Ms Evans should have been released. Whether the governor was actually, *as a matter of fact considered at the time of acting*, mistaken, was not relevant.[363] What was important was that he was retroactively deemed to have been mistaken.[364] It is clear from the previous authorities that the governor did, in fact, act as the law as interpreted by the courts at the time of the imprisonment obliged him to do.[365] For that reason the House of Lords emphasised that he was not personally to be blamed.[366] Nonetheless, whether what he did was actually in accordance with the law at the time that he did it was not in issue. Instead, what was in issue was whether what he did was in accordance with the law as it was later deemed to have been at the time that he acted.[367] So characterised, there was a straightforward case of false imprisonment.

It is worth starkly summarising the implications of this decision. At the time that the governor continued Ms Evans' imprisonment, he acted in accordance with the law as it was then interpreted by the courts, the decisions of which he was bound to follow. At the time of the litigation brought by Ms Evans, the Divisional Court changed the law and applied the new rule to Ms Evans' case, deeming the law at the time of her imprisonment to have been something other than it in fact was, with the result that the governor was liable for false imprisonment.

361 A similar claim was successful in *Cowell v Corrective Services Commission of New South Wales* (1988) 13 NSWLR 714.

362 [2001] 2 AC 19, 26, 27, 28, 35 (HL). See also *Cowell v Corrective Services Commission of New South Wales* (1988) 13 NSWLR 714, 743.

363 On the theoretical distinction between an executive act being apparently lawful, *as a matter of fact*, and a later court decision that, *as a matter of law*, such an executive act was always void, see C Forsyth '"The Metaphysic of Nullity" Invalidity, Conceptual Reasoning and the Rule of Law' in *The Golden Metwand and the Crooked Cord: Essays on Public Law in Honour of Sir William Wade QC* C Forsyth and I Hare (eds) (Clarendon Press Oxford 1998) 141, 147–8.

364 Cf the discussion of *Kleinwort Benson v Lincoln City Council* [1999] 2 AC 349 (HL) in Ch 5 Pt D(1).

365 Contra *Kleinwort Benson* in which there was no judicial authority prior to *Hazell v Hammersmith and Fulham London Borough Council* [1992] 2 AC 1 (HL) on the question of whether transactions of the kind in that case were *intra vires* and there was no question of any party being *obliged* as opposed to merely *permitted* to act in a certain way.

366 [2001] 2 AC 19, 26, 27 (HL).

367 Contra *R(Lunn) v Governor of Moorland Prison* [2006] 1 WLR 2870, especially at [30]–[31] (CA).

Lord Steyn thought that it was 'a matter of judgment how the weight of the competing principles in the present case should be assessed'.[368] The principles to which Lord Steyn referred were, on the one hand, that the governor was acting as the law at the time of his actions required him to do, and on the other hand, that Ms Evans was imprisoned for 59 days longer than allowed by the view of the law ultimately held to be correct.[369] Lord Steyn was particularly influenced by the fact that the case involved deprivation of individual liberty by the executive government.[370] Lords Hope[371] and Hobhouse[372] also emphasised this characteristic of the case, as did Priestley JA in *Cowell*.[373] The fact that individual liberty was at stake militated towards a result favouring the individual.[374]

The concern for liberty that motivated the decision in *Evans* was different to the type of liberty that provides a rationale for the presumption against retroactivity. The rationale for the presumption is concerned, for example, with individuals who, at the time of acting, enjoyed a freedom so to act, not later being deprived of that freedom with the deprivation being deemed effective at the time of acting.[375] This did not arise in *Evans*. For the whole time that Ms Evans was imprisoned the law was that she was rightly imprisoned. In *Evans* the concern was to constrain the state's power to deprive people of their personal liberty by imprisoning them. Because the change in law was in favour of individual liberty the judges were not dissuaded from making it by the retroactive effect of doing so. When individual liberty militates towards the new rule, then that result will, as it was in *Evans*, be difficult to resist on the basis of its retroactivity.

4 Conclusions on Public Law

A common theme of the cases discussed in this part, and of most public law cases, is that the primary judicial concern is to keep the exercise of executive power within lawful limits. Many prominent public law cases that developed or changed the law concern the availability, standard or grounds of judicial review. In addition to the cases selected for discussion above, it may be mentioned that, for example, *Ridge v Baldwin*[376] recognized a right to be afforded natural justice, but not to any particular outcome, and *Minister of State for Immigration and Ethnic Affairs v Teoh* recognized a new basis for a procedural legitimate expectation, but not any

[368] [2001] 2 AC 19, 28 (HL).

[369] *Ibid*. See also *Cowell v Corrective Services Commission of New South Wales* (1988) 13 NSWLR 714, 717–18.

[370] [2001] 2 AC 19, 28–9 (HL).

[371] *Ibid* 35, 37.

[372] *Ibid* 43.

[373] (1988) 13 NSWLR 714, 717–718.

[374] See also *D v Home Office* [2006] 1 WLR 1003, [69]–[70] (CA) and *R(Lunn) v Governor of Moorland Prison* [2006] 1 WLR 2870, [30] (CA).

[375] See further Ch 3 Pt C(3).

[376] [1964] AC 40 (HL).

right for an executive power to be exercised in any particular way.[377] Because of the nature of what was at stake in these cases, and others like them, the ability to rely on the law is often not as relevant as it is in other fields of law.

Nonetheless, sometimes, as in *Conway v Rimmer*, *Coughlan*, *Vestey* and *Evans*, the executive may have an interest in relying on the law as stated by the courts. When changing the law is proposed in such cases, it is necessary to weigh the desirability of the executive being able to rely on the law against the desirability of the executive being prevented from exceeding what the court considers to be the best view of the bounds of the executive's lawful power.[378] Because in such cases a person will have been subject to what is subsequently considered to have been an excess of executive power, the courts have typically favoured the protection of private interests and individual liberty over the ability of the executive to rely on the law at the time that it acted. It should also be observed that many seminal public law cases were decided in favour of an individual seeking to control the exercise of executive power,[379] thus overcoming any objection to changing the law that might otherwise be made on the basis of the impact on individual liberty caused by the retroactive effect of doing so. The frequent absence of private reliance interests from public law cases combined with the fact that individual freedom from excessive executive power may often be furthered rather than hampered by changing the law with retroactive effect, mean that overcoming presumptive concerns about the retroactive effects of developing or changing the law is relatively easily done in a public law context.

G Criminal Law

Discussion of many of the issues associated with adjudicative retroactivity in criminal law has already been prompted by the consideration above of the marital rape cases.[380] In particular, change to the law being gradual and foreseeable,[381] the conduct criminalised being heinous even if not strictly illegal at the time that it occurred,[382] the desirability of the law keeping pace with changed social conditions,[383] and the desirability of the law being both internally logical and consistent

[377] (1995) 183 CLR 273, 291–2, 302, 313.

[378] Cf J Harris 'Towards Principles of Overruling—When Should a Final Court of Appeal Second Guess?' (1990) 10 Oxford Journal of Legal Studies 135, 172.

[379] Not only *Anisminic v Foreign Compensation Commission* [1969] 2 AC 147 (HL) and *O'Reilly v Mackman* [1983] 2 AC 237 (HL) as discussed above, but also *Conway v Rimmer* [1968] AC 910 (HL), *R v Secretary of State for the Home Department, ex p Khawaja* [1984] 1 AC 74 (HL), *Vestey v Inland Revenue Commissioners* [1980] AC 1148 (HL), *R v Governor of Brockhill Prison, ex p Evans (No 2)* [2001] 2 AC 19 (HL), *Ridge v Baldwin* [1964] AC 40 (HL), *Minister of State for Immigration and Ethnic Affairs v Teoh* (1995) 183 CLR 273, and *R v North and East Devon Health Authority, ex p Coughlan* [2001] QB 213 (CA).

[380] Ch 5 Pt C.

[381] Ch 5 Pt C(2).

[382] Ch 5 Pt C(3).

[383] Ch 5 Pt C(4).

with fundamental common law principle,[384] have been discussed as reasons that may militate towards overcoming the prohibition on retroactivity in exceptional cases. The presence of all of these factors in one case, as occurred in the marital rape cases, is unusual, if not unique. Other cases in which the criminal law has been changed with retroactive effect have not always contained the same number nor strength of reasons in favour of retroactivity and so are often more open to question than the marital rape cases. The general prohibition that must be borne in mind is that a person who acts in a way that is not, at the time of acting, criminal, should not subsequently be deemed to have been responsible for a criminal offence. Strong reasons in exceptional circumstances are required to defeat that prohibition.

1 The Creation of New Law without Overruling Prior Authority

(a) Judicial Response to New Factual Circumstances

Joyce v DPP[385] involved an appeal from a conviction for treason. The appellant was not a British subject, but had obtained and travelled on a British passport after stating, falsely, that he was a British subject. He 'broadcast propaganda on behalf of the enemy'[386] in 1939. He was arrested by the British in Germany in 1945 and, in England, was tried and convicted of treason. He appealed on the basis, inter alia, that treason against the King could not be committed by an alien abroad and purported to rely on authority for that proposition. Lord Jowitt, with whom Lords Simon, Macmillan and Wright agreed, held that there was no authority for that proposition and rather that there was authority for the proposition that an alien abroad enjoying the 'protection' of the British Crown could be guilty of treason.[387] The relevant form of 'protection' in this case, and this appears to have been a novel point,[388] was the holding of a British passport. Before so concluding Lord Jowitt observed that 'it is by the application of principle to changing circumstances that our law has developed'.[389] Lord Jowitt continued:

> It is not for His Majesty's judges to create new offences or to extend any penal law and particularly the law of high treason, but new conditions may demand a reconsideration of the scope of the principle. It is not an extension of a penal law to apply its principle to circumstances unforeseen at the time of its enactment, so long as the case is fairly brought within its language.[390]

In *Joyce* the House of Lords considered that the existing law of treason was being applied to the unusual facts that arose in the case. The House did not consider that

[384] Ch 5 Pt C(5).
[385] [1946] AC 347 (HL).
[386] *Ibid* 349.
[387] *Ibid* 366–8.
[388] G Williams 'The Correlation of Allegiance and Protection' (1948) 10 Cambridge Law Journal 54, 60.
[389] [1946] AC 347, 366 (HL).
[390] *Ibid.*

it was creating a new crime. It is certainly true that the crime of treason, of which he was ultimately convicted, existed at the time of Mr Joyce's actions. The more important question, however, is whether, to borrow the language of article 7 of the ECHR, Joyce's actions constituted a criminal offence at the time that they occurred. Glanville Williams commented in response to *Joyce* that it 'is always a difficult question of degree whether an apparently new determination is an application of old rules or an extension of them'.[391] In the case of *Joyce* that question can be straightforwardly framed, though not easily answered. The question is whether, at the time of Joyce acting, the possession of a British passport was itself, as a matter of law,[392] sufficient to give rise to a duty of allegiance, breach of which could amount to treason. If not, then *Joyce* involved retroactive criminal liability. The answer to that question hinges on areas of law into which the present discussion need not delve and on which different views have been taken.[393]

After *Joyce*, Glanville Williams thought, in a comment making the link between adjudicative and statutory retroactivity, that:

> Everyone now agrees that the judges should not extend the criminal law under the guise of applying it, however detestable the conduct of which the prisoner has been guilty. We no longer tolerate Acts of Attainder, and so we cannot, consistently with our own views, approve the same result being attained by unavowed departure from the existing law.[394]

He could not know that less than 15 years later moral conservatism in the House of Lords would outweigh respect for the prohibition on retroactive criminal liability.

(b) Perceived Immorality

In *Shaw v DPP*[395] a man who published and sold booklets advertising the names, addresses and, in some instances, photographs and mention of the particular services, of prostitutes, who paid him a fee for the advertisement, was tried and convicted of, relevantly, conspiracy to corrupt public morals. The Court of Criminal Appeal was at pains to discuss old authorities on the basis of which it concluded that that:

> it is an established principle of common law that conduct calculated or intended to corrupt public morals . . . is an indictable misdemeanour. As the reports show, the conduct to which that principle is applicable may vary considerably, but the principle itself does not, and in our view the facts of the present case fall plainly within it.[396]

[391] G Williams 'The Correlation of Allegiance and Protection' (1948) 10 Cambridge Law Journal 54, 55. Cf *R v Kataja* [1943] VLR 145, 146.

[392] Contra the dissenting opinion of Lord Porter in *Joyce* [1946] AC 347, 374–6 (HL).

[393] G Williams 'The Correlation of Allegiance and Protection' (1948) 10 Cambridge Law Journal 54; and Mr Justice Barry 'Treason, Passports and the Ideal of a Fair Trial' (1956) 7 Res Judicate 276; contra H Lauterpacht 'Allegiance, Diplomatic Protection and Criminal Jurisdiction over Aliens' (1947) 9 Cambridge Law Journal 330.

[394] G Williams 'The Correlation of Allegiance and Protection' (1948) 10 Cambridge Law Journal 54, 55.

[395] [1962] AC 220 (HL).

[396] [1962] AC 220, 233 (CCA).

The Court of Criminal Appeal emphasised that the:

> courts in the relevant cases were not creating new offences or making new law: they were applying existing law to new facts.[397]

The Court of Criminal Appeal considered itself to be engaged in the same modest enterprise. On one view of the decision of the House of Lords, it too primarily rested its judgment on this point.[398] If that approach is adopted, *Shaw*, along with its application in *R v Knuller*,[399] merits criticism on the basis that an offence of corruption of public morals does not define the conduct that is proscribed with a sufficient degree of precision to allow a person to know in advance of acting the ways in which his liberty is confined.[400] Whether an action that has never before been held to be criminal constitutes the existing crime of corruption of public morals, or conspiracy to do so, is left within the potentially arbitrary discretion of a jury.[401] These criticisms are related to the prohibition on retroactivity in the sense that, like the prohibition on retroactivity, they are motivated by the principle of legality.[402]

The more relevant aspect of *Shaw* for present purposes is Viscount Simonds' claim that:

> In the sphere of criminal law I entertain no doubt that there remains in the courts of law a residual power to enforce the supreme and fundamental purpose of the law, to conserve not only the safety and order but also the moral welfare of the State, and that it is their

[397] *Ibid* 234.

[398] [1962] AC 220, 266–7 (HL) (Viscount Simonds, with whom Lords Morris and Hodson agreed).

[399] [1973] AC 435 (HL), and its precursors such as *The Queen v Wellard* (1884) 14 QBD 63, 67 in which Huddleston B thought that it 'seems to be established that, speaking generally, whatever openly outrages decency and is injurious to public morals is a misdemeanour at common law'.

[400] Cf *Advisory Opinion of the Permanent Court of International Justice on the 'Consistency of Certain Legislative Decrees with the Constitution of the Free City'* (1935) PCIJ Series A/B No 65, 41, 52–3, 56, 57. The decision in *Manley v DPP* [1933] 1 KB 529, 534 (CCA) involving a conviction for unlawfully effecting a public mischief also deserves the same criticism, particularly insofar as it relied on the farcically wide statement of Lawrence J in *R v Higgins* (1801) 2 East 5, 21; 102 ER 269, 275 that 'all offences of a public nature, that is, all such acts or attempts as tend to the prejudice of the community, are indictable'. See *R v Newland* [1954] 1 QB 158, 167–8 (CCA); *R v Bailey* [1956] NI 15, 18–24; WTS Stallybrass 'Public Mischief' (1933) 49 Law Quarterly Review 183, 183 who thought *Manley* a decision 'which opens up a gloomy vista of indefinite criminal liability'; and *DPP v Withers* [1975] AC 842, 858, 861, 867 (HL) in which Viscount Dilhorne described *Manley* 'as an exercise of the inherent power claimed in earlier days to declare acts to be offences' and indicated his 'hope that in future such a vague expression as "public mischief" will not be included in criminal charges' and Lord Simon thought that on the authorities and 'on principle' the best view was that, contrary to *Manley*, there was no offence of effecting a public mischief known to English law.

[401] [1962] AC 220, 281–2 (HL) (Lord Reid, dissenting); *R v Knuller* [1973] AC 435, 479–80 (HL); *DPP v Withers* [1975] AC 842, 857, 861, 870 (HL); contra [1962] AC 220, 269, 292, 294 (HL); [1973] AC 435, 460–63 (HL); cf J Waldron 'Torture and Positive Law: Jurisprudence for the Whitehouse' (2005) 105 Columbia Law Review 1681, 1701.

[402] Cf the jurisprudence on the extended meaning of art 7 of the ECHR: *Kokkinakis v Greece* (1994) 17 EHRR 397, [52]; *SW v United Kingdom* (1996) 21 EHRR 363, [35]; *Cantoni v France* ECtHR (1996) Series A No 20, 1614, [29]; *Baskaya v Turkey* (2001) 31 EHRR 10, [36]; *Coeme v Belgium* ECtHR, 2000-VII 75, [145]; *Veeber v Estonia (No 2)* (2004) 39 EHRR 6, [31]. Also cf J Rawls *A Theory of Justice* (Revised edn Oxford University Press 1999) 209.

> duty to guard it against attacks which may be the more insidious because they are novel and unprepared for.[403]

Viscount Simonds continued:

> When Lord Mansfield . . . said[404] that the Court of King's Bench was the custos morum of the people and had the superintendency of offences contra bonos mores, he was asserting, as I now assert, that there is in that court a residual power, where no statute has yet intervened to supersede the common law, to superintend those offences which are prejudicial to the public welfare. Such occasions will be rare. . . . But gaps remain and will always remain since no one can foresee every way in which the wickedness of man may disrupt the order of society.[405]

Viscount Simonds said that it was 'for her Majesty's judges to play the part which Lord Mansfield pointed out to them'.[406]

If this is the basis on which *Shaw* was decided[407] then the case involved the imposition of criminal liability on the basis of the perceived immorality of the conduct notwithstanding the fact that at the time that the conduct occurred it was not criminal. If that is so, then it is necessary to examine whether the reasons that motivated the House of Lords to impose retroactive criminal liability were strong enough to overcome the general prohibition on retroactivity in criminal law. A majority of their Lordships were expressly motivated by their perception of public morality, which they believed to be informed by traditional precepts of Christianity.[408]

Lord Morris said that:

> There are certain manifestations of conduct which are an affront to and an attack upon recognised public standards of morals and decency, and which all well-disposed persons would stigmatise and condemn as deserving of punishment.[409]

This claim might be defensible if limited to extreme cases of immoral behaviour, but the pressing question in *Shaw* should have been whether the publication of a directory of prostitutes fell within that category, not whether the category existed. The conclusion that the publication of a directory of prostitutes did fall within a category of conduct so immoral as to justify retroactive criminal liability, assuming that is what happened in Shaw, was supported by nothing more than a view held by a majority of the House of Lords, informed by their view of Christianity, of what constituted public morality. This is clearly insufficient to warrant trumping the prohibition on retroactive criminal liability. That was the view taken by Lord Reid in dissent.

403 [1962] AC 220, 267 (HL). Contra JF Stephen *History of the Criminal Law of England* (Reprint of the original 1883 edn Routledge/Thoemmes Press London 1996) vol 3, 359–360; *Frey v Fedoruk* [1950] SCR 517, 525–30.

404 Citing *R v Delaval* (1763) 3 Burr 1434, 1438–1439; 97 ER 913, 915.

405 [1962] AC 220, 268 (HL).

406 *Ibid.*

407 Contra the explanation offerred by Lord Kilbrandon in *R v Knuller* [1973] AC 435, 496 (HL).

408 [1962] AC 220, 293–4 (HL).

409 *Ibid* 292.

Lord Reid thought that there was 'no such general offence known to the law as conspiracy to corrupt public morals'[410] and that 'it is now established that the courts cannot create new offences by individuals'.[411] Nonetheless, addressing himself to the decision reached by the other members of the House in Shaw, Lord Reid added:

> Even if there is still a vestigial power of this kind it ought not, in my view, to be used unless there appears to be general agreement that the offence to which it is applied ought to be criminal if committed by an individual.[412]

It is not the role of the courts to enter moral controversies on which the public is divided and on which parliament has not taken a view with the result that an individual whose acts were not criminal at the time that they occurred is subjected to retroactive criminal liability. Here individual liberty is centrally concerned. Assuming Mr Shaw's acts did not constitute a criminal offence at the time that he performed them, he enjoyed a liberty to act as he did. Many people, including members of the House of Lords, may have found the exercise of that liberty offensive and have considered it immoral, but that does not detract from the fact that the liberty existed. In assessing whether that liberty should have been deemed, by retroactive decision of the courts, not to have existed, whether the conduct could be regarded as unquestionably heinous and at all times deserving of punishment, as, for example, in the case of marital rape, should have been the decisive factor in the Law Lords' deliberations. Unfortunately little regard was had to this consideration and instead the majority's own view of morality seems to have been decisive on a morally controversial point,[413] to the detriment of individual liberty.

A related concern arising from this interpretation of Shaw is the decision's lack of respect for the ability of individuals to rely on the law to plan their affairs.[414] A publisher who wishes to publish something about which there is doubt as to its legality takes the risk that there will be a legal decision against her. However, if the decision is about whether to publish something about which there is doubt only as to its morality, then she should be able to rely on the existing law that definitely does not criminalise such publication and not be frightened that what is legal today will tomorrow be held to have been criminal yesterday.

Fuller thought that:

> where law is largely a reflection of extralegal morality, what appears in form as retrospective legislation may in substance represent merely the confirmation of views already widely held, or in process of development toward the rule finally enacted.[415]

[410] *Ibid* 272.
[411] *Ibid* 274.
[412] *Ibid* 275.
[413] A Ashworth *Principles of Criminal Law* (5th edn Oxford University Press 2006) 69.
[414] *Ibid*; [1962] AC 220, 281 (HL).
[415] L Fuller *The Morality of Law* (Revised edn Yale University Press New Haven CT 1969) 92.

By contrast, Glanville Williams thought that opinions:

> about what people ought morally to do are almost as numerous as human beings, but opinions about what people are obliged legally to do should be capable of being ascertained by legal research.[416]

Fuller's view is accurate in cases where the act in question is heinous on any credible moral standard. Marital rape and, in international criminal law, war crimes and crimes against humanity,[417] are examples that are now seen as belonging to this exceptional category. In the case of marital rape, the announcement of the legal rule may have been the culmination of a process of development of public morality. At a more contestable level of immorality, Glanville Williams' view holds sway. Deciding into which category a case falls is a matter of judgment. That is why there are judges. Sometimes, as in *Shaw*, judges have too readily placed a case in the exceptional category and individual liberty has suffered as a result. The chances of a similar mistake being repeated have diminished in light of indications by members of the House of Lords that the courts no longer enjoy the power to create new offences.[418]

2 The Creation of New Law by Overruling Prior Authority

(a) Prior Authority Wrong in Principle

A trio of cases dealing with the availability of the defence of duress to a charge of murder deserves discussion from the perspective of a concern with retroactivity. At a general level it is unrealistic to think that the content of the law on the topic of duress could have any effect on how a person under duress would act.[419] However, changes made by judicial decision to the availability of the defence of duress to a charge of murder changed the law by which personal liberty was constrained in circumstances of duress and so invite discussion for that reason. If duress was, at the time of killing, a defence available to a person who killed another under circumstances fulfilling the requirements of duress, then that person's acts

[416] G Williams *Criminal Law: The General Part* (2nd edn Stevens and Sons London 1961) 576.

[417] On which see H Kelsen 'Collective and Individual Responsibility in International Law with Particular Regard to the Punishment of War Criminals' (1943) 31 California Law Review 530, 544; H Kelsen 'Will the Judgment in the Nuremberg Trial Constitute a Precedent in International Law?' (1947) 1 International Law Quarterly 153, 165.

[418] *R v Knuller* [1973] AC 435, 457–8, 464–5, 474–5, 490, 496 (HL); *DPP v Withers* [1975] AC 842, 857, 860, 863, 867, 877 (HL); *Abbott v The Queen* [1977] AC 755, 767 (PC); *R v Rimmington* [2006] 1 AC 459, [33], [49], [58] (HL). See generally ATH Smith 'Judicial Law Making in the Criminal Law' (1984) 100 Law Quarterly Review 46. But contra *R v Tan* [1983] QB 1053, especially 1062–3; *R v R* [1992] 1 AC 599 (HL), discussed in Ch 5 Pt C; *S v HM Advocate* 1989 SLT 469; *Khaliq v HM Advocate* 1983 SCCR 483, especially 486–7, 492–4. On the latter 2 cases see TH Jones 'Common Law and Criminal Law: The Scottish Example' [1990] Criminal Law Review 292.

[419] A similar point could be made about the judicial approach to the statutory formulation of provocation as a partial defence to a charge of murder, about which *A-G (Jersey) v Holley* [2005] 2 AC 580 (PC) (followed in *R v James* [2006] QB 588 (CA) and *R v Moses* [2006] EWCA Crim 1721) departed from *R v Smith* [2001] 1 AC 146 (HL).

would not, at the time of acting, constitute a criminal offence. If the law was retroactively changed to remove the availability of the defence of duress from such a person, then that person would retroactively become subject to criminal liability to which he was not subject at the time of acting.[420]

In *DPP for Northern Ireland v Lynch*[421] the House of Lords departed from the longstanding common law rule that duress was not an available defence to any charge of murder,[422] to hold that it was available in circumstances in which the accused was charged with murder on the basis of aiding and abetting another person who actually killed the victim. This decision had retroactive effect in the sense that the appellant, who claimed that he had been forced, in fear of his life, to drive others to the scene of the murder, was granted a retrial, on the basis of the new rule, that he would otherwise not have been entitled to. Because this was retroactivity in favour of an individual defendant, and because the consequence was a retrial rather than an acquittal, this example of retroactivity did not create any problematic issues.

Potentially more problematic was the decision of the House of Lords in *R v Howe*.[423] In *Lynch* the House of Lords left open the question of whether the defence of duress was available to a person who was responsible for actually killing the victim.[424] In *Abbott v The Queen*[425] the Privy Council refused to extend the defence of duress to such a person. The primary question in *Howe* was whether the approach taken in *Abbott* should be followed in English law, but the House of Lords also took the opportunity, on the invitation of the Crown, to reconsider its decision in *Lynch* that duress was available to someone charged with murder who did not actually kill the victim. Whether this gave rise to problematic retroactivity can only be assessed by close attention to the particular circumstances that arose in *Howe*.

The report of *Howe* incorporates two conjoined appeals, each of which had two appellants. For one of these four appellants, duress was not in issue. Two of the appellants had been convicted of the same three counts as each other. For one count of murder, in which they did not perform the actual killing, and one count of conspiracy to murder, in which there was no actual killing, the trial judge left duress to the jury, which rejected it on the facts. The other count relevant to those two appellants was a second count of murder in which they were the actual killers. On the basis of existing authority, duress was not left to the jury on that count and they were found guilty of it. For the fourth appellant, there was one count of murder with the same relevant characteristics, ie he was found guilty of being the actual killer and his claim of duress was ruled inadmissible at trial.

[420] Cf, on changing the law on self-defence, *Zecevic v DPP (Victoria)* (1987) 162 CLR 645, 664.

[421] [1975] AC 653 (HL).

[422] M Hale *History of the Pleas of the Crown* (New edn Emlyn London 1800) vol 1, 50 (51 in original MS); W Blackstone *Commentaries on the Laws of England* (16th edn Cadell London 1825) vol 4, 30.

[423] [1987] 1 AC 417 (HL).

[424] [1975] AC 653, 671, 685, cf 715 (HL).

[425] [1977] AC 755 (PC).

It was never the law that an actual killer could claim duress. *Lynch* did not go that far and *Abbott* refused to extend it. After *Abbott* the law, at least as held by the Privy Council, was clearly that duress was not available to an actual killer. The House of Lords confirmed that view in *Howe* which meant that the appeals on the counts in which the appellants actually killed their victims were unsuccessful, but that decision did not involve any retroactivity because it involved the confirmation of existing authority. The point for which *Lynch* was authority, because it related only to murder in circumstances where the accused did not actually kill the victim but only aided and abetted the actual killer, was irrelevant to those two counts. That left only two counts, relating to two appellants, to which *Lynch* was applicable.

The House of Lords did overrule *Lynch* and so retroactively changed the law, but because in the two counts in which the point arose duress had already been left to the jury and rejected by it on the facts, the appellants in *Howe* were not prejudiced by that change in the law.[426] It was probably this confluence of circumstances that led Lord Hailsham to observe in *Howe* that the case afforded:

> an ideal and never to be repeated opportunity to consider as we were invited expressly to do by the respondent [Crown], the whole question afresh.[427]

However, the change in the law made in *Howe*, that *Lynch* should be overruled and the rule that duress was not available for any charge of murder reinstated, whether the accused actually killed the victim or not, was thereafter applicable to all cases in which the point arose, including those in which the facts occurred after *Lynch* and before *Howe*, at which time the law was that duress was an available defence to a charge of murder in which the accused did not perform the actual killing. Thus, although the absence of prejudice to the particular appellants before the court in *Howe* removes what would otherwise have been a significant objection to the retroactivity of the decision, it is necessary to consider whether its retroactivity was otherwise defensible—explicit consideration of which was absent from the judgments in *Howe*.

Whether duress should be an available excusatory defence to a charge of murder remains a controversial question.[428] Without entering the substance of that controversy, the present suggestion is that the judgments in *Howe*, assuming them to be correct as a matter of substantive law, contain multiple reasons supporting the defeat of the prohibition on retroactivity in the case. First, the departure from existing authority and breach of fundamental principle in *Lynch* meant that it was wrong in principle and wrong when it was decided,[429] and was not merely subject

426 See also *A-G (Jersey) v Holley* [2005] 2 AC 580, [39]–[40] (PC), in which, because of an undertaking given by the Attorney-General, the approach to provocation was changed without any retroactive effect on the defendant in that case.

427 [1987] 1 AC 417, 427 (HL).

428 Law Commission *A New Homicide Act for England and Wales?* (Consultation Paper No 177, 2005) Pt 7.

429 [1987] 1 AC 417, 437 (HL). Cf J Harris 'Towards Principles of Overruling—When Should a Final Court of Appeal Second Guess?' (1990) 10 Oxford Journal of Legal Studies 135, 184–9.

to reversal on the basis of a change in conditions[430] or on the adoption of a different but equally plausible view of the law.[431] Thus, *Howe* was an exercise in 'restoring' the true position rather than creating a brand new rule.[432] Second, this was not some trifling matter. The sanctity of human life was at stake and *Lynch* failed to respect the common law's longstanding reverence, including, for example, in *R v Dudley and Stephens*,[433] for that sanctity, in some circumstances at the cost of the likely sacrifice of one's own life.[434] Third, the change made in *Lynch*, combined with the refusal to extend it in *Abbott*, meant that the law was left in what was thought to be a logically unattractive position in which it allowed duress as a defence for those who did not do the actual killing but not for those who did, regardless of the fact that a person who did not actually kill may be more morally culpable than someone who did.[435] These reasons are additional to the fact that duress is an area in which reliance could not be in issue, in contrast, for example, to *Shaw v DPP*,[436] and that the particular appellants before the House were not prejudiced by the retroactivity of the decision. Cumulatively, these reasons provided a sound basis for overcoming the prohibition on retroactivity in *Howe*.

(b) Retroactivity in Favour of a Defendant

If an appellate court considers that the criminal law should be changed in favour of a defendant it will not because of the retroactive effects of its decision hesitate to do so. If the consequence of such a change is that the court orders a new trial, then the Crown has lost the effort of the first trial and the knowledge that a conviction has already been secured. These interests are subordinated to the consideration that a person has been convicted of a criminal offence, and perhaps suffered imprisonment, on the basis of a rule no longer thought to be appropriate. In such circumstances the defendant is exposed to the possibility of a new trial, which would occur on the basis of the new rule. In cases in which an appellate court enters an acquittal following its decision to change a legal rule on the basis of which the defendant was convicted, then the Crown might be thought to have suffered greater prejudice. Not only has an existing conviction gained on the basis of the existing law been overturned, but there is no prospect of a new trial on the basis of the newly announced rule. In public law the interest of the individual is preferred where the state exceeds what is later held to be its lawful powers. The interest of the individual in criminal law, with a criminal conviction and penalty at stake, is even stronger, and will always be preferred to any interest in gaining a

[430] Cf *Miliangos v George Frank (Textiles)* [1976] AC 443 (HL), discussed in Ch 5 Pt E(2)(d), in which, in a private law matter, retroactive change was made on this basis.

[431] Cf *The Hannah Blumenthal* [1983] 1 AC 854, 912, 913 (HL), discussed in Ch 5 Pt E(2)(e), in which existing common law authority in a private law matter was not overruled on the grounds that do so would be no more than favouring one plausible approach over another plausible approach.

[432] [1987] 1 AC 417, 427, 430 (HL).

[433] (1884) 14 QBD 273, discussed in *R v Howe* [1987] 1 AC 417, 429–32, 439, 453 (HL).

[434] [1987] 1 AC 417, 430, 439, 444, 453, 456 (HL).

[435] *Ibid* 437, 445, 453.

[436] Discussed in Ch 5 Pt G(1)(b).

conviction on the basis of existing law that may be asserted by the Crown. The state, taken as a whole rather than just the Crown as represented by the prosecution, properly has an interest in criminal convictions obtained on the basis of the best legal rule, not in convictions obtained under rules later deemed to have been inappropriate. Thus the interest of the individual in only being subjected to the force of the criminal law by the most just legal rules, even if only deemed to be so after the facts giving rise to the charge, will always outweigh any other interests in the case. An example is hardly needed in this area, but to illustrate the point, the archetype will be discussed.

In the famous case of *Woolmington v DPP*[437] a man was convicted of murder on the basis of the then traditional direction to the jury that if the prosecution proved that the victim died at the defendant's hands then it was murder unless the defendant could show circumstances alleviating the crime to manslaughter.[438] The House of Lords reviewed the authorities on which this traditional direction was said to be based and concluded that if they did indeed stand for that proposition then they were 'wrong'.[439] The reason for this was that the rule was inconsistent with the 'one golden thread' throughout 'the web of English criminal law' which was 'that it is the duty of the prosecution to prove the prisoner's guilt'.[440] It was not for the accused to satisfy the jury of the circumstances said to alleviate the crime to manslaughter. It was for the prosecution to prove that it was murder. The result in *Woolmington* was that a verdict of acquittal was entered on the basis of a decision that the traditional direction was inconsistent with fundamental principle. In more modern times one might expect a new trial to be ordered in similar circumstances.

3 Overruling a Prior Judicial Interpretation of a Statute

The question stated for the House of Lords in *R v Shivpuri* was:

> Does a person commit an offence under section 1 of the Criminal Attempts Act 1981 where, if the facts were as that person believed them to be, the full offence would have been committed by him, but where on the true facts the offence which that person set out to commit was in law impossible, eg, because the substance imported and believed to be heroin was not heroin but a harmless substance?[441]

The appellant thought that he was receiving, storing and distributing either heroin or cannabis, which was imported into England from India. In fact it was 'snuff or some similar harmless vegetable matter'.[442] The commission of the actual

437 [1935] AC 462 (HL).
438 Based, eg, on M Foster *Discourses upon a Few Branches of the Crown Law* (Clarendon Press Oxford 1762) 255 and *R v Greenacre* (1837) 8 C & P 35, 42; 173 ER 388, 391.
439 [1935] AC 462, 482 (HL).
440 *Ibid* 481.
441 [1987] 1 AC 1, 13 (HL).
442 *Ibid* 14.

offences of being knowingly concerned in dealing with and in harbouring a controlled drug with intent to evade the prohibition of importation[443] was impossible because there was no controlled drug.

Section 1(2) of the Criminal Attempts Act 1981 (Eng) provided that a:

> person may be guilty of attempting to commit an offence to which this section applies even though the facts are such that the commission of the offence is impossible.

In *Anderton v Ryan*,[444] which was decided one year prior to *Shivpuri*, the House of Lords held that a woman who bought a video recorder that she believed to be stolen, but which was in fact not stolen, could not be convicted of an attempt under section 1 of the Criminal Attempts Act on the basis that she was 'objectively' innocent.[445] Lord Bridge, who gave one of the leading speeches in *Anderton v Ryan*, said in *Shivpuri*, in which the other members of the House relevantly agreed with him, that he did not think that any sound principle could be discerned from *Anderton v Ryan* that would allow it to sit with the plain meaning of section 1(2) of the Criminal Attempts Act.[446] He came to the conclusion that *Anderton v Ryan* was 'wrong'[447] and that the proper interpretation of the statute required that someone could be guilty of an attempt to commit an offence even if the facts were such that it was impossible for him actually to commit the offence that he thought he was committing. Lord Bridge thought that *Anderton v Ryan* could not validly be distinguished and so considered whether it should be overruled, 'notwithstanding the especial need for certainty in the criminal law'.[448]

In reaching the decision that it should be overruled, Lord Bridge was influenced by, inter alia, the fact that following *Anderton v Ryan* would involve a denial of the reform of the law that the Criminal Attempts Act plainly sought to make,[449] and that no one:

> could have acted in reliance on the law as propounded in Anderton v Ryan in the belief that he was acting innocently and now find that, after all, he is to be held to have committed a criminal offence.[450]

Indeed, at all times the appellant believed himself to be involved in receiving, storing and distributing a controlled drug, and it would hardly lie in his mouth to complain that he should have been able to rely on the law being that if he thought he was doing something criminal but in fact he was dealing with a substance that was not controlled, that he should not be guilty of a criminal attempt. The very nature of an attempt was inconsistent with a person being able to rely on the rule in *Anderton v Ryan*.

443 Misuse of Drugs Act 1971 (UK) s 3(1) and Customs and Excise Management Act 1979 (UK) s 170(1)(b).
444 [1985] AC 560 (HL).
445 *Ibid* 580, 582–3.
446 [1987] 1 AC 1, 20–22 (HL).
447 *Ibid* 23.
448 *Ibid*; *Practice Statement (Judicial Precedent)* [1966] 1 WLR 1234 (HL).
449 [1987] 1 AC 1, 23 (HL).
450 *Ibid*.

The issue of Mr Shivpuri's liberty is more difficult, though it was not expressly considered by the House of Lords. At the time of the relevant events in *Shivpuri*, *Anderton v Ryan* had not yet been decided. Thus a simple way out of the problem would be that Mr Shivpuri's liberty was, at the time of his acting, constrained by the Criminal Attempts Act, and that Act was given its natural meaning in his case. The brief interlude in which *Anderton v Ryan* was the law fell, in its entirety, between the events in *Shivpuri*, and the House of Lords decision in *Shivpuri*. Alhough it semantically disposes of the problem of liberty in this particular case, that sort of argument would not be of any application to other cases in which the rule applicable at the time of acting was departed from in a later case, so let it be assumed for the sake of argument that *Anderton v Ryan* represented the law at the time of the facts in *Shivpuri* and that the point somehow fell to be determined on appeal to the House of Lords. At the time of his acts, Mr Shivpuri would have committed no crime. In that sense, he was free to do what he did. A person being free to attempt to commit a crime if circumstances unknown to him made it impossible actually to commit that crime is a strange sounding sort of liberty. It cannot be the sort of liberty that is founded on respect for personal autonomy, because those particular circumstances are, by definition, not circumstances that someone could choose; and more importantly such a conception of liberty does not sit comfortably with common sense. The absence of sensible reliance or liberty considerations in the case meant that the prohibition on criminal retroactivity was, without diminishing the strength of that prohibition in general, eminently susceptible to being justifiably overcome in *Shivpuri*. Once the rule in *Anderton v Ryan* was shown to be wrong in principle, in the sense of being inconsistent with the plain meaning of the statute, the absence of the rationales for the prohibition on retroactivity in the particular circumstances of the case meant that, exceptionally, retroactivity was justifiable.

The case for retroactive change was even stronger in *R v G*.[451] Because the change to the law was in favour of criminal defendants, individual liberty was not in issue. In *R v G* the House of Lords overruled existing authority that 'reckless' in section 1 of the Criminal Damage Act 1971 (Eng) could be satisfied where a defendant did not actually appreciate the risk that she took if it was a risk that would have been obvious to an ordinary prudent person.[452] The House adopted an interpretation by which a person can only be 'reckless' if she actually appreciates the risk and then unreasonably takes it. The reasons expressed for changing the rule provide additional justifications for the retroactive effect of the change. These justifications are that the House's earlier decision in *R v Caldwell* was wrong when it was decided,[453] that it was inconsistent with the fundamental principle that to be guilty of a serious crime a defendant must have a culpable state of mind,[454] that experience showed that the rule led to injustice (including in the

451 [2004] 1 AC 1034 (HL).

452 Most notably *R v Caldwell* [1982] AC 341 (HL).

453 [2004] 1 AC 1034, [35], [45]–[51], [64] (HL).

454 *Ibid* [32], [55].

present case which involved children),[455] and that it had been subject to sustained academic and judicial criticism.[456]

4 Conclusions on Criminal Law

In criminal law individual liberty is usually acutely at issue, and the ability to rely on the law is sometimes at issue, so when consideration is given to changing the law by judicial decision, the prohibition on retroactivity will typically be very difficult to overcome. It should be overcome only by the most compelling reasons or unusual circumstances, or if the retroactivity is favourable to the accused. This cautious approach to retroactive criminal liability has not always been followed in the common law. As well as the blatant inconsistency with such an approach of some of the historical examples discussed in Chapter two,[457] even some more modern cases suggest that wariness is needed about judicial assertions that existing criminal law can cover new factual scenarios, because in circumstances where what was not criminal when it was done is, by this technique, later deemed to have been criminal, then retroactive criminal liability is the result.

The suggestion that the prohibition on retroactive criminality can, through the retroactivity that accompanies common law adjudication, be overcome at all might at first glance be thought to be inconsistent with article 7 of the ECHR, which enshrines *nullum crimen sine lege antea exstanti* as a rule with only limited exceptions and from which derogation is not permitted. On closer analysis, however, two factors limit the extent of possible inconsistency between the common law and article 7. First, article 7, as it has been interpreted by the Strasbourg Court, in practice allows changes in the law to be made by way of common law decision, to the detriment of the accused, in exceptional circumstances.[458] Second, common law decisions in criminal law, at least since half way through last century, are usually cautious about changes to the law that will have retroactive effect to the detriment of the particular accused. It may be overly optimistic to describe the common law approach to adjudicative retroactivity as 'entirely consistent' with article 7 of the ECHR, as Lord Bingham did in *R v Rimmington*,[459] but the factors just mentioned do at least limit the extent of any inconsistency, and it may be hoped that the spectre of article 7 will further constrain adjudicative retroactivity in English criminal law.

455 [2004] 1 AC 1034, [33], [52]–[54].

456 *Ibid* [34], [57], [65]–[67]. One of the leading objectors to the rule in *R v Caldwell* referred to it, after the decision in *R v G*, as an 'academic bête noir': ATH Smith 'Criminal Law: The Future' [2004] Criminal Law Review 971, 978.

457 Ch 2 Pt C.

458 *SW v United Kingdom* (1996) 21 EHRR 363. See the discussion in Ch 5 Pt C(6). See also S Atrill '*Nulla Poena Sine Lege* in Comparative Perspective: Retrospectivity under the ECHR and US Constitution' [2005] Public Law 107, 124–6 and *R v Rimmington* [2006] 1 AC 459, [35] (HL).

459 [2006] 1 AC 459, [33]–[35] (HL)

Although the common law's caution about retroactive effects in criminal law, created in part by respect for the doctrine of precedent, has probably never been more than a strong *presumption* against retroactivity, which has occasionally been defeated rather too cavalierly, it is preferable to refer to a *prohibition* on retroactive criminal laws, to which exceptions may be established by compelling reasons. This preference is motivated by the venerability, including in the common law, of the maxim *nullum crimen sine lege antea exstanti*, by the strength of the terms of article 7 of the ECHR and the equivalent provision in article 15 of the International Covenant on Civil and Political Rights, and most of all by the fact that the subject matter of what is at stake in criminal law will typically make overcoming objections to retroactivity more difficult than in other areas of the law, where the term *presumption* is more appropriate. The conceptual difference between a presumption defeasible only to strong reasons in exceptional circumstances, and a prohibition to which exceptions may be established by strong reasons in exceptional circumstances may be slight, or non-existent. 'Prohibition' is a preferable term in criminal law only because it better conveys the difficulty of justly achieving a contrary result to that indicated by the prohibition.

Although the approach of the common law and of article 7 are closer than they might at first appear, one point of potential future conflict may arise from the tendency of common law judges in criminal matters to focus only on the particular accused. If the circumstances of a case mean that retroactive change is made without prejudice to the accused before the court, the possibility remains that the new rule will be applied to a subsequent case in which the facts arose before the change to the law was made and in which the accused is prejudiced by the retroactive change.[460] If the reasons for the change in the law were of the exceptional kind that would justify retroactive criminal liability, then there would be no difficulty applying those reasons to the subsequent case. But if the law was changed in the first case only because the particular circumstances meant that there would be no retroactive effect on the defendant in that case, then harder questions will arise.

H Overruling and the Age of a Decision

General conclusions about adjudicative retroactivity will be made in the concluding chapter, but it is convenient separately to address one issue that cuts across private, public and criminal law. When a court is considering whether to overrule a decision, it is not clear from existing cases and literature the relevance, if any, of the age of that decision. There are some obvious possibilities. First, that age is a neutral factor.[461] Second, that the more recent a decision, the more reticent a court

[460] Cf *R v Graham L* [2003] EWCA Crim 1512, [20]; *R v C* [2004] 1 WLR 2098, [22], [25] (CA).

[461] *R v Secretary of State for the Home Department, ex p Khawaja* [1984] 1 AC 74, 106, 125 (HL); *Jones v Secretary of State for Social Services* [1972] AC 944, 1014–15 (HL); J Harris 'Towards Principles of Overruling—When Should a Final Court of Appeal Second Guess?' (1990) 10 OJLS 135, 150.

should be to overrule it.[462] Third, by contrast, that a recent decision thought to be mistaken should be promptly overruled.[463] Fourth, and perhaps most obviously, that the longer a decision has stood, the more reticent a court should be to overrule it.[464] A variation on this fourth approach is that a precedent 'may be compared to wine which "improves with age", up to a certain point, and then begins to "go off" ',[465] possibly because of changes in factual or legal circumstances. Willingness to overrule recent decisions and reticence to overrule old ones could co-exist. Arguably, reticence to overrule very recent decisions *and* very old decisions could co-exist, the result of which would be that 'middle aged' decisions would be most amenable to overruling while the very old and the very new would be less amenable. This would be difficult to defend on any rational basis.[466] The best approach is none of the possibilities just listed.

Consideration should first be given to factors, other than age, relevant to whether a decision should be overruled. If there are factors pointing strongly against overruling, such as reliance, then those factors will be multiplied by the age of the decision. If there are strong reliance considerations and the decision is an old one, then it will be most difficult to establish that the decision should be overruled. But even a recent decision that has given rise to significant reliance may still, either because of that reliance alone or by multiplying it even by the tender age of the decision, not be amenable to overruling. If there are no strong reasons to object to overruling, then multiplying those reasons by the age of the decision will not greatly increase their strength, even if the decision is of great antiquity.[467] The source of this approach is Julius Stone's observation that the age of a decision is 'a basic multiplier of all other factors'.[468] This approach treats age not as a factor of primary relevance to whether a decision should be overruled, but as a multiplier of primary factors.

[462] *Conway v Rimmer* [1968] AC 910, 938 (HL); *R v Knuller* [1973] AC 435, 496 (HL); *DPP v Nock* [1978] AC 979, 997 (HL).

[463] *Jones v Secretary of State for Social Services* [1972] AC 944, 993 (HL); *R v Shivpuri* [1987] 1 AC 1, 11, 23 (HL); *Queensland v The Commonwealth of Australia* (1977) 139 CLR 585, 592–4.

[464] *Geelong Harbour Trust Commissioners v Gibbs Bright* (1970) 122 CLR 504, 517–18; *Brodie v Singleton Shire Council* (2001) 206 CLR 512, [218]; C Sampford *Retrospectivity and the Rule of Law* (Oxford University Press 2006) 186. Contra *Miliangos v George Frank (Textiles)* [1976] AC 443, 469 (HL); *Ross Smith v Ross Smith* [1963] AC 280, 293 (HL).

[465] CK Allen *Law in the Making* (7th edn Clarendon Press Oxford 1964) 257.

[466] *Queensland v The Commonwealth of Australia* (1977) 139 CLR 585, 631.

[467] Eg *Robinson Brothers (Brewers) v Durham County Assessment Committee* [1938] AC 321, 339–40 (HL); cf The Albazero [1977] AC 774, 846 (HL).

[468] J Stone *Precedent and Law* (Butterworths Sydney 1985) 184. Cf *Jones v Secretary of State for Social Services* [1972] AC 944, 993, 1015 (HL); *Brodie v Singleton Shire Council* (2001) 206 CLR 512, [218]; C Sampford *Retrospectivity and the Rule of Law* (Oxford University Press 2006) 186.

6

Prospective Overruling

A What is Prospective Overruling?

One way to control the retroactive effect of judicial decisions that develop or change the law would be to allow 'prospective overruling'. This umbrella term includes a number of techniques that may be used either when a previous authority is overruled or, despite the limited nomenclature, when a new rule is created without the need to 'overrule' an existing authority.[1] 'Non-retroactive judicial law making' would be a more accurate, but more cumbersome expression. Because 'prospective overruling' is an established term, its use will be continued here.

The techniques described by this expression include, first, that the court might announce a new rule that will be applicable only to future cases involving a cause of action arising after the announcement of the new rule. If this approach were to be adopted, the newly announced rule would not apply to the dispute before the court in which it was announced. The instant dispute would be governed by the old rule. The old rule would also govern any causes of action arising prior to the announcement of the new rule but determined after that announcement. A second alternative would be for the court to announce a new rule that will be applicable only to future cases involving a cause of action arising after the announcement of the new rule, but, by way of exception, also apply the new rule to the case in which it is announced. All other causes of action arising prior to the announcement of the new rule, and determined after that announcement, would be governed by the old rule. A third variation would be that as well as applying to the case in which it was announced, the new rule would apply to all other cases already pending at the time of the announcement, but not to cases in which the cause of action predated the announcement of the new rule but in which proceedings had not already been commenced at the time of the announcement of the new rule. A fourth possibility would be to announce a new rule, which does not have retroactive effect, but to suspend the entry into force of that new rule until some future date to allow the legislature time to enact a different rule should it wish to do so and/or to allow the parties affected by the change, particularly if one such party is the executive government, time to regulate their affairs in accordance

[1] Cf *Chamberlains v Sun Poi Lai* [2006] NZSC 70, [134]; AGL Nicol 'Prospective Overruling: A New Device for English Courts?' (1976) 39 Modern Law Review 542, 546.

with the new rule. On this approach the dispute in which the new rule was announced, and all other causes of action arising before the delayed entry into force of the new rule, would not be governed by that new rule, but instead by the old rule.

There is already a significant body of literature on prospective overruling,[2] but as this book addresses problems of retroactivity in common law decision making, and because some jurists consider that prospective overruling provides an appropriate solution to such problems, consideration of prospective overruling is called for here. Prospective overruling techniques are often discussed in the context of litigation about whether legislation is void for inconsistency with a written constitution. Because they are not the subject of this book, such cases will be discussed only insofar as necessary properly to consider prospective overruling. Prospective overruling has a long and less than straightforward history in the United States.[3] Whilst acknowledging the importance of decisions made in the United States jurisdictions, and in India,[4] to the issue of prospective overruling, the present discussion is limited to the jurisdictions under consideration in this book more generally.

B The Status Quo

1 England

Prospective overruling has been the subject of comment by a number of Law Lords since they granted themselves the power to overrule their own decisions in 1966.[5] Some have expressed curiosity about what happens in the United States,[6] some have cautiously advocated its appearance in English law, either by judicial decision[7] or

[2] Eg MDA Freeman 'Standards of Adjudication, Judicial Law-Making and Prospective Overruling' [1973] Current Legal Problems 166, 200–7; AGL Nicol 'Prospective Overruling: A New Device for English Courts?' (1976) 39 Modern Law Review 542; Lord Lloyd *Introduction to Jurisprudence* (4th edn Stevens London 1979) 856–9; J Stone *Precedent and Law* (Butterworths Sydney 1985) 184–94; K Mason 'Prospective Overruling' (1989) 63 Australian Law Journal 526; R Cross and J Harris *Precedent in English Law* (4th edn Clarendon Press Oxford 1991) 228–32; M Arden 'Prospective Overruling' (2004) 120 Law Quarterly Review 7; *Re Edward and Edward* (1987) 39 DLR (4th) 654, 660–64; *Ha v New South Wales* (1997) 189 CLR 465, 503–4, 515; *Re Spectrum Plus (in liquidation)* [2005] 2 AC 680 (HL); *Chamberlains v Sun Poi Lai* [2006] NZSC 70, [129]–[154].

[3] The modern genesis of which was *Great Northern Railway Co v Sunburst Oil and Refining Co* 287 US 358, 364–6 (1932). A brief summary of the position in the United States is provided by Lord Nicholls in *Re Spectrum Plus (in liquidation)* [2005] 2 AC 680, [18]–[19] (HL).

[4] Relevant Indian constitutional cases are mentioned in *Re Spectrum Plus (in liquidation)* [2005] 2 AC 680, [20] (HL).

[5] *Practice Statement (Judicial Precedent)* [1966] 1 WLR 1234 (HL).

[6] Eg Lord Reid 'The Judge as Lawmaker' (1972) 12 Journal of the Society of Public Teachers of Law 22, 23; *Jones v Secretary of State for Social Services* [1972] AC 944, 1015 (HL) (Lord Diplock).

[7] Eg *R v Governor of Brockhill Prison, ex p Evans (No 2)* [2001] 2 AC 19, 26–7 (HL) (Lord Slynn).

legislation,[8] and some have denounced it as inconsistent with the English legal system.[9] A notable example of the latter occurred in *Kleinwort Benson v Lincoln County Council*, in which Lord Goff, having opined that retroactivity of judicial decisions was inevitable, said:

> The only alternative, as I see it, is to adopt a system of prospective overruling. But such a system, although it has occasionally been adopted elsewhere with, I understand, somewhat controversial results, has no place in our legal system.[10]

Arguably a form of prospective overruling occurred in *Royal Bank of Scotland v Etridge (No 2)*[11] in which it was asserted that the practical steps announced in that decision that, once put on inquiry, a bank should take to satisfy itself that a surety is not acting under the undue influence of the debtor, were applicable only 'for the future', whilst the earlier, and different advice given in *Barclays Bank v O'Brien*[12] was 'applicable to past transactions'. There was no consideration of the potential constitutional significance of this approach which, in any event, related more to practical advice about how to comply with the law than with substantive changes to the law itself.

Lord Hope advocated what was unquestionably a form of prospective overruling in *Hall v Simons*,[13] but no other member of the House commented on Lord Hope's view or otherwise discussed prospective overruling. The change in the law that was made in *Hall v Simons* has subsequently been applied with retroactive effect.[14]

In *Re Spectrum Plus (in liquidation)*,[15] the House of Lords, after reviewing arguments for and against prospective overruling and reviewing experience with prospective overruling in other jurisdictions,[16] departed from Lord Goff's statement in *Kleinwort Benson* and adopted a 'never say never' approach to prospective overruling.[17] Lord Nicholls summarised the case for prospective overruling thus:

> There could be cases where a decision on an issue of law, whether common law or statute law, was unavoidable but the decision would have such gravely unfair and disruptive consequences for past transactions or happenings that this House would be compelled to depart from the normal principles relating to the retrospective and prospective effect of court decisions.[18]

Despite it being acknowledged as a theoretical possibility in rare cases, there was no prospective overruling in *Spectrum*. The new rule had the usual retroactive

[8] Eg *Jones v Secretary of State for Social Services* [1972] AC 944, 1026–27 (HL) (Lord Simon); *Miliangos v George Frank (Textiles)* [1976] AC 443, 490 (HL) (Lord Simon).

[9] Eg Lord Devlin 'Judges and Lawmakers' (1976) Modern Law Review 1, 11; *R v Governor of Brockhill Prison, ex p Evans (No 2)* [2001] 2 AC 19, 48 (HL) (Lord Hobhouse); *Birmingham Corporation v West Midland Baptist (Trust) Association* [1970] AC 874, 898–9 (HL) (Lord Reid).

[10] [1999] 2 AC 349, 379 (HL).

[11] [2002] 2 AC 773, [50], [89] (HL).

[12] [1994] 1 AC 180 (HL).

[13] [2002] 1 AC 615, 710, 726 (HL). Discussed in Ch 5 Pt E(2)(e).

[14] *Awoyomi v Radford* [2007] EWHC 1671 (QB).

[15] [2005] 2 AC 680 (HL).

[16] *Ibid* [8]–[42], [65]–[74], [121]–[127].

[17] *Ibid* [39]–[41], [45], [74], [126], [162], [165].

[18] *Ibid* [40].

effect.[19] Thus, despite sporadic interest in the technique, no English court has ever really done it, as Lord Hope pointed out in *Spectrum*.[20] The highest that it could be put is that in *Spectrum* the House decided that prospective overruling is theoretically possible for the House of Lords.

This appears to have superseded earlier doubts about whether, even if the act of prospective overruling is constitutionally permissible, it would be possible and desirable for the House of Lords to utilise the technique without a statutory grant of power to do so.[21] As well as the House of Lords deciding that, in theory, it has the power to issue prospective overrulings, it should further be noted that the legislature of the United Kingdom has granted power to courts deciding devolution matters to control the intertemporal effect of judicial decisions which decide that legislation passed by a devolved legislature is beyond the competence of that legislature, or that subordinate legislation is beyond the competence of the devolved executive authority which purports to promulgate it.[22] This power has never been exercised, and its scope will be the subject of comment below.

The situation has been thought to be more complicated when the application by English courts of certain decisions of the Strasbourg Court and the European Court of Justice in Luxembourg are considered. Those courts do, on rare occasions, deliver decisions said to have only prospective effect.[23] If a decision of the Strasbourg or Luxembourg Court that has only prospective effect is applied by an English court, the question may arise as to whether the English court should apply the same temporal limit to the decision. Before determining whether limited temporal effect should be granted to a judgment of the Strasbourg or Luxembourg Court in the English legal order, close attention must be paid to the precise temporal effect of the Strasbourg or Luxembourg judgment. Lord Rodger comments that in *Goodwin v United Kingdom*[24] the Strasbourg judges were 'careful . . . to frame their judgment so as to make it prospective only',[25] and suggests that such effect would be transported to the English legal order.[26] In *Spectrum*, Lord Nicholls also appeared to treat *Goodwin* as an example of prospective overruling.[27] Accordingly, *Goodwin* requires examination.

[19] Discussed in Ch 5 Pt E(2)(b).

[20] [2005] 2 AC 680, [66] (HL).

[21] Most notably, *Jones v Secretary of State for Social Services* [1972] AC 944, 1026–27 (HL) (Lord Simon).

[22] Scotland Act 1998 (UK) s 102, Government of Wales Act 1998 (UK) s 110 and Northern Ireland Act 1998 (UK) s 81.

[23] Eg *Defrenne v Sabena* [1976] ECR 455, [69]–[75]; *Marckx v Belgium* (1979) 2 EHRR 330, [58]. On judgments of the Luxembourg Court, see FAR Bennion *Statutory Interpretation* (4th edn Butterworths London 2002) 268; E Campbell 'The Retrospectivity of Judicial Decisions and the Legality of Governmental Acts' (2003) 29 Monash University Law Review 49, 72–3; *R(Bidar) v Ealing London Borough Council* [2005] ECR I-2119, [64]–[71].

[24] (2002) 35 EHRR 18.

[25] Lord Rodger 'A Time for Everything under the Law: Some Reflections on Retrospectivity' (2005) 121 Law Quarterly Review 57, 76.

[26] *Ibid* 76–7.

[27] [2005] 2 AC 680, [24]–[25] (HL).

In *Goodwin* the Strasbourg Court emphasised its established 'dynamic and evolutive approach'[28] to interpreting the ECHR. The court had previously found legal and administrative measures relating to transsexuals in the United Kingdom to comply with the right to private life protected by article 8 of the ECHR and the right to marry protected by article 12 of the ECHR.[29] However, the increased social acceptance of transsexuals and the inactivity of the government of the United Kingdom in addressing the concerns expressed by the Strasbourg Court in earlier judgments, meant that the court was no longer willing to excuse the treatment of transsexuals on the basis of the 'margin of appreciation' afforded to states in the interpretation of Convention rights.[30] The Strasbourg Court did not explicitly overrule its previous decisions but rather held that the 'balance' of considerations pertaining to the issue 'now tilts decisively in favour of the applicant'.[31] In part because treatment similar to that suffered by the applicant had, until the judgment in *Goodwin*, been found to be within the margin of appreciation, the court in *Goodwin* declined to award pecuniary damages to the applicant in that case.[32] That is not prospective overruling.

Although not awarding pecuniary damages, the court held that the applicant *had suffered* violations of her Convention rights, even though that sufferance occurred at a time when the Strasbourg Court's earlier, and contrary, decisions on similar issues were good law. Nor was there any limitation expressed by the court by which only causes of action arising after the decision in *Goodwin*, perhaps along with cases already pending at that time, could enjoy its protection. The court was explicit that the rule was being changed because conditions had changed, not because the old rule was always wrong; but in making that change it applied the new rule to the case before it, in which the facts occurred when the rule was otherwise, and took no steps to limit the retroactive application of the new rule to other cases. Thus the approach of the Strasbourg Court in *Goodwin* may be compared to the approach of common law courts in cases that announce a new legal rule that is thought to be necessary because of changed social conditions, not because the old rule was wrong at the time that it was decided.[33] In such cases the court, although not explicitly criticising the past existence of the old rule, nonetheless retroactively applies the new rule to facts arising prior to its announcement, which is to say at a time at which the old rule was operative. Just because a rule may evolve to meet social conditions does not mean that the announcement of such an evolution, and the application of the newly evolved rule to facts arising prior to its announcement, does not have retroactive effect.

[28] (2002) 35 EHRR 18, [74].

[29] Eg in *Rees v United Kingdom* (1987) 9 EHRR 56 and *Sheffield v United Kingdom* (1999) 27 EHRR 163.

[30] (2002) 35 EHRR 18, [93], [103].

[31] *Ibid* [93].

[32] *Ibid* [119]–[120].

[33] See Ch 5 Pt E(2)(d), especially the discussion of *Miliangos v George Frank (Textiles)* [1976] AC 443 (HL). See also *Dyson Holdings v Fox* [1976] 1 QB 503 (CA), mentioned in Ch 5 Pt E(2)(c).

Lord Nicholls in *Spectrum* thought that because the Strasbourg Court could give decisions with prospective effect only, that the case for the House of Lords being able to give decisions on the interpretation and application of the ECHR that had prospective effect only 'seems irresistible'.[34] Lord Nicholls' view apparently extended to the House of Lords issuing non-retroactive rulings not only in situations in which the House is applying a decision of the Strasbourg Court which was expressed by that court to have only prospective effect, but also to decisions on ECHR points decided by the House absent a temporally limited Strasbourg decision. This broader claim, in relation to which Lord Nicholls[35] cited Lord Rodger,[36] differs from the situation described by Lord Rodger, which is limited to the application by English courts of decisions from Strasbourg or Luxembourg the effects of which are temporally limited by the court that first decides them.

If the Luxembourg or Strasbourg Court announces that its decision is to have prospective effect only, then if an English court is called upon to apply such a decision it is difficult to imagine circumstances in which it would be proper for the English court not to apply the same temporal limit to the rule under consideration, particularly given the existence of a statutory command to take into account decisions of the Strasbourg Court[37] and the direct effect of the law of the European Community within the English legal order. In doing so, the English court would be taking account of the ambit of the decision of the Luxembourg or Strasbourg Court, issued in accordance with the powers claimed by those courts. That does not mean that English courts can, or should, on the back of powers claimed by the Strasbourg or Luxembourg Courts, claim similar powers for English courts in cases in which they are not applying temporally limited judgments of the Strasbourg or Luxembourg Courts.

2 Australia

The High Court of Australia has been emphatic, if brief, in its rejection of prospective overruling. That court has held that it 'has no power to overrule cases prospectively'[38] and added that if 'an earlier case is erroneous and it is necessary to overrule it, it would be a perversion of judicial power to maintain in force that which is acknowledged not to be the law'.[39] This approach, adopted in the context of a decision about whether a statute was inconsistent with the Australian Constitution, has closed off discussion in Australian jurisprudence of prospective overruling more generally, including as regards its potential use in decisions on common law rules.

[34] [2005] 2 AC 680, [42] (HL).

[35] *Ibid.*

[36] Lord Rodger 'A Time for Everything under the Law: Some Reflections on Retrospectivity' (2005) 121 Law Quarterly Review 57, 77.

[37] Human Rights Act 1998 (UK), s 2(1)(a).

[38] *Ha v New South Wales* (1997) 189 CLR 465, 503, see also 515.

[39] *Ibid* 504. Contra *Re Eurig Estate* [1998] 2 SCR 565, 586–7.

3 New Zealand

Until recently, the traditional common law approach to the retroactive effect of judicial decisions that develop or change common law rules had not been seriously challenged in New Zealand. However, in *Chamberlains v Sun Poi Lai*,[40] two members of the New Zealand Supreme Court considered it theoretically possible for the court to declare a new rule and for that rule to 'save for the immediate parties, apply only to events occurring after the date of the judgment which effects the change'.[41] All five judges in the case were, however, agreed that the particular case at hand, which involved the abolition of advocate's immunity from suit for work done in court or intimately connected to such work, was not an appropriate one for any form of prospective overruling to occur.[42] The issue is unlikely to fade away, as evidenced by its brief appearance in the Court of Appeal decision in *The Queen v Alo*.[43]

4 Canada

The Saskatchewan Court of Appeal, in *Re Edward and Edward*,[44] expressed traditional disfavour for prospective overruling on the basis that by 'deciding an existing case under the old rule but warning that future cases will be decided under a new rule now being announced, a court is really usurping the function of the legislature'.[45] The Supreme Court of Canada was, however, in the celebrated case of *Re Manitoba Language Rights*,[46] willing to deem temporarily valid statutes that it held to have been always unconstitutional. Section 23 of the Manitoba Act 1870 (Can), which is constitutionally entrenched by section 52(2)(b) of The Constitution Act 1982 (Can), provided, relevantly, that the Acts of the Manitoban legislature 'shall be' published in both the English language and the French language. In 1890 the Manitoban legislature passed an Act[47] asserting that its Acts need only be published in English. Thereafter the Manitoban legislature published its Acts only in English, ignoring decisions of the Manitoban courts that this purported repudiation of the Canadian legislature's Manitoba Act by the Manitoban legislature was ultra vires the Manitoban legislature.[48] Eventually the issue came before the Supreme Court of Canada, which did not 'overrule' any prior decision.

[40] [2006] NZSC 70, [129]–[154] (Tipping J), [205] (Thomas J) cf [95].

[41] *Ibid* [147].

[42] *Ibid* [95], [149]–[154], [205]. Contra *Hall v Simons* [2002] 1 AC 615, 710, 726 (HL).

[43] [2007] NZCA 172, [66](d), [79], [84].

[44] (1987) 39 DLR (4th) 654, 660–64.

[45] *Ibid* 664.

[46] [1985] 1 SCR 721. For a detailed account of this case and the circumstances surrounding it, see WJ Newman 'The Principles of the Rule of Law and Parliamentary Sovereignty in Constitutional Theory and Litigation' (2005) 16 National Journal of Constitutional Law 175, 240–6.

[47] An Act to Provide that the English Language shall be the Official Language of the Province of Manitoba 1890 (Man).

[48] See [1985] 1 SCR 721, 732–3.

Indeed its decision was in accord with longstanding decisions of the Manitoban courts that had been ignored by the Manitoban legislature.

Provisions dealing with Acts of provincial legislatures that were inconsistent with the Constitution of Canada or other Acts of the Canadian parliament made it explicit that an inconsistent provincial Act was, to the extent of the inconsistency, of 'no force and effect',[49] or 'absolutely void and inoperative'.[50] It was obvious that the Manitoban legislature had been continuously obliged since 1870 to publish its Acts in both languages. Accordingly, the Supreme Court of Canada held that all unilingual Acts of the Manitoban legislature were 'invalid and of no force or effect'.[51] If the Supreme Court's decision had the ordinary intertemporal effect, the court opined, 'legal chaos'[52] would ensue in Manitoba because almost every Manitoban Act since 1890 was unilingual and would be void ab initio, and any bilingual Manitoban Acts validly passed prior to 1890 would continue in force even if purportedly repealed by a subsequent unilingual Act.[53] The court's view of the rule of law, a principle included in the preamble of the Constitution of Canada, was thought by the court to require it to avoid the legal chaos that might otherwise follow its decision.[54]

The court fulfilled its constitutional duty[55] to declare that all 'unilingually enacted Acts of the Manitoba Legislature are, *and always have been*, invalid and of no force or effect', [emphasis added][56] and additionally felt compelled 'to take such steps as will ensure the rule of law in the Province of Manitoba'.[57] Accordingly the court held that:

> All Acts of the Manitoba Legislature which would currently be valid and of force and effect, were it not for their constitutional defect, are deemed temporarily valid and effective from the date of this judgment to the expiry of the minimum period necessary for translation, re-enactment, printing and publishing.[58]

The unusual step taken by the Court was to deem the unconstitutional laws to be temporarily valid until a later time, and so, in essence, to suspend the effect of its judgment. It asserted the power to do so in these extraordinary circumstances largely on the basis of an analogy with the doctrine of state necessity.[59] However, the Court did not decide that the law was one thing before its decision and another thing from the time of the decision onwards. There was no prospective overruling in that sense.[60] The court was emphatic that the relevant Acts were always uncon-

[49] The Constitution Act 1982 (Can) s 52.
[50] Colonial Laws Validity Act 1865 (UK) 28 and 29 Vict c 63 s 2.
[51] [1985] 1 SCR 721, 747.
[52] *Ibid.*
[53] *Ibid* 747–8.
[54] *Ibid* 748–54, 758.
[55] *Ibid* 754.
[56] *Ibid* 767
[57] *Ibid* 754.
[58] *Ibid* 767.
[59] *Ibid* 758–67.
[60] Cf *Canada (Attorney General) v Hislop* [2007] SCC 10, [140], [161]; J Lovell 'From Now On: Temporal Issues in Constitutional Adjudication' (2005) 18 National Journal of Constitutional Law 17, 20.

stitutional and therefore void ab initio. Once the period of grace had passed, the court's judgment would apply in the usual way and all unilingual statutes would be void ab initio.[61]

The court held that all 'rights, obligations and any other effects'[62] that had purportedly arisen under unilingual, and therefore void, legislation and which were not protected by the de facto doctrine,[63] res judicata,[64] mistake of law[65] or some other doctrine, though temporarily protected by the suspension of the effect of the court's order, would, on the expiration of the temporary period, fall with the Acts under which they arose 'unless the Acts under which they arose have been translated, re-enacted, printed and published in both languages'. The court did not explicitly state that such enactment would have to have retroactive effect if it were to cover events preceding the date of bilingual enactment. Nonetheless, because the previous legislation was void ab initio, it follows as a matter of logic that for the chaos feared by the court to be avoided, it was necessary for the new bilingual legislation to have retroactive effect. Accordingly, by way of example of the various statutes passed by the Manitoban legislature in response to the court's judgment, section 8 of The Re-Enacted Statutes of Manitoba 1987 (Man), provides that:

> The Re-enacted Statutes of Manitoba, 1987, shall not be held to operate as new law but shall be construed and have effect as a consolidation and as declaratory of the law as contained in the Acts repealed by section 5 and for which the Re-enacted Statutes of Manitoba, 1987, are substituted.[66]

This retroactivity might be thought unfair to monolingual francophones subject to Manitoban jurisdiction. However, in order to avoid the chaos that would otherwise follow from the court's declaration of the invalidity of the Manitoban legislature's unilingual legislation, the Manitoban legislature might be thought justified in bilingually re-enacting its legislation with retroactive effect. Because the Supreme Court did not decide that the law until its judgment had been one thing, but since its decision was to be something else, and instead suspended the effect of its judgment which otherwise had the usual intertemporal effect, the decision about how to react to the potential chaos caused by the legislature's failure to comply with its constitutional obligation to enact bilingual laws, was left to the legislature itself.

One potential problem with the legislature passing retroactive curative legislation, however, might be thought to have arisen because of section 11(g) of the

[61] The same pattern has been followed in subsequent exceptional cases, eg *R v Swain* [1991] 1 SCR 933, 1021–2; *Re Eurig Estate* [1998] 2 SCR 565, 586–7. Cf *Canada (Attorney General) v Hislop* [2007] SCC 10, [92].

[62] [1985] 1 SCR 721, 768.

[63] *Ibid* 755–7.

[64] *Ibid* 757.

[65] *Ibid.*

[66] The curative legislation passed in Ontario after *Re Eurig Estate* [1998] 2 SCR 565, in which the order was suspended, also had retroactive effect. See J Lovell 'From Now On: Temporal Issues in Constitutional Adjudication' (2005) 18 National Journal of Constitutional Law 17, 35.

Canadian Charter of Rights and Freedoms, which provides that no one can be convicted of a criminal offence for something that was not criminal at the time that he did it. Any statutory offence prior to bilingual re-enactment was void and so no criminal offence existed under such a statute. Convictions for which the time for appeal had passed were unassailable. Furthermore, arguments that the statute under which conviction occurred was void could not succeed during the period of temporary validity of unconstitutional monolingual statutes.[67] However, any conduct occurring prior to bilingual enactment that did not attract a statute of limitation and was not the subject of a conviction that was res judicata would come within the protection of the prohibition on retroactive criminal liability—which the re-enacted statutes purported to impose.[68] This is a specific example of the more general point that retroactive curative legislation can only follow a court's decision that legislation is constitutionally infirm and therefore void ab initio if there is a constitutionally permissible way for a parliament to legislate retroactively to alleviate the intertemporal effects of the court's judgment.[69]

The Supreme Court of Canada has recently shown deference to a legislative response to its temporarily suspended judgment in *M v H*[70] that has the effect of limiting the intertemporal reach of that judgment. *M v H* held that for the purpose of pension payments, the survivor of a same sex relationship in which one partner has died is constitutionally required to be treated like any other spouse. In *Canada (Attorney General) v Hislop*[71] the court considered the constitutionality of ameliorative legislation passed in response to *M v H* that allowed such a survivor to claim benefits only from a particular date onwards, and not from the latter of the relevant death or the commencement of the Canadian Charter of Rights and Freedoms, as one might have expected under conventional principles. Although the judgment in *Hislop* was phrased in the language of 'prospective remedies',[72] the court was not required expressly to limit the intertemporal effect of its judgment in that case. However, the court in *Hislop* did give its imprimatur to legislation ameliorative, although not retroactively curative, of the constitutional invalidity announced in *M v H*. The practical result was that the holding in *M v H*, by virtue of its temporary suspension and the consequent legislation approved in *Hislop*, was given limited temporal effect.

[67] *Bilodeau v A-G (Manitoba)* [1986] 1 SCR 449.

[68] There do not appear to be any cases on this point.

[69] J Lovell 'From Now On: Temporal Issues in Constitutional Adjudication' (2005) 18 National Journal of Constitutional Law 17, 36. Cf *University of Wollongong v Metwally* (1984) 158 CLR 447, 457, 474–5, 478–9.

[70] [1999] 2 SCR 3.

[71] [2007] SCC 10.

[72] Eg *ibid* [99], [78], [92]–[93].

C Evaluation of Prospective Overruling

Prospective overruling arises as an issue because appellate courts perform at least two functions. One is administering justice according to law in particular disputes. Another is, in the course of adjudicating particular disputes, stating the law in sufficiently general form to be of use to persons other than the litigants in the particular case in which the law is stated.[73] Considerations of certainty and liberty do, or should, motivate circumspection in developing or changing the law in such a way as to have retroactive effect on the litigants in a particular case and on any others who may be affected by a retroactive change in the law. This curtails the freedom of courts to develop or change the law.

If the judicial function of administering justice according to law in a particular dispute can be separated from the judicial function of making general pronouncements of law, then the possibility is raised of appellate courts developing or changing common law rules without being restrained by the retroactive effect of doing so. This possibility would mean that a rule that an appellate court no longer considers to be the best legal rule, but which has given rise to an ability to rely on it or has defined the parameters of individual liberty in a particular way, can be applied to those who were entitled to rely on it or had their liberty defined by it, but can simultaneously be replaced by a new rule that does not have retroactive effect. This superficially convenient technique requires careful scrutiny from at least two related perspectives. The first is whether it is inconsistent with the judicial role in common law systems. The second is whether it gives rise to arbitrary results.

1 Inconsistency with the Proper Scope of the Judicial Function in Common Law Systems

If the type of prospective overruling under consideration is that in which the rule newly announced has effect only for the future, either immediately or after a specified delay, so that any cause of action arising before the announcement, including that in the case before the court, is governed by the law as it was prior to the announcement, then there is a *manifest severance* between the court's function in the case before it and the more general announcement of a new, and non-retroactive, rule. This is sometimes called 'pure' prospective overruling. It might be thought that this would be an enhanced form of obiter dicta.[74] However, prospective overruling differs from obiter dicta in at least two important ways. First, and most importantly, obiter dicta does not have the effect that the rights

[73] AGL Nicol 'Prospective Overruling: A New Device for English Courts?' (1976) 39 Modern Law Review 542, 542; K Mason 'Prospective Overruling' (1989) 63 Australian Law Journal 526, 526. Cf R Cross and J Harris *Precedent in English Law* (4th edn Clarendon Press Oxford 1991) 232.

[74] Cf Lord Rodger, "A Time for Everything under the Law: Some Reflections on Retrospectivity" (2005) 121 Law Quarterly Review 57, 78.

between the parties in the case before the court are held to be one thing, whereas the same dispute arising between different parties will attract a different rule in future cases. Obiter dicta goes beyond what is necessary for the decision in the instant case, but it does not mean that the decision in the instant case will be inconsistent with a future case decided in accordance with the obiter dicta. Second, obiter dicta is not binding which, presumably, prospective overruling would be.

A serious problem with this form of prospective overruling is that if the new rule is not applied to the case at hand, then the party that went to the effort and expense and performed the public service of litigating a point requiring a development or change in the law does not enjoy the benefit of the development or change for which he rightly advocated. This is problematic at the level of individual litigants, who are deprived of their just desserts, and at a systemic level because the spectre of prospective overruling of this kind may discourage litigation that seeks to change the law, except perhaps amongst criminal appellants who have nothing to lose by trying their luck, and institutional repeat litigants who are concerned with what the rule will be in the future as well as with what it will be held to have been in a particular case. This is sometimes classed as a 'practical' problem,[75] as though it were merely a question of incentive to litigate or just a transitional difficulty *en route* to a new rule. But this problem is linked to the fundamental point that the primary purpose of common law litigation is to adjudicate between the parties before the court in the instant case. A technique that applies one rule in the exercise of that function and simultaneously announces that the rule that is being applied is not the best rule and that a different rule will be applicable in the future, is problematic.

It is appropriate to emphasise that courts' primary function is adjudicating between parties.[76] In a case in which a court develops or changes the law, the court may deem those rights to have been other than what they in fact were at the time when the cause of action arose. However, the court's function does not include declaring the rights between the parties to be, and have been, one thing, whilst deciding that in the future the rights between any similar parties shall be something else. In the course of their adjudicative function, appellate courts properly make broad pronouncements about legal rules, including in some cases developing or changing a common law rule, but it would be wrong for such a pronouncement to be *inconsistent with*, as opposed to just unnecessary for, the rule being applied in the case in which the pronouncement is made. It is not that common law courts should not develop or change the law. It is that they should not do so where the rule announced as being applicable for the future is inconsistent with the rule being applied in the very case in which that announcement is made.

If a court severs the link between the case before it and the new rule that the court espouses in the course of that case, then the court's function becomes blatantly legislative—in the sense that it announces a new rule binding for the future

[75] Eg *Re Spectrum Plus (in liquidation)* [2005] 2 AC 680, [26]–[27] (HL).
[76] Cross and Harris, Precedent in English Law (4th edn Clarendon Press Oxford 1991) 232.

but inconsistent with the case before it. The court is not developing the common law interstitially to meet the needs of the case before it. It is difficult to reconcile such an activity with the constitutional role of common law courts—which is primarily adjudicative and only incidentally creative. Advocates of prospective overruling accurately point out its systemic benefits, particularly with regards to the protection of the certain application of the law to past events. However, though common law courts may take into account systemic considerations in deciding whether or not to develop or change a common law rule, they cannot pursue systemic benefits that are inconsistent with the demands of the case that has engaged their jurisdiction.

In order to avoid a situation in which the newly announced rule is not applied to the litigants that have contested the point, a possible form of prospective overruling, as mentioned above, is that the new rule not, in general, have retroactive effect, but, by way of exception, be deemed to have been applicable to the instant case, or, more broadly, to the instant case and other proceedings commenced prior to the announcement of the new rule. This is sometimes regarded as avoiding the difficulties associated with the party that advocates the new rule not enjoying its benefit, whilst not upsetting the legal status of past events of unknowable quantity. What must also be appreciated is that, under such a model, the unsuccessful party in the litigation in which the rule is changed, and perhaps her equivalents in pending litigation, who acted in accordance with the law as it was at the time of the relevant events are also subjected, to their disadvantage, to the new, and, so far as their cases are concerned, retroactive, rule. This is the very characteristic of traditional common law decision making sought to be avoided by prospective overruling. It should be remembered that the correlative of exceptions to prospective overruling is retroactive application of a new rule in all cases to which the exception applies. It is by no means clear that if prospective overruling is desirable that 'some' prospective overruling is better than none. The reason for this is the arbitrariness to which it gives rise.

Furthermore, a decision to adopt a limited form of prospective overruling may lead a court to feel free to develop a new rule without properly considering, and presumptively resisting, the retroactive effects that would arise in the particular case before the court due to the application of the new rule to that case. An unsuccessful litigant in such a case may find that retroactive adoption of a new rule is not as strongly resisted by the court as it would be if the retroactivity was to have general effect, because it is only his case, or only his case and pending cases, that will be affected. Retroactivity is therefore suffered by one or a few so that the new rule can be introduced for the many. This might be tolerable if the retroactive effect on the case before the court is recognised and thought a necessary price for the development of the common law. It is not tolerable if the court were to assume that it need not consider retroactive effects because it was prospectively overruling. Those effects, under this type of prospective overruling, would still be felt by those before the court and, potentially, by others with litigation pending.

2 Arbitrariness

Under the form of prospective overruling just mentioned the new rule is, exceptionally, retroactively applied to the case in which the new rule is announced, and perhaps also to cases already pending at the time of that announcement. Whether the new rule or the old rule applies to a case is determined by whether the case at hand gave rise to the litigation in which the rule was changed or, on the broader version, whether proceedings had been commenced at the time that the new rule was announced. Cases in which the same cause of action arose at the same time will be determined according to a different rule on the basis of when proceedings were determined or commenced. Accordingly, for cases contemporaneous with the one in which the new rule is announced and applied, the primary determinant of the applicable rule is not the requirements of justice in a particular case, or a court's view of which, in general, is the best legal rule, but instead the primary determinant of the applicable rule is the date on which proceedings are either determined or commenced. These dates do not seem, in general, to be logically defensible bases for choosing which rule applies.

Amongst those who would allow the possibility of prospective overruling there seems to be an acknowledgement that, although there are alternatives, the most workable form of prospective overruling would be one which, at least ordinarily, would apply the newly announced rule to the case in which the announcement was made.[77] By necessary logic, the new rule would be deemed to have existed at least as long ago as the events giving rise to the litigation in which the new rule is announced. For the new rule to apply to the case at hand, and still qualify as prospective overruling, the old rule would have to continue to apply to at least some other cases in which the cause of action arose prior to the announcement of the new rule.

If a newly announced rule is applied to some cases within its ambit, but not others, then in an attempt to avoid retroactivity, but at the same time provide the fruits of victory to litigants who successfully argue for a change in the law, the change ends up being retroactive for some, but not others. That is arbitrary in the following sense. The legal rule has been announced and applied. The cases in question are all within its ambit and within any relevant time limit. The application of the new rule to any of them would be retroactive because all of the causes of action in question arose prior to the announcement of the new rule. The only distinction between the case or cases to which the rule is held to apply and those to which it is held not to apply would be the time at which they were decided or commenced. The submission is that variation in such dates does not validly distinguish between otherwise congruent cases.

It has been said that such arbitrariness 'must be accepted in the interests of the law as a whole',[78] but it is not clear why there is an imperative to accept results

[77] Eg *Chamberlains v Sun Poi Lai* [2006] NZSC 70, [147]. Cf *Re Spectrum Plus (in liquidation)* [2005] 2 AC 680, [72] (HL); K Mason 'Prospective Overruling' (1989) 63 Australian Law Journal 526, 528.

[78] *Chamberlains v Sun Poi Lai* [2006] NZSC 70, [145].

admitted to be arbitrary. The fact that statutes of limitation, and the doctrines of merger and res judicata may mean that the rule governing causes of action arising at the same time may differ according to when proceedings were commenced or determined has been said to be no more arbitrary than the lack of generality that accompanies prospective overruling.[79] Merger, res judicata, statutes of limitation, issue estoppel and the equitable defence of laches, are directed towards *finality* and, within their spheres of operation, other considerations are subordinate to the protection of finality. The arbitrariness created by prospective overruling has nothing to do with finality. It occurs amongst causes of action that are within time and yet to be finally determined.

Statutes of limitation prevent a claim from being agitated by applying a rule of a different *kind* (ie one of limitation) to the rule that would be applied if the claim was allowed to proceed to determination on its substantive merits. Statutes of limitation do not require, as prospective overruling does, that one cause of action be determined on its substantive merits by one rule and that, in a different, though contemporaneous case involving the same cause of action, it be determined on its substantive merits by a different rule *of the same kind.*

In unusual cases it may be appropriate for the legislature to respond to a court decision developing or changing a common law rule by enacting a limitation scheme tailored to protect a measure of finality whilst also respecting the application of the new common law rule. The statutory limitation scheme recommended by the Law Commission in response to the decision of the House of Lords in *Kleinwort Benson v Lincoln County Council*[80] is one example.[81]

A possibility that might go some way to alleviating concerns about arbitrariness would be for the new rule to apply to all causes of action arising at or after the time of the cause of action giving rise to the case in which the new rule is announced. The date of retroactive applicability might be considered arbitrary in the sense that it would be determined by the date of the cause of action arising in the case that first reached an appellate court willing to announce a new rule. However, for all causes of action arising after that time and not yet finally determined, the same rule would be applicable regardless, subject to statutes of limitation and laches, of when proceedings were commenced or determined. This possibility is a long way from 'pure' prospective overruling in which the new rule applies *only* to causes of action arising after the announcement of the new rule, meaning that the new rule does not even apply to the case in which it is announced. Indeed this possibility is different from the ordinary retroactive effect of judicial decisions only in the sense that causes of action arising prior to the one giving rise to the case in which the new rule is announced would not be subject to the new rule. In those cases, courts would apply the old rule at a time when its replacement, retroactive to a certain date, had already been announced. This form of prospective overruling would

[79] K Mason 'Prospective Overruling' (1989) 63 Australian Law Journal 526, 530–31. Cf *R v Unger* [1977] 2 NSWLR 990, 995–6.

[80] [1999] 2 AC 349 (HL).

[81] Discussed in Ch 5 Pt D(1).

avoid *some* of the forms of arbitrariness discussed above, but in order to do so, it would forego many of the benefits of prospective overruling by retroactively applying the new rule to a potentially large class of litigants. Because it is so far removed from pure prospective overruling, this technique was not included in the discussion of four potential forms of prospective overruling earlier in this chapter.

A further alternative form of prospective overruling would be for a new rule announced in a case not to be applicable to that case, and perhaps not to any proceedings already commenced at the time of the announcement of the new rule, but for the new rule to be applicable to all other cases decided after the announcement of the new rule regardless of when the cause of action arose. This alternative would preserve the fewest benefits of prospective overruling, because it is closest to the normal retroactive effect of judicial decisions, whilst still creating arbitrary results. It would avoid the new rule having retroactive effect in the case that happened to reach the appellate court first, and perhaps in other cases already pending, but would impose the new rule on all other causes of action yet to be determined, including, with retroactive effect, on those that arose prior to the announcement of the new rule. Because of the characteristics just described, the two forms of prospective overruling just mentioned are not serious candidates for adoption.

All forms of prospective overruling other than pure prospective overruling involve arbitrariness in the application of a new legal rule. Arbitrariness is the antithesis of the rule of law. An innovation advocated by some because of its assumed benefits for legal certainty turns out, on closer inspection, to conflict with a fundamental requirement of the rule of law.

3 Prospective Overruling of Decisions about Statutory and Constitutional Construction

There has been some discussion of whether, even if prospective overruling is permissible for decisions developing or changing a rule that is entirely a creature of the common law, it follows that it is permissible when a court overturns an interpretation previously given to a statute. When the concern is not with the separation of powers, it is clear that the retroactive effect of changing a previous judicial interpretation of a statute may be just as great as changing a common law rule.[82] However, when, as with prospective overruling, concern about the separation of judicial and legislative powers becomes relevant, there is room for argument about whether there is a meaningful difference between these two types of case. One possibility is that by overruling a previous interpretation of a statute, judges change the law just as much as if they were changing a common law rule and so making such a change non-retroactive is just as legitimate when interpreting a statute as it is in changing a common law rule.[83]

[82] See Ch 5 Pt E(3).

[83] Eg *Re Spectrum Plus (in liquidation)* [2005] 2 AC 680, [36]–[40], [74], [162] (HL); *Chamberlains v Sun Poi Lai* [2006] NZSC 70, [141].

A contrary possibility is that when a court overrules a previous judicial interpretation of a statute, even though the practical effect on litigants may be the same as changing a common law rule, the constitutional implications are different. The statute, not the court, is the source of the rule. Regardless of whether changed social conditions have motivated a court to change a previous interpretation without impugning the validity of that previous interpretation in its own time, or whether the court views the earlier interpretation as flawed from the outset, or whether, as in the case of section 3 of the Human Rights Act 1998 (UK), a subsequent statute commands that earlier statutes be interpreted, insofar as possible, in accordance with the provisions of the later statute, it is still the statute, which is a command of the legislature, admittedly as interpreted by the court over time, that is the source of the rule. A rule of statutory source cannot have its application temporally manipulated by a court because a court does not have the power to deny the application of a rule that has been mandated by parliament. This so even if compliance with this constitutional doctrine means that some litigants will be subject to a rule that, for all practical purposes, has retroactive effect.[84]

If prospective overruling in cases of changed judicial interpretation of a statute raises additional issues when compared to cases changing or developing common law rules, then so too do cases of changed constitutional interpretation. If a statute is inconsistent with a written constitution, then it is that constitution, albeit as interpreted by judges, who might change their view over time, that makes it so.[85] If prospective overruling of decisions about the meaning of statutes is constitutionally dubious, so too is prospective overruling of decisions about the meaning of a written constitution.

D Conclusion

These difficulties with prospective overruling in cases of statutory and constitutional interpretation mean that the strongest case for prospective overruling is in cases involving rules that are entirely the creation of courts. However, courts having the ability to develop and change common law rules, and having the ability to control the intertemporal effects of doing so, are different things. Within the class of cases dealing with rules that are entirely the creation of courts, the type of case with the strongest claim for prospective overruling to occur would be one in which certainty or liberty pointed strongly towards the new rule not having retroactive effect, for example if the retroactive introduction of a new rule would create retroactive criminal liability, but other factors specific to the substantive nature of

[84] Eg *Re Spectrum Plus (in liquidation)* [2005] 2 AC 680, [45], [125]–[127] (HL); M Arden 'Prospective Overruling' (2004) 120 Law Quarterly Review 7, 11. Cf *Re Spectrum Plus (in liquidation)* [2005] 2 AC 680, [36]–[38] (HL).

[85] *McGinty v Western Australia* (1996) 186 CLR 140, 235; *Canada (Attorney General) v Hislop* [2007] SCC 10, [138], [141]–[144] contra [79]–[89].

the new rule in question, for example that there was a glaring omission in the criminal law, pointed strongly towards its adoption. The apparent convenience of prospective overruling in such cases, and its potential contribution to protection of legal certainty relating to past events, should not deter inquiry into whether, despite its convenience, it is an appropriate *judicial* technique.

The High Court of Australia rested its objection to prospective overruling on the declaratory theory of law—that all judges ever do is declare existing rights and obligations—when its majority stated:

> A hallmark of the judicial process has long been the making of binding declarations of rights and obligations arising from the operation of the law upon past events or conduct.[86] The adjudication of existing rights and obligations as distinct from the creation of rights and obligations distinguishes the judicial power from non-judicial power.[87] Prospective overruling is thus inconsistent with judicial power on the simple ground that the new regime that would be ushered in when the overruling took effect would alter existing rights and obligations.[88]

This objection is only as strong as the idea that judges never alter the existing law. That is not strong. But not accepting the declaratory theory does not mean that accepting prospective overruling automatically follows.[89] The crucial question is whether it is permissible and appropriate for a court that develops or changes a common law rule ever to prevent the new rule having the retroactive effect that it ordinarily would.

In a truly exceptional case, in the strictest sense of the word exceptional, where legal chaos may be expected to flow from a retroactively effective new rule, it may be appropriate for a court to exercise its inherent discretion over its orders to suspend the commencement of the legal force of its judgment in order to allow affected parties, particularly the legislative and executive branches of government, to take whatever permissible action such parties may think it necessary to take in response to the court's reasons. That is what happened in *Re Manitoba Language Rights*[90] and it may be all that is permissible under the provisions of the devolution legislation in the United Kingdom that empower courts to control the intertemporal effects of their decisions. The key characteristic is that once a suspended judgment commences its operation, it has retroactive effect in the usual way, subject to any constitutionally permissible retroactive legislation passed during the period of the suspension of the court's order. The parties are bound by the new rule announced in the suspended judgment and, consistently with the

[86] *Precision Data Holdings Ltd v Wills* (1991) 173 CLR 167, 188.

[87] *Rola Co (Australia) v The Commonwealth* (1944) 69 CLR 185, 203.

[88] *Ha v New South Wales* (1997) 189 CLR 465, 503–4 [footnotes in original].

[89] *Deutsche Morgan Grenfell Group v Inland Revenue Commissioners* [2006] UKHL 49, [23].

[90] See also s 16(1)(a) of the Administrative Decisions (Judicial Review) Act 1977 (Aus), which vests discretionary power in the Federal Court of Australia and the Australian Federal Magistrates Court to make the operative date of an order quashing an administrative decision later than the date on which the administrative decision was made. This is discussed, along with cases in which the power has been exercised, by E Campbell 'The Retrospectivity of Judicial Decisions and the Legality of Governmental Acts' (2003) 29 Monash University Law Review 49, 70–71.

requirement that the law be general in its application, so are all past causes of action not yet finally determined or lapsed by effluxion of time, as well as all future causes of action.

A court has no business applying one rule to the case before it and simultaneously announcing a new rule for future cases, inconsistent with the rule being applied. To do so would ignore the primacy of the case before the court to common law adjudication.[91] All other forms of prospective overruling, and indeed most forms of prospective overruling in which the new rule is not applied to the case in which it is announced, necessarily have the consequence that one common law rule applies to some causes of action yet to be determined and a different common law rule applies to other causes of action yet to be determined. Which rule applies to which cause of action is determined by factors that, as discussed above, create arbitrary results.

Although the House of Lords in *Spectrum*, the Supreme Court of Canada in *Hislop* and two members of the New Zealand Supreme Court in *Chamberlains* indicated a contrary view, the better view, it is submitted, is that prospective overruling is constitutionally impermissible. In all of its various manifestations it has one or both of the following constitutional defects. First, it announces a new rule inconsistent with the one being applied in the case in which the announcement is made and therefore deviates from the primarily adjudicative function of courts. Second, it disrespects the requirement of the rule of law that legal rules be general in their application, and not arbitrarily applied.

Once a court has taken into account the retroactive effect of introducing a new rule and has decided that, notwithstanding the retroactivity, the law needs to develop or change, the newly announced rule should apply both to the parties in the case in which the announcement is made and to any other cases properly brought in the future, whensoever the cause of action arose. The protection of finality by the doctrines of merger and res judicata,[92] the equitable defence of laches, issue estoppel and appropriately crafted statutes of limitation, means that the retroactive effects need not be limitless.

The potential retroactive effect of their judgments deprives courts of a free hand in announcing new rules. That is not a bad thing. It means that courts should only announce new rules if they have considered, amongst other things, the potential retroactive effects of developing or changing the law and are nonetheless convinced that the new rule is so important, and so clearly within the province of judicial creation and alteration, as to require judicial introduction with retroactive effect on the case before the court and in subsequent cases. If parliament were to lack the time, skills or inclination to deal with an identified problem in a way unavailable to courts, in the form of legislation the temporal effect of which may be specified as thought fit, that would be a reason for parliament to do a better job. It would not be a reason for the courts, by asserting a power to make law without

[91] Cf *R v Governor of Brockhill Prison, ex p Evans* (No 2) [2001] 2 AC 19, 48 (HL).
[92] *R v Unger* [1977] 2 NSWLR 990, 995–6; *R v Gregory* [2002] NSWCCA 199, [33]–45].

retroactive effect, to attempt to arrogate to themselves a power of which they are constitutionally deprived. The relationship between the potential retroactive effect of a new common law rule and a court's decision about whether to introduce that rule, is the core of the next, and concluding, chapter.

7

Conclusions

A Foundations

Julius Stone thought that we 'must . . . reconcile ourselves to the fact that no perfect answer to the retroactivity problem is feasible'.[1] He may have been right, but ignoring the problem, as common lawyers often do, is an inappropriate response to recognition of the impossibility of a perfect solution. The most important goals of this book have been to develop coherent rationales for a general presumption against retroactivity, to examine existing approaches to retroactivity in statutory construction and the adjudication of common law rules, and, ultimately, to suggest improvements to the common law's approach to issues of retroactivity. The core argument that, when making a decision about whether to develop or change a common law rule, courts should draw on their approach to the construction of statutes and, motivated by the same rationales, should explicitly consider and presumptively resist retroactivity in the development or change of common law rules, requires further development.

It is foundational to this book that the rationales for a presumption against retroactivity expressed in Chapter three are applicable regardless of whether a law by which someone is bound is a statute or a common law rule. Whatever the constitutional and theoretical differences between statutes and the common law, it makes no difference to a person who is entitled to rely on a legal rule and whose liberty is affected by that rule, whether the source of that rule is a statute or the common law. It only matters that there is a rule by which she is bound. With that in mind, comparison of some of the cases discussed in Chapter four, on statutory construction, with some of the cases discussed in Chapter five, on adjudicative retroactivity, is instructive.

[1] J Stone *Precedent and Law* (Butterworths Sydney 1985) 192.

B Comparison of Cases of Statutory and Adjudicative Retroactivity

In *Barber v Pigden* the removal by statute of the legal fiction that a wife's identity was fused with her husband's overcame the presumption against retroactivity in part because the statute sought to remove 'the historical interferences by lawyers with the natural rights of woman' and restore women's 'natural status and capacity'.[2] The effect of this change was that a man was liable for his wife's tort at the time that it was committed but, at the time that the claim was litigated, he was retroactively deemed not to have been liable for that tort. This may be compared to the marital rape cases.[3] At the time that each defendant husband had, or attempted to have, non-consensual sex with his wife, he was, subject to an expanding list of exceptions, immune from prosecution for raping his wife. At the time that the cases were tried, the changed common law rule retroactively applied was that husbands were liable to prosecution for marital rape. The immunity had shielded from prosecution men responsible for an act that was eventually seen as naturally and intrinsically wrong. In the marital rape cases and in *Barber v Pigden*, a modern view of marriage and the status and rights of a woman within marriage, meant that objections to retroactively removing an offensive legal fiction were rightly overcome. The old rule came to be seen as so unacceptable that a modern court should not apply it. Retroactivity was a way to achieve that result and was more than an incidental effect of changing the rule.[4] This approach was similar regardless of the fact that one case involved statutory retroactivity and the other adjudicative retroactivity.

Just as the nature of the conduct in the marital rape cases was crucial to the justification for imposing retroactive criminal liability under the common law, the nature of the war time conduct criminalised by the statute under consideration in *Polyukhovich v The Commonwealth of Australia*[5] was crucial to the judicial construction of that statute to impose retroactive criminal liability. If it was ever true that people were at legal liberty to perform what are now called war crimes (or, more precisely, having performed them, to flee to a country in which it was not criminal to have performed them elsewhere), or have non-consensual sex with their wife, the heinousness of such acts justified the retroactive removal of those liberties. The liberty rationale for prima facie prohibiting retroactivity, and the process of justifying exceptions to that prohibition by concentrating on the heinous nature of the acts retroactively criminalised, did not, because one case involved adjudicative retroactivity and the other statutory retroactivity, vary.

2 [1937] 1 KB 664, 678 (CA), discussed in Ch 4 Pt F(3).

3 Discussed in Ch 5 Pt C.

4 See also *R v Bow Road Justices, ex p Adedigba* [1968] 2 QB 572, 579 (CA), discussed in Ch 5 Pt E(3).

5 (1991) 172 CLR 501, discussed in Ch 4 Pt F(3).

Another issue of retroactivity arising from the Second World War appeared in *Starkowski v A-G.*[6] Under the German marriage law in force in Austria in May 1945 a religious marriage was not a legally valid marriage. A woman who was religiously married in Austria at that time subsequently moved to England. Her religious marriage was retroactively validated under Austrian law. The question arose in English proceedings whether or not her retroactively validated marriage in Austria should be recognised in English law. The key factor in the decision of the English court to recognise the retroactive Austrian law, was that certainty of legal status did not militate against doing so. Because a key rationale for the presumption against retroactivity was inapplicable, the presumption could be overcome. A similar approach may be taken to the adjudicative retroactivity involved in changing the common law rule on jurisdiction to grant a divorce. When such a change was made in *Indyka v Indyka*[7] it was judicially assumed that there were no reliance considerations. As discussed in Chapter five, that assumption is open to question, but the case nonetheless indicates an approach whereby a decision that there are no reliance considerations overcomes a core obstacle to retroactivity and, as in *Starkowski*, may lead to rebuttal of the presumption against retroactivity. The cases so far mentioned in this concluding chapter all involved the rebuttal of the presumption against retroactivity. There are also examples where the presumption against retroactivity in statutory construction was not overcome and comparable cases turning on a common law rule did or should have adopted a similar approach.

In *Wijesuriya v Amit*[8] the presumption against retroactivity was applied to prevent a tax ordinance that was fairly obviously intended by the legislature to have retroactive effect from doing so, on the basis that the ordinance did not adequately specify the ways in which, if it operated retroactively, compliance was possible. Judicial concern to protect individual reliance and liberty in a taxation context were also apparent in *Vestey v Inland Revenue Commissioners*,[9] but in that case those concerns favoured adjudicative retroactivity. An existing decision of the House of Lords,[10] if applied to the facts in *Vestey*, would have allowed the Revenue to decide, in its discretion, for what proportion of the income of a trust particular beneficiaries were liable. In departing, with retroactive effect, from its previous decision about the interpretation of the relevant statute, the House was motivated by the importance of people being able to know their tax liabilities in advance, and that those liabilities be imposed by Act of parliament, not by executive discretion. *Wijesuriya* and *Vestey* both demonstrate, in the field of taxation, judicial protection of the rationales for the presumption against retroactivity,[11] but the consequences

[6] [1954] AC 155 (HL), discussed in Ch 4 Pt F(2).

[7] [1969] 1 AC 33 (HL), discussed in Ch 5 Pt E(2)(a).

[8] [1966] AC 372 (PC), discussed in Ch 4 Pt C.

[9] [1980] AC 1148 (HL), discussed in Ch 5 Pt F(3).

[10] *Congreve v Inland Revenue Commissioners* [1948] 1 All ER 948 (HL).

[11] Contra *Lord Howard de Walden v Inland Revenue Commissioners* [1942] 1 KB 389 (CA), discussed in Ch 4 Pt F(3).

of that concern varied. In *Wijesuriya* the presumption against retroactivity was not overcome, but in *Vestey* concern for reliance and liberty led to the prior decision being overruled with retroactive effect. Though a uniform *approach* to retroactivity, motivated by uniform *rationales*, is possible, the *outcome* in any given case will vary according to the particular facts and circumstances.

A uniform approach to retroactivity should have, but did not, lead to a uniform outcome in *Noss Farm Products v Lilico*[12] and *Shaw v DPP*.[13] In *Noss Farm Products* the court was adamant that a statute not be construed to create a result whereby an act lawful when done was later deemed to have been criminal. Humphreys J exclaimed:

> We are asked to say here that the meaning of that provision is, that if a man sells what is perfectly legal and proper according to law, nevertheless a year afterwards—and, it may be said, the law having in the meantime been altered—he is to be brought before a police court and, being a reputable person, is to be charged with a criminal offence. To my mind that is a monstrous proposition.[14]

In *Shaw*, by contrast, the House of Lords, by way of judicial decision with retroactive effect, deemed conduct that was not criminal at the time that it occurred to have been criminal at that time.

As discussed in Chapter five, some of the Law Lords in *Shaw* were influenced by their view that the conduct was not, unlike in *Noss Farm Products*, 'proper' and that the man responsible for it was not 'reputable'. Such impressionistic views should be irrelevant to the question of criminal liability. From Mr Shaw's perspective, whether he was found to have been criminally liable on the basis of a statute with retroactive effect or on the basis of a common law rule with retroactive effect, would also have been irrelevant. Or as Glanville Williams put it, there is, when retroactive effect is at issue, 'no moral difference between legislation and law-making by judicial decision'.[15] It would have been preferable if the House of Lords in *Shaw* had been motivated by the same concern for the protection of individual liberty in its decision about a common law rule as was the Court of King's Bench in *Noss Farm Products* in its construction of a statute.

A final comparison of a case dealing with the presumption against retroactivity in statutory construction and a case of adjudicative retroactivity lies in *Gardner v Lucas*[16] and *Re Spectrum Plus (in liquidation)*.[17] In *Gardner v Lucas* the House of Lords, motivated by a concern for certainty, found that the presumption against retroactivity was not rebutted. The result was that an agreement that was void when it was made was not, because of a later statute, deemed to have been valid when it was made. In *Spectrum* the House was also concerned about certainty, but ultimately held that a decision made by a single judge in the Chancery division on

[12] [1945] 2 All ER 609 (KB), discussed in Ch 4 Pt C.
[13] [1962] AC 220 (HL), discussed in Ch5 Pt G(1)(b).
[14] [1945] 2 All ER 609, 610 (KB).
[15] G Williams *Criminal Law: The General Part* (2nd edn Stevens and Sons London 1961) 602.
[16] (1878) 3 App Cas 582 (HL), discussed in Ch 4 Pt C.
[17] [2005] 2 AC 680 (HL), discussed in Ch 5 Pt E(2)(b).

which there was significant reliance, should be overturned with retroactive effect. *Spectrum* is noteworthy not because it ultimately changed the law, but because before doing so, the importance of certainty and the retroactive effect of changing the law were confronted openly.

These examples demonstrate similar problems of retroactivity arising in statutory construction and in the adjudication of common law rules. Uniform *answers* are not available, but a more uniform and principled *approach* to those problems is both possible and desirable.

C Approaching Rebuttal of the Presumption

Although no general statement can be made about when rebuttal of the presumption against retroactivity will be appropriate,[18] it may be pointed out that when neither certainty nor liberty is engaged by the circumstances of the case, the rebuttal of the presumption will be made more likely by the inapplicability of both of its core rationales.[19] When certainty or liberty actually militates *towards* retroactivity, the rebuttal of the presumption will be even more likely. The most obvious example is the rebuttal of the presumption against retroactivity in cases where a statute provides for a lesser sentence than was applicable at the time of the relevant crime being committed, on the ground that such rebuttal favours individual liberty.[20]

Parallel examples of adjudicative retroactivity in which retroactive effect was desirable because it furthered individual liberty are the decision in *Woolmington v DPP*[21] that the prosecution must *prove* murder, even where the victim died at the defendant's hands and, in public law, the decision in *Vestey v Inland Revenue Commissioners*[22] to overrule an earlier decision that granted the Revenue excessive power and also deprived people of the ability to be certain about their fiscal obligations. The fact that some of these cases involved statutory construction and others involved adjudication of a common law rule is irrelevant to the guiding role of certainty and liberty in each case. Attention to the rationales for the presumption against retroactivity anchors the presumption to its raisons d'etre and, by justifying its rebuttal in appropriate cases, prevents the application of the presumption being a source of injustice.

In addition to cases in which concentration on the rationales for the presumption may lead to its rebuttal, there are cases in which the presumption against retroactivity may be defeated by factors unrelated to certainty and liberty. Those factors may have existed at the time of the conduct retroactively deemed to have

[18] See Ch 3 Pt E(4).

[19] As well as the comparison just above of *Starkowski* and *Indyka*, see also the cases discussed in Ch 5 Pts E(1)(a), E(1)(b), F(2) and G(3).

[20] Discussed in Ch 4 Pt G(2)(c).

[21] [1935] AC 462 (HL), discussed in Ch 5 Pt G(2)(b).

[22] [1980] AC 1148 (HL), discussed in Ch 5 Pt F(3).

been subject to a new rule, or have come into existence subsequent to that conduct.[23] In such cases other values trump the concern for certainty and liberty manifested in the presumption against retroactivity.

The diversity of individual circumstances detailed in Chapters four and five is such that any more general observations about the circumstances in which the rebuttal of the presumption against retroactivity will be appropriate are not possible. As discussed earlier, 'fairness' is not a valid determinant of the applicability[24] or strength[25] of the presumption against retroactivity. Nor is it a meaningful ground for the rebuttal of the presumption.[26] It may be hoped that when a case, either of statutory construction or adjudication of a common law rule, is approached by beginning with the presumption against retroactivity and then being willing to rebut that presumption only if strong reasons demand, that the result in a particular case, whether ultimately retroactive or not, could accurately be called 'fair'. That does not mean, however, that such a conclusory expression has a legitimate place in the evaluative process leading to that result.

D Legislative and Judicial Processes

Although the concern throughout this book has been with the potential retroactive *effect* of statutes and of decisions developing or changing common law rules, rather than with the nature of the law making processes that give rise to that effect, one relevant difference between the legislative and judicial processes must be considered. Legislatures have the ability to, and most often do, make laws without retroactive effect. When a court applies the presumption against retroactivity to legislation and construes the legislation so that it does not have retroactive effect, the new law made by the legislature still operates non-retroactively. By contrast, when courts make law,[27] although there are some examples in which a particular confluence of circumstances means that they can avoid[28] or limit[29] retroactive effect (at least on the litigants before the court), in which case courts can focus on the question of law distinct from its temporal effect, in general courts can only develop or change the law with retroactive effect. The choice for courts is usually between not making law at all (leaving the legislature to make any change that the legislature may decide to be necessary), and making law with retroactive effect. Retroactivity in common law decisions is to be resisted, but if judges are to

[23] See Ch 3 Pt E(4).
[24] Ch 4 Pts D and G(1)(c).
[25] Ch 4 Pts E and G(1)(d).
[26] Ch 3 Pt E(2).
[27] Usage of this potentially controversial term is discussed in Ch 5 Pts A(2) and A(3).
[28] Ch 5 Pts E(1)(e), E(2)(e) and G(3).
[29] Ch 5 Pts C(2), E(1)(a) and E(1)(c).

improve the common law, then retroactivity is 'inevitable'.[30] This creates an insoluble tension. The best that can be done in the face of that tension is that when a judicial decision about whether to develop or change the law is being made, its potential retroactive effect should openly be considered and presumptively be resisted as part of the overall decision in the particular case.

Some jurists think that retroactivity need not *inevitably* accompany judicial decisions and that one potential way to remove the retroactive effect of judicial decisions that make law would be to adopt a system of prospective overruling. An argument against prospective overruling is developed in Chapter six of this book. In essence, it is submitted that because every form of prospective overruling either announces a new rule inconsistent with the one being applied in the case in which the announcement is made, or disrespects the requirement of the rule of law that legal rules be general in their application and so avoid arbitrariness, or suffers both of those defects, it is constitutionally impermissible for common law courts.

The judicial function is such that judges will sometimes not know whether retroactively changing a rule will adversely affect the parties to litigation in which it is submitted that such change should occur, and will often not know whether non-parties will be adversely affected. Because the presumption against retroactivity protects the *ability* to rely on the law, rather than actual reliance,[31] and because the nature of a presumption is to grant its protection in any case to which it is relevant,[32] without first considering the details of a particular case, the operation of the presumption should be such that if the case is one in which there is an inability to rely on the law or in which any such reliance would not deserve protection, then the presumption might be overcome, but that an inability to demonstrate actual reliance or know the extent of the consequences caused by retroactivity, is not grounds for either the inapplicability or rebuttal of the presumption.

E Final Observations

In criminal law, courts have acknowledged that development or change of the common law has retroactive effect and, because of that acknowledgement, judicial power to impose retroactive criminal liability has been constrained, if not abandoned. Developing or changing the law in other areas has the same *intertemporal* effect, though the effect of the *substantive* change in law may have less severe

[30] *Kleinwort Benson v Lincoln County Council* [1999] 2 AC 349, 378–9 (HL); *Brodie v Singleton Shire Council* (2001) 206 CLR 512, [317]; L Fuller *The Morality of Law* (Revised edn Yale University Press New Haven CT 1969) 55–8; J Waldron 'Retroactive Law: How Dodgy was Duynhoven?' (2004) 10 Otago Law Review 631, 639; J Hall '*Nulla Poena Sine Lege*' (1937) 47 Yale Law Journal 165, 171 cf J Hall *General Principles of Criminal Law* (2nd edn Bobbs-Merrill Indanapolis IN 1960) 61.

[31] Ch 3 Pt B(2).

[32] Ch 4 Pt E.

consequences for individual certainty and, particularly, liberty, than those that arise in criminal law. There has been accordingly less acknowledgement of the retroactive effect of developing or changing common law rules in private or public law.

An approach that would better serve the complementary goals of analytical rigour, open reasoning and the pursuit of justice according to law, would be to acknowledge the retroactive effect caused by developing or changing a common law rule in any area and then openly to confront the issue of whether, despite the retroactivity, the development or change should nonetheless occur. In approaching that question the common law should draw on the rationales for the presumption against retroactivity that inform its approach to the construction of statutes and apply a similar presumption to the adjudication of common law rules. As Chapter five demonstrates, reasons capable of defeating the presumption against adjudicative retroactivity arise readily in public law, less readily in private law and extremely rarely in criminal law.

The conclusions reached are summarised in the following propositions. Retroactivity is a particular kind of retrospectivity and should be defined as the application of a new law to a past event as though it was the law at the time of that event. Common law courts have historically resisted retroactivity in their construction of statutes but, informed by the declaratory theory, have tolerated the retroactive effects of judicial decisions developing or changing a common law rule. Certainty, particularly in the form of an ability to rely on the law, and a conception of negative liberty, constitute rationales for a general presumption against retroactivity at a level of abstraction applicable both to the construction of statutes and to developing or changing common law rules. Those rationales are manifested in the common law principle that, independently of any concern with legislative intent, presumes against a statute having retroactive effect. Courts often fail to consider explicitly the retroactive effect of judicially developing or changing a common law rule. Nonetheless, the doctrine of precedent and judicial attachment to existing principle in novel cases serve to restrict the occasions on which judicial decisions have retroactive effect. When a court considers whether to develop or change a common law rule the retroactive effect of doing so should explicitly be considered and, informed by the common law's approach to statutory construction, presumptively be resisted. In many cases that have developed or changed a common law rule, even without explicitly considering retroactivity or applying an explicit presumption against it, there are identifiable factors that would have overcome such a presumption. Common law courts should not resort to the constitutionally impermissible alternative of prospective overruling in an attempt to control the retroactive effect of making or changing common law rules. In statutory construction and the adjudication of common law rules there should be a consistently strong presumption against retroactivity, motivated by the common law's concern for certainty and liberty, and defeasible only to strong reasons.

BIBLIOGRAPHY

Allen, CK *Law in the Making* (7th edn Clarendon Press Oxford 1964).

Arden, M 'Prospective Overruling' (2004) 120 Law Quarterly Review 7.

Ashworth, A *Principles of Criminal Law* (5th edn Oxford University Press 2006).

Atrill, S '*Nulla Poena Sine Lege* in Comparative Perspective: Retrospectivity under the ECHR and US Constitution' [2005] Public Law 107.

Austin, J *Lectures on Jurisprudence* R Campbell (ed) (5th edn Revised John Murray London 1911).

Baker, P 'Retrospective Tax Legislation and the European Convention on Human Rights' [2005] British Tax Review 1.

Mr Justice Barry 'Treason, Passports and the Ideal of a Fair Trial' (1956) 7 Res Judicate 276.

Beddard, R 'Retrospective Crime' (1995) 145 New Law Journal 663.

Bell, J *Policy Arguments in Judicial Decisions* (Clarendon Press Oxford 1983).

Bennion, FAR *Statutory Interpretation* (4th edn Butterworths London 2002).

Bentham, J 'Principles of Penal Law' in *The Works of Jeremy Bentham* J Bowring (ed) (William Tait Edinburgh 1843) vol 1.

— 'Truth versus Ashhurst' in *The Works of Jeremy Bentham* J Bowring (ed) (William Tait Edinburgh 1843) vol 5.

— *A Comment on the Commentaries: A Criticism of William Blackstone's Commentaries on the Laws of England* CW Everett (ed) (Clarendon Press Oxford 1928).

Beyleveld, D, Kirkham, R and Townend, D 'Which Presumption? A Critique of the House of Lords Reasoning on Retrospectivity and the Human Rights Act' (2002) 22 Legal Studies 185.

Lord Bingham 'The Judge as Lawmaker: An English Perspective' in T Bingham *The Business of Judging: Selected Essays and Speeches* (Oxford University Press 2000).

Blackstone, W *Commentaries on the Laws of England* (Facsimile of the 1st edn (1765) University of Chicago Press 1979).

— *Commentaries on the Laws of England* (2nd edn Clarendon Press Oxford 1766).

— *Commentaries on the Laws of England* (16th edn Cadell London 1825).

Bobbett, CS 'Retroactive or Retrospective? A Note on Terminology' [2006] British Tax Review 15.

Burrows, JF *Statute Law in New Zealand* (3rd edn Lexis Nexis Wellington 2003).

Cadoppi, A '*Nulla Poena Sine Lege* and Scots Criminal Law: A Continental Perspective' [1998] Juridical Review 73.

Campbell, E 'The Retrospectivity of Judicial Decisions and the Legality of Governmental Acts' (2003) 29 Monash University Law Review 49.

Cane, P 'The Temporal Element in Law' (2001) 117 Law Quarterly Review 5.

Clark, EC *An Analysis of Criminal Liability* (Cambridge University Press 1880).

Coke, E *The Second Part of the Institutes of the Laws of England* (Brooke London 1797).

— *The Fourth Part of the Institutes of the Laws of England* (Brooke London 1797).

Craig, PP *Administrative Law* (5th edn Sweet and Maxwell London 2003).

Cross, R *Statutory Interpretation* J Bell and G Engle (eds) (3rd edn Butterworths London 1995).

Cross, R and Harris, J *Precedent in English Law* (4th edn Clarendon Press Oxford 1991).

Lord Devlin 'Judges and Lawmakers' (1976) Modern Law Review 1.

Dicey, AV *Lectures Introductory to the Study of the Law of the Constitution* (MacMillan London 1885).

— *Introduction to the Study of the Law of the Constitution* (3rd edn MacMillan London 1889).

— *A Leap in the Dark or Our New Constitution* (John Murray London 1893).

— *A Leap in the Dark: A Criticism of the Principles of Home Rule as Illustrated by the Bill of 1893* (2nd edn John Murray London 1911).

— *Introduction to the Study of the Law of the Constitution* (10th edn MacMillan London 1959).

Driedger, EA 'The Retrospective Operation of Statutes' in JA Corry, FC Cronkite and FC Whitmore (eds) *Legal Essays in Honour of Arthur Moxon* (University of Toronto Press 1953).

— 'Statutes: Retroactive Retrospective Reflections' (1978) 56 Canadian Bar Review 264.

Dworkin, G *The Theory and Practice of Autonomy* (Cambridge University Press 1988).

Dworkin, R *Law's Empire* (Hart Publishing Oxford 1998).

Edgar, SGG *Craies on Statute Law* (7th edn Sweet and Maxwell London 1971).

Edinger, E 'Retrospectivity in Law' (1995) 29 University of British Columbia Law Review 5.

Ekins, R 'Legislative Intent and Group Action' (M Phil Thesis University of Oxford 2005).

— 'The Relevance of the Rule of Recognition' (2006) 31 Australian Journal of Legal Philosophy 95.

Fawcett, JES *The Application of the European Convention on Human Rights* (2nd edn Clarendon Press Oxford 1987).

Feldman, D 'Commencement, Transition and Retrospective Legislation' (1992) 108 Law Quarterly Review 212.

Finnis, JM 'The Fairy Tale's Moral' (1999) 115 Law Quarterly Review 170.

Forsyth, C ' "The Metaphysic of Nullity" Invalidity, Conceptual Reasoning and the Rule of Law' in *The Golden Metwand and the Crooked Cord: Essays on Public Law in Honour of Sir William Wade QC* C Forsyth and I Hare (eds) (Clarendon Press Oxford 1998) 141.

Foster, M *Discourses upon a Few Branches of the Crown Law* (Clarendon Press Oxford 1762).

Frandberg, A 'Retroactivity, Simulactivity, Infraactivity' in J Bjarup and M Blegvad *Time Law and Society* (Franz Steiner Stuttgart 1995).

Freeman, MDA 'Standards of Adjudication, Judicial Law-Making and Prospective Overruling' [1973] Current Legal Problems 166.

Fuller, L *The Morality of Law* (Revised edn Yale University Press New Haven CT 1969).

Gray, JC *The Nature and Sources of the Law* D Campbell and P Thomas (eds) (New edn Dartmouth Aldershot 1997).

Greenberg, D (ed) *Craies on Legislation* (8th edn Sweet and Maxwell London 2004).

Griffin, J 'First Steps in an Account of Human Rights' (2001) 9 European Journal of Philosophy 306.

Grodecki, JK 'Conflicts of Laws in Time' (1959) 35 British Year Book of International Law 58.

Hale, J *The History and Analysis of the Common Law of England* (Walthoe London 1713).

— *History of the Pleas of the Crown* (New edn S Emlyn London 1800).

— *The History of the Common Law of England* (6th edn Butterworth London 1820).

Hall, J '*Nulla Poena Sine Lege*' (1937) 47 Yale Law Journal 165.

— *General Principles of Criminal Law* (2nd edn Bobbs-Merrill Indianapolis IN 1960).

Hall, L and Seligman, SJ 'Mistake of Law and Mens Rea' (1941) 8 University of Chicago Law Review 641.

Harris, BV 'Final Appellate Courts Overruling Their Own "Wrong" Precedents: The Ongoing Search for Principle' (2002) 118 Law Quarterly Review 408.

Harris, J 'Towards Principles of Overruling—When Should a Final Court of Appeal Second Guess?' (1990) 10 Oxford Journal of Legal Studies 135.

Hart, HLA *The Concept of Law* (2nd edn Clarendon Press Oxford 1994).

Hayek, FA *The Road to Serfdom* (Routledge London 1944).

Heydon, JD 'Limits to the Powers of Ultimate Appellate Courts' (2006) 122 Law Quarterly Review 399.

Higgins, R 'Time and Law' (1997) 46 International and Comparative Law Quarterly 501.

Hobbes, T *Leviathan* (1651) JCA Gaskin (ed) (Oxford University Press 1996).

Holdsworth, WS *History of English Law* (7th edn Methuen London 1956).

Hornung, G '*Nulla Poena Sine Lege* in German Law: A Reply to Cadoppi' [2002] Juridical Review 237.

Howard, AE Dick *Magna Carta: Text and Commentary* (Revised edn University Press of Virginia 1998).

Hudson, W 'A Treatise of the Court of Star Chamber' in F Hargrave (ed) *Collectanea Juridica* (Brooke London 1792).

Irish, LE *Time and Law: Retrospectivity and Prospectivity of Statutes and Judicial Decisions* (D Phil Thesis University of Oxford 1971).

Jones, TH 'Common Law and Criminal Law: The Scottish Example' [1990] Criminal Law Review 292.

Juratowitch, B 'Retroactive Criminal Liability and International Human Rights Law' (2004) 75 British Year Book of International Law 337.

Kelsen, H 'Collective and Individual Responsibility in International Law with Particular Regard to the Punishment of War Criminals' (1943) California Law Review 530.

— *General Theory of Law and State* (1945) A Wedberg (tr) (Russell and Russell New York 1961).

— 'Will the Judgment in the Nuremberg Trial Constitute a Precedent in International Law?' (1947) 1 International Law Quarterly 153.

Krueger, P (ed) *Codex Justinianus* (Berolini Apud Weidmannos 1877).

Lauterpacht, H 'Allegiance, Diplomatic Protection and Criminal Jurisdiction over Aliens' (1947) 9 Cambridge Law Journal 330.

Law Commission *A New Homicide Act for England and Wales?* (Consultation Paper No 177, 2005).

Law Commission of England and Wales *Limitation of Actions* (Law Com No 270, 2001).

Lord Lloyd *Introduction to Jurisprudence* (4th edn Stevens London 1979).

Loomer, GT 'Taxing Out of Time: Parliamentary Supremacy and Retroactive Tax Legislation' [2006] British Tax Review 64.

Lovell, J 'From Now On: Temporal Issues in Constitutional Adjudication' (2005) 18 National Journal of Constitutional Law 17.

Mann, FA 'The Time Element in the Conflict of Laws' (1954) 31 British Year Book of International Law 217.

Mason, K 'Prospective Overruling' (1989) 63 Australian Law Journal 526.

McHugh, M 'The Law-making Function of the Judicial Process—Part I' (1988) 62 Australian Law Journal 15.

McHugh, M 'The Law-making Function of the Judicial Process—Part II' (1988) 62 Australian Law Journal 116.
McKechnie, WS *Magna Carta* (2nd edn Maclehose Glasgow 1914).
Mead, D 'Rights, Relationships and Retrospectivity: The Impact of Convention Rights on Pre-Existing Private Relationships following *Wilson* and *Ghaidan*' [2005] Public Law 459.
Mommsen, T, Krueger, P (eds) and Watson, A (tr) *The Digest of Justinian* (University of Pennsylvania Press 1985).
Morris, JHC 'The Time Factor in the Conflict of Laws' (1966) International and Comparative Law Quarterly 422.
Newman, WJ 'The Principles of the Rule of Law and Parliamentary Sovereignty in Constitutional Theory and Litigation' (2005) 16 National Journal of Constitutional Law 175.
Nicol, AGL 'Prospective Overruling: A New Device for English Courts?' (1976) 39 Modern Law Review 542.
O'Higgins, P 'Wright v Fitzgerald Revisited' (1962) 25 Modern Law Review 413.
Osborne, C 'Does the End Justify the Means? Retrospectivity, Article 7, and the Marital Rape Exemption' [1996] European Human Rights Law Review 406.
Palmer, A and Sampford, C 'Retrospective Legislation in Australia—Looking Back at the 1980s' (1994) 22 Federal Law Review 217.
— Judicial Retrospectivity in Australia' (1995) 4 Griffith Law Review 170.
Pearce, DC and Geddes, RS *Statutory Interpretation in Australia* (4th edn Butterworths Sydney 1996).
Prott, LV 'When Will a Superior Court Overrule Its Own Decision?' (1978) 52 Australian Law Journal 304.
Rawls, J *A Theory of Justice* (Revised edn Oxford University Press 1999).
Raz, J 'The Rule of Law and its Virtue' (1977) 93 Law Quarterly Review 195.
Lord Reid 'The Judge as Lawmaker' (1972) 12 Journal of the Society of Public Teachers of Law 22.
Lord Rodger 'A Time for Everything under the Law: Some Reflections on Retrospectivity' (2005) 121 Law Quarterly Review 57.
Salembier, JP 'Understanding Retroactivity: When the Past Just Ain't What it Used to Be' (2003) 33 Hong Kong Law Journal 99.
Sampford, C *Retrospectivity and the Rule of Law* (Oxford University Press 2006).
von Savigny, FC *Private International Law and the Retrospective Operation of Statutes: A Treatise on the Conflict of Laws and the Limits of their Operation in Respect of Place and Time* W Guthrie (tr) (2nd edn T&T Clark Edinburgh 1880).
Scott, SP (tr and ed) *The Civil Law* (The Central Trust Company Cincinnati OH 1932).
Simester, AP and Sullivan, GR *Criminal Law: Theory and Doctrine* (2nd edn Hart Publishing Oxford 2003).
Smead, EE 'The Rule Against Retroactive Legislation: A Basic Principle of Jurisprudence' (1936) 20 Minnesota Law Review 775.
Smith, ATH 'Judicial Lawmaking in the Criminal Law' (1984) 100 Law Quarterly Review 46
— 'Criminal Law: The Future' [2004] Criminal Law Review 971.
Spigelman, JJ 'Principle of Legality and the Clear Statement Principle' (2005) 79 Australian Law Journal 769.
Spiro, E 'The Incidence of Time in the Conflict of Laws' (1960) 9 International and Comparative Law Quarterly 357.

St J Langan, P (ed) *Maxwell on the Interpretation of Statutes* (12th edn Sweet and Maxwell London 1969).
Stallybrass, WTS 'Public Mischief' (1933) 49 Law Quarterly Review 183.
Steele, I 'Substantive Legitimate Expectations: Striking The Right Balance?' (2005) 121 Law Quarterly Review 300.
Stephen, JF *A History of the Criminal Law of England* (Reprint of the original 1883 edn Routledge/Thoemmes Press London 1996).
Stone, J *Human Law and Human Justice* (Stevens and Sons London 1965).
— *Precedent and Law* (Butterworths Sydney 1985).
Thorne, SE (tr), Woodbine, GE (ed) *Bracton On the Laws and Customs of England* (Belknap Press Cambridge MA 1968).
Vinogradoff, P 'Magna Carta, C 39' in HE Malden (ed) *Magna Carta Commemoration Essays* (Royal Historical Society London 1917).
Waldron, J *Law and Disagreement* (Clarendon Press Oxford 1999).
— 'Retroactive Law: How Dodgy was Duynhoven?' (2004) 10 Otago Law Review 631.
— 'Torture and Positive Law: Jurisprudence for the Whitehouse' (2005) 105 Columbia Law Review 1681.
Wilberforce, E *Statute Law* (Stevens and Sons London 1881).
Williams, G 'The Correlation of Allegiance and Protection' (1948) 10 Cambridge Law Journal 54.
— *Criminal Law: The General Part* (2nd edn Stevens and Sons London 1961).
— 'The Problem of Domestic Rape' (1991) 141 New Law Journal 205 and 246.
Lord Wright 'The Study of Law' (1938) 54 Law Quarterly Review 185.
Woozley, AD 'What is Wrong with Retrospective Law?' (1968) 18 Philosophical Quarterly 41.

Index

Introductory Note

References such as '178–9' indicate (not necessarily continuous) discussion of a topic across a range of pages. Wherever possible in the case of topics with many references, these have been divided into sub-topics. The use of retroactivity and retrospectivity as entry points has been minimised. Information will be found under the corresponding detailed topics, eg 'definitions, retroactivity'.